Energy Security and Sustainability

T0300496

Energy Security and Sustainability

Edited by
Amritanshu Shukla · Atul Sharma

CRC Press
Taylor & Francis Group
Boca Raton London New York

CRC Press is an imprint of the
Taylor & Francis Group, an **informa** business

CRC Press
Taylor & Francis Group
6000 Broken Sound Parkway NW, Suite 300
Boca Raton, FL 33487-2742

First issued in paperback 2020

© 2017 by Taylor & Francis Group, LLC
CRC Press is an imprint of Taylor & Francis Group, an Informa business

No claim to original U.S. Government works

ISBN 13: 978-0-367-57445-1 (pbk)
ISBN 13: 978-1-4987-5443-9 (hbk)

Visit the Taylor & Francis Web site at
http://www.taylorandfrancis.com

and the CRC Press Web site at
http://www.crcpress.com

Contents

Foreword

Energy, in its various forms, has influenced and governed the lifestyle of human society throughout human history. It has also controlled technological progress. Primitive man relied primarily on his muscle power. After learning to how to make fire and taking to agriculture, humans started using animal power and energy derived from combustible materials of biological origin such as biomass, oil, etc. After, the scientific revolution, dependence on fossil fuels increased. Until the middle of the twentieth century, the problem of energy did not receive much attention. In this fossil fuel era it was generally believed that the electric power plants, natural gas, and petroleum derived fuels (diesel, gasoline, etc.) would be available forever and an abundant supply of energy in whatever form was taken for granted. The new oil policy of the Organization of Petroleum Exporting Countries (OPEC) adopted in 1973–1974 changed the entire scenario forever. It affected both developed and developing countries alike. In order to cope with this problem, crash programs to develop alternatives to petroleum-based fuels were launched in many countries of the world.

Intensive research and developmental activities were initiated to develop various forms of renewable energy resources such as active and passive solar energy systems, photovoltaic modules, wind and ocean energy systems, and biomass. As a widely dispersed and abundant carbonaceous resource, biomass became the logical choice as raw material for the production of a broad range of fossil fuel substitutes. Environmental issues such as deteriorating ambient air quality and global climate change were linked to fossil fuel consumption.

Until the end of the first decade of the twenty-first century nearly 1.1 billion people worldwide lacked access to electricity and more than 2.6 billion relied on the traditional use of biomass for cooking. Over 95% of these were located in Asia and sub-Saharan Africa. In 2012, the United

Nations launched its new initiative—"Sustainable Energy For All"—which aims at:

- Providing universal access to electricity and modern heating and cooking fuels.
- Doubling the renewable energy's share from 15 to 30%.
- Doubling the rate of improvement of energy efficiency from 1.2 to 2.4% per year.

The world is on the verge of witnessing a renewable energy revolution as the cost of harnessing renewable energy is likely to reduce drastically with the development of new biomass, solar, and wind energy technologies. Both developed and developing countries have intensified their R&D activities in this direction. The renewable energy sources are expected to account for 18% of the world's primary energy use by 2035 that was around 13% in 2011. China plans to more than triple its installed solar power generating capacity by 2017. In India, large-scale solar farms, rooftop solar, and other off-grid solutions (involving solar as well as biomass, small-scale hydro, and wind) could bring power to more than 200 million people by 2025.

Global environmental issues like climate change and global warming are also responsible for giving impetus to global developmental efforts for harnessing renewable energy sources. Climate change is no longer just an environmental issue as it affects the economy, leads to migration of people, and changes in living standards. There is no trade-off between tackling issues of climate change and building a strong economy. Indeed, success in one area will help us achieve the same in the other. It is the single most important thing that the present generation can do for the future generation. Thus, it has to be one of the highest priority issues for the global community.

Of late for all those involved in developing and formulating energy policy, "Energy Security and Sustainability" has meant mostly securing access to oil and other fossil fuels. With increasingly global, diverse energy markets, however, and increasingly transnational problems resulting from energy transformation and use, the old energy security rationale is no longer valid, and other issues such as climate change and other environmental, economic, and international concerns are becoming increasingly important. As a consequence, a more comprehensive operating definition of "Energy Security and Sustainability" is needed, along with a workable framework for analysis through which future energy paths or scenarios are likely to yield greater energy security in a broader and more comprehensive sense.

The future of global economic growth in the coming decades is going to rely significantly on changes related to energy security as the global energy demand continues to grow. According to the World Energy Outlook, with the United States moving steadily toward meeting almost all of its energy needs, the BRIC economies (especially India and China) and the EU are likely to be the major catalysts of global energy demand growth. Russia and Brazil are other major consumers of energy, but they intend to satisfy their consumptions through their domestic resources.

The editors of this book have come out with a book that discusses the numerous ways in which the natural resources of India and some other countries can be made use of for meeting the energy needs of our millions of citizens without causing further damage to the environment. During my short stay at the Rajeev Gandhi Petroleum Technology Institute, we often had discussions on the future global energy scenario as well as in India. During such discussions, the need to publish a book on energy security and sustainability was felt. I congratulate both Drs. Shukla and Sharma for having come out with the book which will be of immense help to students, practicing managers, and policy makers alike.

Professor S.N. Upadhyay
DAE-Raja Ramanna Fellow, BHU Varanasi
Ex-Director, IIT BHU, Varanasi

Editors

Dr. Amritanshu Shukla received his masters in physics from University of Lucknow (1999) and received his PhD in physics from IIT Kharagpur (2005) and postdoctoral work at the Institute of Physics Bhubaneswar (under Department of Atomic Energy, Govt. of India), University of North Carolina, Chapel Hill, University of Rome, Italy, and Physical Research Laboratory Ahmedabad (under Department of Space, Govt. of India). Currently, he is working as an assistant professor in physics at Rajiv Gandhi Institute of Petroleum Technology (RGIPT) (set up through an Act of Parliament by the Ministry of Petroleum & Natural Gas, Govt. of India as an "Institute of National Importance" on the lines of IITs). The institute is copromoted as an energy domain-specific institute by six leading PSUs—ONGC Ltd., IOCL, OIL, GAIL, BPCL, and HPCL in association with OIDB. The mission of the institute is to work toward promoting energy self-sufficiency in the country through its teaching and R&D efforts.

His research interests include theoretical physics, physics of renewable energy systems, nuclear physics, solar thermal systems, energy storage, and numerical simulation. He has published about 100 research articles in various international journals, conference proceedings of national and international repute. Currently, he is working on the development and simulation of phase change materials based on energy storage applications. He is also supervising several research students and conducting research at the Non-Conventional Energy Laboratory (NCEL), RGIPT. He is actively involved in a number of sponsored research projects and has several national as well as international active research collaborations from India and abroad on the topics of his research interests.

Dr. Atul Sharma completed his MPhil Energy and Environment (August 1998) and PhD on the topic Effect on Thermophysical Properties of PCMs due to Thermal Cycles and Their Utilization for Solar Thermal Energy Storage Systems (June 2003) from School of Energy and Environmental Studies, Devi Ahilya University, Indore, Madhya, Pradesh, India.

He has worked as a scientific officer at Regional Testing Centre Cum Technical Backup Unit for Solar Thermal Devices, at the School of Energy and Environmental Studies, Devi Ahilya University, Indore funded by the Ministry of Non-Conventional Energy Sources of the Government of India. He also worked as a research assistant at the Solar Thermal Research Center, New and Renewable Energy Research Department at Korea Institute of Energy Research, Daejon, South Korea (April 1, 2004–May 31, 2005) and as a visiting professor at Department of Mechanical Engineering, Kun Shan University, Tainan, Taiwan, ROC (August 1, 2005–June 30, 2009).

Dr. Sharma is currently assistant professor at Rajiv Gandhi Institute of Petroleum Technology (RGIPT), which has been set up by the Ministry of Petroleum and Natural Gas, Government of India through an Act of Parliament (RGIPT Act 54/2007) along the lines of the IITs with an "Institute of National Importance" tag. The institute is copromoted as an energy domain-specific institute by six leading PSUs—ONGC Ltd., IOCL, OIL, GAIL, BPCL, and HPCL in association with OIDB. The mission of the institute is to work toward promoting energy self-sufficiency in the country through its teaching and R&D efforts.

Recently, Dr. Sharma published an edited book, *Energy Sustainability through Green Energy* published by Springer (Pvt.) Limited, India. Dr. Sharma has published several research papers in various international journals and conferences. He also published several patents related to the PCM technology in the Taiwan region. He is working on the development and applications of phase change materials, green building, solar water heating system, solar air heating system, solar drying systems, etc. Dr. Sharma is conducting research at the Non-Conventional Energy Laboratory (NCEL), RGIPT and is currently engaged with the Department of Science and Technology (DST), New Delhi sponsored projects at his lab. Further, he served as an editorial board member and was reviewer for many national and international journals, project reports, and book chapters.

Contributors

John Andrews
School of Engineering
Royal Melbourne Institute of
    Technology (RMIT) University
Melbourne, Australia

Giacobbe Braccio
Italian National Agency for
    New Technologies, Energy
    and Sustainable Economic
    Development Research Centre
    Trisaia
Division for Bionergy, Bio-
    refinery and Green Chemistry
    (DTE-BBC)
Rotondella (MT), Italy

Ajay Kumar Chaturvedi
College of Engineering Roorkee
Uttarakhand, India

Abhay Kumar Choubey
Rajiv Gandhi Institute of
    Petroleum Technology
Rae Bareli, Uttar Pradesh, India

Mahendra Joshi
School of Architecture
Babu Banarasi Das (BBD)
    University
Lucknow, Uttar Pradesh, India

Rajarajeswari Kamalanathan
Centre for Green Energy
    Technology
Pondicherry University
Puducherry, India

Karunesh Kant
Non-Conventional Energy
    Laboratory
Rajiv Gandhi Institute of
    Petroleum Technology
Rae Bareli, Uttar Pradesh, India

Sanjay Kumar Kar
Department of Management
    Studies (NOIDA)
Rajiv Gandhi Institute of
    Petroleum Technology
Rae Bareli, Uttar Pradesh, India

Richa Kothari
Department of Environmental
  Science
Babasaheb Bhimrao Ambedkar
  University
Lucknow, Uttar Pradesh, India

Anil Kumar
Energy Technology Research Center
Prince of Songkla University
Hat Yai, Songkhla, Thailand

and

Department of Energy (Energy
  Centre)
Maulana Azad National Institute
  of Technology
Bhopal, India

Alok Kumar Maurya
School of Architecture
Babu Banarasi Das (BBD) University
Lucknow, Uttar Pradesh, India

Ashok Kumar Mishra
Finance
IMIS
Bhubaneswar, India

Saurabh Mishra
Rajiv Gandhi Institute of
  Petroleum Technology
Rae Bareli, Uttar Pradesh, India

Reza Omrani
School of Engineering
Royal Melbourne Institute of
  Technology (RMIT) University
Melbourne, Australia

Vinayak V. Pathak
DST-Centre for Policy Research
Babasaheb Bhimrao Ambedkar
  University
Lucknow, Uttar Pradesh, India

Sreekumar Appukuttan Pillai
Centre for Green Energy
  Technology
Pondicherry University
Puducherry, India

Om Prakash
Department of Mechanical
  Engineering
Birla Institute of Technology
Mesra, Ranchi, India

Saket Pratap
Department of Mechanical
  Engineering
Birla Institute of Technology
Mesra, Ranchi, India

Reena
Rajiv Gandhi Institute of
  Petroleum Technology
Rae Bareli, Uttar Pradesh, India

Geetam Richhariya
Department of Energy (Energy
    Centre)
Maulana Azad National Institute
    of Technology
Bhopal, India

Bahman Shabani
School of Engineering
Royal Melbourne Institute of
    Technology (RMIT) University
Melbourne, Australia

Ankit Sharma
Rajiv Gandhi Institute of
    Petroleum Technology
Rae Bareli, Uttar Pradesh, India

Atul Sharma
Non-Conventional Energy
    Laboratory
Rajiv Gandhi Institute of
    Petroleum Technology
Rae Bareli, Uttar Pradesh, India

Vinod Kumar Sharma
Italian National Agency for
    New Technologies, Energy
    and Sustainable Economic
    Development Research Centre
    Trisaia
Division for Bionergy, Bio-
    refinery and Green Chemistry
    (DTE-BBC)
Rotondella (MT), Italy

Amritanshu Shukla
Non-Conventional Energy
    Laboratory
Rajiv Gandhi Institute of
    Petroleum Technology
Rae Bareli, Uttar Pradesh, India

Priyanka Singh
Rajiv Gandhi Institute of
    Petroleum Technology
Rae Bareli, Uttar Pradesh, India

Satish Kumar Sinha
Rajiv Gandhi Institute of
    Petroleum Technology
Rae Bareli, Uttar Pradesh, India

Helia Teheri
Faculty of Fine Arts
University of Tehran
Tehran, Iran

Vineet V. Tyagi
Department of Energy and
    Management
Shri Mata Vaishno Devi University
Jammu & Kashmir (J&K), India

Balchandra Yadav
Babasaheb Bhimrao Ambedkar
    University
Lucknow, Uttar Pradesh, India

I

Solar PV and Solar Thermal

CHAPTER 1

Solar Energy

An Effective Tool for Value Addition of Foodstuffs

Rajarajeswari Kamalanathan
and Sreekumar Appukuttan Pillai

CONTENTS

1.1 WORLD POPULATION GROWTH AND FOOD IMBALANCE

The world population by 2015 was reported to be 7.6 billion and it is expected to be 9 billion by the year 2050 according to a United Nations, Department of Economic and Social Affairs (UN DESA) report (United Nations 2015). The developing countries contribute the highest percentage of the world population. This alarming increase in population leads to scarcity of food, water, and natural resources. The food imbalance results in malnutrition of many millions of people. Most African countries suffer from hunger and malnutrition, as reported by the UN DESA. The main challenge of the food producers is to feed the 9 billion people by the year 2050. Therefore, substantial attention has been given to increase the food production by 50–70%. On the other hand, food loss and food wastes have to be decreased. The Food and Agricultural Organization (FAO/World Bank 2011) reported that one-third of world food production has been lost or wasted amounting to 1.3 billion tons of food per year leaving 870 million people hungry (World Bank 2011). Reducing food loss is one of the keystones to food security (Affognon et al. 2015). Agriculturalists and experts strongly believe and recommend that reducing postharvest losses leads to food availability, poverty alleviation, and nutrition improvement. One of the main reasons for postharvest loss is lack of adequate storage facilities. Though there are advanced technologies available for storage, they are not within reach of poor food producers and farmers. The factors affecting adoption of improved storage structures are basic education, contact with marketing agents, production experience, technology adoption, and economic position. Therefore, a simple, user-friendly technology for storage with a feasible cost may help in encouraging farmers to adopt food storage.

1.2 FOOD PRESERVATION

Food preservation has been followed from ancient days to avail the crop at nonseasonal times. Food preservation refers to application of various techniques to prevent food from spoilage. There are different methods of food preservation such as drying, canning, freezing, pasteurizing, smoking, adding chemicals, etc. Food spoilage can be caused by attack of pathogens, oxidation, attack by insects, rodents, etc. The following are some basic methods of food preservation adopted for decades to remove these causative agents.

1.2.1 Canning

It is the process of heating the food product at a defined temperature for a particular time in sealed jars or cans specially made for this purpose. The microorganisms are killed during this process, which increases the shelf life of the product. Fruits, vegetables, seafood, and meat can be stored by this method.

1.2.2 Freezing

It is the process of cooling the products to below 0°C. Freezing preserves the food by arresting the growth of microorganisms and slowing down enzyme reactions.

1.2.3 Smoking

Exposing the food to smoke extends the shelf life of food. The smoke from wood has antimicrobial activity and hence helps to prevent the growth of microbes.

1.2.4 Salting

Salting or curing is the process of adding salt, which combines with the water molecules and helps in dehydration. A high level of salinity averts microbial action, which ensures safer storage.

1.2.5 Drying

It is the process of removing moisture content for long-term storage. Dehydration accomplishes preservation in two major ways. First, it removes the water required for the growth of microorganisms and for enzymatic activity. Second, by removing the water, it increases the osmotic pressure by concentration of salts, sugars, and acids creating a chemical environment unfavorable for the growth of many microorganisms.

1.3 FUNDAMENTALS OF DRYING

Drying is a complex process involving simultaneous heat and mass transfer along with several rate processes causing physical and chemical changes to the products. Drying occurs by evaporation of surface moisture at the beginning and then the moisture migration takes place from the interior of the product to the surface and to the surrounding areas. The process of drying is controlled by external and internal parameters. The properties of drying air are said to be external parameters and properties of product to be dried are known as internal parameters. Thermodynamic properties of moist air can be determined by the use of a psychrometric chart.

1.3.1 Psychrometry

The properties of moist air play an important role in designing a drying system. Psychrometric properties are associated with the air–water mixture and their interaction on drying materials. These properties can be accomplished by the use of a psychrometric chart.

A psychrometric chart is available in varied ranges of temperature and pressure. A chart for high temperatures is given in Figure 1.1. Dry bulb temperature and relative humidity are the abscissa and ordinate of the chart, respectively. Knowing any two properties of drying air, other

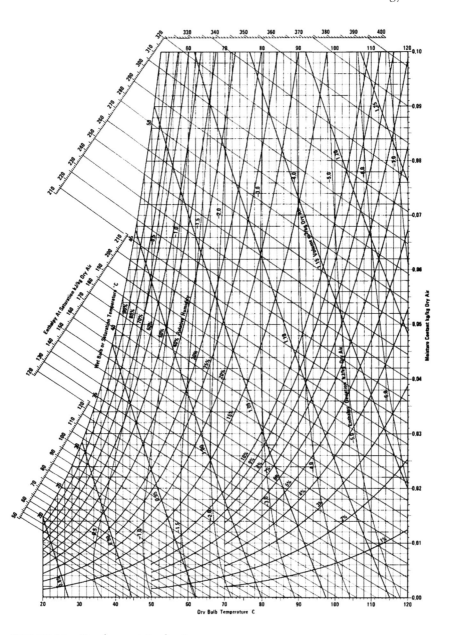

FIGURE 1.1   Psychrometric chart.

parameters can be obtained by using the chart. The properties of the moist air that can be obtained from psychrometric chart are as follows:

Dry bulb temperature: It is the temperature measured by an ordinary thermometer whose sensor is dry.

Wet bulb temperature: It is the temperature indicated by the thermometer whose sensor is wet. It is the temperature of dry air and water vapor mixture.

Dew point temperature: It is the temperature at which the water vapor begins to condense.

Relative humidity: It is measured by the ratio of water vapor pressure in the air to the water vapor pressure in the saturated air.

Enthalpy: It is the total amount of heat energy content in the moist air.

Specific volume: It is the volume occupied by kilogram of moist air.

Humidity ratio: It is defined as the mass of water vapor per unit mass of dry air.

1.3.2 Properties of Product

1.3.2.1 Moisture Content

Moisture content is the mass percentage of water present in a product. Initial moisture content of the product can be obtained by the following equation:

$$M = \frac{w-d}{w} \times 100 \tag{1.1}$$

where w and d are the weights of wet and dry products, respectively.

1.3.2.2 Equilibrium Moisture Content

Equilibrium moisture content is obtained by drying the product for a long enough time. The moisture content of the wet product in equilibrium with the air at a given humidity and temperature is called equilibrium moisture content. Equilibrium is reached when the product stops losing or gaining moisture. The relative humidity of the air at this stage is said to be equilibrium relative humidity.

1.3.3 Effect of Parameters on Drying

1.3.3.1 Temperature

Temperature is the main parameter that affects the quality of the product. High temperature may hinder the germination capacity of seeds. It may also cause shrinkage, cracks, and color change to the product that accounts for the rejection of the product by the consumers. Low temperature drying essentially decreases the drying duration providing a chance for microbial attack. Therefore, an optimum temperature level should be chosen for drying where the optimum temperature changes for different products.

1.3.3.2 Mass Flow Rate

Rate of drying depends on the mass flow rate. Moisture removal per unit time can be increased by increasing the mass flow rate. Drying efficiency depends on the flow rate in the drying chamber.

1.4 METHODS OF DRYING

Drying is the process of removal of moisture from the interior of food products for preservation. To remove moisture from the food, different drying methods are followed.

1.4.1 Hot Air Drying

It is the most common method practiced for food dehydration. In this method, food is exposed to continuously flowing hot air. A schematic representation of hot air drying is given in Figure 1.2. The simultaneous mass

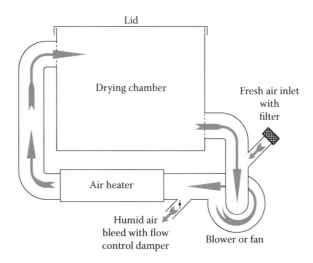

FIGURE 1.2   Schematic representation of hot air drying.

and heat transfer is the phenomenon underlying this process. Depending on the temperature, velocity, and humidity ratio of the drying environment, the drying rate varies. Hot air for drying can be produced by natural solar radiation, electric hot air oven, burning fossil fuels, etc. The hot air by convection removes the surface moisture and then removes the interior moisture content of the product. The product is reduced to equilibrium moisture content for safe storage. Air drying produces dehydrated products of long shelf life but they experience the disadvantage of low quality product with the conventional method of drying.

1.4.2 Freeze Drying

Among the various drying methods available for food, freeze drying is the appropriate method for maintaining desirable function. The principle of freeze drying is that the product to be dried is frozen and the water vapor is removed by sublimation. A schematic representation of a freeze dryer is shown in Figure 1.3. Freeze dried products help to maintain the palatability characteristics of the food. The low temperature requirement and absence of liquid in this process reduces microbial activity and helps it evolve into a high quality dried product. Further, the dried products can be stored for longer duration without refrigeration. Though it is a well-known method of dehydration and producing high quality of food, its main disadvantage is the economics (Litvin, Mannheim, and Miltz 1998). The high running cost and the longer duration of drying for high moisture products is why the economics of the drying method are so high.

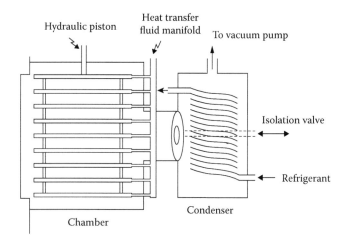

FIGURE 1.3   Schematic representation of a freeze dryer.

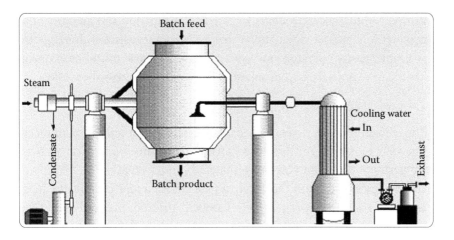

FIGURE 1.4   Schematic representation of a vacuum dryer.

1.4.3 Vacuum Drying

Figure 1.4 shows a schematic representation of a vacuum dryer. In this method of drying, the air around the food product is removed so that evaporation takes place. The water inside the product evaporates rapidly leaving the product dried with high quality. The heat transfer in the vacuum limits the drying rate and the high equipment price builds a large gap between the technology and common food producers. Heat transfer in vacuum may be enhanced by assisting with microwaves or infrared waves (Drouzas, Tsami, and Saravacos 1999). Researchers proved that vacuum drying assisted with microwave radiation resulted in controlled drying of food products.

1.5 SOLAR DRYING TECHNOLOGY FOR FOOD PRESERVATION

Sun is a freely available heat source. The utilization of the free energy is considerably less due to lack of appropriate technology. Solar drying technology is a simple and ancient technology that utilizes solar radiation to generate heat for drying application. A proper design of a solar dryer would yield exportable quality dried products (Amir et al. 1991). Tropical countries are designated with high solar radiation and sudden rainfall. This region of the world cultivates many food crops such as coffee, coconut, cocoa, and vegetables. The products have to be dehydrated to a safe moisture content in short duration with a simple and cost-effective method. Open sun drying is easy and an economic way of drying. But unfortunately, the sudden rainfall, wind, insects, rodents, etc., reduce the quality and quantity of the product to a greater extent. Solar drying is an alternative technology that is simple, easily operated, and cost-effective for agricultural crop drying. There are various designs of solar dryers developed across the world.

1.5.1 Design of Solar Dryer

The efficiency of the dryer depends on the maximum utilization of incoming solar radiation. A solar dryer must possess three basic parts such as a transparent cover, an absorbing material, and insulation. A transparent cover allows maximum radiation to pass through and prevent the longer wave radiation from escaping the chamber. Absorber material should possess high thermal conductivity. Any metal with high conductivity is chosen as an absorber and a selective black coating on the absorber with high absorptivity and low emissivity is used to enhance the absorption of solar radiation. Insulation material is of low thermal conductivity. Materials such as wood, thermocol, polyurethane foam, etc., are used as insulating material. The efficiency of the dryer depends on the solar radiation and mass flow rate.

Collector efficiency can be calculated by

$$\eta = \frac{\dot{m} C_p (t_o - t_i)}{A_c I} \tag{1.2}$$

where $\dot{m}$ is the mass flow rate (kg/s), C_p is the specific heat capacity of air (kJ/kg.K), t_o is the outlet temperature, t_i is the inlet temperature, A_c is the collector area, and I is the solar radiation (W/m²).

Drying efficiency is given by

$$\eta = \frac{m_w h_L}{A_c It} \tag{1.3}$$

where m_w is the mass of water to be removed (kg), h_L is the latent heat of vaporization of water (kJ/kg), and t is the drying time (s).

1.5.2 Types of Solar Dryer

Solar dryers are classified according to the mode of operation and nature of flow. Depending on the mode of operation, solar dryers are classified into three types. They are direct, indirect, and mixed mode dryers. Depending on the air flow, they are classified as passive solar dryers and active solar dryers.

1.5.2.1 Direct Solar Dryers

In these types of dryers, the product to be dried is placed under the transparent cover. The solar radiation transmits through the glass cover and gets absorbed by the products. The reflected radiation from the product keeps the chamber hotter. The evaporation occurs from the product and the air entering the chamber takes away the evaporated moisture through the outlet. Cabinet dryers and solar tunnel dryers fall under this category. Direct solar dryers have limitations such as small capacity, discoloration of crop, moisture condensation, and insufficient rise in crop temperature.

1.5.2.2 Indirect Solar Dryers

In this type, the product is not directly exposed to solar radiation to reduce discoloration and shrinkage. The principle of indirect solar drying is that a separate unit called a solar air heating collector is used for collecting solar radiation. The air heater is connected to a separate drying unit or drying chamber where the products to be dried are kept. Drying takes place due to temperature gradient between the hot air and the surface of the product. Convective heat transfer takes place from hot air to the product surface resulting in moisture removal. Controlled drying is achieved in indirect type dryers and the products are superior in quality (Sreekumar, Manikantan, and Vijayakumar 2008).

1.5.2.3 Mixed Mode Solar Dryers

This type of dryer combines both the features of direct and indirect mode dryers. The product is dried by direct solar radiation and also by natural convection process. This type of dryer subsequently reduces the drying duration (Montero et al. 2010).

1.5.2.4 Passive Solar Dryers

In passive solar dryers, air is circulated by natural wind and pressure and drying takes place by a natural convection process. Cabinet dryers and greenhouse type dryers are examples of passive solar dryers.

1.5.2.5 Active Solar Dryers

In this type of dryer pumping force for air is employed by externally powered fans. The drying process takes place by forced convection method. In all indirect type solar dryers air from the collector is extracted to the chamber by external blower fans. Indirect type and mixed mode dryers are examples of active solar dryers.

1.6 DIFFERENT TYPES OF SOLAR DRYERS IN OPERATION

There are various solar dryers designed, installed, and analyzed in different parts of the world for drying agricultural crops and marine products. The following are a few of them.

1.6.1 Greenhouse Type Solar Dryer for Drying Chili in Thailand

The greenhouse type of solar dryer installed in northern Thailand has a capacity of 1000 kg of fresh product as shown in Figure 1.5. The size of the dryer is 20.0 m × 8.0 m × 3.5 m. DC fans powered by photovoltaic panels are used to drive the moisture out of the dryer. The roof of the dryer is made up of a polycarbonate sheet. The solar radiation passing through the transparent sheet heats the product, air, and components inside the dryer. The hot air passing through the product removes the moisture. The dryer is of direct mode forced convection type. The initial moisture content with 74% of chili loaded in the drier was reduced to 9% in 3 days. The capital cost for construction and installation of a greenhouse dryer was $25,900. Fifty batches of chili can be dried per year resulting in 11,500 kg of dry chili. The payback period of the dryer was estimated to be 2 years (Kaewkiew, Nabnean, and Janjai 2012).

FIGURE 1.5 Large-scale polycarbonate cover greenhouse solar dryer. (From Kaewkiew, J., Nabnean, S., and Janjai, S. *Procedia Engineering* 32 (2012): 433–439. With permission.)

1.6.2 Rack Type Greenhouse Effect Solar Dryer for Wild Ginger Drying in Indonesia

The dryer is the transparent building where the products to be dried are spread on the racks as shown in Figure 1.6. The dryer consists of 144 trays, 4 blowers, biomass stove, burner, and cross flow heat exchanger. Biomass energy was used to maintain the constant drying temperature of 45.5°C. Sixty kilograms of wild ginger with initial moisture content of 80% was reduced to 11% in 30 drying hours (Aritesty and Wulandani 2014).

1.6.3 Concentrated Solar Crop Dryer in Tanzania

The dryer developed in Tanzania for drying tomatoes with concentrating collectors with a reflecting surface of 1.71 m² is shown in Figure 1.7. The dryer has lightweight wooden frames of dimension 1.5 m × 1.8 m × 1 m wrapped in a 4-mm thick plastic sheet supported on four 0.3-m legs. The absorber is corrugated aluminum painted black. Four removable racks are present with mesh on which products to be dried can be placed. Initial moisture content of 92% for tomatoes was brought down to 10.5% in 1.54 h. It was reported that this smaller drying duration is due to the

FIGURE 1.6 Rack type greenhouse effect solar dryer. (From Aritesty, E. and Wulandani, D. *Energy Procedia* 47 (2014): 94–100. With permission.)

FIGURE 1.7 Solar concentrated dryer. (From Ringeisen, B., Barrett, D.M., and Stroeve, P. *Energy for Sustainable Development* 19 (April) (2014): 47–55. With permission.)

addition of concentrating solar collector (Ringeisen, Barrett, and Stroeve 2014).

1.6.4 Parabolic Shaped Solar Tunnel Dryer in Thailand

The parabolic shaped solar tunnel dryer shown in Figure 1.8 was designed for drying *Andrographis paniculata*. The total collector area was 108 m^2. The dryer consists of a flat plate solar collector and a drying tunnel. DC fans powered by 12 W solar cells were used to drive air. The dryer can hold 100 kg of fresh product. Seventy five percent initial moisture content of the product reduced to 7% in 2 to 3 days. Depending on the weather conditions, the drying air temperature varied from 35°C to 75°C (Srisittipokakun, Kirdsiri, and Kaewkhao 2012).

1.6.5 Fruit Solar Dryer Using Concentrating Panels, United States

The mixed mode solar dryer shown in Figure 1.9 was developed at the University of California, Davis, for drying Roma tomatoes. Flat concentrating solar panels were used to increase the incident solar radiation on the dryer. Inclusion of concentrating panels increased the drying rate to 27% and reduced the drying time considerably (Stiling et al. 2012).

FIGURE 1.8   Parabolic shaped solar tunnel dryer. (From Srisittipokakun, N., Kirdsiri, K., Kaewkhao, J. *Procedia Engineering* 32 (January) (2012): 839–846. With permission.)

FIGURE 1.9   Solar dryer and concentrating reflection panels. (From Stiling, J., Li, S., Stroeve, P., Thompson, J., Mjawa, B., Kornbluth, K., and Barrett, D.M. *Energy for Sustainable Development* 16 (2) (2012): 224–230. With permission.)

FIGURE 1.10   Solar tunnel dryer with product. (From Rathore, N.S. and Panwar, N.L. *Applied Energy* 87 (8) (2010): 2764–2767. With permission.)

1.6.6 Hemi-Cylindrical Walk-In Type Solar Tunnel Dryer for Drying Grapes in Rajasthan, India

The dryer installed in Udaipur, Rajasthan shown in Figure 1.10 has a drying area of 37.5 m². The dryer was designed for drying grapes on a large scale. Two hundred micrometer UV stabilized plastic sheet was used as transparent cover. Three hundred and twenty kilograms of fresh grapes can be loaded in the dryer. The maximum drying temperature recorded was 64.3°C. It took 7 days for the dryer to bring down the moisture content of the product to a desired level, where in open sun drying it took more than 11 days (Rathore and Panwar 2010).

1.6.7 Roof Integrated Solar Air Heater with Batch Dryer, India

Figure 1.11 shows a roof integrated solar air heater connected with a batch dryer for drying fruits and vegetables. It is an indirect mode forced convection solar dryer. The batch dryer can hold 200–250 kg of fresh products. The total collector area is 46 m² and the volume of the dryer is 7.24 m³. Two hundred kilograms of pineapple were dried in 8 hours and the economics of the dryer were proved to be more efficient than the conventional fossil fuel dryers (Sreekumar 2010).

1.6.8 Matrix Solar Air Heater Integrated with Drying Chamber, India

An indirect mode solar dryer developed at the Centre for Green Energy Technology, Pondicherry University is shown in Figure 1.12. Solar collectors that are 6 m² are used for radiation capture. A drying chamber

FIGURE 1.11   Roof integrated solar air heater. (From Sreekumar, A. *Energy Conversion and Management* 51 (11) (2010): 2230–2238. With permission.)

FIGURE 1.12   Indirect mode solar air heater. (From Rajarajeswari, K. and Sreekumar, A. *Voice of Research* 3 (3) (2014): 46–53. With permission.)

capable of holding 30 kg of fresh products is connected to the outlet of the solar air heater. The solar air heater is a nonconventional type in which the air flow path is packed with wire mesh matrices. A centrifugal blower with 500 m³/h of volume flow rate was used for driving the hot air from the air heater. The 90.62% initial moisture of tomatoes was reduced to 18.28% in 3 h (Rajarajeswari and Sreekumar 2014).

1.6.9 Solar Tunnel Dryer, India

A mixed mode operated solar tunnel dryer is shown in Figure 1.13. The dryer was designed and installed at the Centre for Green Energy Technology. This dryer is designed for drying agricultural and marine products. An average of 50°C hot air temperature has been recorded. Two centrifugal fans powered by photovoltaic panels are used for driving the moist air out of the dryer. The dryer has a provision to load the products both above and below the absorber plate. Products above the absorber are dried by solar radiation where the dryer runs through direct mode and products below the absorber are dried by convection where the dryer runs through an indirect mode.

1.6.10 Solar Dryer Developed by Sardar Patel Renewable Energy Research Institute (SPRERI)

SPRERI has been foremost in developing solar dryers in India for agricultural crop drying. An indirect type solar dryer was developed for

FIGURE 1.13   Solar tunnel dryer.

drying tomatoes. The collector area was 60 m². The total air flow rate was 3000 m³/h. The system can dry 125 kg of tomatoes whose initial moisture content of 95% reduced to 10%. The drying temperature was about 80°C (Chavda and Kumar 2009).

1.7 ECONOMIC ANALYSIS OF SOLAR DRYER

An economic analysis of a solar dryer can be performed by three methods; annualized cost method, lifetime savings method, and payback period (Sreekumar 2010; Rajarajeswari and Sreekumar 2014). In the annualized cost method, one can compare the cost of drying per unit weight of the product using solar and conventional dryers. The drawback of this method is that the unsteady prices of fossil fuel reserves are not considered. The second method called lifetime savings method includes inflation rate in calculating the present worth of annual savings and cumulative annual savings on using a solar dryer. Payback period is the time required to get back the investment.

1.7.1 Annualized Cost

The economics of drying different products using a solar dryer were estimated by different research. The price of a solar dryer was considered to be more than conventional dryers. The cost of a drying unit weight of pineapple using a solar dryer was ₹11 and that of using an electric dryer was ₹19.73 (Sreekumar 2010). The economics of drying bitter gourd using a solar dryer were presented by Aravindh and Sreekumar (2014). It was reported that the cost of the drying unit weight of bitter gourd was ₹14.43 and that of the electric dryer was ₹29.99. Since the running fuel cost for a solar dryer is 0, the annualized cost for a solar dryer is less than conventional dryers.

1.7.2 Lifetime Savings

Lifetime savings on using solar dryers for drying tomatoes is presented by Rajarajeswari and Sreekumar (2014). Lifetime savings was estimated to be ₹28, 52, and 503 for 20 years of drying.

1.7.3 Payback Period

The payback period of a solar dryer whose investment was ₹550,000 was estimated to be 0.54 year (Sreekumar 2010). A solar tunnel dryer for drying silkworm pupae was economically analyzed and the payback period was recorded as 1.42 years (Usub et al. 2008). The payback

period of a greenhouse dryer with an investment of $25,900 was cal-
culated as 2 years (Kaewkiew, Nabnean, and Janjai 2012). On average,
the lifetime of the solar dryers was considered to be 20 years and the
payback period calculated for the above dryers was much less compared to the lifetime. So the dryers can perform free of cost for the rest
of the period.

1.7.4 Economic Analysis of Matrix Solar Air Heater Developed at the Centre for Green Energy Technology (Pondicherry University)

Economic analysis was done for drying pineapple in a solar dryer. The cost
of the drying unit weight of pineapple using a solar dryer was compared
with an electric dryer. Twenty kilograms of fresh pineapple can be dried
per batch and 962 kg of dried pineapple can be retrieved per year from
the solar dryer. The capital cost of solar dryer was ₹140,000.00 and that of
electric dryer was ₹75,000.00. The cost of the drying unit weight of product
in the solar dryer was found to be ₹18.62 and by using the electric dryer
the cost was ₹25.33. The cost of drying in an electric dryer was higher than
the solar dryer due to the fuel consumption price. The cost and economic
parameters involved in calculation are presented in Table 1.1.

In the life cycle savings method, the savings per day in the base year
has been estimated to be to be ₹268.00. Annual savings, present worth of
annual savings, and cumulative worth of annual savings were calculated
for 20 years and presented in Table 1.2. The cumulative worth of annual
savings at the end of 20 years was estimated to be ₹1,044,119.00. The payback period of the solar dryer was calculated to be 2.2 years.

TABLE 1.1 Cost and Economic Parameters of Solar Dryer

Cost of solar dryer	₹140,000.00
Cost of electric dryer	₹75,000.00
Rate of interest	8%
Inflation rate	6%
Electricity cost	₹4.00/kWh
Cost of fresh pineapple	₹60.00/kg
Cost of dried pineapple	₹400.00/kg
Lifetime of solar dryer	20 years
Maintenance cost	5% of annualized cost
Salvage value	10% of annualized cost

TABLE 1.2   Lifetime Savings of Solar Dryer

Year	Annual Savings (₹)	Present Worth of Annual Savings (₹)	Present Worth of Cumulative Savings (₹)
1	67,000.00	61,975.00	61,975.00
2	71,020.00	60,864.00	122,839.00
3	75,281.00	59,697.00	182,536.00
4	79,798.00	58,651.00	241,187.00
5	84,585.00	57,517.00	298,704.00
6	89,661.00	56,486.00	355,190.00
7	95,040.00	55,408.00	410,598.00
8	100,743.00	54,401.00	464,999.00
9	106,787.00	53,393.00	518,392.00
10	113,195.00	52,409.00	570,801.00
11	119,986.00	51,354.00	622,155.00
12	127,186.00	50,492.00	672,647.00
13	134,817.00	49,477.00	722,124.00
14	142,906.00	48,588.00	770,712.00
15	151,480.00	47,716.00	818,428.00
16	160,569.00	46,886.00	865,314.00
17	170,203.00	45,954.00	911,268.00
18	180,415.00	45,103.00	956,371.00
19	191,240.00	44,367.00	1,000,738.00
20	202,715.00	43,381.00	1,044,119.00

1.8 CONCLUSION

Solar drying technology produces high quality dried food products. The stumbling blocks of the ancient method of drying and the high price of conventional energy dryers can be overcome by the adoption of solar dryers. Manifesting the technology to food producers could considerably reduce the postharvest losses of agricultural products. Developing appropriate designs of solar dryers with thermal energy storage could flourish in uninterrupted drying of products. The case studies show that the solar dryers installed are performing better and producing branded quality food products.

REFERENCES

Affognon, H., Mutungi, C., Sanginga, P., and Borgemeister, C. "Unpacking Postharvest Losses in Sub-Saharan Africa: A Meta-Analysis." *World Development* 66 (February) (2015): 49–68.

Amir, E.J., Grandegger, K., Esper, A., Sumarsono, M., Djaya, C., and Muhlbauer, W. "Development of a Multi-Purpose Solar Tunnel Dryer for Use in Humid Tropics." *Renewable Energy* 1 (2) (1991): 167–176.

Aravindh, M.A. and Sreekumar, A. "Experimental and Economic Analysis of a Solar Matrix Collector for Drying Application." *Current Science* 107 (3) (2014): 350–355.

Aritesty, E. and Wulandani, D. "Performance of the Rack Type-Greenhouse Effect Solar Dryer for Wild Ginger (*Curcuma Xanthorizza* Roxb.) Drying." *Energy Procedia* 47 (2014): 94–100.

Chavda, N.K. "Solar Dryers for High Value Agro Prodcuts At Spreri." *International Solar Food Processing Conference* (2009): 1–5.

Drouzas, A.E., Tsami, E., and Saravacos, G.D. "Microwave/vacuum Drying of Model Fruit Gels." *Journal of Food Engineering* 39 (2) (1991): 117–122.

Kaewkiew, J., Nabnean, S., and Janjai, S. "Experimental Investigation of the Performance of a Large-Scale Greenhouse Type Solar Dryer for Drying Chili in Thailand." *Procedia Engineering* 32 (2012): 433–439.

Litvin, S., Mannheim, C.H., and Miltz, J. "Dehydration of Carrots by a Combination of Freeze Drying, Microwave Heating and Air or Vacuum Drying." *Journal of Food Engineering* 36 (1) (1998): 103–111.

Montero, I., Blanco, J., Miranda, T. et al. "Design, Construction and Performance Testing of a Solar Dryer for Agroindustrial by-Products." *Energy Conversion and Management* 51 (7) (2010): 1510–1521.

Rajarajeswari, K. and Sreekumar, A. "Performance Evaluation of a Wire Mesh Solar Air Heater Voice of Research." *Voice of Research* 3 (3) (2014): 46–53.

Rathore, N.S. and Panwar, N.L. "Experimental Studies on Hemi Cylindrical Walk-in Type Solar Tunnel Dryer for Grape Drying." *Applied Energy* 87 (8) (2010): 2764–2767.

Ringeisen, B., Barrett, D.M., and Stroeve, P. "Concentrated Solar Drying of Tomatoes." *Energy for Sustainable Development* 19 (April) (2014): 47–55.

Sreekumar, A. "Techno-Economic Analysis of a Roof-Integrated Solar Air Heating System for Drying Fruit and Vegetables." *Energy Conversion and Management* 51 (11) (2010): 2230–2238.

Sreekumar, A., Manikantan, P.E., and Vijayakumar, K.P. "Performance of Indirect Solar Cabinet Dryer." *Energy Conversion and Management* 49 (6) (2008): 1388–1395.

Srisittipokakun, N., Kirdsiri, K., and Kaewkhao, J. "Solar Drying of Andrographis Paniculata Using a Parabolicshaped Solar Tunnel Dryer." *Procedia Engineering* 32 (January) (2012): 839–846.

Stiling, J., Li, S., Stroeve, P., Thompson, J., Mjawa, B., Kornbluth, K., and Barrett, D.M. "Performance Evaluation of an Enhanced Fruit Solar Dryer Using Concentrating Panels." *Energy for Sustainable Development* 16 (2) (2012): 224–230.

United Nations. Department of Economic and Social Affairs, Population division. *World Population Prospects: The 2015 Revision, Key Findings and Advance Tables.* 2015.

Usub, T., Lertsatitthanakorn, C. et al. "Experimental Performance of a Solar Tunnel Dryer for Drying Silkworm Pupae." *Biosystems Engineering* 101 (2) (2008): 209–216.

World Bank. Missing food: The case of post harvest losses in Sub-Saharan Africa, The World Bank, Report No. 60371-AFR. The World Bank, Washington, DC, 2011.

CHAPTER 2

Solar Thermal Technologies

Overview and Development Perspectives

Vinod Kumar Sharma and Giacobbe Braccio

CONTENTS

2.1 INTRODUCTION

Rapid industrialization, economic growth, human civilization and its progress, communications, health, shelter, and other basic needs of society are very much restrained by inadequate availability of energy. Moreover, today with billions of tons of carbon emissions into the atmosphere, global temperature rise, threats of climatic changes, and the great obstacles to further development of conventional energy sources, it is very important that due attention be given to a range of environmentally friendly energy technologies which are relevant to us, too, in developing countries. It is in the above context that energy and, in particular, clean energy, is certainly an important scientific topic that needs special attention by the scientific community worldwide and, more so, in the context of developing countries. The relationships between energy and poverty as well as energy and gross domestic product (GDP) are captured in Figures 2.1 and 2.2, while the global population explosion is shown in Figure 2.3.

There is a strong correlation between energy and poverty. For instance, Sweden consumes 15,000 kWh of electricity per person/year, compared with Tanzania's 100 kWh/person year.

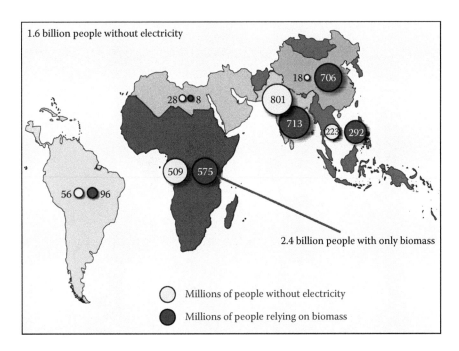

FIGURE 2.1 Correlation between energy and poverty. (From *World Energy Outlook*, Chapter 13, p. 372, 2002. IEA Publications, France.)

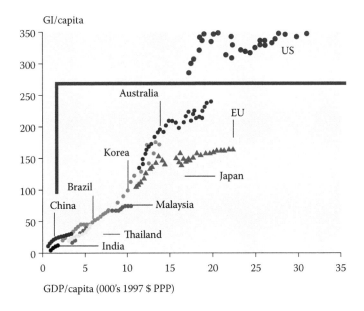

FIGURE 2.2 Correlation between energy and GDP. (From Prof. Carlo Rubia, ICTP Trieste, May 2006.)

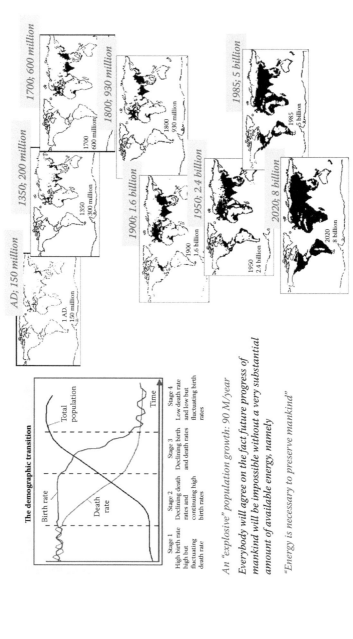

FIGURE 2.3   Global population explosion. (From Prof. Carlo Rubia, ICTP Trieste, May 2006.)

2.2 NEW ENERGY TECHNOLOGIES: WHICH ONES?

Renewable energy should be looked at as the most important instrument for the socioeconomic development, eradication of poverty and unemployment, and an instrument of rural development. The world is certainly moving in this direction and let us commit ourselves as well to the development of pollution-free renewable energy technologies (Figure 2.4). Only two natural resources have the capability for long-term energetic survival of humanity, namely: solar energy and nuclear energy.

As far as solar energy is concerned, it is worth noting that the world's primary energy consumption is only 1/10,000 of that available on the surface of the Earth in sunny countries. Solar energy may be either used directly as heat photovoltaic power or used indirectly through hydro, wind, biomass, and so on. If adequately exploited, solar energy may provide enough energy for future humanity.

2.2.1 Solar Constant

The solar constant is defined as the amount of radiant energy received per second by a unit area of a perfectly black body surface field at a right angle to the direction of the sun's rays at the mean distance of the Earth from the sun (about 149.5 million km).

Solar radiation on the surface comprises:

1. Direct beam solar radiation. This is solar radiation that reaches the Earth without being diffused.

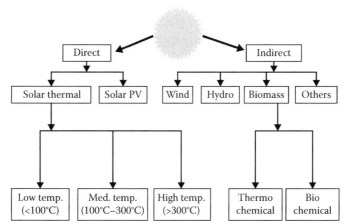

FIGURE 2.4 Classification of RETs.

2. Diffused radiation. As sunlight passes through the atmosphere, some of it is absorbed, scattered, and reflected by air molecules, water vapor, clouds, and dust and pollutants from power plants, forest fires, and volcanoes. This is called diffuse solar radiation.

3. Global solar radiation. This is the sum of the diffuse and direct solar radiation.

2.3 SOLAR THERMAL ENERGY

Solar thermal energy is a technology for harnessing solar energy for thermal energy (heat). Solar thermal collectors are defined as low-, medium-, or high-temperature collectors. Low-temperature collectors are flat plates generally used for domestic water heating and swimming pools. Medium-temperature collectors are also usually flat plates but are used for creating hot water for residential and commercial use. High-temperature collectors concentrate sunlight using mirrors or lenses and are generally used for electric power production. While only 600 MW of solar thermal power is up and running worldwide in October 2009 according to Dr. David Mills (http://www.evergreen-energyllc.com/solar_thermal.htm), another 400 MW is under construction and there are 14,000 MW of the more serious concentrating solar thermal (CST) projects being developed. Solar thermal energy is different from photovoltaic, which converts solar energy directly into electricity.

Today, low-temperature (<100°C) thermal solar technologies are reliable and mature for the market. Worldwide, they help to meet heating needs with the installation of several million square meters of solar collectors per year. These technologies can play a very important role in advanced energy-saving projects, especially in new buildings and structures. The conventional collector is the core element of a solar system for domestic hot water (DHW) or space heating. Low-temperature panels supply the carrier fluid at a temperature usually less than 80°C. As opposed to CST collectors, conventional solar panels work with both direct and diffuse solar irradiation, thus producing hot water even on cloudy days. In general, there are two large classes of solar collectors: glazed and unglazed. Unglazed collectors are cheap, easy to install, and suitable for summer (camping, swimming pools, etc.) use. Water flowing into the panel tubes is instantly heated by the sunbeams and then sent to a storage tank or even directly to the final user since the required water temperature is usually below 50°C.

The most common type of glazed collector (Figure 2.5) is the flat plate collector. In this case, the tubes in which carrier fluid flows are protected by a single or multiple transparent covering made of glass or plastic. This generally improves performance due to the greenhouse effect. The components of a glazed collector and typical energy losses are shown in Figures 2.6 and 2.7, respectively.

The thermal performance of a solar collector is usually represented by means of the collector efficiency curves as shown in Figure 2.8.

FIGURE 2.5 Glazed collectors.

Absorber plate (1)
• Copper and fins enhance heat transfer
• High absorptance and low emissivity thanks to a selective paint
• Includes the tubing grid (2) and the piping connection (3)

Transparent covering (5)
• Typically a relatively thick glass with high solar transmittance
• Designed to reduce reflection
• Tempered to maximize strength and durability

Thermal insulation (6)
• Polyurethane foam or mineral wool
• Surrounding the absorber heat losses from the carrier fluid
• An attached aluminum foil (4) acts as a barrier against out-gassing

Casing (7)
• Plastic or aluminum
• Ensures strength and resistance to the atmospheric agents
• Equipped for roof integration or anchorage to the roof or stand
• Differential expansion of frame and glazing is absorbed by gaskets (8)
• The whole is closed by a back plate (9) usually made of PVC

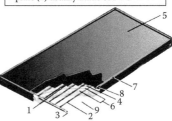

FIGURE 2.6 Components of glazed collectors. (From Sabatelli, V., Proc. Training Course on Renewable Energy: Solar Thermal, sponsored by UNESCO, held at ENEA C.R. Trisaia, Feb. 2005.)

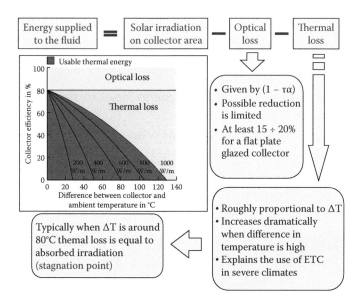

FIGURE 2.7   Energy losses in glazed collectors. (From Sharma, V.K., Proc. 1st International Conference on Mechanical Engineering: Emerging Trends for Sustainability, held at MANIT Bhopal [India], January 29–31, 2014.)

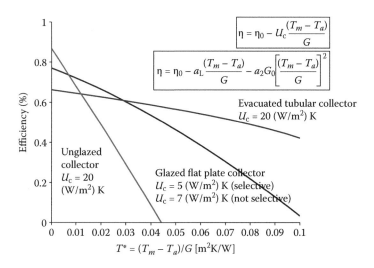

FIGURE 2.8   Collector efficiency curves. (From Sharma, V.K., Proc. 1st International Conference on Mechanical Engineering: Emerging Trends for Sustainability, held at MANIT Bhopal [India], January 29–31, 2014.)

2.4 EVACUATED-TUBE COLLECTORS

Evacuated-tube collectors (ETCs), that is, a type of solar collector that can achieve high temperatures in the range 80°C to 180°C, were introduced in the late 1970s (Figures 2.9 and 2.10). An ECT consists of parallel rows of glass tubes connected to a header pipe. Each tube has the air removed from it to eliminate heat loss through convection and radiation. Several types are available, with the common element being a glass tube surrounding an absorber plate. Most use borosilicate glass to maximize solar transmission to the absorber plate, and use similar absorber coatings to flat-plate collectors. Frames and manifolds for paralleling multiple tubes are available and can hold 4 to 20 tubes or more.

As with flat-plate collectors, multiple banks can be plumbed together to increase system capacity. While overall weights and dimensions are similar between the two types, evacuated tubes usually have an advantage in that individual tubes can be carried to the location and then assembled in place, rather than lifting an entire collector.

It is noteworthy that for the past 10 years or so, ETCs have gained significant market shares. This has partly been due to promising cost/performance ratios and the fact that ETCs tend to perform better than flat plates under some circumstances. Moreover, to avoid the risk that low quality products

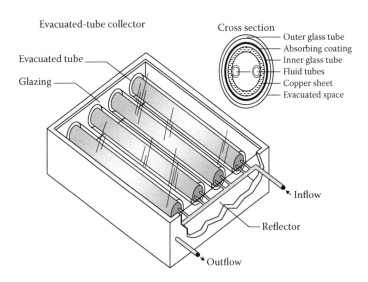

FIGURE 2.9 Evacuated-tube collector. (From http://www.daviddarling.info /encyclopedia/E/AE_evacuated_tube_collector.html.)

FIGURE 2.10   Working principle of ETC. (From http://www.siliconsolar.com /shop/solar-store/solar-hot-water-heaters/solar-evacuated-tube-collectors/.)

will destroy the good reputation of solar thermal technology, it is of the utmost importance that due consideration be given to ETCs. ETCs fall into two main groups.

2.4.1 Direct-Flow Evacuated-Tube Collectors

These consist of a group of glass tubes inside each of which is a flat or curved aluminum fin attached to a metal (usually copper) or glass absorber pipe. The fin is covered with a selective coating that absorbs solar radiation well but inhibits radiative heat loss. The heat transfer fluid is water and circulates through the pipes, one for inlet fluid and the other for outlet fluid.

Direct-flow ETCs come in several varieties distinguished by the arrangement of these pipes.

2.4.1.1 Direct-Flow Evacuated-Tube Collectors

1. Concentric fluid inlet and outlet (glass–metal). These use a single glass tube. Inside this is a copper heat pipe or water flow pipe with attached fin. The glass-metal design is efficient but can suffer reliability problems. The different heat expansion rates of the glass and

metal tubes can cause the seal between them to weaken and fail, resulting in a loss of vacuum.

2. Separated inlet and outlet pipes (glass–metal). This is the traditional type of ETC. The absorber may be flat or curved. As in the case of the concentric tube design, the efficiency can be very high, especially at relatively low working temperatures. The weakness again is the potential loss of vacuum after a few years of operation.

3. Two glass tubes fused together at one end (glass–glass). The inner tube is coated with an integrated cylindrical metal absorber. Glass–glass tubes are not generally as efficient as glass–metal tubes but are cheaper and tend to be more reliable. For very high temperature applications, glass–glass tubes can actually be more efficient than their glass–metal counterparts.

2.4.1.2 Heat Pipe Evacuated-Tube Collectors

Heat pipe ETCs consist of a metal (copper) heat pipe, to which is attached a black copper absorber plate, inside a vacuum-sealed solar tube. The heat pipe is hollow and to promote a change of state of the liquid it contains, the space inside is evacuated. There is a small quantity of liquid, such as alcohol or purified water plus special additives, inside the heat pipe. The vacuum enables the liquid to turn from liquid to vapor at a much lower temperature than it would at normal atmospheric pressure. Water, or glycol, flows through a manifold and picks up the heat, while the fluid in the heat pipe condenses and flows back down the tube for the process to be repeated.

A drawback of heat pipe collectors is that they must be mounted with a minimum tilt angle of around 25° in order to allow the internal fluid of the heat pipe to return to the hot absorber. The glass tubes are fragile, especially so since they are made of annealed glass, which is much more delicate than tempered glass. Care must be taken when transporting and handling the glass tubes.

Finally, ETCs, unlike flat-plate collectors (the surface of which is always warm), do not shed snow. Because the evacuated tubes are such good insulators, little heat escapes them and the snow that accumulates on the tubes can stick for a long time. Their surface is also irregular, so snow packs between the tubes, rendering them ineffective, and the fragility of the glass tubes makes it impossible to scrape the accumulated snow off.

They are well-suited to commercial and industrial heating applications and also for cooling applications (by regenerating refrigeration cycles). They can also be an effective alternative to flat-plate collectors for domestic space heating, especially in regions where it is often cloudy. For domestic hot water heating, flat-plate collectors tend to offer a cheaper and more reliable option.

2.4.2 Influence of the Tilt Angle on the Performance of a Solar Collector with Heat Pipes

The performance of gravity-driven heat pipes is influenced by tilt angle under which the heat pipes are installed. For many collectors, the influence of tilt angle, in general, is small, but it is worth noting that it can be an important variable for specialized collectors such as those incorporating heat pipes. It was in this context that a series of thermal performance tests were performed on an evacuated tube solar collector with heat pipes.

In one of the tests, azimuth and tilt angle were varied in such a way that the incidence angle was close to normal. The three following tests were at tilt angles of 25, 50, and 70°, but following the sun (keeping it in the vertical plane of a tube). The value of 25° was the minimum given by the manufacturer. The value of 70° was the maximum tilt angle of the test bench whereas 50° is an intermediate value. Investigation clearly revealed that the best results were obtained with 50° tilt angle whereas the worst results were obtained with the 70° tilt angle. In particular, it was noticed that varying tilt angle affects especially the thermal loss coefficients.

In the above context it is to be noted that the poorer performance obtained with the 70° tilt angle cannot be attributed solely to the greater incidence angle (compared to the other tests). The tilt angle influences the functioning of the heat pipe. When the heat pipe is horizontal, the efficiency of the collector is near zero. It grows when the tilt angle increases up to a certain value and then decreases.

This decrease is likely due to the circulation patterns of the two phases of the fluid. In the case of the outdoor steady state method, if the tilt angle varies to keep a normal incidence angle, results depend on the season and on the hour of the day. No doubt, it would be better to test the collector at several tilt angles across the operating range but the fact remains that it would certainly not be easy to test the collector with the outdoor steady state method.

Thermal performance tests on evacuated tubular collectors with heat pipes show the influence of the tilt angle on the efficiency. The best performance does not correspond to the greatest inclination. Tilt angle affects especially the thermal loss coefficient. Therefore, a fixed tilt angle, that is, a value suggested either by the manufacturer or fixed by the standard, is recommended.

In brief, it can be stated that since the tilt dependency of heat pipe collectors is still an open issue, it is recommended that future work be conducted on this topic to gain more experience and to come up with a reliable procedure on how to determine the tilt dependency in a reliable and cost-effective way.

2.5 FLAT PLATE VERSUS EVACUATED-TUBE SOLAR HOT WATER COLLECTORS

Solar hot water has come a long way in the last decade, particularly with the introduction of ETCs that are rapidly becoming the preferred option over flat plate systems. So, which is actually better—a flat plate solar hot water system or one that uses ETCs? While evacuated-tube technology is more of an investment, the benefits certainly outweigh the cost. Any additional cost may also be offset by solar hot water rebates.

2.5.1 Evacuated-Tube Collector Based Systems

- Capture sunlight better as they have a greater surface area exposed to the sun at any time.

- Are more efficient in transferring heat—up to 163% demonstrated in Australian conditions.

- Can be used in sub-zero temperatures.

- Are durable and if a tube should be broken, it can be easily and cheaply replaced.

- Provide excellent performance in overcast conditions.

- Require a smaller roof area than comparable flat plate collectors.

- Do not have the same level of corrosion problems as flat plate collectors.

2.5.2 Collector Efficiency Comparisons

The results below speak for themselves as to the improved efficiency of evacuated-tube technology over flat plate collector solar hot water systems. The following figures demonstrate efficiencies of collectors when heating water from ambient temperature to 75°C (data provided by Hills Solar, http://www.energymatters.com.au/solar-hot-water-hills-solar). Flat plate collector efficiency testing was performed at National Solar Test Facility Canada.

2.5.2.1 Sydney, New South Wales

Winter: Based on solar insolation of 426 W/m² and an ambient temperature of 13.1°C in Sydney, the Hills Esteem evacuated-tube solar collector is on average 104% more efficient per m² of aperture compared to a flat plate solar collector.

Summer: Based on solar insolation of 840 W/m² and an ambient temperature of 21.3°C in Sydney, the Hills Esteem evacuated-tube solar collector is on average 50.5% more efficient per m² of aperture (Figure 2.11).

2.5.2.2 Melbourne, Victoria

Winter: Based on solar insolation of 296 W/m² and an ambient temperature of 9.9°C in Melbourne, the Hills Esteem evacuated-tube solar collector is on average 163.5% more efficient per m² of aperture over the flat plate solar collector.

Summer: Based on solar insolation of 861 W/m² and an ambient temperature of 19.8°C in Melbourne, the Hills Esteem evacuated-tube solar collector is on average 51.5% more efficient (Figure 2.12).

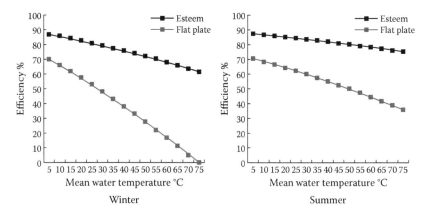

FIGURE 2.11 Sydney seasonal variations in collector efficiency. (From http://www.energymatters.com.au/solar-hot-water/flat-vs-evacuated.)

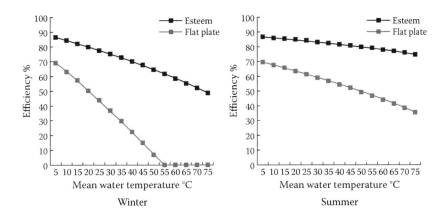

FIGURE 2.12   Melbourne seasonal variations in collector efficiency. (From http:// www.energymatters.com.au/solar-hot-water/flat-vs-evacuated.)

2.5.2.3 Brisbane, Queensland

Winter: Based on solar insolation of 546 W/m² and an ambient temperature of 17.8°C in Brisbane, the Hills Esteem evacuated-tube solar collector is on average 81% more efficient per m² of aperture compared to the flat plate solar collector.

Summer: Based on solar insolation of 828 W/m² and an ambient temperature of 25.2°C in Brisbane, the Hills Esteem evacuated-tube solar collector is on average 54% more efficient (Figure 2.13).

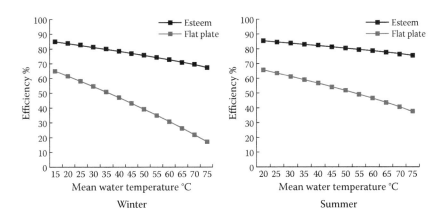

FIGURE 2.13   Brisbane seasonal variations in collector efficiency. (From http:// www.energymatters.com.au/solar-hot-water/flat-vs-evacuated.)

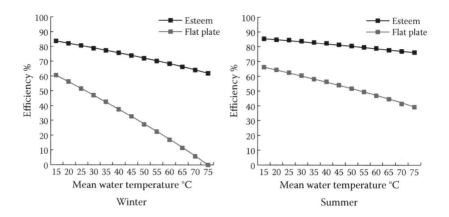

FIGURE 2.14 Adelaide seasonal variations in collector efficiency. (From http://www.energymatters.com.au/solar-hot-water/flat-vs-evacuated.)

2.5.2.4 Adelaide, South Australia

Winter: Based on solar insolation of 452 W/m^2 and an ambient temperature of 10.9°C in Adelaide, the Hills Esteem evacuated-tube solar collector is on average 132% more efficient per m^2 of aperture than the flat plate solar collector.

Summer: Based on solar insolation of 953 W/m^2 and an ambient temperature of 22.1°C in Adelaide, the Hills Esteem evacuated-tube solar collector is on average 52% more efficient (Figure 2.14).

A correctly installed solar hot water system can start saving you money straightaway, while doing your bit toward a smaller carbon footprint.

2.6 OPEN AND CLOSED LOOP HEAT TRANSFER SYSTEMS

The heat transfer in a solar water heating system may be an open loop system or a closed loop system (Figure 2.15). Water circulates using a thermosiphon or pump system.

2.6.1 Open Loop Solar Water Heating System

In an open loop (direct) system, the solar collector is separate from the storage cylinder, and the water from the cylinder that is being heated for consumption circulates through the collector panel by natural thermosiphon (open loop) or by pump. A system such as a temperature controlled pump to allow hot water to be circulated through the panel on cold nights

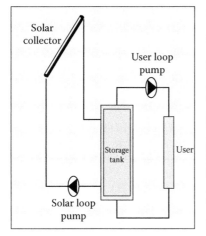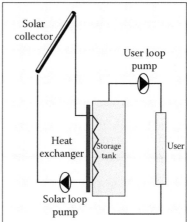

FIGURE 2.15   Open and closed loop systems. (From Sharma, V.K., Proc. Solar Energy Conference and Exhibition [Solaris 2012], February 7–9, 2012, at Varanasi, U. P., India.)

to prevent freezing must be integrated into the circuit. The open loop system has the advantage of simplicity and economy and is suitable for warm, nonfreezing climates.

2.6.2 Closed Loop Solar Water Heating System

In a closed loop (indirect) system, the solar collector is separate from the storage cylinder. A heat transfer fluid such as glycol (which does not freeze) circulates through the collector panel (closed loop) to the cylinder using either thermo-siphon or a pump. The fluid absorbs heat in the solar panels, which is then transferred to the water in the cylinder through a heat exchanger. The heat transfer fluid does not come into direct contact with the water being heated. Closed loop systems are slightly less efficient than open loop systems as there is some heat loss through the heat exchanger. Their advantage is that they can use a freeze-resistant fluid and so are more suitable for frost-prone areas.

For both open and closed loop systems, heat loss between the solar panels and the storage cylinder can be reduced by (1) keeping the distance between the two as short as possible, (2) insulating all pipes, and (3) running pipes through warm areas of the house.

2.6.3 Systems for Circulating Water or Heat Exchange Fluid

2.6.3.1 Thermo-Siphon System

In a thermo-siphon (or passive) system, as water is heated in the solar panel, it rises by convection into a storage tank located above. Cold water is then drawn into the panel for heating. This type of system is simple and low-maintenance, and uses no energy, but the cylinder must be located above the solar collectors and the pipes must have a continuous rise. Water flow with a thermo-siphon system is relatively slow. This can significantly increase heat losses from the pipes.

2.6.3.2 Pump System

To optimize performance, a pump controlled by the water temperature can be used to circulate the water/heat exchange fluid. This can provide flexibility in the location of the panel and the cylinder, and increase the form part of the frost protection system by activating a reverse flow through an open loop system when there is risk of frost.

2.7 CLASSIFICATION OF SOLAR THERMAL SYSTEMS

Solar heating systems can be distinguished into two categories, that is, factory made solar heating systems and custom built solar heating systems. The classification of a system as factory made or custom built is a choice of the final supplier, in accordance with the following definitions.

Factory made solar heating systems are batch products with one trade name, sold as complete and ready to install kits, with fixed configurations. Systems of this category are considered a single product and assessed as a whole. If a factory made solar heating system is modified by changing its configuration or by changing one or more of its components, the modified system is considered a new system.

Custom built solar heating systems are either uniquely built or assembled by choosing from an assortment of components. Systems of this category are regarded as a set of components. The components are separately tested and test results are integrated to an assessment of the whole system. Custom built solar heating systems are subdivided into two categories:

- Large custom built systems are uniquely designed for a specific situation. In general, HVAC engineers, manufacturers, or other experts design them.

- Small custom built systems offered by a company are described in a so-called assortment file, in which all components and possible system configurations, marketed by the company, are specified. Each possible combination of a system configuration with components from the assortment is considered as one custom built system.

Forced circulation systems can be classified either as factory made or as custom built, depending on the market approach chosen by the final supplier.

A factory made system for domestic hot water preparation may have an option for space heating; however, this option should not be used or considered during testing as a factory made system.

Factory made solar heating systems are batch products with a trade name sold as complete and ready to install kits with fixed configuration (Figure 2.16). A custom built solar heating system is either uniquely built or assembled by choosing from an assortment of components (Figure 2.17).

Table 2.1 shows the major differences between the system types.

FIGURE 2.16   Factory made solar systems for homes.

FIGURE 2.17   Custom-built solar systems.

TABLE 2.1   Categories of Factory Made and Custom Built Solar Heating Systems

Factory Made Solar Heating Systems	Custom Built Solar Heating Systems
Integrated collector storage systems for domestic hot water preparation	Forced-circulation systems for hot water preparation and/or space heating, assembled using components and configurations described in an assortment file (mostly small systems)
Thermo-siphon systems for domestic hot water preparation	
Forced-circulation systems as batch product with fixed configuration for domestic hot water preparation	Uniquely designed and assembled systems for hot water preparation and/or space heating (mostly large systems)

2.8 SOLAR ENERGY FOR DISTRICT HEATING

District and block heating applications offer good conditions for the use of solar thermal for existing buildings and there are a number of demonstration plants with ground-mounted as well as roof-mounted collector arrays. A major advantage is that the solar plant can be of considerable size which leads to lower specific costs.

The largest solar district heating plant comprises 18.300 m² of collector area (~10 MW thermal capacity). The main barriers to growth are low alternative fuel costs and lack of confidence for solar heating in thermal utilities.

Once cost-effective seasonal heat storage becomes widely available, large-scale applications will become more competitive, resulting in a strong increase of the potential for solar thermal. District and block heating applications offer good conditions for the use of solar thermal for existing buildings and there are a number of demonstration plants with ground-mounted as well as roof-mounted collector arrays.

In Central and Northern Europe it has become common to install solar thermal systems that provide heat both for domestic hot water and for space heating. The collector size of these so-called combi-systems is typically in the range of 7–20 m² and the tank(s) in the range of 300–2000 L. Combi-systems are often more complex than solar systems supplying DHW only. As a consequence, system design must be adapted to the specific requirements of the building. Different practices are used in different countries. In Southern Europe, combi-systems are still rarely used, but there is a big potential for systems generating space heating in winter, air-conditioning in summer, and DHW throughout the year.

2.9 SOLAR THERMAL (EU COMPETITIVENESS)

The industrialized countries should act as examples for the economically developing "sun-belt" countries, where active solar systems could play a much more important role. These countries are more important destinations for the technology than "well developed" energy economies. This could have a major impact on the realization of the worldwide active solar potential. The current market for active solar systems appears to be particularly suited to SMEs. With further development of market, larger companies may become interested in the technology.

2.10 QUALITY ASSURANCE

Solar thermal is becoming big business: The solar thermal business is one of the fastest growing businesses in Europe. This corresponds to an annual turnover—collectors only—of about 300 million Euros. Including the other components and the installation of the solar thermal system, the annual turnover reaches above 1 billion Euros.

Ensuring high-quality solar thermal products is important for the industry. Solar Keymark is the first internationally recognized quality mark for solar thermal products. Standard test methods exist to check durability, safety, and performance. These procedures are specified in European

TABLE 2.2   Standard Norms for Collector Systems

System Type	Standard Test
1. Solar collectors	EN 12975
2. Factory-made systems	EN 12976
3. Custom-built systems	EN 12977

Standards (EN). Developing the market of solar thermal products has a very high political priority. National and regional subsidies are given in most places all over Europe, but only if the products are certified—and the common European level of certification is already the requirement in the new European standards. Although the Keymark is a voluntary mark—and that goes for the Solar Keymark too—there is a very high motivation from the industry to have this certificate because of the possibility of obtaining a subsidy. Solar Keymark states conformity with these European standards and is valid almost all over Europe. Ensuring high-quality solar thermal products is important for the industry. Table 2.2 lists "quality assurance" norms that are used for different collector types.

2.11 EUROPEAN STANDARDS FOR SOLAR THERMAL PRODUCTS

EN 12975-1:2012 "Thermal solar systems and components—Solar collectors—Part 1: General Requirements." (Revised version available by end of 2014.)

EN ISO 9806: Oct. 2014 "Thermal solar systems and components—Solar collectors—Part 2: Test Methods."

(Recently, EN ISO 9806, i.e., fusion of EN 12975-2 with the international standard ISO 9806-1-2-3, has taken place. This international standard has cancelled and replaced the first/second/... editions of ISO 9806-1:1994, ISO 9806-2:1995, ISO 9806-3:1995, and European Standard EN 12975-2:2006.)

FprEN 12976-1:2015 "Thermal solar systems and components—Factory made systems Part 1: General requirements." Revised version to be available by May 2016.

FprEN 12976-2:2015 "Thermal solar systems and components—Factory Made System Part 2: Test methods." Revised version to be available by May 2016.

EN 12977-1: 2012 "Thermal solar systems and components—Custom built systems—Part 1: General requirements for solar water heaters and combi-systems." (Under revision)

EN 12977-2: 2012 "Thermal solar systems and components—Custom built systems—Part 2: Test methods for solar water heaters and combi-systems." (Under revision)

EN 12977-3: 2012 "Thermal solar systems and components—Custom built systems—Part 3: Performance test methods for solar water heater stores." (Under revision)

EN 12977-4: 2012 "Thermal solar systems and components—Custom built systems—Part 4: Performance test methods for solar combi-stores." (Under revision)

EN 12977-5: 2012 "Thermal solar systems and components—Custom built systems—Part 5: Performance test methods for control equipment." (Under revision)

2.12 SOLAR THERMAL FOR ELECTRICITY PRODUCTION

Medium temperature (about 550°C) heat collection and storage is primarily intended for electricity generation, whereas high temperature (about 800°C) heat collection and storage is primarily intended for hydrogen generation. Both of these applications are of priority strategic interest, in terms of their impact on the national energy and environmental sectors, as well as in terms of technological innovation aimed at increasing the competitive edge of Italian companies.

2.12.1 Advantages of CSP

The inherent advantage of CSP technologies is their unique integrity into conventional thermal plants, since all of them can be integrated as a "solar burner" in parallel with a fossil burner into conventional thermal cycles (see Figure 2.18). Again, with thermal storage, solar thermal plants can provide firm capacity without the need for separate backup power plants and without stochastic perturbations of the grid. Other combined cycle configurations (Figures 2.19 through 2.21) also exist.

The Archimedes project combining the best technology of today with that of tomorrow consists of a solar field, a storage system, and a steam generator, the first of its kind in the world was inaugurated in Italy on July 15, 2010.

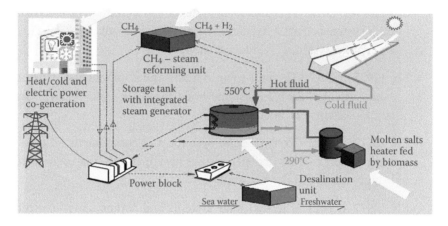

FIGURE 2.18 New ENEA technology for small and medium modular CSP. (From Fabrizi, F., Proc. Workshop Solar Energy [Concentrated Solar Power], Athens, Greece, December 9, 2011.)

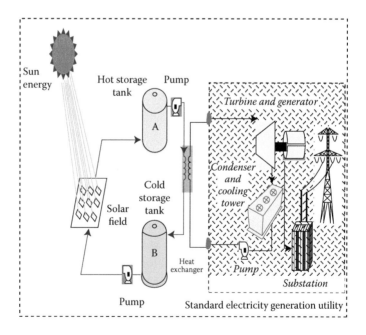

FIGURE 2.19 Integrated thermal cycle. (From Vignolini, M., CSP—ENEA technology for solar power plants. Archimedes' Solar Energy, http://www.archimedes olarenergy.it.)

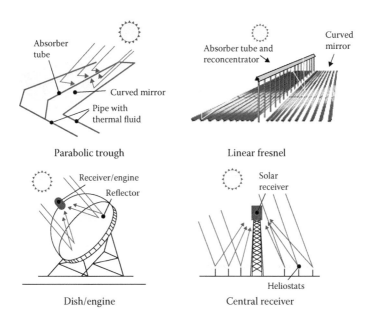

FIGURE 2.20 Stand-alone CSP plants. (From Technology Roadmap, Solar Thermal Electricity. International Energy Agency, 2014 edition.)

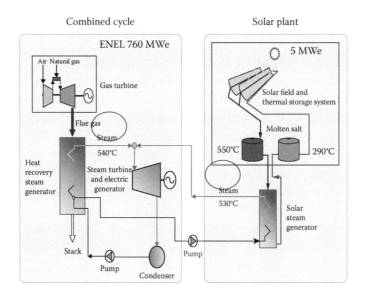

FIGURE 2.21 The Archimedes project is integration of solar plant with natural gas combined plant. (From Donatini, F., Zamparelli, C. Maccari, A., and Vignolini, M., *Clean Electrical Power*, 770–776, 2007.)

In the modular solar field, the solar energy is collected in 360 linear parabolic collectors. The movable collectors are arranged in parallel rows each forming a single string. ENEA introduced a new fluid heat carrier (molten salt eutectic mixture, 60% $NaNO_3$–40% KNO_3) in order to increase the operating temperature and the possibility of storing heat. Another innovation of ENEA is the design of a new type of concentrator based on thinner mirrors that saves construction and installation costs.

The use of large-scale heat storage (another innovation in the Archimedes project) enables the plant to provide heat to the steam generator at a constant rate of 24 hours a day, regardless of variations in solar energy availability. The steam generator consists of "tube and shell" heat exchangers in which heat is transferred to water to produce super-heated steam for use in a conventional thermoelectric plant.

A 5 MW capacity solar plant costing nearly 60 million Euros has a unique characteristic to collect and conserve thermal energy of the sun for many hours thus enabling the plant to generate electricity both during off sunshine hours and overcast sky. Although the cost for 1 kWh produced through CSP is nearly five or six times more compared to the cost of energy generated using conventional fuels, about 2.100 tons of oil saved and 3.250 tons of carbon dioxide emission is reduced in a year, making the present achievement an important milestone.

2.13 100% RENEWABLE-BASED EU (RE-THINKING 2050)

The European Renewable Energy Council (EREC) outlines in its new report RE-thinking 2050 a pathway toward a 100% renewable energy system for the EU as the only sustainable option in economic, environmental, and social terms. It assesses how the different renewable energy technologies can contribute to a fully sustainable energy supply by 2050 provided there is strong political, public, and economic support for all renewable energy technologies. The potential benefits of a future based on renewable energy are multiple: mitigating climate change, ensuring energy security, and creating sustainable future-oriented jobs.

Renewable energy deployment by 2020 will reduce annual energy-related CO_2 emissions by about 1200 million tons against 1990 emissions. By 2050, the EU would be able to reduce its energy-related CO_2 emissions by more than 90%. This reduction would result in an additional total CO_2 benefit in 2050 of €3800 billion. Higher upfront investments for renewable energy do pay off in the long-run, as the capital investment cost will be outweighed by the avoided fossil fuel and CO_2 costs. Considering the pathway set out in RE-thinking 2050, it is estimated that the renewable energy sector will employ more than 2.7 million people in 2020 and about 4.4 million in 2030 in the EU. By 2050, employment will bring 6.1 million people into work.

"Clearly, the precondition for this to happen is that the commitment toward a 100% renewable energy system for the EU needs to be established as the guiding principle for all European policies in the fields of energy, climate, R&D, industry, regional development and international cooperation." Achieving a 100% renewable energy fuelled economy is not a matter of availability of technologies; rather it is a matter of political will and of setting the course today for a sustainable energy future for the EU. A 100% renewable energy society is one where the benefits greatly outweigh the costs, be it in economic terms or in social terms, and the renewable industry is ready to prove it.

2.14 SOLAR THERMAL IS BECOMING BIG BUSINESS

The solar thermal business is one of the fastest growing businesses in Europe having a growth rate of about 30% a year and absolute annual market of 1.5 million m² of collectors in 2001. This corresponds to an annual turnover—collectors only—of about 300 million Euros. With the cost of other components and the installation of the solar thermal system, the annual turnover reaches above 1 billion Euros a year.

2.15 THE SOLAR KEYMARK WILL BE NECESSARY FOR OBTAINING SUBSIDIES

Although the Keymark is a voluntary mark—and that goes for the solar Keymark too—there is very high motivation from the industry to have this certificate because of the possibility of obtaining subsidies. Developing the market of solar thermal products has a very high political priority: National and regional subsidies are given in most of the places all over Europe, but only if the products are certified, and the common European level of certification is already the requirements in the new European standards. Solar Keymark states conformity with these European standards and is valid almost all over Europe.

EU-wide market for testing: As the solar Keymark is valid all over Europe, the test lab looks into not only its own national market, but into the total European market. The solar Keymark network (SKN) sees an urgent need to transfer solar Keymark certification into a global certification mark (Figure 2.22).

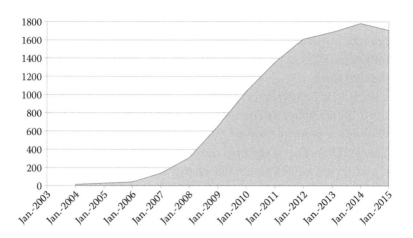

FIGURE 2.22 Number of solar Keymark licenses. (From http://www.estif.org /solarkeymarknew/images/graphs/2015%20Solar%20Keymark%20Licences.jpg.)

In this framework, general certification rules will be revised in such a way that certification bodies all over the world have the possibility to grant solar Keymark certificates similar to the ones issued by the certification bodies located in Europe, thus ensuring a fair and transparent competition.

For that purpose, major steps have already been taken for the establishment of a global solar certification network with members from the European solar industry, certification bodies, and test laboratories.

2.16 CONTRIBUTION OF SOLAR THERMAL TO THE EU 20% RENEWABLE ENERGY TARGET

To reach 20% share of renewable across the EU-27 countries by 2020, the contribution of solar thermal would be 12% according to the "Full R&D and Policy" (RDP) scenario (which includes substantial financial and political support mechanisms, energy efficiency measures, and research activities), 4.5% according to the Advanced Market Deployment (AMD) scenario, and 2.9% in the Business As Usual (BAU) scenario.

To reach the goals of the RDP scenario, a 26% average annual growth rate of the European solar thermal market is needed up to 2020. A 15% average annual growth rate is required to reach the goals of the AMD scenario and a 7% growth rate for the BAU scenario. The resulting total collector area by 2020 would be between 97 million m^2 (BAU) and 388 million m^2 (RDP). These collector areas correspond to total installed capacities of 67.9 GWth and 271.6 GWth, respectively.

2.17 LONG-TERM POTENTIAL—BEYOND DOMESTIC HOT WATER

In 2050, the solar thermal contribution to the European Union's (EU-27) low temperature heat demand will range from 47% (RDP scenario) to 8% (BAU scenario). The corresponding annual solar yields are 1552 TWh (RDP) and 391 TWh (BAU). The collector area needed to reach these goals is between 8 m^2 (RDP) and 2 m^2 (BAU) per inhabitant in the EU-27. The resulting total collector area is between 3.88 billion m^2 (RDP) and 970 million m^2 (BAU).

If solar thermal is to contribute significantly to the long-term heating and cooling demand in EU-27 countries, then the primary focus in central and northern Europe must be on systems for space heating (solar combi-systems) and in the Mediterranean area on systems providing space heating, hot water, and air conditioning (solar combi-systems).

It is worth noting that another most important segment with considerable potential is the low-temperature process heat for industry (up to 250°C).

2.18 SOLAR THERMAL—FUTURE R&D

The future R&D needs can be divided into two groups, namely, market pull and technology push. For market pull, large-scale systems should be promoted in the tourism sector and for large family house applications. This may be achieved by using demonstration installations.

R&D needs for market pull will involve demonstration of space heating and cooling systems as well as other industrial uses. Future R&D needs for technology push will involve technical and economic optimization of the systems, which is expected to result in cost reduction, especially for space heating systems. Development of design assistance services could also come in handy in this effort. There is also a need to develop new technologies for cooling systems.

2.19 CONCLUSIONS

Modern solar thermal technologies are reliable, efficient, and absolutely safe, and can be successfully applied to a broad range of heat demand including domestic water heating, space heating, and drying. Domestic water heating is currently by far the largest application for solar thermal in Europe. These systems are normally designed to cover 100% of the hot water demand in summertime and 50–80% of the total annual hot water demand.

The solar thermal industry has a high interest in delivering high-quality products, to further enhance the positive image of our technology. Public authorities that support solar thermal want to make sure that the products comply with the relevant norms. Companies are concerned to make test and certification procedures as smooth as possible.

The Solar Keymark is the quality label for solar thermal products in Europe. It certifies compliance with the relevant EN standards for solar thermal products: EN 12975 (solar collectors) and EN 12976 (factory made system). It has been established in 2003 and is since then getting more and more recognition.

New exciting areas of applications are being developed, in particular solar assisted cooling. System design, costs, and solar yield are being constantly improved.

It is true that during the past quarter century, a significant effort has gone into the development, trial, induction, and promotion of solar energy (covering varieties of applications) but truly speaking many R&D efforts still need to be undertaken to exploit fully the large potential of solar energy use in both the domestic and industrial sectors.

Keeping in view the large scope for R&D collaboration, possibilities for the exchange of technical know-how (especially in the field of solar thermal at low-medium temperature) together with significant financial contribution available from different financing institutions such as World Bank/GEF and Kfw of Germany, it is highly recommended that appropriate initiatives must be taken at the ministerial level to establish scientific contacts, seek investment by foreign investors, and promote solar business.

ACKNOWLEDGMENTS

Dr. V.K. Sharma expresses his sincere thanks to Ing. Agostino Iacobazzi, Ing. Mauro Vignolini, and Ing. Domenico Marano for their valuable cooperation.

REFERENCES

David Mills. http://www.evergreen-energyllc.com/solar_thermal.htm.
Hills Solar. http://www.energymatters.com.au/solar-hot-water-hills-solar, South Melbourne, Australia.

CHAPTER 3

Use of Building Integrated Photovoltaic (BIPV)

A Significant Step toward Green Buildings

Karunesh Kant, Amritanshu Shukla, and Atul Sharma

CONTENTS

3.1 INTRODUCTION

The projection of world energy demand will more than double by 2050 and triple by the end of the century. Incremental growth in existing energy networks will not be acceptable to supply this demand in a sustainable approach. Discovering sufficient supplies of clean energy for the future is one of society's most daunting challenges. Sunlight provides by far the largest of all carbon-neutral energy sources. More energy from the Sun strikes the Earth in one hour (4.3×10^{20} J) than is consumed on the planet in a year (4.1×10^{20} J) [1]. Presently solar resource is exploited through solar electricity—$7.5 billion industry growing at a rate of 35–40% per annum—and solar-derived fuel from biomass, which delivers the primary energy source for over 1 billion people. Worldwide, it's well known that fossil fuels will gradually decline out of common use by humans. Due to that happening in the Earth's atmosphere, it can be concluded that the environment is completely going to change as well as it will also force the planet to behave differently. The weather has been spiking to new highs or dropping to new lows every year. The water level in the world has risen and yet the amount of fresh water, which is used for drinking purposes, has decreased. It is now common knowledge that lower energy necessity is a basic requirement to surviving in the modern era. Choosing to construct using eco-friendly and sustainable techniques helps society worldwide to save a significant amount of energy. Eco-friendly products not only have lower emissions and waste, but also they are constructed in a manner wherein less energy is used in their production thereby reducing their carbon emissions [2].

Not only do eco-friendly methods help save nature, they also help to save money. For example, using insulated glass helps regulate the temperature of a home by allowing in less sunlight on sunny days and more sunlight during the winter. Thus, less is spent on heating and cooling systems in order to keep the temperature maintained inside at the desired level. Due to the environmental crisis, the green building design revolves around a wide range of issues: habitat destruction, air pollution, stormwater run-off, resource use, and climate change. However, the ongoing consumption of energy to operate, condition, and light a building, as well as the energy embodied in ongoing protection, is the largest single source of environmental harm and resource expenditure due to buildings. Carbon emissions and energy security have signaled an even stronger focus on energy in green buildings, mainly as the energy utilization growth rate of countries such as China, India, Russia, and Brazil is boosted. Energy efficient appliances may help to reduce electricity costs significantly. Dropping the operational energy use and rising durability should be the prime concerns of architects who wish to design and build "green" buildings. The conclusion was made after spending a number of years looking at actual building energy consumption, reviewing countless computer simulations, and being involved in numerous green building charrettes. It had even been suggested that 80% of a green architect's concern should be concentrated toward dropping energy expenditure during operation [3]. Figure 3.1 shows the global energy use by different sectors.

3.1.1 What Is Green Building?

A green building uses less energy, water, and other natural resources, creates less waste and greenhouse gases, and is healthy for people living or working inside as compared to a standard building. Another sense of a green structure is a clean environment, water, and healthy living. Building

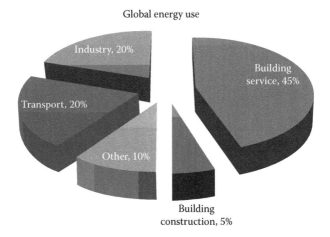

FIGURE 3.1 Global energy consumption in buildings. (From Mohanasundaram, V. *International Journal of Multidisciplinary Research*, 2.4 (2012): 66–73.)

green is not about a little more efficiency. It is about making buildings that optimize the local ecology, use of local materials, and most prominently they are built to cut power, water, and material necessities. Thus, if these things are kept in mind, then we will realize that our traditional archi- tecture was in fact very green. The major intake of energy in buildings is throughout construction and later in lighting or air-conditioning systems. This consumption must be minimized. Possibly, this should be limited to about 80–100 watts per square meter [4].

3.1.2 Needs for Green Buildings

On a national and global scale, green building offers one of the most sig- nificant and exciting prospects for sustainable development. The design of our built environment influences us all, as well as our economies and environment. The benefits of green building are as follows.

3.1.2.1 Generating Sustainable Growth

The building sector is a driver of gross domestic product (GDP), which is a measure of a country's economic performance, and green building offers an opportunity for increased output with decreased impact. Global con- struction output is projected to develop considerably by 2020, and with markets moving to greater resource productivity, policy makers have a vital role to play in ensuring European companies are at the forefront of the global green building market (Figure 3.2).

FIGURE 3.2 The Federation of Korean Industries 28-1, Yeoeuido-dong Yeongdeungpo-gu, Seoul South Korea. (From http://www.nbmcw.com/articles /green-tall-construction/15837-need-for-developing-green-building-concept-in -the-country.html.)

3.1.2.2 Creating Jobs

The construction industry employs billions of people, but it suffers from a skills shortfall. Getting talent and investment is one of the key challenges for employers. Green building gives a chance to people to become a part of the solution to worldwide challenges, to search new and exciting technologies, and to learn skills that will stay relevant.

3.1.2.3 Increasing Energy Security and Reducing Fuel Poverty

Many countries are importing oil and natural gas, which cost hundreds of billions of dollars per year. With greater energy efficiency across the world, buildings will help reduce this excessive cost, in addition to reducing the need for new expensive infrastructure. Individual energy security is also essential, and those whose fuel bills denote a significant portion of income are helped by enlarging efficiency too.

3.1.2.4 Improving the Delivery of Public Services

The power of a strong public sector leadership in green building is not just about helping lead the wider market. Green building can reduce the cost of running public buildings, grow the efficiency of service delivery, and help create the right environment to retain and foster the brightest talent.

3.1.2.5 Adding and Retaining Financial Value

Green buildings attract sales, rental premiums, and help in reducing capital expenses and diminish the risk of regulation requiring expensive alterations to buildings. Energy- and water-efficient buildings also save businesses' and consumers' money during the lifetime of the property.

The 10 best sustainable building locations range from Santa Monica, California, to Hyderabad, India, to Brisbane, Australia, and Budapest, Hungary, which shows that countries across the globe are embracing sustainability and the importance of becoming more energy efficient with new construction [5].

1. Robert Redford Building—The Robert Redford Building in Santa Monica, California is the headquarters of National Resources Defense Council. The building was named a LEED Version 2 Platinum green building rating. The building had the highest possible level of sustainable design.

2. Bank of America Tower—Bank of America Tower located at One Bryant Park in New York City received the U.S. Green Building Council's LEED Core & Shell Platinum certification.

3. Council House 2—Council House 2 is an office building located in Melbourne, Australia that is occupied by the City of Melbourne council. In 2005, it turned into the first purpose-built office building in Australia to attain a maximum Six Green Star rating, certified by the Green Building Council of Australia.

4. Adam Joseph Lewis Center for Environmental Studies—Adam Joseph Lewis Center for Environmental Studies, on the campus of Oberlin College in Ohio, uses sustainable building practices to keep it energy-efficient and comfortable. The geothermal wells are used for heating and cooling of buildings, and for generation of electricity, a photovoltaic system was installed on the roof. For purifying and treatment of water, a water treatment system was also installed and treated water can be reused for toilets.

5. Sohrabji Godrej Green Business Centre—CII-Sohrabji Godrej Green Business Centre in Hyderabad, India offers advisory services to the industry in the areas of green buildings, water management, energy efficiency, renewable energy, environmental management, green business incubation, and climate change activities.

6. Santos Place—The building has a 6 Star Green Star in Brisbane, Australia, which opened in 2009. The property includes the latest tools in environmentally sustainable design and energy efficient initiatives to achieve a 5.5 star target NABERS energy rating.

7. Clinton Presidential Library—The William J. Clinton Presidential Library at 1200 President Clinton Ave, Little Rock, Arkansas has been chosen as one of the most energy proficient and environmentally friendly places to work in the United States by the U.S. Green Buildings Council under its Direction of Energy and Environmental Design Green Building Program.

8. K&H Bank Headquarters—The K&H Bank Headquarters in Budapest on the banks of the River Danube in Hungary is the country's first LEED-NC rated building. The energy-saving design and technologies have resulted in a building that consumes around 22% less than a comparable conventional building, while providing optimum occupant comfort.

9. Park Hotel in Hyderabad—The Park Hotel in Hyderabad, India is a 270-room hotel notable for its remarkable facade of punched metallic, which helps as a sun and rain screen that guards the building's high-performance windows. Daylighting, orientation, solar gain, and local climate were all taken into account during the design of the building to maximize light and minimize heat gain.

10. Marco Polo Tower—Marco Polo Tower (Figure 3.3), which is situated alongside the new Unilever headquarters and on the river Elbe, is a noticeable place in Hamburg, Germany. A vacuum collector on the roof of a tower with heat exchanger helps to turn the heat into the cooling system for the apartments. Innovative sound insulated air louvers, in the sleeping areas, make natural ventilation possible without increased noise pollution from outside.

FIGURE 3.3   Marco Polo Tower in Hamburg, Germany. (From http://www.energy digital.com/top10/2735/Top-10-sustainable-buildings-in-the-world.)

3.2 KEY APPROACHES FOR DEVELOPING GREEN BUILDINGS

The inefficient building design and the equipment associated with it have an adverse effect on health and comfort, due to unnecessary water and energy use. Optimum use of resources by improving the design of indoor environments for industrial, institutional, and commercial buildings can be done by engineers to help building owners, tenants, and other customers.

3.2.1 Building Design and Construction

In general, highly energy-efficient buildings use reduced amounts of natural resources and energy, are less expensive to run, and create fewer adverse ecological effects than conventional buildings. However, the process of designing, renovating, or constructing a high-performance building is different from the traditional design/build methods. The approach to whole building architectural design is well thought-out with its energetic design. Mechanical and electrical system's capacity can be minimized by integrating passive solar technologies to help meet indoor space-conditioning requirements and electricity consumption. Building simulation software can guide decisions to achieve this strategy.

To increase energy efficiency of a building, a variety of measures are employed such as proper site selection and building orientation, which leads to greater heat gain by taking simple steps such as sealing air leaks around doors and windows. Renewable energy systems, active solar space heating systems, such as solar water preheaters, and solar electric (photovoltaic) panels used to offset some of a building's electric usage through self-generation and net metering are also becoming more popular.

3.2.1.1 Passive Solar Design Techniques

In building design, construction, and planning, passive solar techniques are those that take advantage of solar heat and light to offset the need for gas or electric heating, air conditioning, and lighting. These kinds of techniques are different from active solar systems like photovoltaic solar panels, which transform solar rays into electricity for home use.

Common passive solar tactics include south-facing building orientations that absorb and store solar heat during the winter and deflect solar heat during the summer, and "daylighting," or maximizing the use of windows and full-glass exterior walls, often covered with a heat-deflecting glaze, to allow natural lighting into the building's interior work spaces, while minimizing the heat gain that might normally result.

3.2.1.2 Thermal Storage

Thermal storage may be implemented in individual building projects in numerous ways. Some of the most common strategies include strategic window placement and daylighting design, selection of appropriate glazing for windows and skylights, appropriate shading of glass to prevent undesirable heat gain, use of light-colored materials or paint for building envelopes and roofs, careful siting and orientation, and appropriate landscaping.

Passive solar heating systems in a building with south-facing orientation can be combined with solar heat-storing trombe walls or floors made with concrete, tile, brick, stone, or masonry that absorb solar heat, store it, and then slowly release the heat into the building. Due to the angle at which solar rays reach the Earth's surface during winter, a south-facing building with a large overhang will be able to absorb the heat of the sun, lessening the need for energy-consuming heating systems. During summer months when solar rays arrive at a much higher angle, the overhang shades the building, eliminating much of the heat gain that would otherwise result and reducing air conditioning use.

According to the U.S. Department of Energy, energy cost reductions of 30–50% below national averages are possible with 45 cents to 75 cents per square foot annual savings in new office building designs if an optimum mix of energy conservation and thermal storage design strategies are applied (building "thermal"). However, the department noted that it is rarely feasible to meet 100% of a building heating or cooling load with passive solar, where an optimum design is based on minimizing life-cycle cost.

3.2.1.3 Cooling Strategies

During the summer months, air conditioning systems consume much electricity. Alternative passive cooling strategies, especially when used in conjunction with thermal storage techniques that prevent heat absorption, may reduce the need for heavy air conditioning. Such cooling techniques include the use of natural ventilation, ceiling fans, atria and stairwell towers, evaporative cooling systems for dry climates, dehumidification systems, and geothermal cooling and heat pump systems. These methods can effectively remove heat from the interior of a building without the use of energy-intensive conventional air conditioning systems.

3.2.1.4 Daylighting

Daylighting techniques involve the incorporation of natural daylight into the mix of a building's interior illumination. When appropriately designed and joined with electric lighting, daylighting can propose significant energy savings by offsetting a portion of the electric lighting required. A side benefit of daylighting is that it also reduces the internal heat gain from electric lighting, thereby reducing required cooling capacity. Results of recent studies imply improved productivity and health in daylighted schools and offices. Windows—the principal source of daylight—also provide visual relief, a visual portal to the world outside the building, time orientation, and a possible source of ventilation and emergency egress (U.S. Dept. of Energy, Building Daylighting). Other sources of daylight include light pipes with mirrored inner surfaces that bring natural light deep into a building interior, skylights, sky domes, and reflective devices and surfaces that spread daylight more evenly in occupied interior spaces.

3.2.1.5 High-Performance Insulation

A type of superinsulating material increasingly used for residential and light commercial buildings is structural insulated panels used in floors, walls, and roofs. The panels are manufactured by forming a sandwich of rigid foam plastic insulation between two panels of plywood. The panels generally cost about the same as building with wood-frame construction, but labor costs and job-site waste are reduced (structural).

In early 2007, the American Institute of Architects; the American Society of Heating, Refrigerating and Air Conditioning Engineers; Architecture 2030; the Illuminating Engineering Society of North America; and the U.S. Green Building Council, with the support of the U.S. Department of Energy, finalized an agreement of understanding establishing a common benchmark and the goal of net zero energy buildings. The ultimate goal is carbon-neutral buildings by 2030. To reach that goal, the alliance partners agreed to define the baseline for their common target goals.

3.2.2 Methods to Decrease Energy Use by Building Operating Systems

Most large, multistory buildings employ sophisticated, computer-based building control systems that integrate key subsystems such as lighting, security, fire protection, heating and air conditioning, occupancy sensors, and large networks of programmable thermostats. Such operating and control systems afford a high degree of fine-tuning capability and operating flexibility for differential environmental control in various locations of a building, depending on their exposure to daylight and weather conditions. Other methods include rooftop wind turbines and geothermal heat pumps.

3.2.3 Commercially Viable Options

There are emerging technologies being developed to increase energy efficiency. One such technology is electro chromic windows that can instantly switch from transparent to varying shades of gray in response to a small, applied current. A large view window made with electro chromic materials could be programmed to respond to incoming natural light by stepping down its setting to minimize light transmittance. When integrated with daylight and occupancy sensors and programmable controls, electro chromic windows could be set to automatic and incrementally shade indoor environments in synch with the sun's arc across the sky.

Computer-simulation programs may impact and improve building energy efficiency. Today's building energy calculation software is growing in sophistication and could eventually lead to whole-building energy simulation analytical tools that could evaluate low-energy use design factors and optimize incorporation of renewable energy systems.

3.3 BIPV: CONCEPT TO REALITY

Solar photovoltaic technology, applied in residential buildings, is generally used for photovoltaic conversion and lighting. Building integrated photovoltaic (BIPV) is a novel concept for the application of solar power, in brief, fitting the solar photovoltaic unit on the surface of the maintenance structure of the building to provide electricity [6]. Photovoltaic arrays do not take up additional floor space when integrated with the construction, and is the best installation of a photovoltaic generation system, thus attracting much attention. BIPV can be divided into two categories according to the forms that the photovoltaic array is integrated with the buildings [7]. One is the combination of photovoltaic array with building, installing the PV array on the building, and the building plays a supporting role as a photovoltaic carrier (Figure 3.4; [8,9]). The other is the integration of the photovoltaic array with the building. PV modules appear as the building material, and the photovoltaic array becomes the integral part of the construction, such as photoelectric curtain walls, photoelectric tile roof, photoelectric lighting roof, etc. (Figure 3.5; [10,11]).

(a)

(b)

FIGURE 3.4 Ways of the solar PV arrays combined with the residential building. (a) Combined with the roof. (From http://sinovoltaics.com/learning-center/bipv /building-integrated-photovoltaics-bipv/.) (b) Combined with the façade. (From http://www.renewableenergyfocus.com/view/39779/spotlight-on-bipv/.)

3.3.1 Building Integration of Photovoltaic Cells

The four main options for building integration of PV cells are on inclined roofs, flat roofs, facades, and shading systems. South-facing inclined roofs are generally best fit for PV installation because of the favorable angle with the sun. One option is to mount PV modules above the roofing system.

(a)

(b)

FIGURE 3.5 Ways of the solar PV arrays integrated with the residential building. (a) Photoelectric tile roof. (From Solar Thermal Magazine, The curved solar power rooftop tile, homeowners now have better looking options, http://www.solarthermalmagazine.com/2010/10/23/the-curved-solar-power-roof top-tile-homeowners-now-have-better-looking-options/S, October 23, 2010.) (b) Photoelectric lighting roof. (From Global Energy Network Institute, Suntech to develop 20% of BIPV solar rooftop program projects, http://www.geni.org /globalenergy/library/technical-articles/generation/solar/pv-tech.org/suntech -to-develope-20%25-of-bivp-solar-rooftop-program-projects,-china/index.shtmlS, November 13, 2009.)

Another option is PV modules that replace conventional building materials in parts of the building envelopes, like the roofs or facades, that is, BIPVs. "BIPV is considered a functional part of the building, or they are architecturally incorporated into the building's design" [12]. The BIPV system serves as building envelope material and a power generator simultaneously [13]. This can provide savings in materials and labor, and also reduce the electricity costs, but obviously increases the importance of water tightness and durability of the BIPV product.

At higher temperature, the performance of the solar cells, especially for mono- and polycrystalline modules decreases. Therefore, an air gap beneath the module is essential to decrease the temperature. The thin-film products, on the other hand, perform more independently of the temperature.

3.3.2 Architectural Aspects of BIPVs

BIPV systems provide many opportunities for innovative architectural design and can be aesthetically appealing. BIPVs can act as shading devices and also form semitransparent elements of fenestration [14]. Amorphous silicon tiles can be used to make a BIPV roof look very much like a standard tiled roof (as shown in Figure 3.5a), while on the other hand semitransparent modules can be used in facades or glass ceilings to create different visual effects (as shown in Figure 3.5b). Some architects enjoy presenting a BIPV roof as a roof giving a clear visual impression, while others want the BIPV roof to look as much like a standard roof as possible. Further information about building integration of solar energy systems in general and architectural integration of PV and BIPV in particular, may be found in the studies by Hestnes [15], Farkas et al. [16], and Peng et al. [12], respectively. The PVs can be integrated in two types as follows.

1. Architectural integration

2. Building integration

Integration of PV into buildings has the following advantages [17]:

- Part of the building is used for PV installation and so additional land is not required. This is particularly significant in densely populated areas in cities.

- The expense of the PV divider or rooftop can be counterbalanced in contrast to the expense of the building component it replaces.

- Power is generated on site and replaces electricity that would otherwise be purchased at commercial rates and avoids distribution losses.

- PV, if grid connected, ensures security of supply and high cost of storage is avoided.

- Architecturally elegant, well-integrated systems will increase market acceptance.

3.3.2.1 Roof Integration of PV

A PV system can be integrated into the roof in several ways. One choice is for the integrated system to be part of the external skin and therefore part of an impermeable layer in the construction. The other type is that the PV is glued onto insulation material. This kind of warm roof construction arrangement is very well suited to renovating large flat roofs. Using PV modules as roof covering reduces the amount of building materials needed, which is very favorable for a sustainable building and can help to reduce costs. There are also many products for small-scale use, to suit the scale of the roof covering, for example, PV shingles and tiles. The roof integration of PV can be categorized as follows.

- PVs on flat roof

- PVs on inclined/pitched roof

- Roof with integrated PV tiles

- PV in saw-toothed north light roof/sky light

- PVs on curved roof/wall

- PVs in atrium/skylights

For PVs on a flat roof, the PVs are laid horizontally on the flat roofs which are normally not visible from the ground and hence the significance of the aesthetic part of integration can be less. Photovoltaic facilities on inclined or pitched roofs when facing in the right direction are suitable for good energy yield. Architectural aesthetics should be taken into consideration while integrating as these are the visible parts of the building unlike the flat roofs (Figure 3.6a). A roof with integrated PV tiles has been

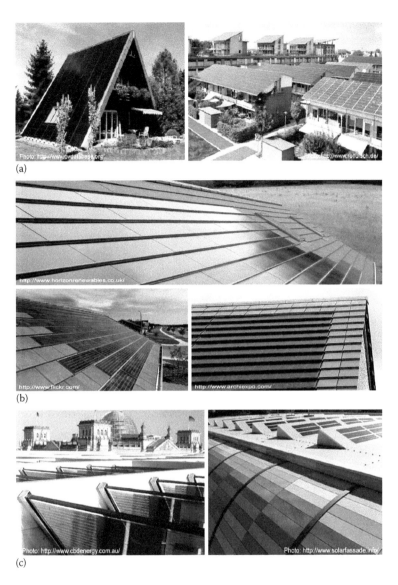

FIGURE 3.6 (a) (Left) Integrated PV on the pitched roof of a vacation house in Bartholomä-Park in Germany. (Right) Integrated PV roofs in Schlierberg Solar Settlement in Freiburg. (From http://www.pvdatabase.org/, http://www.rolfdisch .de/.) (b) Integrated PV roof tiles on the roof. (From http://www.horizonrenewables .co.uk/, http://www.flickr.com/, http://www.archiexpo.com/.) (c) (Left) Integrated PV on the sawtoothed glass roof of Paul Lobe Haus, Berlin. (Right) Sawtooth roof with PV integration, DIY store, Hamburg. (From http://www.cbdenergy.com .au/, http://www.solarfassade.info/.) *(Continued)*

(d)

(e)

FIGURE 3.6 (CONTINUED)   (d) PV integration on the curved roof of BP solar show-case in Birmingham. (From http://www.solartechnologies.co.uk/.) (e) (Left) Atrium with PV modules, Ludesch/Vlbg., Austria; (right) PV on colored skylights at Bejar Market, Salamnca, Spain. (From http://www.solarfassade.info/, http://www.onyxsolar.com/.)

a normal practice or integrated with larger standard modules of PV on the roof for energy yield. However, when the integration is to be done on traditional tiled roofs, it may not always be possible to use large modules and the character of the roof may also be ruined (Figure 3.6b).

Sawtooth roofs can be implemented as (semi-) transparent or opaque. Glass sawtooth roofs make optimal use of daylight, protect in contrast to direct sunlight, and thus reduce a building's cooling load. The world's largest integration of thin-film PV systems on the sawtoothed glass roof of Paul

Lobe Haus, Berlin optimizes interior light conditions in addition to producing clean energy (Figure 3.6c, left). The flexibility with the integration of PV is further emphasized by the fact that PV modules can also be mounted on curved load-bearing surfaces. Arched surfaces and roofs are equally suited for use with PV systems. This allows added freedom of design involving PV integration. The BP solar showcase in Birmingham, UK is a good example of PV integration of a curved roof (Figure 3.6d). PVs can equally be integrated as multifunctional elements in transparent roof structures or atriums that allow controlled light into the interior. As a semitransparent roof unit, they can protect the building from heat, sunlight, glare, and the weather (Figure 3.6e).

3.3.2.2 Facade Integration of PV

It is a normal building practice that the external walls of buildings are covered with insulation and protective cladding. This covering can be wood, metal sheets, panels, glass, or PV modules. For luxury office buildings, where the cladding is often expensive, integrating PV modules as cladding on opaque parts of the building is not more expensive than other commonly used materials like natural stones, granite, or aluminium cladding. In the Solar XXI building, vertical bands of photovoltaic panels are integrated into the south facade, with an alternative rhythm with the glazing, resulting in an elevation based on the concept of modularity and repetition (Figure 3.7).

FIGURE 3.7 PV integrated into the opaque parts of the façade of Solar XXI building, Portugal. (From http://csc.esbensen.dk.)

Façade integration of PV module is installed in two ways on walls depending on inclination.

- PV on inclined walls

- PVs as sunshades

It is quite interesting to incline the façade where PV is integrated basically for two reasons; first because it would then be easy to optimize the PV modules' position for maximum energy yield and second because this would further add to the elegance of the façade. The west side of the Vocational College in Tirol, Austria is treated in a similar fashion. The PV integrated façade is curved and inclined, which is one of the main features of the architectural expression of the building (Figure 3.8). In energy efficient buildings, south-facing glazing acts as an energy absorber and hence the building can be designed to enable all the solar heat energy to be distributed from the south façade. However, problems can arise in the summer when the building overheats and becomes uncomfortable. High solar heat gain will increase the demand for air conditioning, which will in turn increase the building's energy requirement. To avoid the energy need for air conditioning, external sunshades could be a good option to prevent

FIGURE 3.8   Inclined PV integrated glazed façade of Vocational College in Tirol, Austria. (Credit: http://www.m9-architekten.at/.)

FIGURE 3.9   Inclined PV integrated façade of Solar-Fabrik building, Freiburg, Germany. (Credit: http://www.solar-fabrik.de/.)

the heat from transmitting into the interior of the building. Typically, sun shades can take the form of a fixed or controlled glass louver system and can be installed either vertically or horizontally on the façade of a building. These shades can be both fixed or movable. Besides, opaque PV modules can equally be used in a similar way as a conventional shading device. The south-glazed PV façade of the Solar-Fabrik building in Freiburg also has integrated PV shades to prevent overheating inside (Figure 3.9).

3.3.3 BIPV Products

There is a wide range of different BIPV products available on the market, which can be categorized in different ways. In this work, the classification is mostly taking into account how the maker depicts the item, and what other sort of material the item is altered to be joined with. The product categories considered are foils, tiles, modules, and solar cell glazing products. Some products hold a variety of properties, therefore making it more difficult to categorize them. This chapter is limited to BIPVs. Nevertheless, there is one more type of PV system classification named building attached photovoltaic (BAPV) products that are not BIPVs, or it is uncertain regarding how the product is mounted. Peng et al. [12] refers to BAPV as an add-on to the building, thus not directly related to the structure's functional aspects.

3.3.3.1 BIPV Foil Products

Because of light weight and adaptability, foil items are perfect for establishment and the weight constraints most rooftops have. The PV cells are regularly produced using thin-film cells to keep up the adaptability in the foil and the productivity with respect to high temperatures for utilization on nonventilated rooftop arrangements. Unfortunately, there are few manufacturers in the market that offer weather-tight solutions. Table 3.1 presents an example of a foil product, displaying the open circuit potential/voltage U_{OC}, short circuit current I_{SC}, maximum power point P_{max}, and the fill factor FF.

3.3.3.2 BIPV Tile Products

The BIPV tile products can cover the entire roof or just parts of the roof. They are normally arranged in modules with the appearance and properties of standard roof tiles and substitute a certain number of tiles. This is a good option for retrofitting of roofs. The cell type and tile shape vary. Some tile products look like curved ceramic tiles (see Figure 3.5a) and will not be area effective owing to the curved surface area, but may be more aesthetically attractive. Table 3.2 gives examples of four photovoltaic tile products that are on the market today.

3.3.3.3 BIPV Module Products

The BIPV module products presented are slightly similar to conventional PV modules. The dissimilarity, however, is that they are prepared with weather skin solutions. Some of the products can replace dissimilar kinds of roofing, or they are suitable for a particular roof application produced by its manufacturer, for example, Rheinzink's "Solar PV Click Roll Cap System" [18]. These mounting systems raise the simplicity of installation. There is a huge amount of products on the market and some of them are promoted as BIPV products without functioning as weather skin. Other products are not specific on how they are installed, which leads to uncertainty whether they are BIPVs or BAPVs. Some of the products in this type are premade modules with isolation or other elements incorporated in the body. Table 3.3 gives examples of BIPV module products.

3.3.3.4 Solar Cell Glazing Products

Solar cell glazing products give an awesome assortment of alternatives for windows, glassed or tiled exteriors, and rooftops. Distinctive hues and transparencies can make various tastefully satisfying results conceivable.

TABLE 3.1 Literature Data for One of the BIPV Foil Products

Manufacturer	Product[a]	η (%)	U_{OC} (V)	I_{SC} (A)	P_{max} (W)	FF	Area (mm × mm)	P_{max}/Area (W/m²)	Material
Alwitra GmbH & Co.	Evalon V Solar 408		138.6	5.1	408/ module	0.58	1550 × 6000	42.9	Amorphous silicon cells
	Evalon V Solar 136		46.2	5.1	136/ module	0.58	1050 × 3360	38.5	Amorphous silicon cells

[a] Several models are available from the producer in the Evalon V Solar series.

TABLE 3.2 Literature Data for Some of the BIPV Tile Products

Manufacturer	Product[a]	η (%)	U_{OC} (V)	I_{SC} (A)	P_{max} (W)	FF	Area (mm × mm)	P_{max}/Area (W/m²)	Material
Solar-dachstein	STEP-design		23.15	2.4	1.36/cell	0.76	8 units 100 × 100	136	Poly-crystalline silicon cells
SRS Energy	Solé Powertile		6.3	4.6	15.75/module	0.54	868 × 457.2	39.7	Amorphous silicon cells from Uni-Solar
Lumeta	Solar Flat Tile		7.4	5.2	28/module	0.73	432 × 905	71.6	Mono-crystalline silicon cells
Solar Century	C21e Tile	20/cell	12	5.55	52/module	0.78	1220 × 420	101.5	Mono-crystalline cells

[a] Several models are available from the producer.

TABLE 3.3 Literature Data for Some of the BIPV Module Products

Manufacturer	Product[a]	η (%)	U_{OC} (V)	I_{SC} (A)	P_{max} (W)	FF	Area (mm × mm)	P_{max}/Area (W/m²)	Material
Creaton AG	Creaton Solesia		13.86	8.46	90/module	0.77	1778 × 355	142.6	Mono-crystalline silicon cells
Rheinzink	PV Quickstep		17.1	5.12	68/module	0.78	2000 × 365	93.2	Crystalline silicon cells
Abakus Solar AG	Peak On P220-60	13.2	36.77	8.22	220	0.73	1667 × 1000	132	Poly-crystalline silicon cells
	Peak On P235-60	14.6	37.21	8.48	235	0.74	1630 × 1000	144.2	Poly-crystalline silicon cells
	ANT P6-60-230	14.07	36.77	8.42	230	0.74	1658 × 986	140.7	Poly-crystalline silicon cells
DuPont	Gevity	17.7	24.20–24.43	8.77–8.87	160–165	0.75–0.76	1332.5 × 929	129.36–133.4	Mono-crystalline silicon cells
Suntech	MSZ-190J-D		45.2	5.62	190/module	0.75	1641 × 834.5	139	Mono-crystalline silicon cells
	MSZ-90J-CH		22.4	5.29	90/module	0.76	879 × 843.5	125	Mono-crystalline silicon cells
Schott Solar	InDax 214	12.5	36.3	8.04			1769 × 999		Poly-crystalline silicon cells
	InDax 225	13.1	33.5	6.6			1769 × 999		Poly-crystalline silicon cells
Solar Century	C21e Slate	20/cell	12	5.55	52	0.78	1174 × 318	139.3	Mono-crystalline silicon cells

a Several models are available from the producer.

TABLE 3.4 Literature Data For Some Solar Cell Glazing Products

Manufacturer	Product[a]	η (%)	U_{OC} (V)	I_{SC} (A)	P_{max} (W)	FF	Area (mm × mm)	P_{max}/Area (W/m²)	Material
Abakus Solar AG	Peak In P210-60		36.5	7.7			2000 × 1066		Poly-crystalline silicon cells
Vidursolar	FV VS16 C36 P120		21.6	7.63			1600 × 720		Poly-crystalline silicon cells
Glaswerke Arnold GmbH & Co KG	Voltarlux-ASI-T-Mono 4-fach		93	1.97	100/module	0.55	2358 × 1027	41.3	Amorphous silicon cells from Schott Solar
Schott Solar	ASI THRU-1-L	6	111	0.55	48	0.79	1122 × 690	62	Amorphous silicon cells
	ASI THRU-4-IO	6	111	2.22	190	0.77	1122 × 2619	64.7	Amorphous silicon cells
Sapa Building System	Amorphous silicon thin film	5/cell			32/cell		576 × 976/cell	50	Amorphous silicon thin film
	Poly-crystalline	16/cell			1.46–3.85/cell		156 × 156/cell	120	Poly-crystalline
	Mono-crystalline high efficient	22/cell			2.90–3.11/cell		125 × 125/cell	155	Mono-crystalline high efficient

[a] Several models are available from the producer.

The modules transmit daylight and function as water and sun shield. "The technology involves spraying a coating of silicon nanoparticles onto the window, which work as solar cells" [19]. The separation between the cells relies on needed transparency level and the criteria for power creation; however, ordinarily the separation is somewhere around 3 and 50 mm. The space in between cells transmits diffuse daylight. Along these lines, both shading and normal lighting is given while creating power. The producers of sunlight-based cell glazing items generally offer recyclable items for the particular project, while Table 3.4 shows some predefined modules. The producers also offer customized modules regarding shape, cell material, color, and transparency level, that is, the distance between cells. Values for the efficiencies are not given for these products, but for Voltarlux an FF value of 0.55 is given with a transparency level of 10%. The transparency level varies from 16% to 41%, respectively, for smallest to largest size, for the Vidursolar models, and is 25% for Abakus' Peak In P210-60.

3.4 MAJOR DEVELOPMENTS

There is a huge potential for the BIPV market all over the world. However, there is an established market in a number of the countries in Europe, that is, Spain, Germany, France, Switzerland, and Italy. Many governments in these countries are sponsoring the BIPV technology by implementing a Feed in Tariff (FiT) system. This concept allows selling back excessive power to the grid at a higher price than the grid price of the electricity. The worldwide growth rate of BIPV during the last seven years is approximately 50% of installed capacity in every year. There is more than 1300 MW of installation to date. The upcoming BIPV market growth is shown in Figure 3.10 to the year 2020 [20]. BIPV installation in 2020 is expected to grow with a growth rate of 30% in each year. The expected installation is more than 8000 MW by end of year 2020. Table 3.5 presents the overall business of PV modules by different companies. It is observed that there is no leading PV module manufacturer in the world. Moreover, manufacturers like Sun Tech occupy only 9.2% of the PV market Table 3.6 [21,22].

Figure 3.11 shows the current BIPV installed systems in the world and some prediction for its future expansion [23]. Figure 3.12 shows the development status of different countries in the BIPV market. In Europe, based on the information on the European Photovoltaic Industry Association in the year 2012 [24], Germany misplaced the top growing market in Italy in 2011; this country is still the biggest PV market in the world. In the year 2011, Germany added 7.5 MW to its previous installation while Italy

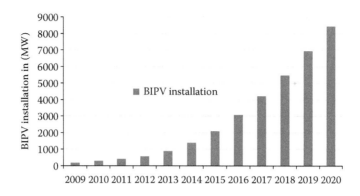

FIGURE 3.10 BIPV market: global installation capacity forecasted till 2020 in MW. (From Frost and Sullivan. European building integrated photovoltaic market. Report. 2008.)

TABLE 3.5   The Competitive Structure of the BIPV Market (Solar Buzz)

PV Module Manufacturer	Country	% of Market Share
Suntech	China	9.2
Yingli Green Energy Energy	China	7.6
Canadian Solar	Canada	7.6
Trina Solar	China	6.9
Sharp Solar	Japan	6
Solar fun	China	5.4
First Solar	US	5.3
Jabil Circuit	US	4.2
Solar World	US	4.1
Sun Power	US	3.6
LDK	China	3.4
Sanyo Electric	US	3.3
REC	Norway	3
Kyocera	Japan	3
JA Solar	China	2.8
Jinko Solar	China	2.6
Ningbo Solar Electric	China	2.5
Renesola	China	2.1
Others		17.4

did almost 9.3 MW and experienced an astonishing growth at the time. The FiT plays a significant role in this achievement (€5.5 billion per year). About half of the PV installations in the world are installed in these two countries. France is the third European country that managed to add more than 1 GW to its market.

TABLE 3.6   List of Major BIPV Projects with Different Photovoltaic Categories

PV Categories	Project Name	Project Location	Latitude/Longitude	Year of Establishment	Capacity of the Project
Roof-top integration	Black River Park commercial Roof Top Solar Project	Cape Town, South Africa	35° 55' S 18° 22' E	2014	1.2 MWp
Roof-top integration	Solar PV plant, Punjab	Amritsar, Punjab, India	31° 37' N 74° 55' E	2014	7.52 MWp
Roof-top integration	Centro Ingrosso Sviluppo compano in Nola	Nola-Naples, Italy	40° 55' 33.96" N 14° 31' 38.64" E	2013	20.252 MWp
Roof-top integration	Riverside Renewable Energy-Holt logistics Refrigerated warehouse	Gloucester City, New Jersey	39° 53' 29.67" N 75° 7' 0.12" W	2012	9 MWp
Roof-top integration	Avidan Energy Solution	Edison, New Jersey	40° 30' 14.4" N 74° 20' 57.84" W	2011	4.26 MWp
Roof-top integration	Goodyear Dunlop logistic center	Philipps burg, Germany	49° 13' 59.88" N 8° 27' E	2011	7.4 MWp
Roof-top integration	Toys "R" Us distribution center	Flanders, New Jersey	40° 50' 52" N 74° 42' 34" W	2011	5.38 MWp
Roof-top integration	Boeing 787 assembly building, South Carolina	North Charleston South Carolina	32° 58' 28.52" N 80° 4' 8.99" W	2011	2.6 MWp
Roof-top integration	Shanghai No. 1/2 Metro operation Co. Ltd.	Hongqiao Railway Station, Shanghai, China	31° 12' N 121° 30' E	2010	6.68 MWp
Roof-top integration	FedEx	Wood bridge, New Jersey	40° 33' 38.88" N 74° 17' 33.36" W	2010	2.42 MWp
Roof-top integration	GSA Bean Federal Centre	Indianapolis, Indiana	39° 47' 27.6" N 86° 8' 52.8" W	2010	2.012 MWp

Source: List of photovoltaic installation. 2014. http://en.wikipedia.org/wiki/List_of_rooftop_photovoltaic_installations.

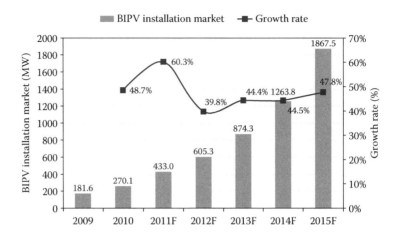

FIGURE 3.11 Global BIPV installation and prediction of its expansion rate. (From Battery, S. BIPV Technology and Market Forecast, 2011.)

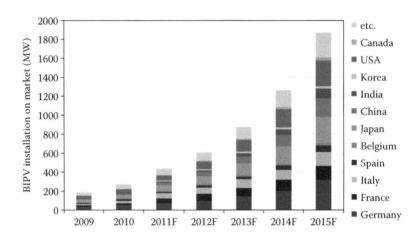

FIGURE 3.12 Development status of different countries in BIPV market and their future progress. (From Battery, S. BIPV Technology and Market Forecast, 2011.)

3.5 BARRIERS AND FUTURE DIRECTIONS

BIPV product improvement has been continuing for the past 30 years, but its practical applications have been slow in contrast to conventional rack-mounted solar PV. Although we can see the substantial rise of tendency toward solar systems all over the world, several problems have to be solved if we want to keep this trend. In this chapter, we have classified the barriers into four main groups as shown in Figure 3.13.

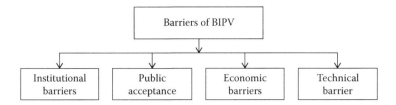

FIGURE 3.13   Main barrier of BIPV.

Institutional barriers can be overcome by making strong permanent supportive policies and plans, governments can empower these programs. Sometimes these plans can entirely revolutionize the situations and open up new channels. For instance, Spain's encouragement of renewable energies was confirmed in 1999 but the big evolution did not happen until 2005 when the promotion of renewable energy (PER) was planned. Consequently, after Germany, Spain holds the second position in the EU ranking in the year 2009. Success or failure in BIPV projects completely depends on citizens' cooperation. Having people educated about the importance of consuming renewable energy and the risks of using fossil fuels such as oil and coal imposed on us and our planet are critical. In view of the low productivity of panels and the amount of energy that we can produce by them is not huge, these projects require more opportunity to end up prominent. So civilians have to be patient and administrations should devote sufficient time and funds to upsurge their knowledge and provoke novel ideas. Rules and regulations should also be simplified enough to become more understandable to the public. Economics is the foremost barrier that obstructs our goals. Without government collaborations, projects will certainly fail. The important impact of strong policy making and enough economic incentives and supports such as loans with low interests and long-term durability, grants and reduced taxes for conducting progressive BIPV projects are stated in various studies. Investing in BIPV systems is a long-term investment and its best result will be revealed 20 years later. Thus, convincing companies and people to work with this investment depends on the government's power and concerns.

One of the main reasons for limited markets and practical applications is that the technical barriers, which span from design phase through to commissioning and maintenance phases, have not been understood by shareholders. All of these barriers can not necessarily be removed by a single solitary branch of knowledge, but rather it needs interdisciplinary

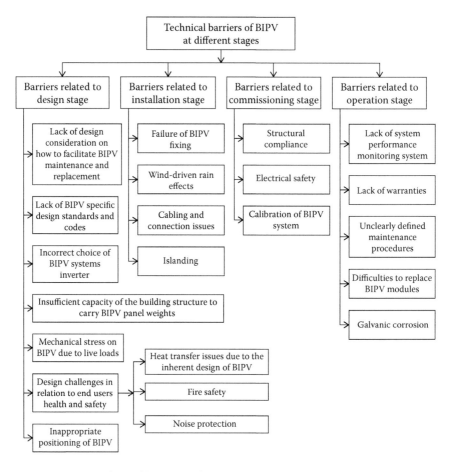

FIGURE 3.14   Technical barriers of BIPV at different stages.

efforts. The technical barriers of BIPV at different stages are given in Figure 3.14.

3.5.1 Future Direction

3.5.1.1 New Materials and Solutions for BIPVs

The future research opportunities are in view of the current products. Huge numbers of items can accomplish a higher proficiency with better materials and better solutions. Actually, advances in the improvement of PV materials will prompt advances for the BIPV frameworks. The challenge is accomplishing this at a suitable expense.

New PV technologies that may start and progress new developments, which may be developed into BIPV, may be found in different fields, for example, (a) ultra-low cost, low-medium efficiency, organic based modules, (b) ultra-high efficiency modules, (c) solar concentrator and/or solar trapping systems embedded in the solar cell surface and material beneath, and (d) flexible lightweight inorganic thin film solar cells, or others. The development of new PV materials and technologies in the future will contribute to new and improved BIPV products, for example, with higher solar efficiencies.

The new solutions in the PV industry are many and various. There is usually room for improvement in each specific system, for example, regarding ventilation rate, positioning, removing of snow, etc. For good integration results, the BIPV system has to be included early in the planning process. Communication between the planners and manufacturers of BIPV products is important for the development of new BIPV solutions. If the PV cells used are mono- or polycrystalline, it is very important to achieve a sufficient ventilation rate, as the solar cell efficiency normally decreases with increasing temperature, and should therefore be planned ahead of the construction phase. If the temperatures reach high levels, one might have to install compensating solutions, such as fans, etc., although this is usually not optimal regarding maintenance and energy efficiency. The BIPV might be formed as a trough at a material level and hence lead to improved efficiency and reduced costs of the building integrated PV cells. Figure 3.15 [25] shows research cell efficiency records of NREL up to 2015.

3.5.1.2 Long-Term Durability of New Materials and Solutions

It is imperative that the new building materials, integrated technology, and solutions are arranged all the while with the building covering. This incorporates prerequisites for rainfall, wind and air tightness, building physical contemplations, and long-term durability with respect to atmospheric exposure. Building physical considerations include investigation of the moisture transport and with this the condensation risk. With new materials the moisture transport and distribution within the building element might change and knowledge about these aspects is important. The long-term durability versus the numerous climate exposure issues needs to be deliberated. Examples of this are as follows [26]:

- Solar radiation (UV–VIS–NIR)

- Ambient infrared (IR) heat radiation

- High and low temperatures

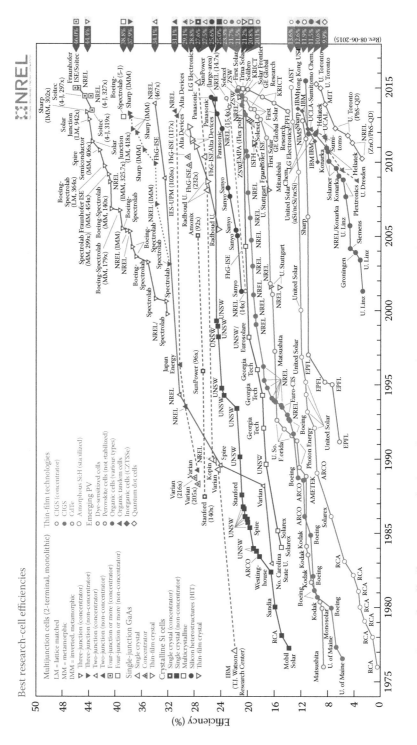

FIGURE 3.15   Research cell efficiency records. (From http://www.nrel.gov/ncpv/images/efficiency_chart.jpg.)

- Temperature changes/cycles giving freezing/thawing processes

- Water, for example, moisture and wind-driven rain

- Physical strains, for example, snow loads

- Wind

- Erosion, also from the above factors

- Pollutions, for example, gases and particles in air

- Microorganisms

- Oxygen

- Time for all the factors above to work

The main aims of BIPV is replacing conventional roof and facade materials with photovoltaic materials, which act as a covering materials as well as generating electricity.

3.6 SUMMARY AND CONCLUSIONS

BIPV is a standout among the most encouraging and exquisite methods for creating on location power straightforward from the sun—quietly, without environmental harm, pollution, or exhaustion of assets. With BIPV innovation, solar energy collection is integrated into the building envelope as a major aspect of the outline. The PV modules fill a double need: they replace building envelope materials and they produce power. While this innovation has been consolidated into the outline of numerous new structures, it is still a rising practice in the world. The introductory expense of BIPV is balanced by decreasing the sum spent on ordinary building materials and labor that would typically be utilized to develop that part of the building. When the building is in operation, there are extra investment funds as the daylight produces electrical vitality. These favorable circumstances make BIPV one of the quickest developing parts of the photovoltaic business.

There are numerous parts of the building that can be effortlessly substituted with photovoltaics: spandrel glass, bay skylights, rooftops, windows, and exteriors. In these applications, BIPV is a part of the structure and the look of a building, not an add-on. New advances are a work in progress and will later on give BIPVs higher efficiencies and lower generation costs. This will enhance the economic viability and prudent payback time for

BIPV installation. A percentage of the new ideas are organic-based PVs, for example, dye sensitized TiO_2 cells, and high proficiency modules. New arrangements can likewise both decrease expenses and increase the market share among others in the retrofitting business. The solutions ought to be effectively pertinent, and a case of future visions is paint utilizations of PV cells. Every single new technology and solution ought to be altogether tried and endorsed as per existing principles. Moreover, with new items there is a requirement for advancement of new measures and techniques, for example, concerning term strength versus atmosphere presentation.

REFERENCES

1. Lu, K. (2014). *Materials in Energy Conversion, Harvesting, and Storage.* John Wiley & Sons. Chapter 4.
2. Mohanasundaram, V. Green marketing–challenges and opportunities. *International Journal of Multidisciplinary Research,* 2.4 (2012): 66–73.
3. Lstiburek, J. Building America, *ASHRAE Journal,* Dec. 2008.
4. http://www.nbmcw.com/articles/green-tall-construction/15837-need-for-developing-green-building-concept-in-the-country.html.
5. http://www.energydigital.com/top10/2735/Top-10-sustainable-buildings-in-the-world.
6. Zhang, L.R. The application of motor control unit in the cement, *Journal of Equipment Manufacturing Technology,* 8 (2011): 208–209.
7. W. Jin, Application of building integrated photovoltaic (BIPV) in green buildings, *Journal of Architecture Technology,* 42(10) (2011): 907–908.
8. http://sinovoltaics.com/learning-center/bipv/building-integrated-photo voltaics-bipv/.
9. http://www.renewableenergyfocus.com/view/39779/spotlight on bipv/.
10. *Solar Thermal Magazine,* The curved solar power rooftop tile, homeowners now have better looking options, http://www.solarthermalmagazine .com/2010/10/23/the-curved-solar-power-rooftop-tile-homeowners-now -have-better-looking-options/S, October 23, 2010.
11. Global Energy Network Institute, Suntech to develop 20% of BIPV solar rooftop program projects, http://www.geni.org/globalenergy/library/technical-arti cles/generation/solar/pv-tech.org/suntech-to-develope-20%25-of-bivp-solar -rooftop-program-projects,-china/index.shtmlS, November 13, 2009.
12. Peng, C., Huang, Y., and Wu, Z. Building-integrated photovoltaics (BIPV) in architectural design in China, *Energy and Buildings,* 43 (2011): 3592–3598.
13. Strong, S. Building integrated photovoltaics (BIPV), whole building design guide, http://www.wbdg.org/resources/bipv.php, June 9, 2010.
14. Norton, B., Eames, P.C., Mallick, T.K., Huang, M.J., McCormack, S.J., Mondol, J.D., and Yohanis, Y.G. Enhancing the performance of building integrated photovoltaics, *Solar Energy,* 85 (2011): 1629–1664.
15. Hestnes, A.G. Building integration of solar energy systems, *Solar Energy,* 67 (2000): 181–187.

16. Farkas, K., Andresen, I., and Hestnes, A.G. Architectural integration of photovoltaic cells—Overview of materials and products from an architectural point of view. *Proceedings of the 3rd CIB International Conference on Smart and Sustainable Built Environments (SASBE)*, Delft, the Netherlands, June 15–19, 2009.
17. Luque, A. and Hegedus, S. Eds. *Handbook of Photovoltaic Science and Engineering.* John Wiley & Sons, 2011.
18. Rheinzink, Solar PV click roll cap, http://www.rheinzink.com/en/products/roof-systems/solar-systems/solar-pv-click-roll-cap/S, 2011 (accessed December 1, 2011).
19. Jelle, B.P., Hynd, A., Gustavsen, A., Arasteh, D., Goudey, H., and Hart, R. Fenestration of today and tomorrow: A state-of-the-art review and future research opportunities, *Solar Energy Materials and Solar Cells*, 96 (1) (2012): 1–28.
20. Frost and Sullivan. European building integrated photovoltaic market report, (2008). Frost and Sullivan, http://ww2.frost.com/.
21. Tripathy, M. and Sadhu, P.K. Building integrated photovoltaic market trend and its applications. *Indonesian Journal of Electrical Engineering and Computer Science,* 14 (2015): 185–190. doi:10.11591/telkomnika.v14i2.7338.
22. List of photovoltaic installation. 2014. http://en.wikipedia.org/wiki/List_of_rooftop_photovoltaic_installations.
23. Battery, S. BIPV Technology and Market Forecast, 2011.
24. European Photovoltaic Industry Assosiation. Global Market Outlook for Photovoltaics until 2016; May 2012.
25. http://www.nrel.gov/ncpv/images/efficiency_chart.jpg.
26. Jelle, B.P., Nilsen, T.-N., Hovde, P.J., and Gustavsen, A. Accelerated climate aging of building materials and characterization by Fourier transform infrared radiation analysis, *Journal of Building Physics*, doi: 10.1177/1744259111423367.

CHAPTER 4

Review on Performance Affected Parameters for Dye Sensitized Solar Cell

Geetam Richhariya and Anil Kumar

CONTENTS

4.1 INTRODUCTION

The application of renewable energy sources saves the environment and resources and thus results in a clean and healthy environment for energy generation [1]. Among the various renewable energy sources, solar energy plays an important role as a pollution-free, noiseless operation [2,3].

Solar energy can be divided into routes: first is the solar thermal system and second is the solar photovoltaic system [4]. A solar photovoltaic system converts solar radiations into electricity through solar modules [5]. The main concern of this chapter is dye sensitized solar cells that come into the category of a solar photovoltaic system.

The emerging generation of the solar cell is the dye sensitized solar cell. The crystalline solar cell and thin film solar cells are considered the first and second generation of the solar cell, respectively [6]. In 1991, O'Regan and Gratzel presented the first dye solar cell based on photosynthesis that had an efficiency of 7.1–7.9% [7]. The efficiency of the crystalline solar cell is about 25% while that of the thin film solar cell is 19.8% as shown in Table 4.1 [8]. The dye sensitized solar cell (DSSC); has a simple structure, is less costly, uses easy fabrication techniques, and is high in efficiency. These special features of the cell make it differ from other generations of the solar cell [9].

This chapter briefly discusses the working operation and constructional parts of the dye sensitized solar cell. In this chapter, various performance parameters of the dye solar cell such as substrate, semiconductor, sensitizer, electrolyte, and counter electrode are discussed.

TABLE 4.1 Generations of the Solar Cell

Parameters	I Generation (Crystalline Silicon Solar Cell)	II Generation (Thin Film Solar Cell)	III Generation (Dye Sensitizer Solar Cell)	Refs.
Fabrication technique employed	Czochralski method [10]	Roll to roll screen printing methodology [11]	Roll to roll screen printing methodology [11]	[10,11]
Efficiency	24% (Monocrystalline) [13]	6–9% (CdTe) [13]	12% (Liquid electrolyte) [12,14]	[12–14]
Life span	30 years	25 years	20 years	[15]

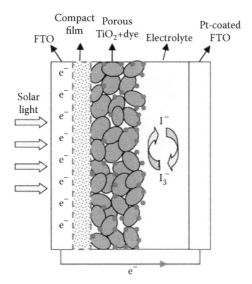

FIGURE 4.1 Constructional parts of a dye sensitized solar cell. (From Gong J, Liang J, Sumathy K. *Renew Sustain Energy Rev* (2012): 5848–5860.)

4.2 STRUCTURE OF DSSC

A schematic structure of the DSSC is shown in Figure 4.1 showing all the parts of the cell [16]. The construction of a dye solar cell is different from the crystalline solar cell as well as from thin film structures. The DSSC has a solid and liquid parts that makes it different from other generations of solar cells.

A dye solar cell consists of mainly five components as shown in Figure 4.1: (1) transparent conductive oxide (TCO) as a working substrate, (2) a semiconductor that is usually titanium dioxide (TiO_2) due to its matched characteristics with DSSC, (3) a sensitizer that absorbs solar radiation and adsorbs on to the layer of titanium dioxide, (4) an electrolyte that causes transition of electrons, and (5) a counter electrode used to regenerate the electrolyte [17].

4.2.1 Substrate

The mesoporous layer of titanium dioxide (semiconductor) is deposited onto the working substrate. The substrate must fulfill the following characteristics [18]:

1. High conductivity

2. Low sheet resistance that is independent of temperature

3. High transparency

4. High stability

5. Capable to prevent impurities, that is, water and oxygen

6. Less cost

Various substrate materials have been used for fabrication of dye solar cells. These are TCO, plastic foils, and metal sheets. Among them TCO is the traditional choice having the advantage of high transparency and high efficiency but high cost, heavy weight, and rigidity are the various obstacles for their use. The most common TCOs are indium doped tin oxide (ITO) and fluorine doped tin oxide (FTO). There are various parameters where ITO differs from FTO. The transmittance of the indium tin oxide is 80% while that of fluorine is 75%. On the other hand, the sheet resistance of the ITO and FTO is 18 ohm/cm² and 8.5 ohm/cm², respectively. During the sintering process, the sheet resistance of the ITO is drastically increased while that of the FTO is constant. Also, the efficiency of the dye solar cell with ITO is 2.4% while that with FTO is 9.4% as shown in Table 4.2 [19,20]. Therefore, FTO is the main choice for DSSC fabrication.

Sung et al. observed the performance of the dye solar cell using transparent conductive ITO, titanium-doped indium oxide (ITiO), and FTO films. It has been found that the efficiency of DSSC using ITiO, ITO, and FTO was 5.64%, 2.73%, and 6.47%, respectively at 100m W/cm² light intensity. Table 4.3 shows the performance parameter of DSSC using ITiO, ITO, and FTO [21].

Many researchers are concentrating on the transparent conductive oxide due to its high cell efficiency and greater transparency. Table 4.4 shows the various advantages and disadvantages of the different substrates.

TABLE 4.2 Differences between ITO and FTO

Parameters	ITO	FTO
Transmittance	80%	75%
Sheet resistance	18 ohm/cm²	8.5 ohm/cm²
Effect on raising temperature (during sintering)	Sheet resistance increases with increasing temperature, that is, 18 to 52 ohm/cm²	Sheet resistance remains the same
Cell efficiency	2.4%	9.4%

Source: Sima, C., Grigoriu, C., and Antohe, S. *Thin Solid Films* 519 (2010):595–597; Wu, S., Yuan, S., and Shi, L. *J Colloid Interface Sci* 346 (2010):12–16.

TABLE 4.3   Performance Parameter of DSSC using ITiO, ITO, and FTO

Performance Parameters	ITiO	ITO	FTO
Voc	0.75	0.63	0.78
Isc	2.94	2.59	3.06
FF	0.47	0.37	0.53
Efficiency (%)	5.64	2.73	6.47

Source: Kwak, D.J., Moon, B.H., and Lee, D.K. *J Elect Eng Technol* 6; 5 (2011):684–687.

TABLE 4.4   Substrates for the Dye Solar Cell

Substrate	Advantages	Disadvantages	Refs.
Transparent conductive oxide (TCO)	High efficiency Transparent	Breakable Rigid construction	[22,23]
Polymers	Flexible Low cost	Low efficiency Low temperature tolerance High sheet resistance	[24,25]
Metals (stainless steel, tungsten, titanium, etc.)	High efficiency Superior electrical conductivity	Corrosion High cost	[26]

The metal sheets have low sheet resistance, robust, high electrical conductivity [27], and are less costly compared to TCOs but are not transparent to the visible spectral regions which makes them unsuitable for DSSCs [28]. The plastic foils have the characteristics that are suitable for a good substrate. The light weight, flexibility, and sufficient transparency are the various features of the plastic foils but they also have a stability problem [29].

4.2.2 Semiconductor

In a dye sensitized solar cell, usually titanium dioxide is used as a semiconductor. The semiconductor material should be chemically stable. Onto the working substrate a layer of nanocystalline porous TiO_2 is deposited.

In nature, TiO_2 is available in three crystalline forms: anatase, rutile, and brookite, out of which the anatase structure is the most suitable for fabricating a dye solar cell. The anatase crystalline form of semiconductor has a high conduction band as compared to the rutile. The anatase is more chemically stable and also has fast electron transition. The rutile shows less adsorption for dye as compared to the anatase. Table 4.5

TABLE 4.5   Properties of Anatase and Rutile Crystalline Form of Titanium Dioxide Semiconductor

Properties	Anatase	Rutile
Conduction band	3.2 eV	3.0 Ev
Chemical stability	More stable	Less stable
Electron transition	Fast	Slow
Adsorption of dye	More	Less

Source: Landmann, M., Rauls, E., and Schmidt, W.G. *J Phys Condens Matter* 24 (2012):1–6; Park, N.G., Lagemaat, J., and Frank, A.J. *J Phys Chem B* 104 (2000):8989–8994.

shows the different properties of anatase and rutile form of titanium dioxide [30,31].

The efficiency of the dye solar cell with titanium dioxide as a semiconductor is high when compared to other alternatives. Also, TiO_2 has good electronic binding with the sensitizer. Zinc oxide, tin oxide, MgO, and Al_2O_3 are also alternatives to titanium dioxide. Following are the various characteristics of the different semiconductors:

1. TiO_2—More porous, high efficiency of cell.

2. Zinc oxide (ZnO)—Less efficiency, high mobility, less dye absorption.

3. Tin oxide (SnO_2)—Less efficiency [16].

4. MgO, Al_2O_2—Increases interfacial resistance, thus restricts the recombination of electrons [32].

A semiconductor should have the following characteristics that suit the performance of the DSSC [33,34]:

1. High surface area

2. Highly porous in nature

3. Suitable band gap that matches the sensitizer

4. Stability

5. Less costly

6. Easy availability

7. Nontoxic

4.2.3 Sensitizer

In a dye solar cell, the sensitizer plays a key role in photon absorption. The main function of the sensitizer is to absorb the incident visible light and transmit the excited electrons to the semiconductor.

The properties of an ideal sensitizer are as follows:

1. It should show more absorbance in the whole visible range of the solar spectrum.

2. It should have a carboxyl and hydroxyl group for providing good electronic binding between semiconductors [17].

3. It should inject electrons to the conduction band of the semiconductor [17].

4. It should not degrade fast.

5. It should have a high extinction coefficient [22].

Basically, there are three kinds of sensitizer [35]:

1. Metal complex sensitizers

2. Metal-free organic sensitizers

3. Natural sensitizers

4.2.3.1 Metal Complex Sensitizers

Various metal complex sensitizers are found by researchers. Most of these used for the dye solar cell are ruthenium complexes such as N3, N719, black dye, Z907, etc. due to their high absorbance under the visible light and thus high efficiency [36].

Sekar et al. discussed the various performance parameters of the ruthenium complexes. The ruthenium complexes are widely used as sensitizers for the dye solar cells. Different ruthenium complexes show different optical properties. The cell efficiency using N3, N719, black dye, and Z907 has been shown as 10%, 11.18%, 10.40%, and 11.10%, respectively, as shown in Table 4.6 [37]. The N719 dye showed the highest efficiency among all ruthenium complexes. Figure 4.2 shows the structure of N3, N719, and black dye [38–40].

TABLE 4.6   Performance Parameters of the Synthetic Dye Solar Cell

Complexes	Absorbance (nm)	IPCE (%)	Jsc (mA)	Voc (mV)	FF (%)	Efficiency (%)
N3	534	83	18.20	720	0.73	10
N719	532	85	17.73	846	0.75	11.18
Black dye	605	80	20.53	720	0.704	10.40
Z907	526	72	13.6	721	0.69	11.10

Source: Sekar, N. and Gehlot, V.Y. *Resonance* (2010):819–831.

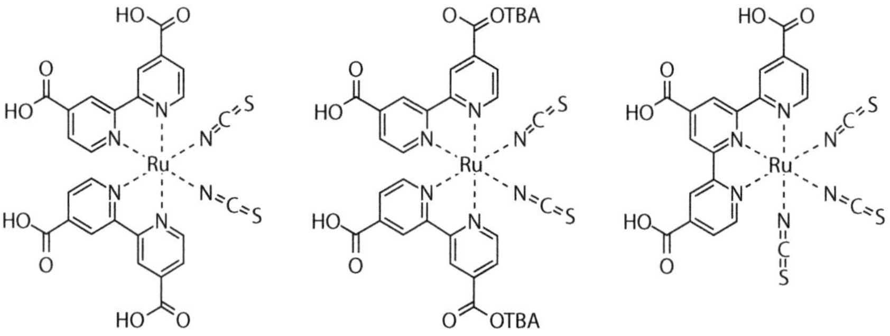

FIGURE 4.2   Structure of N3 (a), N719 (b), and black dye (c). (From Nazeeruddin MK, Kay A, Rodicio I. *J Am Chem Soc* 115 (1993):6382–6390; Nazeeruddin MK, Zakeeruddin SM, Baker RH. *Inorg Chem* 38:26 (1999):6298–6305; Nazeeruddin MK, Pechy P, Gratzel M. *Chem Comm* 18 (1997):1705–1706.)

Ludin et al. measured the absorption of two different dyes namely N719 and SQ1 applied on the titanium dioxide semiconductor. The UV results have shown the maximum absorption at 230 nm with N719 dye while SQ1 dye has shown peak absorption at 630 nm. It was concluded that the peak absorption has not reached the NIR region of the spectrum [41].

4.2.3.2 Metal-Free Organic Sensitizers
Metal free organic sensitizers are less costly than metal complex sensitizers and they also provide good electronic properties.

Kim et al. developed three organic photo-sensitizers such as: Single, double, and triple CBZ containing one, two, or three carbazole-based chromophores, respectively. Among them triple CBZ containing three carbazole chromophores and a bulky tris(hexyloxyphenyl) ethane (THPE) spacer showed the best results. The open circuit voltage, current density, fill factor, and the efficiency with the triple CBZ sensitizer was 0.715 V, 2.31 mA/cm², 64.56%, and 1.075%, respectively, as shown in Table 4.7 [42].

TABLE 4.7   Performance Parameters of DSSC

Sensitizers	Voc (V)	Jsc (mA/cm²)	FF (%)	Efficiency (%)
Single CBZ	0.540	1.29	60.03	0.42
Double CBZ	0.565	1.97	62.15	0.69
Triple CBZ	0.715	2.31	64.56	1.07

Source: Kim, M.S., Yanga, H.S., and Junga, D.Y. *Physico Chem. Eng. Aspects.* 420 (2013): 22–29.

4.2.3.3 Natural Sensitizers

The application of natural dyes extracted from fruits, flowers, leaves, roots, and bark through simple procedures is less costly, environmentally friendly, and no complicated chemical synthesis is required for their extraction. The natural dye can be formed from the various flowers, fruits, and leaves of the plants through a simple extraction process [9]. Hemalatha et al. fabricated a dye sensitized solar cell from anthocyanin pigments extracted natural dye from the flowers of the Rhododendron species with three different colors: pink, red, and violet. The highest efficiency has been shown by the pink and red dyes when treated with acetic acid. The conversion efficiency from pink dyes was 0.35% while 0.36% from the red dyes. FT-IR spectra of the anthocyanin pigment extracts is shown in Figure 4.3 [43].

Iha et al. fabricated a dye solar cell using Jaboticaba and Calafate as a dye. The open circuit voltage, current density, fill factor, and maximum power using Jaboticaba was 0.59 V, 9.0 mA/cm², 0.54 and 1.9 mW/cm²,

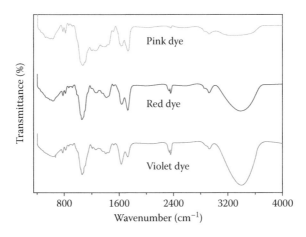

FIGURE 4.3   FT-IR spectra of the anthocyanin pigment extracts. (From Kim HJ, Bin YT, Karthick SN, *Int J Electrochem. Sci* 8 (2013): 6734–6743.)

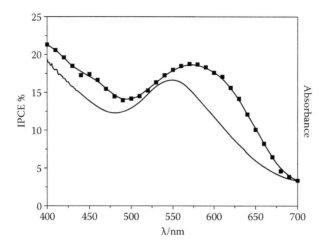

FIGURE 4.4 Incident photon to current efficiency (IPCE) (dotted line) and absorbance of the solar cell using Jaboticaba. (From Polo AS, Iha NYM. *Sol Energy Mater. Sol Cells* 90 (2006):1936–1944.)

respectively. Figure 4.4 shows the incident photon to current efficiency (IPCE) (dotted line) and absorbance of the solar cell using Jaboticaba. When Calafate is used as a dye, the open circuit voltage, current density, fill factor, and maximum power was noted as 0.47 V, 6.2 mA/cm², 0.36 and 1.1 mW/cm², respectively, as shown in Table 4.8. The cell efficiency was high with Jaboticaba used as the dye. Figure 4.5 shows the absorption spectra of Calafate before (plain line) and after being absorbed onto the semiconductor surface (dotted line) [44].

4.2.4 Electrolyte

The function of the electrolyte is to regenerate the dye. An electrolyte contains a redox couple that plays an important role in the dye solar cell. The open circuit voltage of the solar cell depends on the redox couple of the electrolyte that affects the efficiency of the cell. The electrolyte acts as a charge transport medium to transfer electrons from cathode electrode to

TABLE 4.8 Performance Parameters of the Natural Dye Solar Cell

Dye	Voc (V)	Jsc (mA/cm²)	FF	Pmax (mW/cm²)
Jaboticaba	0.59	9.0	0.54	1.9
Calafate	0.47	6.2	0.36	1.1

Source: Polo, A.S. and Iha, N.Y.M. *Sol Energy Mater. Sol Cells* 90 (2006):1936–1944.

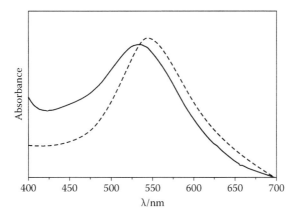

FIGURE 4.5   Absorption spectra of Calafate before (plain line) and after being absorbed onto a semiconductor surface (dotted line). (From Polo AS, Iha NYM. *Sol Energy Mater. Sol Cells* 90 (2006):1936–1944.)

anode electrode. There are four kinds of electrolytes, namely organic liquid electrolyte, ionic liquid electrolyte, quasi solid state electrolyte, and solid electrolyte.

The most common electrolyte used in DSSC is iodide tri-iodide redox couple (ionic liquid electrolyte). However, it is corrosive in nature [45].

The properties of an ideal electrolyte are as follows [46–48]:

1. It should have good solubility.

2. It must regenerate the dye fast.

3. It should show low photon absorbance in the visible region.

4. Slow recombination of electrons.

5. It should possess high electrical conductivity.

6. It must be less viscous for high rate electron transition.

Shelke et al. fabricated DSSCs using two different electrolytes, namely potassium iodide and a solution of iodide and iodine. It has been observed that the potassium electrolyte has shown high conductivity as compared to iodide-iodine electrolyte. Figure 4.6 shows the power and efficiency of the cell using potassium iodide electrolyte and iodide iodine electrolyte [49].

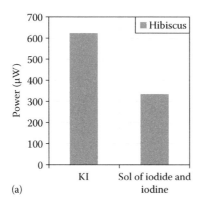 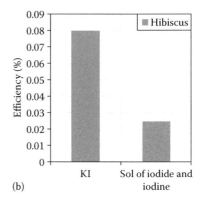

(a) (b)

FIGURE 4.6 Power (a) and efficiency (b) for potassium iodide and iodide iodine electrolyte. (From Shelke RS, Thombre SB, Patrikar SR. *Inter J Res in Sci Advanc Technol* 3 (2013):131–136.)

4.2.5 Counter Electrode

A counter electrode regenerates the electrolyte [17]. A catalytic material is deposited over the transparent conductive oxide substrate to accelerate the chemical reaction.

The counter electrode should have the following features [50]:

1. Chemically stable

2. Low charge transfer resistance

3. Mechanically stable

Generally, carbon is used because of less cost, easy availability, and chemical stability [51]. Whereas platinum is the best catalytic material for the counter cathode having a low resistance and good electro catalytic activity [52].

4.3 MECHANISM OF DSSC

When the sunlight strikes the dye solar cell, the electrons are excited and move from the ground level to the excited level of the sensitizer. The excited dye gives electrons to the conduction band of the sensitizer and thus the dye gets oxidized [53]. The electrons then travel through the transparent conductive oxide (i.e., working substrate) to the electrical load and finally reach the counter electrode as shown in Figure 4.7 [54]. The cathode has a coating of transition material so that the electrons move

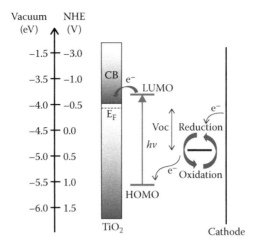

FIGURE 4.7 Working of the dye solar cell. (From Stathatos E. *J Eng Sci Technol Rev* 4 (2012): 9–13.)

toward the electrolyte and thus regenerates the electrolyte. The electrolyte is oxidized by the sensitizer [55]. And thus completes the reaction. There are three following backward reactions that also happen with the above forward reactions that affect the efficiency of the cell:

1. The electrons move from conduction band of the semiconductor to the electrolyte.

2. Electrons move from the excited state to the ground state of the sensitizer.

3. The transparent conductive oxide is treated with the titanium tetrachloride ($TiCl_4$) solution to avoid the recombination of the electrons during the operation of the cell [56].

The operating cycle can be summarized in chemical reaction terminology as [57]:

$$S + hv \rightarrow S^* \text{ Electron absorption} \tag{4.1}$$

$$S^* \rightarrow S^+ + (TiO_2) \text{ Electron injection} \tag{4.2}$$

$$2S^+ + 3I^- \rightarrow 2S + I^{-3} \text{ Regeneration of dye} \tag{4.3}$$

$$I^{-3} + 2e^{-}(Pt) \rightarrow 3I^{-} \text{ Reaction at cathode} \qquad (4.4)$$

$$e^{-}(Pt) + hv \rightarrow 3I^{-} \text{ Reaction in cell} \qquad (4.5)$$

4.4 FABRICATION OF DSSC

4.4.1 Preparation of Working Substrate

A sheet of transparent conductive oxide is broken into two equal pieces, one for making a working electrode and another for a counter cathode. The working substrate is cleaned using an ultrasonic bath. After drying the substrate, a paste of titanium dioxide that is prepared using an ethanol solution is applied onto it and spread using a glass rod. Now, keep this semiconductor deposited substrate for sintering process at nearly 450°C for half an hour [58]. After that the substrate is allowed to cool down at room temperature and then dipped into the solution of sensitizer for 24 hours [59]. Thus, the semiconductor soaks the sensitizer.

4.4.2 Assembling of Sensitizer

The anthocynain pigment as a dye can be extracted from the flowers and fruits through a simple procedure using ethanol or methanol as a solvent. The flowers are dried to remove the moisture content [60]. The dried flowers are crushed into tiny bits and then dissolved into ethanol solvent for the proper extraction of the natural dye. The solution is placed in a dark room for 24 hours [61].

4.4.3 Preparation of Counter Electrode

The other sheet of transparent conductive oxide is taken and a catalyst material layer is applied using a simple pencil [62]. Thus, a layer of carbon is deposited onto the substrate.

4.4.4 Assembly of the Dye Solar Cell

The working substrate and counter cathode are sandwiched together with a hole drilled onto to the top for providing the electrolyte solution [63]. The electrolyte solution is filled between the two substrates through the hole. Finally, combine the two substrates using binder clips [64].

4.5 MAJOR ISSUES WITH DSSC

A dye sensitized solar cell has various merits over the other solar cells and also requires a simple fabricating methodology but these have obstacles that are less efficiency, only approximately 15% [65], which is less when compared to other generations of the solar cell. The life of the DSSC is also less. The use of liquid electrolyte causes leakage problems during variations in the temperature. The liquid electrolyte freezes at low temperature while at high temperature it expands. The application of iodide and tri-iodide as a redox couple is corrosive in nature which affects the performance of the electrodes, especially in the case of metal substrates [66].

4.6 CONCLUSIONS

From this study, it is concluded that the DSSCs have less costly fabrication, less maintenance cost, are environmentally friendly, and are less sensitive to impurities. Although the application of the metal complex sensitizer causes environmental problems, natural sensitizers are the best alternative as these are nonpolluting and less costly. However, these have less adsorption on the surface of the semiconductor which causes less efficiency of the cell. The performance of the dye solar cell depends on various fabrication parameters such as transparent conductive oxide, semiconductor, sensitizer, electrolyte, etc.

It is summarized that the performance of dye solar cell increases using iodide tri-iodide used as an electrolyte, the best semiconductor for the dye solar cell is titanium dioxide, while the highest efficiency occurred with N719 ruthenium complex as a sensitizer and the transparent conductive oxide used as a substrate showed the maximum efficiency of the dye solar cell.

REFERENCES

1. Sharma A, Srivastava J, Kumar A, "A comprehensive overview of renewable energy status in India." *Environ Sustain*. Springer (2015).
2. Richhariya G, Kumar A, "Grid interactive renewable power in India." *J AISECT Uni* 3 (2014).
3. Shan F, Tang F, Cao L, Fang G, "Performance evaluations and applications of photovoltaic thermal collectors and systems." *Renew Sustain Energy Rev* 33 (2014): 467–483.
4. Kumar A, Richhariya G, Sharma A, "Solar photovoltaic technology and its sustainability." *Energy Sustainability through Green Energy*, edited by Atul Sharma, Sanjay Kumar Kar. Chapter 1. (2015):3–25. Springer. ISBN: 978-81-322-2336-8.
5. Shan F, Cao L, Fang G, "Dynamic performances modelling of a photovoltaic thermal collector with water heating in buildings." *Energy Buildings* 66 (2013): 485–494.

6. Sharma GD, Zervaki GE, Angaridis PA, "Stepwise co-sensitization as a useful tool for enhancement of power conversion efficiency of dye-sensitized solar cells: The case of an unsymmetrical porphyrin dyad and a metal-free organic dye." *Org Electro* 15 (2014): 1324–1337.

7. O'Regan B, Gratzel M, "A low-cost, high-efficiency solar cell based on dye sensitized colloidal TiO_2 films." *Nature* 353 (1991): 737–740.

8. Fan J, Jia B, Gu M, "Perovskite based low cost and high efficiency hybrid halide solar cells." *Photon Res* 2 (2014): 111–120.

9. Zhou H, Wu L, Gao Y, Ma T, "Dye sensitized solar cells using 20 natural dyes as sensitizers." *J Photochem Photobiol A: Chem* 219 (2011): 188–194.

10. Kumar A, Banerjee J, Muralidhar K, "Thermal modeling of crystal growth by the Czochralski method including radius control." *J Sci Ind Res* 61 (2002): 607–616.

11. Sondergaard R, Hosel M, Angmo D, Thue T, Olsen L, Krebs FC, "Roll to roll fabrication of polymer solar cells." *Mater Today* 15 (2012): 36–49.

12. Li Q, Chen X, Tang Q, "Enhanced photovoltaic performances of quasi-solid state dye sensitized solar cells using a novel conducting gel electrolyte." *J Power Sources* 248 (2014): 923–930.

13. Pavlovic T, Milosavljevic D, Radonjic I, "Application of solar cells made of different materials in 1 mw pv solar plants in banja luka." *Renew Energy Sources* 2 (2011): 155–163.

14. Upadhyaya HM, Senthilarasu S, Hsu MH, "Recent progress and the status of dye sensitized solar cell (DSSC) technology with state of the art conversion efficiencies." *Sol Energy Mater Sol Cells* 119 (2013): 291–295.

15. Parisi ML, S. Maranghi S, Basosi R, "The evolution of the dye sensitized solar cells from Gratzel prototype to up-scaled solar applications: A life cycle assessment approach." *Renew Sustain Energy Rev* 39 (2014): 124–138.

16. Gong J, Liang J, Sumathy K, "Review on dye-sensitized solar cells (DSSCs): Fundamental concepts and novel materials." *Renew Sustain Energy Rev* (2012): 5848–5860.

17. Mehmood U, Rahman S, Harrabi K, "Review article: Recent advances in dye sensitized solar cells." *Adv Mater Sci Eng* (2014): 1–13.

18. Heo JH, Jung KY, Kwak DJ, "Fabrication of titanium-doped indium oxide films for dye-sensitized solar cell application using reactive RF magnetron sputter method." *IEEE Transaction on Plasma Science* 37 (2009): 1586–1592.

19. Sima C, Grigoriu C, Antohe S, "Comparison of the dye-sensitized solar cells performances based on transparent conductive ITO and FTO." *Thin Solid Films* 519 (2010): 595–597.

20. Wu S, Yuan S, Shi L, "Preparation characterization and electrical properties of fluorine-doped tin dioxide nanocrystals." *J Colloid Interface Sci* 346 (2010): 12–16.

21. Kwak DJ, Moon BH, Lee DK, "Comparison of transparent conductive indium tin oxide, titanium-doped indium oxide, and fluorine-doped tin oxide films for dye-sensitized solar cell application." *J Elect Eng Technol* 6; 5 (2011): 684–687.

22. Ludin NA, Mahmoud AMA, Mahamad AB, "Review on the development of natural dye photo sensitizer for dye sensitized solar cells." *Renew Sustain Energy Rev* 31 (2014): 386–396.

23. Bauer C, Boschloo G, Mukhtar E, "Interfacial electron-transfer dynamics inRu(tcterpy)(NCS)3-sensitized TiO_2 nanocrystalline solar cells." *J Phys Chem B* 106 (2002): 12693–12704.

24. Murakami TN, Kijitori Y, Kawashima N, "Low temperature preparation of mesoporous TiO_2 films for efficient dye-sensitized photo-electrode by chemical vapor deposition combined with UV light irradiation." *J Photochem Photobiol A Chem* 164 (2004): 187–191.

25. Weerasinghe HC, Huang F, Cheng YB, "Fabrication of flexible dye sensitized solar cells on plastic substrates." *Nano Energy* 2 (2013): 174–189.

26. Jun Y, Kim J, Kang MG, "A study of stainless steel based dye-sensitized solar cells and modules." *Sol Energy Mater Sol Cells* 91 (2007): 779–784.

27. Onoda K, Ngamsinlapasathian S, Fujieda T, "The superiority of Ti plate as the substrate of dye- sensitized solar cells." *Sol Energy Mater Sol Cells* 91 (2007): 1176–1181.

28. Miettunen K, Halme J, Toivola M, "Initial performance of dye solar cells on stainless steel substrates." *J Phys Chem C* 112 (2008): 4011–4017.

29. Pasquier AD, Stewart M, Spitler T, Coleman M. "Aqueous coating of efficient flexible TiO_2 dye solar cell photo anodes." *Sol Energy Mater Sol Cells* 93; 4 (2009): 528–535.

30. Landmann M, Rauls E, Schmidt WG. "The electronic structure and optical response of rutile, anatase and brookite TiO_2." *J Phys Condens Matter* 24 (2012): 1–6.

31. Park NG, Lagemaat J, Frank AJ, "Comparison of dye-sensitized rutile and anatase based TiO_2 solar cells." *J Phys Chem B* 104 (2000): 8989–8994.

32. Choi H, Nahm C, Kim J, "The effect of $TiCl_4$ treated TiO_2 compact layer on the performance of dye-sensitized solar cell." *Curr Appl Phys* 12 (2012): 737–741.

33. Mbonyiriyuze A, Omollo I, Ngom BD, "Natural dye sensitizer for Gratzel cells: Sepia melanin." *Physics and Material Chemistry* 3 (2015): 1–6.

34. Law M, Greene LE, Johnson JC, "Nano wire dye sensitized solar cell." *Nat Mater* 4 (2005): 455–459.

35. Polo AS, Itokazu MK, Iha NYM, "Metal complex sensitizers in dye-sensitized solar cells." *Coord Chem Rev* 248 (2004): 1343–1361.

36. Narayan MR, "Review: Dye sensitized solar cells based on natural photo-sensitizers." *Renew Sustain Energy Rev* 16; 1 (2012): 208–215.

37. Sekar N, Gehlot VY, "Metal complex dyes for dye-sensitized solar cells: Recent developments." *Resonance* (2010):819–831.

38. Nazeeruddin MK, Kay A, Rodicio I, "Conversion of light to electricity by cis-X_2(dcbpy)$_2$Ru(II) CT sensitizers on nanocrystalline TiO_2 electrodes." *J Am Chem Soc* 115 (1993): 6382–6390.

39. Nazeeruddin MK, Zakeeruddin SM, Baker RH, "Acid-base equilibria of (2,2′-bipyridyl-4,4′-dicarboxylic acid)ruthenium(II) complexes and the effect of protonation on charge-transfer sensitization of nanocrystalline titania." *Inorg Chem* 38:26 (1999): 6298–6305.

40. Nazeeruddin MK, Pechy P, Gratzel M, "Efficient panchromatic sensitization of nanocrystalline TiO_2 films by a black dye based on atrithiocyanato ruthenium complex." *Chem Comm* 18 (1997): 1705–1706.
41. Ludin NA, Karim NA, Teridi MAM, "Absorption spectrum of N719 and SQ1 dye on TiO_2 surface of dye sensitized solar cell." *Latest Trends in Renew Energy Environ Inform.* 175:3 (2013): 255–58.
42. Kim MS, Yanga HS, Jung DY, "Effects of the number of chromophores and the bulkiness of a non-conjugated spacer in a dye molecule on the performance of dye-sensitized solar cells." Colloids. Surfaces. A: *Physico Chem. Eng. Aspects.* 420 (2013): 420: 22–29.
43. Kim HJ, Bin YT, Karthick SN, "Natural dye extracted from rhododendron species flowers as a photo-sensitizer in dye sensitized solar cell." *Int J Electrochem. Sci* 8 (2013): 6734–6743.
44. Polo AS, Iha NYM, "Blue sensitizers for solar cells: Natural dyes from Calafate and Jaboticaba." *Sol Energy Mater. Sol Cells* 90 (2006): 1936–1944.
45. Boschloo G, Hagfeldt A, "Characteristics of the iodide/triiodide redox. Mediator in dye-sensitized solar cells." *Acco Chem Res* 42 (2009): 1819–1826.
46. Kusama H, Arakawa H, "Influence of pyrazole derivatives in I^-/I_3^- redox electrolyte solution on Ru(II)-dye-sensitized TiO_2 solar cell performance." *Sol Energy Mater Sol Cells* 85:3 (2005): 333–344.
47. Nogueira AF, Longo C, Paoli MAD. "Polymers in dye sensitized solar cells: Overview and perspectives." *Coord Chem Rev* 248 (2004): 1455–1468.
48. Wu J, Lan Z, Hao S, "Progress on the electrolytes for dye-sensitized solar cells." *Pure Appl Chem* 80 (2008): 2241–2258.
49. Shelke RS, Thombre SB, Patrikar SR, "Comparative performance of dye sensitized solar cell using two electrolytes." *Inter J Res in Sci Advanc Technol* 3 (2013): 131–136.
50. Kay A, Gratzel M, "Low cost photovoltaic modules based on dye sensitized nanocrystalline titanium dioxide and carbon powder." *Sol Energy Mater Sol Cells* 44 (1996): 99–117.
51. Chen J, Li K, Luo Y, "A flexible carbon counter electrode for dye-sensitized solar cells." *Carbon* 47 (2009): 2704–2708.
52. Hagfeldt A, Boschloo G, Sun L, "Dye sensitized solar cell." *Chem Rev* 110 (2010): 6595–6663.
53. Hara K, Arakawa H, Dye-sensitized solar cells, in: S.H. Antonio Luque (Ed.) *Handbook of Photovoltaic Science and Engineering.* England: John Wiley & Sons Ltd (2003).
54. Stathatos E, "Dye sensitized solar cells: A new prospective to the solar to electrical energy conversion Issues to be solved for efficient energy harvesting." *J Eng Sci Technol Rev* 5:4 (2012): 9–13.
55. Chen HY, Kuang DB, Su CY. "Hierarchically micro/nanostructured photoanode materials for dye sensitized solar cells." *J Mater Chem* 22 (2012): 475–489.
56. Sedghi A, Miankushki HN, "Influence of TiO_2 electrode properties on performance of dye sensitized solar cells." *Int J Electrochem Sci* 7 (2012): 12078–12089.

57. Matthews D, Infelta P, Gratzel M. "Calculation of the photocurrent-potential characteristic for regenerative sensitized semiconductor electrodes." *Sol Energy Mater Sol Cells* 44 (1996): 119–155.
58. Kelvin O, Ekpunobi, "Fabrication and characterization of dye sensitized solar cell using anarcardium occidentale sensitizer." *Adv Appl Sci Res* 3 (2012): 3390–3395.
59. Taya SA, El-Agez TM, El-Ghamri HS, "Dye-sensitized solar cells using fresh and dried natural dyes." *Int J Mater Sci Appl* 2 (2013): 37–42.
60. Latif MSA, Agez TMEl, Taya SA, "Plant seeds-based dye-sensitized solar cells." *Mater Sci Appl* 4 (2013): 516–520.
61. Latif MSA, Abuiriban MB, Dahoudi NA, "Dye-sensitized solar cells using fifteen natural dyes as sensitizers of nanocrystalline TiO_2." *Sci Technol Develop* 34; 3 (2015): 135–139.
62. Jasim KE, "Natural dye-sensitized solar cell based on nanocrystalline TiO_2." *Sains Malaysiana* 41:8 (2012): 1011–1016.
63. Kumara NTRN, Ekanayake P, Lim A, "Layered co-sensitization for enhancement of conversion efficiency of natural dye sensitized solar cells." *J Alloys Compoun* 581 (2013): 186–191.
64. Usha K, Mondal B, Sengupta D, "Fabrication of dye sensitized solar cell using nanocrystalline TiO_2 and optical characterization of photo-anode." *Nanosci Nanoeng* 2:2 (2014): 29–35.
65. Fan J, Jia B, Gu M, "Perovskite based low cost and high efficiency hybrid halide solar cells." *Photon Res* 2 (2014): 111–120.
66. Hashmi G, Miettunen K, Peltola T, "Review of materials and manufacturing options for large area flexible dye solar cells." *Renew Sustain Energy Rev* 15 (2011): 3717–3732.

CHAPTER 5

A Role of Phase Change Materials in Building Applications

Helia Teheri and Atul Sharma

CONTENTS

5.1 INTRODUCTION

Nowadays, two factors lead us to utilize various sources of renewable energy; these factors are the increasing level of greenhouse gas emissions and the growth of fuel prices. In many parts of the world, the direct solar radiation, which reaches the earth, is significant and should be considered one of the most prospective sources of energy. To use this source of energy, some standards and legislation related to the thermal regulations become more and more stringent toward the energy efficiency in building. The requirements of energy saving have to be in compliance with the thermal comfort of building occupants. To reach this goal, one of the options is to develop energy storage devices, which is as important as developing new sources of energy. Thermal storage not only reduces the mismatch between the amount of supply and demand, but also improves the performance of the energy systems and plays important roles in conserving the energy (Garg et al. 1985). Thermal storage can store energy in the period of time in which the building does not need energy and use the saved energy in the needed periods. By using this system, buildings can benefit from peak load shifting. In addition, the size of the HVAC (heating, ventilation, and air conditioning) systems reduces and the efficiency of them increases.

One of the most beneficial thermal storage systems is a latent heat storage system in which phase change materials (PCMs) are one of the most important types. In comparing with sensible heat storage, which is the common way to store heat in a material with changes in temperature, latent heat storage can store more heat in certain volume and mass; therefore, PCMs can store more heat in smaller volume and mass than sensible heat storage materials. This aspect of PCMs expands their usage in contemporary lightweight buildings; therefore, in the last decades, various researchers have studied PCMs in building applications because of their considerable benefits.

The main purpose of this chapter is discussing the applications of PCMs which are used in building surfaces such as walls, ceilings, floors, and windows.

5.2 THERMAL STORAGE

Heat can change the internal energy of thermal storage and it can be stored in three ways. These ways are sensible heat, latent heat, and thermochemical. Also, heat can be stored through a combination of these three ways.

5.2.1 Sensible Heat

The common way of storing heat is changing temperature of the materials and there is no change in the phase of them. This method is called sensible heat storage (SHS). The instrument that can measure sensible heat is a thermometer; the amount of heat that is stored in the material through SHS depends on three factors which are classified below:

1. The specific heat of the material,

2. The temperature change, and

3. The mass of the material.

These systems use specific heat and temperature change during charge and discharge processes (Lane 1983).

High specific heat for the materials causes a time lag in using heat energy and use at the required time of the day. For instance, if we have a 4-in. concrete wall, its time lag is 4 hours. If we increase the thickness of the concrete wall to 24 in., the power of the storage on the wall is received in 18 hours. In common for the passive systems we define 4 to 12 hours for the storage and time lag. We should select the material, among the vast number of them, which can adapt with our building characteristics (Taheri and Sharma 2015).

5.2.2 Latent Heat

Latent heat is the heat released or absorbed by a body or a thermodynamic system during a constant-temperature process. Latent heat storage (LHS) is based on the heat absorption or release when a storage material has a phase transition from solid to liquid or liquid to gas or vice versa. In specific mass, LHS has more capacity in storing heat than SHS. An example of phase transition that is common and noticeable in everybody's life is ice melting or water boiling. In LHS, the heat transfer causes a volume change while the thermodynamic system's temperature is constant. Therefore, this energy doesn't sense directly, and can't be measured by a thermometer.

The LHS may be classified on the basis of the phase change process as solid–solid, solid–liquid, solid–gas, and liquid–gas. Solid–gas and liquid–gas transformations are generally not employed for energy storage in spite of their higher latent heats, since gases occupy large volumes. Among many types of phase transitions, liquid–solid and solid–liquid transitions are more practical and usable in applications (Sharma et al. 2009, Taheri and Sharma 2015). Despite all of the advantages of this method, it causes some problems such as decrease in thermal conductivity, changes in density during the phase change process, phase segregation, etc.

5.2.3 Thermochemical

This method relies on the energy that is absorbed and released in breaking and reforming molecular bonds in a completely reversible chemical reaction. In this case, the heat that is stored depends on the amount of storage material, the endothermic heat of reaction, and the extent of conversion. All of the chemical reactions are along with a change in energy. There are two kinds of reactions due to energy: endothermic and exothermic. The endothermic reaction is the reaction that gains energy from the ambient during the reaction and causes a decrease in ambient energy. The exothermic reaction is the reaction that releases the energy during the process and causes an increase in ambient energy (Sharma et al. 2009, Taheri and Sharma 2015).

5.3 HOW DO PCMs REDUCE BUILDING LOADS?

In traditional architecture, architects are interested in using thermal energy storage systems due to some benefits and reasons. Some of these reasons are as follows:

- During certain hours of the day, solar energy is greater than the requirement of the applications; in such cases, thermal energy storage can store this energy for the hours in which there is a need for energy but there is no access to solar energy.

- In thermal energy storage, the coldness of the night can be saved and later be used for cooling during hot summer days and the heat in winter days can be saved and used for heating during cold winter nights; therefore, natural sources of heating and cooling during the winter and summer could be matched with thermal energy storage systems.

- Thermal energy storage systems lead us to use the heating and cooling units efficiently.

As mentioned above, there are three types of thermal energy storage methods. PCMs, which are the LHS materials, have been studied for more than 40 years. These materials store heat through latent heat fusion, which is about 100 times more than SHS ones; therefore, PCMs store heat 5–14 times more than SHS materials. These aspects of LHS, which are low volume and high thermal storage, are significant in contemporary light-weight buildings (Sharma et al. 2009).

The LHS materials are used to store energy in the periods of the day and night in which the building faces more energy than it needs and after this period it uses stored energy in the required time of the day. This process causes a reduction in the temperature fluctuations and the loads of the buildings. Because of these advantages, the PCM applications in buildings are increased in contemporary architecture.

5.4 PHASE CHANGE MATERIALS (PCMs)

5.4.1 Classification

From the aspects of melting temperature and latent heat of fusion, there are a large number of materials that can be identified as PCMs. However, the majority of PCMs are not efficient for an adequate storage material. As there is not any single material that can have all required and sufficient properties for ideal thermal storage, one has to use the available materials and try to improve the physical properties by adequate design. Among the most thorough references related to PCMs, one can cite Abhat et al. (1981), Lane (1983), and Sharma et al. (2009).

There are two types of PCMs: (1) organic and (2) inorganic. Each of these two types has some subsets, which are explained in the following paragraphs.

5.4.2 Organic Phase Change Materials

Organic PCMs are divided into paraffin and nonparaffin materials. Organic materials have some characteristics such as (1) they have congruent melting, which means that they can melt and freeze repeatedly without phase segregation, (2) self-nucleation, which means that they crystallize with little or no supercooling, and (3) usually they are noncorrosive (Sharma et al. 2009).

5.4.2.1 Paraffin

Paraffin wax is one of the types of organic PCMs that consists of a mixture of mostly straight chain n-alkanes $CH_3–(CH_2)–CH_3$. The crystallization of the (CH_3)-chain releases a large amount of latent heat energy. Both the melting point and latent heat of fusion enhance with increase in chain

TABLE 5.1   Advantages and Disadvantages of Paraffin PCMs

	Advantages	Disadvantages
Paraffin	• High latent heat storage (200–250 kJ/kg) • Odorless and nontoxic • Low volume change in phase transition • Long melting-freezing cycle • Accessible and low price • Noncorrosive • No phase segregation • Chemical stability • Low vapor pressure	• Supercooling during freezing process • Low thermal conductivity (0.2 W/m.K) • Incompatible with plastic • Approximately flammable (It should be mentioned that these disadvantages can be resolved by improving paraffin wax and thermal storage.)

length (Sharma et al. 2009). Table 5.1 shows advantages and disadvantages of paraffin PCMs.

5.4.2.2 Nonparaffin

Nonparaffin wax is one of the types of organic PCMs that is the most numerous type of the PCMs with highly variable properties. Each material has its own properties. Abhat et al. (1981) have conducted an extensive survey of nonparaffin materials and have identified a number of esters, fatty acids, alcohols and glycols suitable for energy storage. Table 5.2 shows advantages and disadvantages of nonparaffin PCMs.

5.4.3 Inorganic PCMs

Inorganic PCMs have a less versatile range of melting points and working temperatures, but they are compatible with the range of temperatures required for construction applications between 15°C and 70°C (Pons et al. 2014). Inorganic materials are further classified as salt hydrate and metallic.

5.4.3.1 Salt Hydrates

The most important categories of inorganic PCMs are salt hydrates. Salt hydrates may be regarded as alloys of inorganic salts and water forming a typical crystalline solid of general formula AB_nH_2O. The solid–liquid transformation of salt hydrates is actually a dehydration of the hydrated salt, although this process resembles melting or freezing thermodynamically. At the melting point, the hydrate crystals break up into water and hydrous salt, or into a lower hydrate and water.

TABLE 5.2 Advantages and Disadvantages of Nonparaffin PCMs

		Advantages	Disadvantages
Nonparaffin	Fatty acids	• Nontoxic • High heat fusion • Thermal and chemical stability • Latent heat between 153 and 182 kJ/kg • No supercooling during freezing process • Repeatable melting and freezing behavior • Appropriate melting point (30–60°C) for many of the applications	• 2 or 2.5 times more expensive than paraffin wax • Approximately corrosive • Flammable • Low thermal conductivity
	Glycols	• Appropriate melting point for many of the applications • Thermal and chemical stability • Low vapor pressure in melting process • Nontoxic and noncorrosive • High heat fusion • Nonflammable and low price	• Low thermal conductivity
	Alcohols	• Long lasting • Low volume change • No phase segregation • High heat in phase change transition • High enthalpy in solid-solid phase change • Repeatable solid–liquid cycle	• Low thermal conductivity • Flammable • Phase change in high temperatures (for solving this problem it can use 2 or 3 combinations of these materials)

One problem with most salt hydrates is that of incongruent melting caused by the fact that the released water of crystallization is not sufficient to dissolve all the solid phase present (Sharma et al. 2009).

5.4.3.2 Metallic

Metallics are low melting metals and eutectics. These metallics have not yet been seriously considered for PCM technology because of weight penalties. However, when volume is a consideration, they are likely candidates because of the high heat fusion per unit volume.

Some of the features of these materials are as follows: (1) low heat fusion per unit weight, (2) high heat fusion per unit volume, (3) high thermal

TABLE 5.3   Advantages and Disadvantages of PCMs

Advantages	Disadvantages
• High latent heat • Low volume change during phase transition • Frequent phase transition • Thermal stability in solid–liquid phase transition and vice versa • High density • Chemical stability • Noncorrosive, nontoxic, and not flammable • Low cost • Accessible	• Low thermal conductivity • Super cooling during crystallization • Need for container in order to prevent PCM leakage

conductivity, (4) low specific heat, and (5) relatively low vapor pressure (Sharma et al. 2009).

5.4.3.3 Eutectics

A eutectic PCM is a combination of two or more compounds of either organic, inorganic, or both. A eutectic is a minimum-melting composition of two or more components, which usually do not interact to form a new chemical compound, which at certain ratios inhibit the crystallization process of one another, but result in a system having a lower melting point than either of the components (George 1989, Stott et al. 1998). Eutectics nearly always melt and freeze without segregation since they freeze to an intimate mixture of crystals, leaving little opportunity for the components to separate (Sharma et al. 2009). A considerable number of eutectics may be developed according to the desired melting point for thermal energy storage systems. As the use of these materials is very new to thermal storage application, only limited data are available on thermo-physical properties. Therefore, the stability of the thermal properties of the new eutectics is needed to ensure the long-term performance of thermal energy storage (Rathod and Jyotirmay 2012). A comparison of the advantages and disadvantages of PCMs is given in Table 5.3.

5.5 ROLE OF PCMs IN BUILDING SURFACES

The usage of PCMs in lightweight building applications has been expanded in the last few decades; therefore, researchers have done many studies on this issue. Nowadays studying on PCMs and the usage of them in building applications as latent heat storage materials has become more and more attractive for optimization of heating and cooling loads of buildings.

The usage of PCMs as LHS materials has two specific building applications. One of them has been used to increase the shield effect of the building envelope (Schossig 2005, Lemma 2006, 2007) and the other has been applied to control the internal gains through buffering. The control of the internal gains by means of PCM-based building components has been achieved either passively, which is done by integrating the PCM into the indoor facing layers of walls (Kuznik 2008), or actively, which is applied by developing new components that include facilities for discharging the heat stored in the PCM layer (natural ventilation, cooling pipes, etc.). Most of the PCM building application should possess at least three components:

1. A suitable PCM with its melting point in the desired temperature range;

2. A suitable heat exchange surface; and

3. A suitable container compatible with the PCM volume change (Abhat 1981).

In this part of the chapter, the authors focus on the PCM building applications that are used in building surfaces and help to decrease the loads of buildings.

5.5.1 PCM Applications in Walls

The integration of PCMs in building walls is the way to enhance the storage capacity of the building envelope and to rationalize the use of renewable and nonrenewable energies. PCM wallboards are the most common and one of the simplest and cheapest ways of using PCMs in building applications. This usage of PCM utilizes natural heat and cold, so it acts in a passive way. Many studies have been conducted on this application and there are many companies in the world that produce PCM wallboards for this purpose. Evola et al. (2013a) studied a case that contains organic PCMs in the partition walls of a lightweight office building (Figure 5.1). The purpose of this study was improving the summer thermal comfort with PCM wallboards and measuring their effectiveness. This study showed that the PCM did not use all of its latent heat capacity during the 24 hours of the day and it only takes advantage of an average 45% of its latent heat (it depends on the period of measurement and the climate). Another result of this study was that the energy saving in

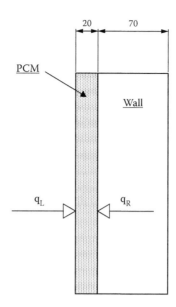

FIGURE 5.1   A PCM wallboard (size in mm).

Chambery (France, temperature climate) is more than it in Catania (Italy, hot Mediterranean climate).

Evola et al. (2013b) studied wallboards that contain micro-encapsulated PCMs and installed them at a certain distance from an existing partition wall; fresh outdoor air can circulate in the narrow cavity, so boosting the rate of heat flux exchanged by the PCM and enhance its solidification process. The purpose of this study was improving the summer thermal comfort. The results show that the studied case allowed reducing the average room operative temperature in July about 0.4°C with respect to the common practice of attaching PCM wall boards directly on the partition wall. As a result, the indoor conditions are in a comfortable range for a longer time. The reason for this outcome is that the heat stored by PCMs during the daytime is effectively rejected at night to the air flowing into the cavity, instead of being released to the air in the room.

Feldman et al. (1989a,b, 1991) studied the use of organic compounds for LHS. In addition to the studies, research was also conducted on energy storage materials, which act as PCM absorbers. Various materials were considered, such as different types of concrete and gypsum. The PCM gypsum board contained about 25% by weight proportion of PCM. The PCM used in this study was butyl stearate. The result of this study was an increase in the thermal storage capacity in the range of 10–130%.

Certain aggregate and filler materials were selected after detailed laboratory study as possible constituents of the proposed composite. Absorption of PCM and the retention thereof in materials such as expanded shale, volcanic rock, activated charcoal, gypsum, and vermiculite were determined. Composite specimens were prepared using coarse aggregates, gypsum, cement, sawdust, and vermiculite and sand with water. Several mix compositions with different proportions of these materials were prepared. These gypsum/cement concrete specimens were cured, dried, and impregnated with PCM. The absorption capacities of PCM in the specimens were determined and compressive strength tests, differential scanning calorimetry analysis, infrared spectroscopy, and thermal conductivity tests were performed.

The composite, depending on the mix composition, is capable of storing up to 30 wt% of PCM. In order to ensure complete encapsulation of PCM, the composite specimens were coated with a film of polyester resin. This, however, resulted in lowering of the heat transfer capability of the composite. Thermal conductivity tests showed great improvement on introduction of aluminum or lignin powders in the resin. The composite can be produced in the form of floor, wall, or ceiling tiles capable of storing energy up to 766 kJ/m^2.

For wallboards heated by direct solar radiation, Drake (1987) found the optimal melt temperature to be proportional to the absorbed solar energy. Peippo et al. (1991) also considered heating only by direct solar radiation, and concluded that optimal diurnal storage occurs with a melt temperature of 1–3°C above the average room temperature.

Muruganantham and Phelan (2010) conducted a study on using PCM panels (Figure 5.2) in walls and compared it with walls without PCMs.

FIGURE 5.2   The PCM panel.

Their results showed that the maximum decrease in consumption for heating and cooling demand was during September (26%) and November (30%). This method can shift the peak load by about 60 min in the month of June.

Ahmad et al. (2006) presented the performance of a test-cell with a new structure of light wallboards containing PCMs subjected to climatic variation and a comparison made with a test-cell without PCMs. To improve the wallboard efficiency, a vacuum insulation panel was associated with the PCM panel. The results showed that such a system can be constructed with commonly available materials and equipment, the optimal use of solar energy remains an essential element of the problems in the current context.

5.5.2 PCM Applications in Ceilings

This application of PCMs is mostly used in the active way and in suspended ceilings with the purpose of using for shifting loads and increasing the HVAC efficiency by decreasing their loads and fluctuations. This application has many advantages; therefore, many studies have been done on this issue. Yahaya and Ahmad (2011) studied the effectiveness of PCM integrated with gypsum ceiling panel as heat energy storage to reduce the cooling load of a single space house in Subang Jaya (Malaysia). The PCM, which was used in this study, was a eutectic mixture of lauric-stearic acid that can be obtained from a palm oil product. In addition, the higher melting point and latent heat capacity of this mixture are the main factors that make it possible to be applied with the ceiling panels to maximize the heat absorption capacity. The determination of energy and indoor air temperature reduction through numerical prediction indicated that the strategy might be practical to minimize the dependency level of building users to the active cooling system. Therefore, the application of PCM in the gypsum board as a ceiling component is highly recommended to improve thermal performance and energy savings, especially in single story buildings.

Koschenz and Lehmann (2004) designed a new ceiling panel that exploits the properties of the paraffin PCM. The overall concept for the ceiling panels adopts the following arrangement (Figure 5.3): a sheet steel tray is used as a container for the PCM/gypsum composite while providing the panels with the required mechanical stability. A mix comprising microencapsulated PCM and gypsum is poured into the tray (5 cm layer of 25% wt PCM). Active control of thermal mass is achieved by the

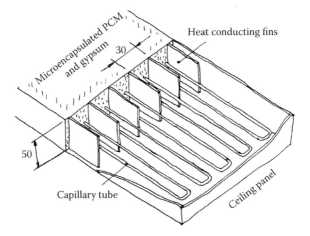

FIGURE 5.3   Schematic drawing of thermally activated ceiling panel with PCM.

incorporation of a capillary water tube system in the gypsum compound. If required, thermal conduction in the composite may be improved by the inclusion of aluminum fins. While the panel is primarily designed for ceiling installation, fitting to walls is equally straightforward (Figure 5.4). The results showed that the system's feature makes it ideal for use in lightweight structures, the incorporation of additional thermal mass offering an efficient means of moderating temperature amplitudes in this type of building.

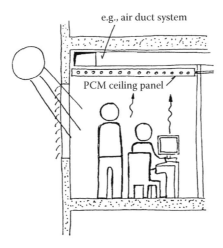

FIGURE 5.4   Installation of ceiling panels in building interior as a suspended ceiling.

Kondo and Ibamoto (2002) conducted a study on using thermal storage (PCM) in the ceiling and they used PCM with a melting point of 25°C. At night thermal storage was cooled by cool air from the HVAC that flows into the ceiling chamber space and stores cooling thermal energy. During peak load period, the air from the room returns to the HVAC via the ceiling chamber space. As a result of passing through the cooled PCM ceiling board, the warm air returning from the room cools down before returning to the HVAC. The maximum thermal load and the capacity of heat source can thus be reduced. In this study, the thermal capacity of the PCM ceiling board was measured by using a small experimental chamber. The thermal capacity of the PCM ceiling board is approximately 663 kJ/m², which is 4.9 times that of an ordinary rock wool ceiling board. The maximum thermal load using the PCM ceiling board was 85.2% of that using the rock wool ceiling board. As the maximum thermal load was reduced by 14.8% by the rock wool ceiling board, it can reduce the load on the HVAC. However, the integrated thermal load was 5.3% greater than that using the rock wool ceiling board. The transition rate of the thermal load to the night was 25.1%. Discounted nighttime electricity, which is 75% cheaper than daytime electricity, is used in Japan. The running cost is 91.6% lower than that by using the rock wool ceiling board. The schematic sketch is shown in Figure 5.5.

5.5.3 PCM Applications in Floors

Radiant heating has a number of advantages over convective air heating systems. One of its advantages is saving the living and working space since it is integrated into the building envelope. In addition, thermal mass integrated into a floor heating system can be used for off-peak storage of thermal energy. Thus, peak loads may be reduced and shifted to nighttime when electricity costs are lower. One of the applications of PCMs is using it in floor heating. This type of PCM usage can be used in two ways: passive and active. In the last decades, many studies have been done on floor heating integrated with PCMs and some researchers optimized the amount of PCMs used in floor heating.

In the passive concept of floor heating with the usage of PCMs, the heat stored in PCMs by using utilities such as HVACs is omitted. In the following paragraphs, this application will be discussed by some studies.

Athienties and Chen (2000) investigated the transient heat transfer in floor heating systems. Their study focused on the influence of the cover layer and incident solar radiation on the floor temperature distribution and energy consumption. Experimental and simulation results in an outdoor

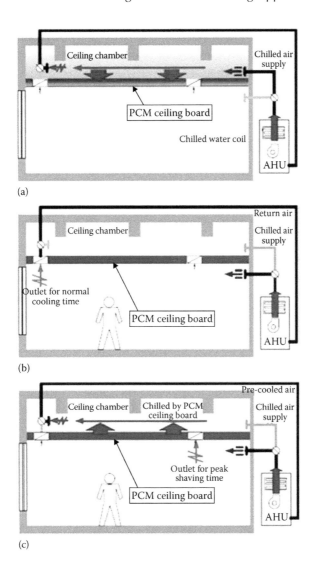

(a)

(b)

(c)

FIGURE 5.5 Schematic diagram showing an outline of the ceiling board system having PCM. (a) Overnight thermal storage time, (b) normal cooling time, and (c) peak shaving control time.

test room reveal that solar beam radiation can cause a local floor surface temperature in the illuminated area of 8°C higher than that in the shaded area. Partial carpet covers further increases the floor surface temperature difference up to 15°C when solar radiation was absorbed. Solar radiation stored in the floor thermal mass was found to reduce heating energy consumption significantly (30% or more).

Active concept of floor heating with the usage of PCMs can be used for off-peak storage of thermal energy in buildings. Therefore, peak loads may be reduced and shifted to nighttime when electricity costs are lower. Barzin et al. (2015) studied on DuPont Energin in wallboard in combination with an under floor heating system incorporating PCMs. An experimental study was carried out using two identical test chambers at the Tamaki Campus, University of Auckland (Figure 5.6).

The PCMs used in the floor is 10 mm impregnated gypsum board used in combination with an under floor heating system, its peak melting point is 28°C and the latent heat storage capacity is 120 J/g (Figure 5.7). The wall boards are 5.2 mm DuPont Energin with a 21.7°C melting point and a latent heat storage capacity of 70 kJ/kg.

The results showed that a total energy saving and electrical cost saving equal to 18.8% and 28.8%, respectively, were achieved from a 5-day experimented measurement. The highest energy saving achieved during this period was 35%, with a corresponding cost saving of 44.4%.

Farid and Chen (1999) studied the active floor-heating concept. In this study, they used an electrical under floor heating system with paraffin wax (melting point 40°C) as PCM. A 30-mm layer of PCM was placed between the heating surface and the floor tiles. The results of the simulation show that when PCM storage is used, the heat output of the floor can be raised significantly from 30 to 75 W/m².

FIGURE 5.6   Experimental chamber at Tamaki Campus, University of Auckland.

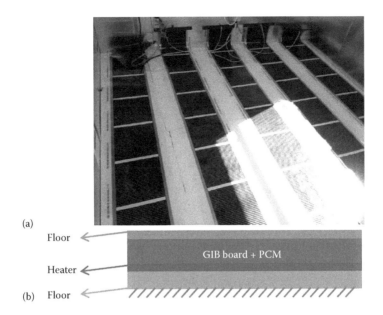

(a)

Floor ←

GIB board + PCM

Heater ←

(b) Floor ←

FIGURE 5.7 The under floor heating system used in the chamber with PCM (a) foil heaters, (b) under floor heating system layout.

Lin et al. (2005) studied electric radiant floor heating systems in buildings using SSPCM plate. Their study used 75% wt paraffin wax, which is used as PCM with 25% wt polyethylene as assistance material. The melting point of paraffin is 52°C. This indicates that PCM having sufficiently high melting point is applied as an example, unlike PCMs that have melting points between 20 and 30°C in typical buildings. One of the results is that the room temperature of the system increased without increasing the thermal difference. The other result, which is made based on the study, is that the temperature of the PCM plate is preserved for a long time after the heating is stopped, which offers effective economic profit based on the difference in electricity charges because more than half of the entire electric thermal energy is moved from the peak load to the nonpeak load. The last results of the study are that the difference in the indoor temperature according to the vertical directions is small because the radiant floor heating system heats the indoor air comfortably and efficiently.

5.5.4 PCM Applications in Transparent Building Elements

In the last few years, a tendency toward integrating PCMs into transparent envelope components has been observed. The passive solar mechanism of PCM glazing systems is offered by the outer and inner insulating glazing units. Transparent PCM is a material that allows light to pass through, but absorbs the infrared part of the spectrum and this increases the temperature of the PCM up to the melting point, which as in all PCMs is done at constant temperature. The PCM can be transparent to the internal space, and act like a window.

Many studies with new details were done on this type of PCM application and satisfying results were achieved. The earliest study of PCM applications in translucent elements was done by Manz et al. (1997). The researchers of this study purposed a two-layered passive wall system, combining a salt hydrate used as a PCM and a transparent honeycomb-type insulation material (Figure 5.8). The PCM was filled into glass containers, which were commercially available glass blocks.

One of the companies that produces transparent panels with PCMs is GlassX (in Switzerland). GlassX Company produces panels that were used in the façade and let the natural light come in. They studied the effects of using these panels and the results are very significant. In the solid phase, these panels are semitransparent and in the liquid phase, they are transparent, which helps buildings to improve the quality of the spaces, in addition to reducing the heating and cooling load of the buildings.

The phase transition is shown in Figure 5.9 (Taheri and Sharma 2015).

The outer insulated glazing unit with a suspended prismatic filter between the panes of glass reflects the higher angle sunlight back out, transmitting the low-angle sunlight into the inner unit that is filled with sealed polycarbonates into which the PCM is encapsulated. As a result, the strong sunlight of the summer is kept out of the building, while the lower

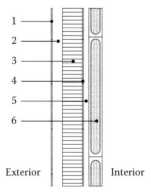

Layer Id	Description
1	Glass pane
2	Air gap
3	Transparent insulation material
4	Glass pane
5	Air gap
6	PCM in a glass container

FIGURE 5.8 Layout of TIM-PCM external wall system. (From Manz H, Egolf PW, Suter P, Goetzberger A, *Solar Energy* 61 (1997): 369–379.)

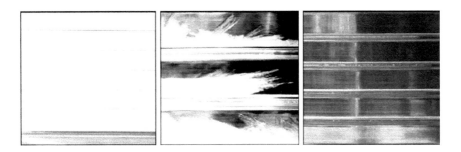

FIGURE 5.9   Transition phase of the PCM in GlassX product.

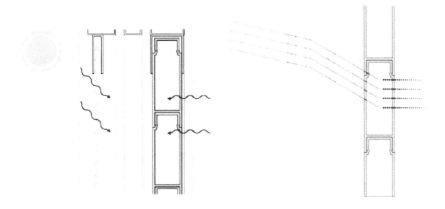

FIGURE 5.10   Fundamentals of operation of GlassX product.

angle winter sunlight is allowed to be captured by the PCM as shown in Figure 5.10 (Fokaides et al. 2015).

5.6 CONCLUSION

In comparison with sensible heat storage systems, PCMs have a lot of advantages because of the lower mass and the volume of the system and the more energy that is stored at a relatively constant temperature. The phase change temperature of the PCM should be close to the average room temperature and appropriate properties will be required for latent heat and thermal conductivity. A few additional properties such as fire characteristics, long-term stability, and low cost should also be considered for organic and inorganic PCMs, respectively.

This chapter is the state-of-the-art of PCMs integrated in a building, that is, in the walls, ceilings, floors, and transparent elements. All of the relevant PCMs and the ones discussed in this chapter have good potential for reducing heating and cooling loads by enhancing the storage capacity of the building envelope. Researchers have made a great effort to investigate integration techniques between building applications and PCMs. However, several problems such as long-term thermal behavior, durability of PCM-impregnated wallboards, fire rating and heat transfer enhancement, combined with active systems, etc., still need to be focused on in future work.

REFERENCES

Abhat A. "Low temperature latent heat thermal energy storage." In *Thermal Energy Storage*. D. Reidel Publication Co., Dordrecht, 1981.

Ahmad M, Bontemps A, Sallée H, Quenard D. "Thermal testing and numerical simulation of a prototype cell using light wallboards coupling vacuum isolation panels and phase change material." *Energy Build* 38 (2006): 673–681.

Athienities A, Chen Y. "The effect of solar radiation on dynamic thermal performance of floor heating systems." *Sol Energy* 69 (2000): 229–237.

Barzing R, Chen JJJ, Yon BR, Farid MM. "Application of PCM underfloor heating in combination with PCM wallboards for space heating using prices base control system." *Applied Energy* 148 (2015): 39–48.

Drake JB. "A study of the optimal transition temperature of PCM wallboard for solar energy storage." Oak Ridge National Laboratory report ORNL/TM-10210 available from National Technical Information Service, Springfield, VA, 1987.

Evola G, Marletta L, Sicurella F. "A methodology for investigating the effectiveness of PCM wallboard for summer thermal comfort in buildings." *Building and Environment* 59 (2013a): 517–527.

Evola G, Marletta L, Sicurella F. "Simulation of a ventilated cavity to enhance the effectiveness of PCM wallboards for summer thermal comfort in buildings." *Energy and Buildings* (2013b).

Farid MM, Chen XD. "Domestic electrical space heating with heat storage." *Proc Inst Mech Eng* 213 (1999): 83–92.

Feldman D, Banu D, Hawes D, Ghanbari E. "Obtaining an energy storing building material by direct incorporation of an organic phase change material in gypsum wallboard." *Sol Energy Mater* 22 (1991): 231–242.

Feldman D, Khan MA, Banu D. "Energy storage composite with an organic phase change material." *Sol Energy Mater* 18 (1989a): 333–341.

Feldman D, Shapiro M, Banu D, Fuks CJ. "Fatty acids and their mixtures as phase change materials for thermal energy storage." *Sol Energy Mater* 18 (1989b): 201–216.

Fokaides PA, Khlili A, Kalogirou SA. "Phase change materials (PCMs) Integrated into transparent building elements: A review." *Material Review Sustainable Energy* (2015): 4–6.

Garg HP, Mullick SC, Bhargava AK. *Solar Thermal Energy Storage*. D. Reidel Publishing Co., Dordrecht, 1985.

George A. "Phase change thermal storage materials." In *Handbook of Applied Thermal Design*. McGraw Hill Book Co., 1989.

Kodo T, Ibamoto T. "Research on using the PCM for ceiling board." IEA ECESIA, Annex 17, 3rd workshop, Tokyo, Japan, Oct. 1–2, 2002.

Koschenz M, Lehmann B. "Development of a thermally activated ceiling panel with PCM application in lightweight and retrofitted buildings." *Energy and Buildings* 36 (2004): 567–578.

Kuznik F, Virgone J, Roux J. "Energetic efficiency of room wall containing PCM wallboard: A full scale experimental investigation." *Energy and Building* 40 (2008): 148–156.

Lane GA. *Solar Heat Storage-Latent Heat Materials*. Vol. 1. CRC Press, Boca Raton, FL, 1983.

Lemma M, Carbonari A. "Procedure for energy saving estimation due to insertion of PCM in buildings' envelopes." Proceeding of 3 Congresso Internazionale Ar.Tec.: L'involucro Edilizio—una progettazione complessa, Italy, November 2007.

Lemma M, De Grassi M, Imperadori M. "A new enclosure heat storage system (a brief history of C-tide craft research)." Proceeding of CIB Joint International Symposium, Roma, Italy, October 2006.

Lin K, Zhang Y, Xu X, Di H, Yang R, Qin P. "Experimental study of under floor electric heating system with shape-stabilized PCM plates." *Energy Build* 37 (2005): 215–220.

Manz H, Egolf PW, Suter P, Goetzberger A. "TIM-PCM external wall system for solar space heating and daylighting." *Solar Energy* 61 (1997): 369–379.

Muruganantham K, Phelan P. "Experimental investigation of a bio-based phase change material to improve building energy performance." 4th International Conference on Energy Sustainability, Phoenix, AZ, May 2010.

Peippo K, Kauranen P, Lund PD. "A multi-component PCM wall optimized for passive solar heating." *Energy Build* 17 (1991): 259–270.

Pons O, Aguado A, Fernández AI, Cabeza LF, Chimenos JM. "Review of the use of phase change materials (PCMs) in buildings with reinforced concrete structures," Materiales de Construcción 64 (315), July–September 2014, e031. doi: http://dx.doi.org/10.3989/mc.2014.05613.

Rathod MK, Banerjee J. "Thermal stability of phase change materials used in latent heat energy storage systems: A review." *Renewable and Sustainable Energy Reviews* 18 (2013): 246–258.

Schossing P, Henning HM, Gschwander S, Haussmann T. "Microencapsulated phase change materials integrated into construction materials." *Solar Energy Materials and Solar Cells* 89 (2005): 297–306.

Sharma A, Tyagi VV, Chen CR, Buddhi D. "Review on thermal energy storage with phase change materials and applications." *Renewable and Sustainable Energy Review* 13 (2009): 318–345.

Stott PW, Williams AC, Barry BW. "Transdermal delivery from eutectic systems: Enhanced permeation of a model drug, ibuprofen." *J Control Release* 50 (1998): 297–308.

Taheri H, Sharma A. "An overview of phase change materials for building applications." In *Energy Sustainability Through Green Energy*, Springer, 2015.

Yahaya NA, Ahmad H. "Numerical investigation of indoor air temperature with the application of PCM gypsum board as ceiling panel in buildings." *Procedia Engineering* 20 (2011): 238–248.

II

Hydrogen Cells and Biofuels

CHAPTER 6

The Hydrogen Initiative

Technological Advancements and Storage Challenges

Abhay Kumar Choubey and Reena

CONTENTS

6.1 INTRODUCTION

Presently the society in which people are living is facing high fuel prices, environmental pollution problems, global warming threats, etc. These are mainly because of extensive use of existing traditional fossil fuels such as coal and petroleum-based fuels. Consumption of energy worldwide will be doubled. The doubling of the world's energy consumption over the next 50 years [1] will require significant modifications in the way people produce, store, distribute, and consume energy. An important step in this process is to reduce our dependency on carbon-based fossil fuels. The rapidly growing global demand for oil will likely outpace production in the near future. Of course, record crude oil prices combined with public interest in energy security have resulted in increased attention to especially a potential transportation economy based on hydrogen fuel. Therefore, there is an urgent and critical need for education and workforce development in clean energy technologies. For more than a decade, hydrogen, a most promising and clean fuel, as an alternative to traditional energy sources such as oil and natural gas has been the focus of research and development efforts globally. It is strongly believed that hydrogen can help to address the growing demand for energy and slow down global climate change. In fact, hydrogen can be produced from a variety of sources including fossil fuels, renewables, and water (by means of nuclear, wind, or solar energy). It is nontoxic and extremely environmentally benign since water is the only exhaust product when hydrogen is converted into energy. Hydrogen is a versatile, clean energy carrier that can be produced from natural gas reforming and a variety of carbon-free energy sources such as solar, wind, and nuclear energy through water electrolysis. Hydrogen can easily be converted into mechanical or electrical energy through a combustion reaction or fuel cell, respectively. In both cases, the hydrogen reacts with oxygen to produce water and energy. If hydrogen is to be used on a large-scale basis, the storage of hydrogen becomes a crucial issue for mobility and transport applications. Fuel cell technology would be practical, if hydrogen could be stored in a safe, efficient, compact, and economic manner [2].

Despite obvious benefits, immediate inclusion of hydrogen into the world economy faces a number of challenges. Unlike oil and gas, hydrogen has no large-scale infrastructure supporting its transportation. Although it is routinely used by chemical and petroleum refining industries, the cost of hydrogen storage and delivery is very high for many energy applications, thus impeding the introduction of the hydrogen economy in which energy is stored and transported using hydrogen as a major energy carrier.

While hydrogen production and conversion are already technologically feasible, its delivery and storage face serious challenges. For example, due to possible hydrogen embrittlement of steel, existing natural gas transmission systems may be unsuitable for the transportation of pure hydrogen gas. Therefore, other options such as blending with natural gas, compressed gas, or cryogenic liquid delivery as well as alternative hydrogen carriers (methanol, ethanol, and other organic liquids) are being considered. Currently, none of the options in the market satisfy the needs of end users, which explains the growing interest and investment in hydrogen energy related research and development.

6.2 HYDROGEN STORAGE

Storing enough hydrogen on-board a vehicle to achieve a driving range of greater than 300 miles is a significant challenge. On a weight basis, hydrogen has nearly three times the energy content of gasoline; however, on a volume basis, the situation is reversed. Hydrogen can be stored as a gas or a liquid. Storage of hydrogen as a gas requires high-pressure tanks (5000–10,000 psi tank pressure) and as a liquid it requires cryogenic temperatures because the boiling point of hydrogen at 1 atm pressure is –252.8°C.

6.3 HYDROGEN STORAGE TECHNOLOGY

Currently hydrogen storage technologies include compressing hydrogen at high pressures (350 or 700 bar), liquefying hydrogen at low temperatures (below 20.3 K), or storing hydrogen as chemical/metal hydrides. These technologies, however, suffer from high costs, low energy densities, loss of hydrogen, and safety issues. Storage of hydrogen is a materials science challenge because, for all the storage methods currently being investigated, materials with either a strong interaction with hydrogen or without any reaction are needed. Besides conventional storage methods, that is, high pressure gas cylinders and liquid hydrogen, the physisorption of hydrogen on materials with a high specific surface area, hydrogen inclusion in metals and complex hydrides, and storage of hydrogen based on metals and water are reviewed. Storage of hydrogen remains one of the challenging technological barriers to the advancement of hydrogen fuel cell technologies for mobile applications. Since hydrogen is a gas at standard pressure and temperature (SPT), it has a low volumetric density. Although 1 kg of H_2 can replace about 3 kg or 1 gallon (3.79 L) of gasoline, on a volumetric scale more than 3500 gallons (1.3×104 L ≈ volume of a midsize car) of H_2 gas is necessary to replace just 1 gallon (3.79 L) of gasoline at SPT.

As mentioned above, there are a variety of ways to store hydrogen [3], and the more conventional methods include compressed gas and liquefaction, where the hydrogen is cooled to below its boiling point. However, these options require extremely high pressures or low temperatures to achieve reasonable hydrogen densities. Solid-state hydrogen storage, where the hydrogen is either attached onto the surface (adsorption) or inserted into a host material, offers improved volumetric energy densities at moderate pressures and temperatures. In fact, many metal hydrides have a hydrogen density greater than that of liquid hydrogen. Most hydrogen storage materials can be divided into two categories, those that bind molecular hydrogen to surfaces via weak dipole (van der Waals) interactions (typically <10 kJ/mol H_2) or chemisorbed or included in solid state materials in atomic form [4].

6.4 HYDROGEN STORAGE MATERIALS

Of the light elements that can support chemistry with hydrogen, the element nitrogen has received a great deal of attention. The initial starting point for these nitrogen-related studies was the compound Li_3N and its hydrogenated cousin $LiNH_2$. These compounds form the foundation for hydrogen storage using amides, imides, and nitrides. Li_3N is an example of a relatively straightforward binary alkali metal nitride. It is a fast lithium ion conductor that has made it a potential solid state electrolyte for lithium batteries. Recently the hydrogen uptake properties of Li_3N have been investigated as the basis for a new route to reversible hydrogen storage materials.

The $2LiNH_2 + MgH_2$ system possesses limited hydrogen storage capacities. When the molar ratio of reactants changes, new reactions between lithium amide and simple or complex metal hydrides can take place, opening up new reaction sequences with higher ultimate hydrogen production. So, changes in the initial stoichiometry of mixed components can really perform as a different hydrogen storage system. Investigators have investigated the hydrogen desorption/adsorption properties of $1:1LiNH_2 + MgH_2$. It turns out that this stoichiometry allows the formation of the fully dehydrogenated product LiMgN on desorption of H_2 as given in the following reaction for $1:1MgH_2/LiNH_2$:

$$MgH_2 + LiNH_2 \rightarrow LiMgN + 2H_2$$

The above reaction represents the complete dehydrogenation—LiMgN would be an important candidate material for the storage of hydrogen if the dehydrogenation takes place at low temperature and if it were shown to be reversible. Thermo gravimetric analysis (TGA) and XRD studies of the above reaction have confirmed the presence of LiMgN in the fully dehydrogenated state.

In order to find suitable systems for the storage of hydrogen, amide-imide systems have been found to show promising results. A comparative study of the $LiNH_2$–MgH_2 hydrogen storage system has been made by researchers [5], and several additives such as $LiBH_4$, KH, and $ZrCoH_3$ have been tested as single catalysts and in various combinations in order to study potential synergistic effects. It was found that $LiBH_4$ and KH significantly improved the de-/rehydrogenation kinetics. However, KH results in irreversible reactions.

Testing of catalyst combinations has shown that a system composed of 2 $LiNH_2$–1.1 MgH_2–0.1 $LiBH_4$–3 mass% $ZrCoH_3$ shows superior absorption/desorption kinetics, with a reversible capacity of 4.2 mass% H at a temperature of 180°C.

For favorable thermodynamics and the considerable kinetics of the hydrogen reaction, Li–Mg–N–H compounds hold promise as novel hydrogen storage materials for on-board usage in metal amide hydrogen storage systems. To further improve their performance, effort has been made by researchers to define the fundamental properties of metal amides such as electronic structure and the energetics of their hydrogen reactions. Though understanding the amino anion transition in the hydrogen reaction is essential for further development, the role of the amino anion in metal amides/imides for hydrogen storage is still unclear. Study by investigators [6] has been directed toward the electronic structures and chemical bonds of $Mg(NH_2)_2$, $LiNH_2$, and $Li_2MgN_2H_2$ by way of a first principle approach. The H vacancy formation energies in $LiNH_2$ and $Li_2MgN_2H_2$ were estimated to comprehend the stability of the amino anion in metal amides/imides and its effect on the thermodynamics and kinetics of the hydrogen reaction.

One of the promising hydrogen storage techniques relies on liquid-phase chemical hydrogen storage materials, in particular, aqueous sodium borohydride, ammonia borane, hydrazine, hydrazine borane, and formic acid. The use of these materials in hydrogen storage provides high gravimetric and volumetric hydrogen densities, low potential risk, and low capital investment because it is largely compatible with the current transport infrastructure. In the present review, the research progresses in hydrogen generation from these liquid-phase chemical hydrogen storage materials and their regeneration is considered [7].

The compound sodium borohydride, also known as sodium tetrahydridoborate and sodium tetrahydroborate ($NaBH_4$, SB), is considered a promising hydrogen storage material and an attractive fuel (aqueous solution) of the direct fuel cell (or direct liquid-feed fuel cell). Chemical hydrides such as $NaBH_4$, LiH, and NaH are known as high hydrogen containing materials. $NaBH_4$, in particular, is stable compared with other chemical hydrides, easy to handle, and can be synthesized from common natural resources. As we know by mixing $NaBH_4$ and H_2O at room temperature, only a small amount of the theoretical yield of hydrogen is liberated. Pt-$LiCoO_2$ has been found to be an excellent catalyst for releasing hydrogen by hydrolysis of $NaBH_4$ solution. Using the catalyst with a stoichiometric amount of water (H_2O/$NaBH_4$: 2mol/mol) at a high H_2 pressure above 0.6 MPa produced nearly the theoretical H_2 yield. The 10-kW scale hydrogen generator comprised a storage vessel of $NaBH_4$ solution, a solution pump, a byproduct storage tank for the $NaBO_2$ solution, a separator, and a hydride reactor. The reactor contained a honeycomb monolith coated with the Pt-$LiCoO_2$ catalyst. $NaBH_4$ was synthesized by annealing $NaBO_2$ with MgH_2 under high H_2 pressure [8].

If we compare and think of similarities and dissimilarities between sodium borohydride and ammonia borane (NH_3BH_3, AB) compounds, as far as the use as hydrogen storage material is concerned, there are many similarities between SB and AB in their features and applications. Nevertheless SB and AB as hydrogen storage materials do not compete. Rather, SB is intended more for portable technologies while AB for vehicular applications. Otherwise, when these hydrides are utilized as fuels for direct fuel cells, one question arises: what can be the advantage of developing the AB-powered fuel cell when it seems to be less effective, practical, and more complex than the SB-powered fuel cell [9]?

Hydrogen has attracted considerable attention as a globally accepted clean energy carrier. Currently, the search for safe and efficient hydrogen storage materials is one of the most difficult challenges for the transformation to a hydrogen-powered society as a long-term solution for a secure energy future. There has been a large number of reports on hydrogen storage materials. However, big challenges still remain. Ammonia borane (NH_3BH_3, AB) has a hydrogen capacity as high as 19.6 wt%, exceeding that of gasoline and making it an attractive candidate for chemical hydrogen storage applications. This chemical hydrogen storage material uses the elements nitrogen and boron to chemically bind hydrogen. In these chemical hydrogen storage materials, hydrogen is discharged by a chemical reaction and the hydrogen is recharged by a chemical processing pathway. This makes them unique compared to metal hydride materials or carbon sorbent materials where the hydrogen release and uptake is controlled by temperature and pressure. Ammonia borane, isoelectronic with ethane, is solid at room temperature, stable in air and water, and contains 190 g/kg (100–140 g/L) hydrogen. Intensive efforts have been made to enhance the kinetics of the hydrogen release from this compound from both solid and solution approaches. Some cobalt-based catalysts that exhibit high efficiency for hydrogen generation have been used for the purposes [10]. Core–shell structured Au-Co@SiO_2 nanospheres have been synthesized using a reverse-micelle method. During heat treatment in vacuum, multiple Au-Co nanoparticles (NPs) embedded in SiO_2 nanospheres (Au-Co@SiO_2-RT) merged into single Au-Co NPs in SiO_2 (Au-Co@SiO_2-HT), resulting in a size increase of the Au-Co NPs. The Au-Co@SiO_2-HT nanospheres showed better catalytic activity than that of Au-Co@SiO_2-RT. The higher catalytic activity of Au-Co@SiO_2-HT could be attributed to the decrease in the content of basic ammine by the decomposition of metal ammine complexes during the heat treatment. Compared with their monometallic counterparts, the bimetallic Au-Co NPs embedded in a SiO_2 nanosphere show higher catalytic activity for the hydrolytic dehydrogenation of NH_3BH_3 to generate a stoichiometric amount of hydrogen at room temperature for chemical hydrogen storage. The synergistic effect between Au and Co inside the silica nanospheres plays an important role in the catalytic hydrolysis of NH_3BH_3.

While ammonia borane looks promising for hydrogen storage, given the volumetric and gravimetric density of hydrogen in the material, there are still technical challenges to be addressed. Foremost of these challenges are (1) enhancing the rates of hydrogen release and (2) the discovery of economical chemical processing pathways that will be used to put the hydrogen back on to the dehydrogenated materials.

Promising hydrogen storage capabilities of hydrazine borane, which is readily prepared from the chemical reaction of dihydrazine sulfate with sodium borohydride, have been improved by the researchers adding an equimolar amount of lithium hydride. The resulting mixture was found to contain 14.8 wt% H_2. The hydrogen release behavior of both the pure hydrazine borane and the LiH mixture was studied at various temperatures and showed excellent hydrogen release rates at a reasonable temperature range of 100–150°C [11].

A new material lithium hydrazinidoborane ($LiN_2H_4BH_3$, LiHB) has also been found for solid-state chemical hydrogen storage. Lithium hydrazinidoborane is a polymorphic material, with a stable low-temperature phase and a metastable high-temperature phase. The former is called β-LiHB and the latter α-LiHB. Results from DSC and XRD have shown that the transition phase occurs at around 90°C. On this basis, the crystal structure of the novel β-LiHB phase was solved. The potential of this material for solid-state chemical hydrogen storage was verified using TGA, DSC, and isothermal dehydrogenations. On the formation of the α-LiHB phase, the borane dehydrogenates. At 150°C, it is able to generate 10 wt% of pure H_2 while a solid residue consisting of polymers with linear and cyclic units forms [12].

A compound of $LiNH(BH_3)NH_2BH_3$ (metal-substituted hydrazine bis-borane, HBB), which is synthesized via the reaction between HBB and *n*-butyllithium in ether solution, releases hydrogen at 126 and 170°C with satisfactory purity. This compound has been found to be a promising material for the storage of hydrogen in comparison to HBB [13].

Another kind of promising hydrogen storage material, like hydrazine bisborane ($N_2H_4(BH_3)_2$, HBB) is synthesized by a typical chemical method, which shows relatively low dehydrogenation temperature (around 100°C), effective prevention of any unwanted gaseous products, such as ammonia, diborane, confirming a very high hydrogen release purity of >99%. The activation energy of the first-step dehydrogenation of HBB has been reported to be 106.4 kJ/mol using Kissinger's method [14].

It has also been reported that rhodium nanoparticles (Rh(0) NPs) having particle size of ~5 nm prepared in the presence of hexadecyltrimethyl ammonium bromide are highly effective for catalytic decomposition of hydrous hydrazine to produce H_2 under aqueous and ambient reaction conditions [15].

Formic acid, HCOOH, a well-known chemical having many uses, is liquid at room temperature and has a density of 1.22 g/cm³. This chemical is usually produced through the hydrolysis of methyl formate and can also be obtained by the reduction of CO_2 with H_2 in the presence of an appropriate catalyst. Formic acid is a strong and corrosive acid. It is nontoxic and suitable for easy transportation, handling, and safe storage. Moreover, formic acid, having 4.4 wt% of hydrogen, produces only gaseous products (H_2/CO_2) by decomposition. It has recently been suggested to be a promising hydrogen storage material. There are a number of highly active and robust homogeneous catalysts that selectively decompose formic acid to H_2 and CO_2 near to room temperature. Although the activity and selectivity of heterogeneous catalysts have not yet reached the level of homogeneous systems, this gap is closing [16].

Recent studies on screening of the materials have shown that the Pt-group metals are highly active for formic acid decomposition [17]. For example, Solymosi and co-workers investigated formic acid decomposition over a range of monometallic nanoparticles (Ir, Pd, Pt, Ru or Rh) supported on carbon at 423 K [18].

Adding a secondary metal to an active phase of a catalyst (in this case, the Pt-group metal) is a well-known means to alter catalytic properties because it modifies the electronic structure of the active phase by alloy formation. Many researchers have taken this approach to improve hydrogen selectivities of the Pt-group metals. The improvements in hydrogen selectivity were particularly significant for Pd-Au and Pd-Ag alloy catalysts which produced hydrogen with CO coproduction well below 100 ppm under ambient conditions [19–22].

Other research worthy of attention was done by Ojeda et al., which showed that highly dispersed gold nanoparticles supported on Al_2O_3 can exhibit considerable formic acid decomposition activity, producing virtually CO-free hydrogen [23].

Carbon nanotubes (microscopic tubes of carbon), 2 nm across, store hydrogen in microscopic pores on the tubes and within the tube structures. Similar to metal hydrides, they have the potentiality to store a significant volume of hydrogen [24].

6.5 HYDROGEN STORAGE CHALLENGES

There are various technological and economic challenges that must be addressed to make hydrogen useful for transportation purposes. The main challenge for the storage of hydrogen is how to store the amount of hydrogen required for a conventional driving range (>300 miles) within the vehicular constraints of weight, volume, efficiency, safety, and cost. Durability remains an issue, as does the development of unified international codes and safety standards to facilitate safe deployment of commercial technologies. The key challenges are as follows:

Weight and volume: The weight and volume of hydrogen storage systems are presently very high, resulting in inadequate vehicle range compared to conventional petroleum fueled vehicles. Materials and components are needed to allow compact, lightweight, hydrogen storage systems that allow driving ranges similar to those available today for all light-duty vehicle platforms.

Efficiency: Energy efficiency is also one of the challenges for all hydrogen storage approaches. The energy required to get hydrogen in and out of storage is an issue for reversible solid-state materials storage systems. In addition, the energy associated with compression and liquefaction must be factored in when considering compressed and liquid hydrogen storage technologies.

Durability: Durability of hydrogen storage systems is also not sufficient. Materials and components are needed that allow hydrogen storage systems with a lifetime in excess of 1500 cycles.

Refueling Time: Refueling times are currently long. That needs reduction. Hydrogen storage systems should be there with refueling times of less than 3 minutes over the lifetime of the system.

Codes and Standards: Applicable codes and standards for hydrogen storage systems and interface technologies, which will facilitate implementation/commercialization and assure safety and public acceptance, have not yet been established. Standardized hardware and operating procedures are required.

Cost: The cost of on-board hydrogen storage systems is also very high, particularly in comparison with conventional storage systems for petroleum fuels. Low-cost materials and components for hydrogen storage systems are needed, as well as low-cost, high-volume manufacturing methods.

6.6 CONCLUSION

The materials science challenge of hydrogen storage is to better understand the interaction of hydrogen with other elements, especially metals. Complex compounds such as $Al(BH_4)_3$ have to be investigated and new compounds of lightweight metals and hydrogen need discovery. Hydrogen production, storage, and conversion have reached a technological level, although plenty of improvements and new discoveries are still possible.

Different hydrogen storage methods have been described here. Alongside well-established, high-pressure cylinders for laboratory applications and liquid hydrogen storage methods for air and space applications, metal hydrides and complex hydrides offer a safe and efficient way to store hydrogen. Further research and technical development will lead to higher volumetric and gravimetric hydrogen density. The best materials known today show a volumetric storage density of $150 \text{ kg} \cdot \text{m}^{-3}$, which can still be improved by approximately 50% according to theoretical estimations.

As far as use of different materials for the storage of hydrogen is concerned, considering all the achievements made in catalyst development, using formic acid as a hydrogen storage material seems to be a viable way that offers many benefits as compared to the conventional hydrogen storage technologies. However, it is important to note that the catalyst materials developed thus far are heavily dependent on expensive elements. To commercialize the technology, we are still in need of novel catalyst materials that are not only active and selective for formic acid dehydrogenation but also potentially inexpensive.

In the present review, all aspects of the storage of hydrogen option are considered. There are alternative options also. The author hopes that this presentation will serve the purpose effectively.

REFERENCES

1. Basic research needs for electrical energy storage, Report of the Basic Energy Sciences Workshop on Electrical Energy Storage, US Department of Energy, 2007.
2. A. Bailey, L. Andrews, A. Khot, L. Rubin, J. Young, T.D. Allston, and G.A. Takacs, "Hydrogen storage experiments for an undergraduate laboratory course—Clean energy: Hydrogen/fuel cells," *J. Chem. Educ.*, 92(4), 688–692, 2015.
3. J. Graetz, "Metastable metal hydrides for hydrogen storage," International Scholarly Research Network, ISRN Materials Science, Volume 2012, Article ID 863025, 18 pages.
4. M. Hirscher and B. Panella, "Hydrogen storage in metal organic frameworks," *Scripta Materialia*, 56(10), 809–812, 2007.
5. U. Ulmer, J.J. Hu, M. Franzreb, and M. Fichtner, "Preparation, scale-up and testing of nanoscale, doped amide systems for hydrogen storage," *Int. J. Hyd. Energy,* 38(3), 1439–1449, 2013.
6. Q. Wang, Y. Chen, J. Gai, C. Wu, and M. Tao, "Role of amino anion in metal amides/imides for hydrogen storage: A first principle study," *J. Phys. Chem. C*, 112(46), 18264–18269, 2008.
7. M. Yadav and Q. Xu, "Liquid-phase chemical hydrogen storage materials," *Energy Environ. Sci.*, 5, 9698–9725, 2012.
8. Y. Kojima, "Hydrogen storage and generation using sodium borohydride," *R&D Review of Toyota CRDL*, 40(2), 31–36, 2005.
9. U.B. Demirci and P. Miele, "Sodium borohydride versus ammonia borane, in hydrogen storage and direct fuel cell applications," *Energy Environ. Sci.*, 2, 627–637, 2009.
10. Z.-H. Lu, H.-L. Jiang, M. Yadav, K. Aranishi, and Q. Xu, "Synergistic catalysis of Au-Co@SiO$_2$ nanospheres in hydrolytic dehydrogenation of ammonia borane for chemical hydrogen storage," *J. Mater. Chem.*, 22, 5065–5071, 2012.
11. T. Hügle, M.F. Kühnel, and D. Lentz, "Hydrazine borane: A promising hydrogen storage material," *J. Am. Chem. Soc.*, 131(21), 7444–7446, 2009.
12. R. Moury, U.B. Demirci, V. Ban, Y. Filinchuk, T. Ichikawa, L. Zeng, K. Goshome, and P. Miele, "Lithium hydrazinidoborane: A polymorphic material with potential for chemical hydrogen storage," *Chem. Mater.*, 26(10), 3249–3255, 2014.
13. H. Fu, J. Yang, X. Wang, G. Xin, J. Zheng, and X. Li, Preparation and dehydrogenation properties of lithium hydrazidobis(borane) (LiNH(BH$_3$) NH$_2$BH$_3$), *Inorg. Chem.*, 53(14), 7334–7339, 2014.
14. W. Sun, Q. Gu, Y. Guo, Z. Guo, H. Liu, and X. Xu, "Hydrazine bisborane as a promising material for chemical hydrogen storage." *Int. J. Hyd. Energy*, 36(21), 13640–13644, 2011.
15. S.K. Singh, X.-B. Zhang, and Q. Xu, "Room-temperature hydrogen generation from hydrous hydrazine for chemical hydrogen storage," *J. Am. Chem. Soc.*, 131(29), 9894–9895, 2009.

16. M. Grasemann and G. Laurenczy, "Formic acid as a hydrogen source—Recent developments and future trends," *Energy Environ. Sci.*, 5, 8171–8181, 2012.
17. D.A. Bulushev, S. Beloshapkin, and J.R.H. Ross, "Hydrogen from formic acid decomposition over Pd and Au catalysts," *Catal. Today* 154, 7, 2010.
18. F. Solymosi et al., "Production of CO-free H_2 from formic acid. A comparative study of the catalytic behavior of Pt metals on a carbon support," *J. Catal.* 279, 213, 2011.
19. Y. Huang et al., "Novel PdAu@Au/C core-shell catalyst: Superior activity and selectivity in formic acid decomposition for hydrogen generation," *Chem. Mater.* 22, 5122, 2010.
20. X. Zhou et al., "High-quality hydrogen from the catalyzed decomposition of formic acid by Pd-Au/C and Pd-Ag/C," *Chem. Commun.*, 30, 3540, 2008.
21. K. Tedsree et al., "Hydrogen Production from formic acid decomposition at room temperature using a Ag-Pd core-shell nanocatalyst," *Nat. Nanotechnol.* 6, 302, 2011.
22. S. Zhang et al., "Monodisperse AgPd alloy nanoparticles and their superior catalysis for the dehydrogenation of formic acid," *Angew. Chem. Int. Ed.* 52, 3681, 2013.
23. M. Ojeda and E. Iglesia, "Formic acid dehydrogenation on Au-based catalysts at near-ambient temperatures," *Angew. Chem. Int. Ed.* 121, 4894, 2009.
24. M. Becher, M. Haluska, M. Hirscher et al., "Hydrogen storage in carbon nanotubes," *C R Phys* 4, 1055–1062, 2003.

CHAPTER 7

Energy Security and Sustainability for Road Transport Sector

The Role of Hydrogen Fuel Cell Technology

Bahman Shabani, Reza Omrani, and John Andrews

CONTENTS

7.1 INTRODUCTION

Global energy supply and demand are increasingly dominated by concerns about a range of factors, most notably climate change, shortage of oil supply and price increase, rising population levels, and energy consumption per capita. Therefore, it is of vital importance to have an undisrupted supply of energy in a sustainable and secure way to meet the energy demand and maintain and improve the well-being of the community. Energy security is a critical element of regional security and stability. The classic concept of energy security, which arose during the oil crisis in 1970s, was based on reliable and cheap supply of oil (Yergin 1988). Energy security was of less importance during the 1990s due to the relative stability in oil price and oil supplying regions. However, in the twenty-first century, energy security has become a topic of debate again. Many factors including rapid increase of energy consumption, gas supply disruptions to Europe, political turmoil and armed conflicts, the urgent need for climate change mitigation measures, and accidents such as the Fukushima nuclear disaster have played roles. Sustainability and the environment are now critical parts of energy security with respect to undisrupted supply of energy with stable prices.

Due to the ever-evolving nature and complex interrelation of factors driving energy security, a universal definition has not been provided to address energy security in all aspects globally. An unexhausted list of definitions can be found in the literature for energy security. Several organizations such as World Energy Council (WEC) (2013) and International Energy Agency (IEA) (2011) have provided definitions for energy security. According to IEA, energy security is defined as "the uninterrupted physical availability at a price which is affordable, while respecting environmental concerns" (IEA 2011).

Attributes of energy security in different definitions (APERC 2007, IEA 2011, Sovacool and Mukherjee 2011, Winzer 2012, WEC 2013) are affordability, availability, acceptability, accessibility, adequacy, sustainability, diversity, reliability, and quality. The Asia Pacific Energy Research Centre (APERC) (2007) introduced the four "As" of energy security: affordability, availability, acceptability, and accessibility; this concept is widely being used by energy experts and policy makers. Affordability refers to the economic viability of the energy source such as production and delivery costs and the price fluctuations. Availability is defined as the geological existence of the energy sources. Acceptability addresses the negative impacts of the energy system on the environment and sustainability. Finally, accessibility refers to the challenges and barriers involved in harnessing an energy source. An energy system must satisfy these factors in order to provide energy security. Therefore, considering the energy security according to the current global situations, fossil fuels fall short in providing energy security. Fossil fuels do not satisfy any of these four "As" from the energy security point of view. The prices have been either experiencing an overall upward trend or strong fluctuations due to the global economic recession, depletion of oil and gas reserves, and conflicts in parts of the oil supplying regions. It is not accessible as many countries rely heavily on imported petroleum fuels, and this is highly sensitive to political and military conflicts around the globe and particularly those countries that are largely involved in supplying oil to the rest of the world. The acceptability of fossil fuels is under question as they are the main contributor to greenhouse gas (GHG) emissions and climate change. Finally, their availability is of a huge concern as the existing reserves are diminishing.

Over 82% of the global energy demand is met through the consumption of fossil fuels, primarily through combustion processes. One of the most energy-intensive sectors is transport. The transport sector, in 2012, made up 28% (IEA 2014a) of the total energy consumption and 23% (IEA 2014b) of total GHG emission. Currently the main fossil fuel that global transportation relies on is oil. For example, the dependency of the European Union's transport sector on oil is around 93% (Capros et al. 2014) of which 86.4% is imported (European Union 2014) causing insecurity in fuel supply due to the instability in some oil producing regions. On average, more than 90% of the global transport sector relies on oil (van Vliet et al. 2011), whereby transportation alone consumes around 49% of oil production and is the most rapidly growing consumer of the world's energy (Amjad et al. 2010). According to projections by IEA (2014a), world transport energy demand will grow by about 33% by 2035 compared to 2012 levels. One of the most optimistic projections provided by Aftabuzzaman and Mazloumi (2011) predicts that oil production would reach its peak of 106 mb/d in 2030, just over 30% above the 2008 level; whereas others have predicted lower amounts such as 96.8 (IEA 2012) and 98 mb/d (Okullo et al. 2015) in 2035. Substantial increase and instability in the price of oil will be a direct consequence of any peaking in global oil production, which will put the economic prosperity of all oil-importing countries at risk (Kim and Moon 2008). In other words, the combined impact of increasing global energy demand and eventual depletion of resources (i.e., fossil fuels) poses serious long-term challenges to maintaining security of energy supply at an economically affordable level (Hal 2006).

GHG emissions are another major concern associated with increasing use of fossil fuels in the transport sector (Cuda et al. 2012). According to IEA (2014b), the transport sector is the second-largest source of GHG emissions at the global level, by emitting about 7187 Mt CO_2 (2012) into the atmosphere, representing 23% of global CO_2 emissions in 2009, with road transport as the largest contributor (about 5374 Mt CO_2) accounting for 17% of total GHG emissions from fuel consumption. While the transport sector made up 19% of the global energy consumption in 2012 (IEA 2014a), only 3.5% of global renewable energy is consumed in this sector (IEA 2015a).

The transport sector, as of 2012, consumes 63.7% of the global oil production (IEA 2014c). Given the highs and lows of the oil prices, and also instability in some oil-producing countries and implementation of environmental policies such as carbon tax and emission trading schemes, finding an alternative to petroleum-based fossil fuels for the transport sector is critically important. For a sustainable energy system, a mix of technological solutions including hydrogen energy, batteries, and other zero-emission alternative fuels such as biofuel are required along with energy efficiency practices (Andrews and Shabani 2012b). Many research studies have concluded that hydrogen will have a significant role to play as a future alternative transport fuel (Ramesohl and Merten 2006, Zhao and Melaina 2006, Offer et al. 2010, Andrews and Shabani 2012b, 2014). Hydrogen can power vehicles either by combustion in internal-combustion engines (ICEs) or electrochemical reaction in fuel cells. Contrary to ICEs, power generation using fuel cells running on high-purity hydrogen can supply electrical power and heat with no emissions since the only reaction product is water (Shabani et al. 2010a). Hence, if the hydrogen is generated using renewable energy sources such as solar or wind as well (i.e., zero-emission generation) the whole process of manufacturing and consumption of hydrogen would involve no emissions (Shabani et al. 2010b, Shabani and Andrews 2011). However, the hydrogen role in a sustainable energy system needs great support by implementing appropriate policies, investment in research and development, and extensive technology demonstration at different levels to facilitate the commercialization of potential technologies (Andrews and Shabani 2012b).

In this chapter, we critically review a number of available zero or low emission technologies and their feasibility for introducing sustainability and energy security to road transport, namely biofuels, battery electric vehicles (BEVs), hydrogen ICE, and fuel cell vehicles. This chapter has a special emphasis on the zero-emission hydrogen fuel cell option and its role to introduce energy security and sustainability to the road transport sector. The hurdles confronting the development of hydrogen fuel cell technology for road transport will be discussed and some practical strategies for future development will be provided.

7.2 RENEWABLE ENERGY TO SUPPORT THE ROAD TRANSPORT SECTOR WITH ENERGY SECURITY AND SUSTAINABILITY

As mentioned earlier, the transport sector is the second largest sector in terms of energy consumption after industry by 28% share in the total energy consumption and contributing to 23% of the total GHG emission. According to the predictions of EIA (2015) under different scenarios the energy consumption of the transport sector in 2040 will be between 25 and 31 exajoule compared to 28 exajoule in 2013 (Figure 7.1). The high dependency of the transport sector on oil makes it both vulnerable to energy supply insecurity and GHG intensive. The majority of the emissions come from road transport. Consequently, it poses a great threat to national

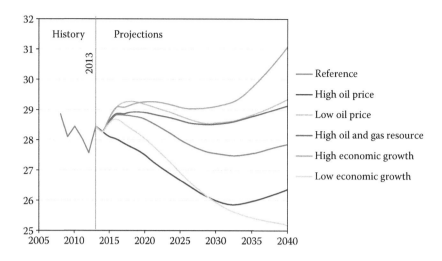

FIGURE 7.1 Transport sector energy consumption (in exajoule) under six different scenarios. (Modified from EIA (2015). Annual Energy Outlook 2015, U.S. Energy Information Administration (EIA).)

security and contributes to the climate change dilemma. Therefore, it is vital to reduce the energy consumption in this sector and substitute oil with green alternative fuels. It is of great importance for countries that are heavily dependent on imported oil such as many EU countries, Australia, Japan, and Korea.

Currently, there are approximately 900 million light-duty vehicles (LDV) on the roads and they are expected to reach 2 billion by 2050 (IEA 2015b). Clearly, this significant jump in the number of vehicles calls for GHG mitigation plans. In the short term, improvement of the existing conventional technologies by efficiency increase of ICEs, design enhancement of the vehicles to reduce the losses, and hybridization can bring the energy consumption and GHG emissions to a lower level. However, these measures cannot be effective more than a certain level and will soon reach their limit. Therefore, in the long run, the only viable option is to shift from fossil fuels to renewable energy sources. Renewable energies can be harvested locally and hence significantly reduce the dependency on energy import or increase the export of oil producing countries by cutting domestic consumption. Also, by local generation of energy, the high cost of energy distribution can be avoided, especially in countries such as Australia with long freight distances.

In order to achieve sustainability in the transport sector, it is necessary to address the demand to reduce the per-capita freight and passenger task, decrease energy intensity through mode shifts, and replace fossil fuels by clean alternative fuels such as hydrogen sourced by renewable energies (Andrews and Shabani 2012b). Consequently, lowering the transport sector energy consumption makes it more practical and achievable to meet this demand through zero-emission energy resources. Two effective measures to decrease the energy demand are reduction of average distance travelled, through urban restructuring, and promoting a modal shift toward public transport and rail freight (Andrews and Shabani 2014, Maniatopoulos et al. 2015).

Andrews and Shabani (2014) suggested that both hydrogen fuel cell and battery electric technologies have roles to play in curbing the emissions from the transport sector and bringing security to the energy supply. Due to the relatively high roundtrip energy efficiency and limited driving range, BEVs are suitable for local and short trips, less than 100 km, whereas hydrogen fuel cell vehicles (HFCVs) are more favorable for longer distances thanks to their higher range.

7.3 THE TECHNOLOGICAL OPTIONS FOR ZERO-EMISSION ROAD TRANSPORTATION

7.3.1 The Options

The principal zero-emission solutions for transport that are being considered are ICE vehicles running on biofuels such as ethanol, methanol, or bio-oils produced from biomass crops; electric vehicles (EVs) charged from the main electricity grid, assuming the electricity supply derives from zero-emission sources; and development of ICEs and HFCVs consuming hydrogen produced from renewables (Andrews and Shabani 2012b). A suitable technological solution for transport has to be chosen in situ with the application (Offer et al. 2010). Figure 7.2 illustrates different levels of electrification in vehicles and various combinations of fuel cell and batteries.

7.3.2 Biofuels for Road Vehicles

An alternative fuel for road vehicles is biofuel, including principally ethanol, various bio-oils, and biodiesel (i.e., biofuel suitable for direct use in diesel engines). Interestingly, the idea of using biofuel in diesel engines originated with the demonstration of the first diesel engine invented by Rudolf Diesel before 1900 using peanut oil as the fuel (Yusuf et al. 2011). The global production of biodiesel has increased from only 11 Ml/year in 1990 to nearly 25,000 Ml/year in 2012, which clearly shows growing

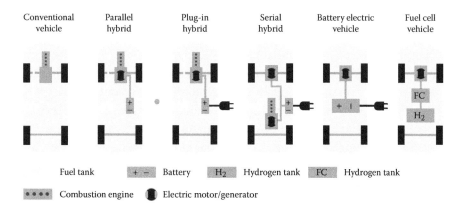

| Conventional vehicle | Parallel hybrid | Plug-in hybrid | Serial hybrid | Battery electric vehicle | Fuel cell vehicle |

Fuel tank   + − Battery   H₂ Hydrogen tank   FC Hydrogen tank

Combustion engine   Electric motor/generator

FIGURE 7.2   Different level and combinations of electric vehicles. (From e-mobil BW (2011). Structure Study BWᵉ mobile 2011, Baden-Württemberg on the way to electromobility, e-mobil BW.)

interest in this technology. The growth in using ethanol for transport was also strong, from about 16,000 Ml/year in 1990 to about 85,000 Ml/year in 2010 (Sorda et al. 2010). Notably, although the total global production of biodiesel has been relatively smaller than that for ethanol, the rate of growth in production of biodiesel around the world has been much faster than that for ethanol in the past two decades. For instance, the growth in biodiesel production between 2004 and 2009 is provided in Figure 7.3 by Timilsina and Shrestha (2011).

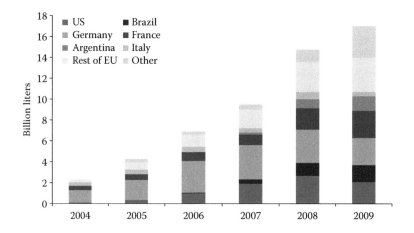

FIGURE 7.3   World biodiesel production. (From Timilsina, G. R. and A. Shrestha (2011). *Energy* **36**(4): 2055–2069. With permission.)

To many, biofuels are seen as a readily implementable substitute for petroleum fuels. Biofuels, for transport, can be used as blends with existing fuels without any modification to today's ICEs, the remainder of vehicle technology, and fuel distribution, storage and delivery infrastructure; and they can be used as 100% alternatives with relatively minor changes to the existing engines and fuel distribution infrastructure (Dwivedi et al. 2011). Biofuels are all produced from organic materials—starch, sugar or cellulosic plants, or algae—that have absorbed carbon dioxide from the atmosphere by photosynthesis during their growth phase. So, by combustion, the same quantity of carbon dioxide is emitted once again. Provided that the energy used to produce and distribute these biofuels is also obtained from renewable resources, they are zero-GHG-emission options.

A key advantage of biofuel over petroleum diesel for trucks is that the biodiesel is biodegradable, which makes its handling and waste management more environmentally friendly (Yusuf et al. 2011). Using biofuel does not emit sulfates and sulfuric acid in the atmosphere as they are mainly vegetable oils with no sulfur content; moreover, the higher oxygen content of biofuels helps improve the combustion quality in diesel engines that leads to cleaner operation, particularly by reducing particulate and CO emissions (Liaquat et al. 2010). Most of the research studies on biodiesel have, however, reported a higher level of NO_x emission than conventional diesel engines, due to the higher combustion temperature (Liaquat et al. 2010), although a few studies have found a reduction in NO_x, (Panwar et al. 2010). Using biodiesel in a diesel engine may slightly reduce its maximum power by up to 5% (due to less energy content compared to diesel fuel), but engine wear may be less than using conventional diesel (Dwivedi et al. 2011).

The environmental benefits of using biofuels are also controversial. Although biofuels consumption can reduce GHG emissions in theory, while arguably increasing NO_x, there are concerns about change of land use (e.g., clearing forests to create land for growing crops) and increase in chemical fertilizer utilization. These factors can generate negative environmental impacts such as water contamination introducing detrimental changes to the natural ecosystems (Stoeglehner and Narodoslawsky 2009, Havlík et al. 2011). Havlík et al. (2011) predicted up to over 150 million hectares (M ha) of deforestation based on an estimate of liquid biofuel production of 277 million tonnes of oil equivalent (toe) in 2030 (mainly used in the transport sector). If the required land is prepared through deforestation, it results in increased GHG emissions, which can reverse the emission reduction through biofuel production.

Another issue mainly discussed regarding biofuels is its possible adverse effect on food security. The crops are also used as food and their dual use results in a price increase. In addition, land use for biofuel production increases the land price, which also affects the food price. On the other hand, biofuel production can assist in agricultural development. The decisive parameter is the feedstock supply own-price-elasticity. The feedstock with higher price elasticity promotes supply by price increase, boosting the agricultural development (Koizumi 2015).

As for the economics of this technology, there is an unanswered question: whether biofuels would be a solution to the likely high cost of petroleum-based fuels in the future or not. Hence, the raw materials used to produce biofuels are also expected to experience a similar order of increase in their prices as that predicted for the price of oil-based fuels themselves and eventually such an effect will be reflected in the final price of biofuels. Some experts believe that a comprehensive economic analysis of biofuel technology has to take into account the effect of biofuel production on the food prices, as some land would be inevitably dedicated to production of raw materials to be used in biofuels production (Stoeglehner and Narodoslawsky 2009). It is reported that even the current implementation level of technology has already had considerable impact on food prices and supply; this situation would call the future widespread adoption of biofuels into question. Using enzymes to produce biofuels efficiently from biomass (Xing et al. 2012) is another factor to be taken into account when evaluating the economics of this technology as this can increase the biofuel production cost considerably (Mohammadi et al. 2011), and may also involve an extensive use of genetically engineered crops. As reported by Klein-Marcuschamer et al. (2012) while using enzymes can add to the cost of biofuel production, some researchers believe that the cost contribution of enzymes will be negligible in the future with the expected technological innovations and advances in this area.

There are also some other social concerns such as the lack of an established sustainability standard focused on the social aspect of the technology, as well as public scepticism about 100% compatibility of these fuels (e.g., E10) with the current engines; that both encourage a public reluctance for using biofuels.

Andrea Wild from CSIRO Australia (2012) believes that moving on from first-generation technologies (using sugar or starch to produce ethanol, and waste oil to produce biodiesel) to the second generation biofuels using non-food biomass, such as lignocellulose to make biodiesel and ethanol, would be the best way to proceed in order to avoid potential problems related to food concerns being raised (refer to first generation of biofuels). As quoted by the Washington Post (2008), according to the US Department of Energy, using algae for production of biofuels would require 30 times less land compared to that needed using land crops such as soybeans; also, per land area productivity of microalgae, as distinct from seaweed or macroalgae, is 100 times more than that for soybeans or any other terrestrial oil-producing crop (DoE 2007).

Notwithstanding the promising aspects of biofuels, major uncertainties remain about their sustainability if substituted for petroleum fuels in transport on a very large scale. Some researchers are still in doubt about the effect of using non-food based cellulosic (second generation) biofuels when considering the effect of developing this technology on changing the land use patterns and hence the indirect impact on food supply on local and global levels (Stoeglehner and Narodoslawsky 2009). According to CSIRO's report by Wild (2012), utilizing less productive lands for production of second generation biofuels (e.g., algae can be grown on nonarable lands) can add to the sustainability of this technology and prepare the ground for further contribution of these fuels into the Australian transport system; however, this raises a question why these types of lands have remained unproductive (lack of water supply?) and how this reason can contribute to making the practice of growing algae in such lands unsustainable.

Assuming the proven capacity of manufacturing about 1300 L of biodiesel per hectare per year (UN 2008), about 13–14 million km^2 of land, almost two times the area of Australia, is required to be dedicated to biodiesel production in order to meet global demand of diesel fuel in 2014, which is over 1750 billion liters per year; this is based on the assumption that the consumption would remain the same if the engines consume the same rate of fuel when shifting from petroleum-based diesel fuel to biodiesel. By considering the land use in each country and the required land for generation of biodiesel, it can be determined what percentage of the diesel demand is possible to be produced domestically in a sustainable manner.

However, considering the attributes of energy security, biofuels cannot meet all the requirements and their role and contribution in the future energy systems are not expected to exceed above a certain level. The main shortcoming of biofuels is their acceptability. As mentioned earlier, biofuels can have many negative impacts on the environment and also food security. Also, availability remains questionable, as a vast area is needed for their production. Moreover, production in many areas can be affected by extreme weather conditions that impact both price and availability. As a result, biofuels may not be reliable solutions from the energy security and sustainability point of view.

7.3.3 Hybrid and Battery Electric Vehicles

Electric cars were first invented and used in late nineteenth century and early twentieth century. In 1891, William Morrison built the first successful electric automobile in the United States; his invention soon became very popular such that 28% of the total cars produced in the United States in 1900 were powered by electricity (IEEE 2012). However, advances in internal combustion engines in the early twentieth century shifted attention away from battery electric vehicles (BEVs) and, consequently, the use of this technology declined. Now, after nearly one century of domination of the automotive market by ICEs, BEVs have regained attention. Brown et al. (2010) estimate that the total number of electric cars sold will grow from 500,000 in 2008 to 11 million by 2020, equivalent to 13% of the global passenger car market in the latter year.

For BEVs, the on-board components required are the battery bank, including a thermal management system, the associated charge regulation and control system, and the electric motors. The electricity required to charge the batteries is drawn from the main grid and a local charging station outside of the vehicle (Andrews and Shabani 2012b). Present day electric cars are mainly plug-in hybrid electric vehicles (PHEVs), which employ ICEs in addition to the standard components used in BEVs, and the batteries can be charged either through the grid or on-board ICE. PHEVs are expected to serve as a bridging technology towards BEVs, charged solely via the main electricity grid. Electric cars can employ regenerative braking to recover the energy usually dissipated when applying the brakes to slow down, halt, or when going downhill. The ICE, used in PHEVs, is designed to be operated close to its rated power all the time in order to deliver power at its highest efficiency. The vehicle is powered by batteries to the maximum extent possible, while the ICE is off; when the energy level of the batteries is low, the ICE is turned on at full load to recharge the battery and contribute in powering the vehicle. When the batteries are fully charged, the ICE is turned off again (Çağatay Bayindir et al. 2011). Although PHEVs may offer a lower emission transport (provided low-emission electricity is used to charge batteries), they are still dependent on petrol and contribute to GHG emissions to the atmosphere (Amjad et al. 2010).

Nickel metal hydride (NiMH) and lithium-ion (Li-ion) batteries are currently the preferred choices for plug-in hybrid electric vehicles from the energy density point of view (Amjadet al. 2010, Young et al. 2013). However, the relatively low power densities of these batteries have encouraged researchers to use ultra-capacitors in conjunction with the battery storage system in order to improve the performance of BEVs during both acceleration and regenerative braking modes (Clarke et al. 2010, Arbizzani et al. 2015). Using ultra-capacitors can also protect batteries from deep discharge, extending their lifetime. Furthermore, ultra-capacitors endure cold weather climate, shocks, vibration, and repeated cycles for many years without degradation. Nevertheless, at their current level of technological development, ultra-capacitors cannot totally eliminate the batteries as their energy storage capacities are substantially lower than batteries (Çağatay Bayindir et al. 2011). There are also some other barriers and challenges to be overcome before BEVs are widely used globally. These challenges are mainly related to the weight of the batteries, their limited gravimetric and volumetric energy densities, which limit their range, long recharging time, lack of recharging infrastructure, and short lifetime of batteries. Obviously, future market penetration of the BEVs will depend on whether technical solutions can be found to help remove such barriers (Çağatay Bayindir et al. 2011, Andrews and Shabani 2012b).

Apart from the concern associated with the cost and mass of BEVs or PBEVs, there is also a concern about the need for increasing the size of the existing power generation capacities, which must be achieved by enhancing the renewable energy input to the grid if net reductions in GHG emissions are to be achieved. The costs of these grid capacity increases must be added to other infrastructure costs associated with a transition to EVs. For example, Vliet et al. (2011) showed that uncoordinated charging would lead to increases of 7% in the Dutch grid national peak load and 54% in the household peak at only 30% penetration rate of EVs, which may exceed the capacity of existing electricity distribution infrastructure. Accordingly, some researchers have proposed recharging during off-peak times (e.g., night time) to minimize the impact on peak demand and the need to increase total generating capacity (Brown et al. 2010, van Vliet et al. 2011). However, this strategy implicitly assumes that the majority of power stations continue to be fossil-fuelled (or nuclear-fission powered) and hence available at all times of the day. As there is a whole scale shift to renewable energy sources of electricity—solar, wind and water power— to meet say the commonly accepted goal of an 80% reduction in global GHG emissions by 2050 compared to 2000 (Metz et al. 2007), there will no longer be surplus power at night time (when solar energy is zero and wind energy supply is low). Thus, in general, the charging requirements of BEVs will not match the availability of electrical energy, unless major storage capacity is introduced to the grid. The introduction of smart-grid has delivered more control and communication features. In order to use the potential of smart-grid, vehicle to grid (V2G) has been developed. V2G can be applied in plug-in EVs to enable the smart-grid to communicate with the vehicle and control the energy exchange between the EV and grid depending on whether it is peak or off-peak demand time. Participating customers will be paid for the power supply to the grid during the peak demand. For further details on V2G and different V2G services and the corresponding issues, the reader is referred to the review papers by Liu et al. (2015) and Tan et al. (2016).

Thermal management of batteries is required in order to achieve a balance between charging phase, exhibiting a net cooling effect, and discharging phase, which is highly exothermic (Al-Hallaj and Selman 2002). Operating the batteries outside their recommended temperature range would affect their charging and discharging performance as well as their useful life (Hamut et al. 2012). Thermal management becomes particularly critical in extreme climate conditions (either very cold or very hot), which is another technical challenge yet to be met by battery technology (Shabani and Biju 2015). For example, extremely high temperatures (caused by high ambient temperature and/or rapid discharge during acceleration) can render the battery system unsafe (Amjad et al. 2010, Rao and Wang 2011, Huber and Kuhn 2015); or exposure to cold weather (below 0°C) can have a negative impact on the charging performance of the batteries and consequently on the range available (Al-Hallaj and Selman 2002, Kim et al. 2014).

Despite all these challenges, the potential benefits of BEVs are encouraging many automakers, globally, to move toward this technology with a view to take a significant share of the future vehicle market. Globally, the total number of electric vehicles on the road is approximately 740,000, of which around 340,000 have been registered in 2014 (ZWS 2015). This figure falls behind the earlier predictions of the International Energy Agency

(2013) that was nearly 2.5 million electric cars by 2015; this number is expected to be approximately 20 million by 2020 in this report. However, still a strong growth in the annual sale has been experienced over the last few years. It is worth mentioning that the key role of policies is promoting the implementation of green vehicles in supporting this technology. In the United States, the federal government is offering $7500 tax credit (IRS 2015) while it is backed up by additional incentives from state governments. On the other hand, despite having some pioneering car manufacturers, Germany falls behind other European countries in terms of EV adoption due to implementation of subsidies on R&D and not on the direct sales. As a result, the introduction of incentives for end users is being considered to achieve the goal of 1 million electric cars in Germany by 2020 (Reuters 2015).

7.3.4 Hydrogen Technologies

7.3.4.1 Sustainable Hydrogen Systems for Road Transport Sector

A hydrogen energy system consists of a hydrogen production system—depending on the implemented method different arrangements are possible; hydrogen storage, distribution, and delivery facilities; and equipment to convert the energy stored in the hydrogen into the users' preferred form of energy such as electrical, thermal, or mechanical energy (Figure 7.4). Hydrogen can be produced from a diverse range of resources including fossil fuels, biomass, and water. Depending on the source and method used, the level of GHG emission varies (Shabani and Andrews 2015). Currently, natural gas reforming is the most economical method to generate hydrogen (Anstrom 2014). Hydrogen sourced by this method if used in HFCVs can reduce the emission by almost 50% compared to ICEs. However, in order to fully take advantage of hydrogen energy systems in addressing climate change, it is necessary to reduce the emissions to the lowest possible level. Currently, the most promising method is water electrolysis, and the hydrogen produced through this method can be used for both stationary and mobile applications (Gray et al. 2011, Aris and Shabani 2015, Maniatopoulos et al. 2015). By implementing renewable energy, we can obtain zero-emission transportation—in terms of direct energy consumption—on a life-cycle basis. Therefore, in the long term, the shift toward renewable energy sources should be the goal of the policies, and fossil fuel sources should be implemented in the introduction phase to facilitate the transition toward sustainable energy solutions.

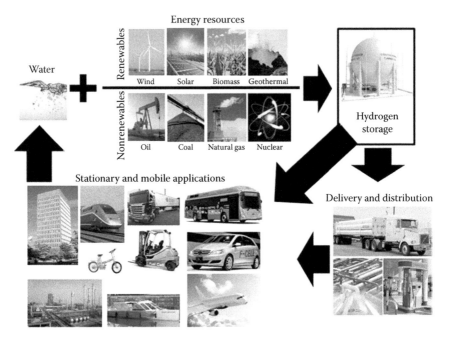

FIGURE 7.4 Hydrogen energy cycle: generation, storage, distribution, and consumption. (From Shabani, B. and J. Andrews (2015). Hydrogen and fuel cells. In: *Energy Sustainability Through Green Energy*. A. Sharma and S. K. Kar, Eds. Springer India, pp. 453–491. With permission.)

Another main challenge in a hydrogen energy system is the distribution of hydrogen. Currently, most of the hydrogen generated is being sourced on-site or at a close distance to minimize the need for a hydrogen distribution network (Shabani and Andrews 2015). While large-scale hydrogen generation sites can benefit from economies of scale to reduce the capital cost of hydrogen production plants, the technical challenges and the high cost involved to establish an extensive hydrogen distribution network consisting of pipeline, compressor stations, and storage facilities all from scratch is one of the main reasons that policy makers and potential investors are opposed to hydrogen technology. To overcome this barrier, decentralized hydrogen production along with the existing power grid can significantly simplify the distribution network and eliminate extensive transfer lines (Figure 7.5) (McDowall and Eames 2007, Andrews and Shabani 2012b). In this scenario, hydrogen will be produced either locally to be consumed on the spot or regionally with a storage system to supply the fuel of the refueling stations. Preferably, in the long term, the hydrogen

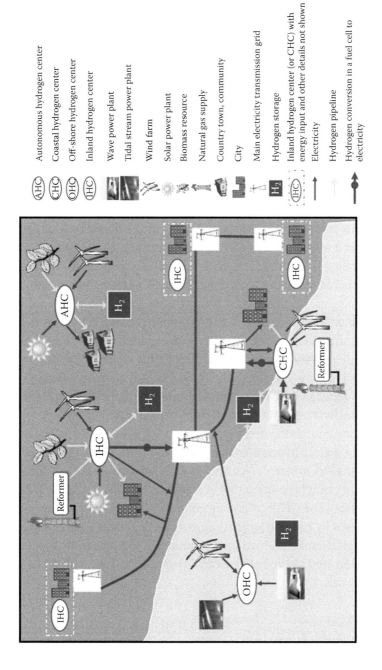

FIGURE 7.5 A schematic illustration of the proposed hierarchy of sustainable hydrogen centers showing the principal RE inputs to each type of center, the local hydrogen distribution system, and the interconnection of higher-order centers via the main electricity grid. (From Andrews, J. and B. Shabani (2012b). *International Journal of Hydrogen Energy* **37**(2): 1184–1203. With permission.)

Autonomous hydrogen center
Coastal hydrogen center
Off-shore hydrogen center
Inland hydrogen center
Wave power plant
Tidal stream power plant
Wind farm
Solar power plant
Biomass resource
Natural gas supply
Country town, community
City
Main electricity transmission grid
Hydrogen storage
Inland hydrogen center (or CHC) with energy input and other details not shown
Electricity
Hydrogen pipeline
Hydrogen conversion in a fuel cell to electricity

production should be carried by zero-emission technologies such as water electrolysis powered by renewable energies. Decentralized and local hydrogen production centers are potential investment for car manufacturers. Currently, companies such as Toyota, Honda, Nissan (Nissan Motor Corporation 2015), and Daimler (Hayter 2014) are establishing local refueling stations with hydrogen production facilities and progressively improve the performance and efficiency while cutting down the costs. An increase in the number of refueling stations hastens the widespread commercialization of HFCVs, which in turn makes the investment in fuelling stations more attractive. These initiatives with proper measures and policies from the government can realize the transition to a sustainable road transport (Andrews and Shabani 2012c).

The main advantage of a hydrogen-based energy system is the diversity in the feedstock and technologies that can be used for hydrogen production. From an energy security point of view, the diversity is of prime importance as it affects all the four "A's" of energy security (APERC 2007). First, availability is improved as each region can source the hydrogen from the available resources from natural gas to water and based on different technologies. Second, hydrogen on mass implementation can be an affordable energy carrier as it can be produced locally, and it is not considerably affected by factors such as weather conditions, political and military conflicts, natural disasters, and economic recessions to the same extent as fossil fuels or even biofuels. Third, hydrogen energy systems can substantially reduce GHG emissions and mitigate climate change effects even when the hydrogen is obtained from natural gas. Finally, hydrogen production does not suffer from geopolitical barriers as it is possible to shift from one source to another to produce the hydrogen, and the needs for import can be eliminated, resulting in national security. Let's highlight this important point here again that eventual viable solution for hydrogen production, from the GHG emissions point of view, should be water electrolysis powered by renewables that suggests no GHG signature. However, for having a zero-emission hydrogen production, some technical barriers have to be addressed to produce a clean energy carrier (i.e., hydrogen) at a competitive price.

7.3.4.2 Hydrogen-Based Technological Options
Hydrogen has the potential to be a mainstream zero-emission transportation fuel in the future, provided that hydrogen is produced using renewable energy sources (e.g., solar, wind, or hydro-electricity) to split water

via electrolysis, direct water splitting by sunlight using photolysis, or conversion of biomass to hydrogen (Larminie and Dicks 2003). Andrews and Shabani (2012b) have recently proposed a model for a hydrogen-based sustainable transport that relies on decentralized renewable energy sources of diverse forms that does not require an extensive new hydrogen pipeline system to take hydrogen from production centers to distribution outlets. The fact that there are many different methods and sources available for production of hydrogen is seen as a unique feature and advantage of this alternative fuel (Verhelst and Wallner 2009).

Based on the model developed by Floris et al. (2010) within the Dutch energy transition policy framework, the shift to hydrogen-based transport is seen as a major contributor to a sustainable transport system. Hydrogen power can be employed for transport either through combustion in ICEs or electrochemical reaction in fuel cells. Unlike batteries, this energy carrier can be used as long-term storage without any concern about self-discharging (Andrews and Shabani 2012a). Despite the existing challenges relating to the on-board storage of hydrogen, the feasibility of using hydrogen for long-range driving, close to higher than that for petrol cars (~500 km), has already been proven, for example, in Honda's FCX Clarity car with 372 km, Hyundai Tucson with 426 km, and Toyota Mirai with over 500 km (DoE n.d.).

Hydrogen can be used directly as an alternative fuel in ICEs. As Verhelst and Wallner (2009) reported, Musashi Institute of Technology, BMW, and Ford Motor Company have all played major roles in the development and demonstration of hydrogen ICEs. Some major car manufacturers (e.g., BMW) have seen hydrogen ICEs as a bridging technology that allowed continued use of ICEs and the associated production lines and vehicle maintenance infrastructure and technical expertise until hydrogen fuel cell technologies and electric drive trains reach maturity and a competitive price to minimize the investment risks. However, in late 2000s, BMW abandoned hydrogen ICE and shifted its focus to fuel cell technology (Beissmann 2009). While hydrogen ICEs can deliver some advantage over conventional ICEs such as higher efficiency and GHG emission reduction, several technical challenges including low power and energy density, high NO_x emission levels, backfiring, surface ignition, and high flame speeds (Berckmuller, Rottengruber et al. 2003, Verhelst and Wallner 2009) have discouraged car manufacturers from further investments on this option.

Hydrogen fuel cell technology is another option for generating propulsion power from hydrogen while achieving zero-emission. Fuel cells draw on energy stored in hydrogen through the electrochemical reaction of recombining hydrogen and oxygen in a fuel cell to form water (and heat as by-product). Such a method is potentially up to twice as efficient as an ICE in converting hydrogen energy to mechanical power (Hoffmann 2001, Mock and Schmid 2009). The high energy efficiency of fuel cells (about 55%), particularly at part load, and their zero-emission and silent operation are the main reasons for the continuing global interest in fuel cell-based engines (Marbán and Valdés-Solís 2007). The capacity of early fuel cells designed and manufactured for automotive applications was very low (e.g., 0.4 kW Ballard MK3 fuel cell). Today, fuel cells of around 150 kW power are being manufactured (e.g., HD6 fuel cell modules by Ballard fuel cell) (Ballard 2012) for use in vehicles.

Among many different types of fuel cell, proton exchange membrane (PEM) fuel cells have emerged as the most promising for automotive applications because of their high power densities, relatively low operating temperature, quick start up time (in the order of existing ICEs), and quick response to dynamic loads (Islam et al. 2015). PEM fuel cells have been improved considerably over the past two decades in terms of price, performance, durability, and power density, while further enhancements are continuously being made aimed at making them a competitive technology for road vehicles. For example, both volumetric and gravimetric power densities of fuel cells at stack and cell levels have been improved in the past 50 years to achieve better packaging configurations and performance. The first PEM fuel cell used by NASA (NASA GEMINI-1960) had 20 W/l and 15 W/kg of stack volumetric and gravimetric power densities, respectively, and the first fuel cell used in a vehicle by Mercedes-Benz had a gravimetric power density of 62.5 W/kg, while comparable figures for the fuel cell used in Honda's FCX Clarity fuel cell car are 1900 W/l and 1500 W/kg, respectively. Honda has increased the volumetric power density for its upcoming FCV (2016) by 60% over the FCX clarity to deliver 3100 W/l (Honda Motor 2014) similar to Toyota Mirai (Toyota Motor Corporation 2015).

Most major automotive companies such as Toyota (Toyota Motor Corporation 2015), Honda (Honda Motor 2014), BMW (Behrmann 2015), GM (GM 2015), Ford (Ford Motor Company 2014); Daimler-Chrysler (Daimler AG 2011), Nissan (Nissan Motor Corporation n.d.), Kia (Kia Motors Corporation 2015), and Hyundai (Hyundai 2015) have shown their interest in hydrogen fuel cell vehicles by developing demonstration models of their popular products running on hydrogen and also initial commercial releases such as Mirai by Toyota and Tucson by Hyundai.

HFCVs currently may not offer strong economic advantages over conventional ICE vehicles attractive to the end customers. Added values such as low/zero emissions and low noise levels, if appealing to the users, do not justify the higher price. In order to be successful in sales, manufacturers should improve the performance, range, or additional features over the competent ICE vehicles. Features such as Honda's "Power Exporter" (Honda Motor 2014) introduced for their upcoming 2016 FCV similar to that offered by Toyota Mirai (Toyota Motor Corporation 2015) can be a strong selling point. Both of these vehicles are capable of powering external electric devices or a small household, which can be very attractive to some customers. Toyota Mirai can supply a typical house power demand for a week by providing around 60 kWh of electricity, with a maximum 9 kW DC power output (Toyota Motor Corporation 2014c, 2015).

7.4 APPLICATION OF HFCS IN ROAD VEHICLES

7.4.1 Overview

Hydrogen fuel cells can deliver efficiencies as high as 50–60% while ICEs have efficiencies around 30% or less. The high efficiency, zero-emission potential, and high energy content of hydrogen support the technology to be promising for shifting toward sustainable and low-emission transportation. HFCVs have zero tailpipe emissions; however, in order to be zero-emission from a life-cycle perspective, the hydrogen should be obtained from zero-emission sources and methods.

The overall efficiency of HFCVs is almost double the efficiency of ICEs (Hoffman 2012) thanks to the high efficiency of fuel cell and illumination of the gearbox on HFCVs. As a result, the energy (fuel) consumption of HFCVs is nearly half of the ICE. Therefore, despite the fact that the energy loss in the hydrogen production and distribution is higher than fossil fuel delivery, the well-to-tank efficiency of HFCVs is still higher. They can also deliver ranges higher than battery electric vehicles and comparable to (and even more than) ICEs.

The fuel cells have been implemented in a range of road vehicles such as passenger cars, vans and low duty trucks, buses and heavy-duty trucks. They can be used as the main power source to form a hybrid fuel cell vehicle in conjunction with a battery or be used as a range extender to assist batteries.

7.4.2 Recent Developments

7.4.2.1 Passenger Cars

The uncertainty about the future of HFCVs, which is highly dependent on the development of refueling stations in a timely manner, discourages some of the major car manufacturers from significant investment in fuel cell technology because of the risks involved. Some manufacturers such as BMW started the implementation of fuel cell technology later than the rest and initially preferred to invest in the ICEs based on hydrogen due to the maturity of the technology and less modification required for the whole system. However, these companies have now adopted fuel cell technologies and have scheduled their future entrance into the HFCV market. The aforementioned problems with the hydrogen internal combustion engines including low power and energy density, high NO_x emission levels, backfiring, surface ignition, and high flame speeds (Verhelst and Wallner 2009) have almost resulted in phasing out of this technology and the majority of the car manufacturers have shifted their focus to fuel cells.

Initially, the HFCVs were solely relying on the fuel cell as the power source. The first HFCV was NECAR 1 Mercedes-Benz (1994). Considering the premature fuel cell technology at that time, the hydrogen system occupied all the loading space of the van. The maximum power was 50 kW delivered by 800 kg fuel cell system and providing a range of 130 km (Mercedes-Benz n.d.). However, NECAR 1 is one the greatest breakthroughs in development of HFCVs after its satisfactory trial. Nevertheless, in order to overcome the shortcomings of fuel cells such as lower response and efficiency, and taking advantage of batteries most of the car manufacturers consider hybridization of HFCVs by incorporating batteries and supercapacitors. Generally, the size of the batteries is small and mainly they provide additional power when needed and take advantage of regenerative braking. The advantages of a hybrid HFCV are energy recovery through regenerative braking; sizing of the FC stack based on the base power of the vehicle and therefore smaller FC can be utilized; FC can be operated mostly at relatively high efficiency points and its lifetime improves; start-up time of the FC is improved; and battery lifetime is increased due to the elimination of deep-discharge. Plug-in hybrid fuel vehicles accommodate larger batteries, which can be charged through an external power source as well. Examples of this type of HFCVs are Mercedes-Benz F125! (Daimler AG 2011) and Audi A7 Sportback h-tron quattro (Audi AG 2015). One of the advantages of plug-in HFCVs is the possibility of using both hydrogen refuelling stations (HRSs) and charging stations. Mercedes-Benz F125!, a concept vehicle, has a range of 1000 km. The battery can provide up to 50 km.

Recently, some car manufacturers have started the mass production of fuel cell cars. Toyota has introduced Mirai as the world's first mass produced HFCV (Toyota Motor Corporation 2015); Hyundai's Tucson Fuel Cell (ix35 Fuel Cell) is the first mass produced crossover utility vehicle (Hyundai 2015). Honda has announced that its first mass-produced HFCV will hit the market in 2016 (Honda Motor 2015). Daimler AG, Ford Motor Company and Nissan Motor Co., in 2013, have signed an agreement for development of a common fuel cell system in order to reduce R&D cost and benefit from economies of scale; their target is to deliver affordable HFCV to the market by 2017 (Nissan Motor Corporation n.d.). BMW has partnered with Toyota in 2013 for development of their HFCV, which is planned for delivery after 2020. Toyota will provide the fuel cell system for the BMW-made vehicles (Behrmann 2015). To further speed up the commercialization of HFCVs, Toyota has offered free-of-charge use of 5680 HFCV related patent by other car manufacturers in the early phase of HFCV market introduction from 2015 to 2020 (Carter 2015).

Before the mass-introduction of the HFCVs to the market, several concept cars have been developed, tested, and some trials have been carried out around the world to assess the viability of this technology and discover and address the barriers. Mercedes-Benz as one of the pioneers in development of HFCVs started with the NECAR 1 and then presented the first fuel cell passenger vehicle, NECAR 2, in 1996. The speed was improved from 90 km/h (NECAR 1) to 110 km/h. The weight of the fuel cell system was reduced by two thirds; due to this mass reduction and improvement in the fuel cell performance, the range was increased to 250 km/h, 92% gain over NECAR 1. By introduction of NECAR 3, Mercedes-Benz showcased on-board hydrogen generation through reforming methanol. They continued the development of HFCVs by NECAR 4, NECAR 4a, and NECAR 5. All these vehicles were being tested in limited numbers. The introduction of A-Class F-CELL (2002) and B-Class (2005) F-CELL changed the game, as they were available to limited customers by lease arrangement. Before that, Mercedes has tested Fuel Cell Sprinter in 2001, which was a van (Daimler AG 2007). Toyota introduced its first HFCV in 1996 and its third HFCV, FCHV-4, was publicly tested in Japan and the United States in 2001 (Toyota Motor Corporation 2014a). Other companies such as Ford, GM, Nissan, Hyundai, and Kia have initiated demonstration projects around the world: United States (mainly California), United Kingdom, Japan, South Korea, Denmark, Sweden, and Germany (IPHE 2009, Qin, Raissi et al. 2014).

Currently, in California, seven HFCVs are available to lease. Audi A7 Sportback h-tron quattro, Chevy Fuel Cell EV, Mercedes-Benz B-Class F-CELL, Honda FCX Clarity, Nissan X-Trail, Toyota Mirai (FCV), and Hyundai Tucson Fuel Cell are HFCVs that are available for customers. These cars are receiving fuel from 9 active HRSs and further 47 stations under development (California Fuel Cell Partnership n.d.).

7.4.2.2 Hydrogen Fuel Cell Buses and Trucks

Hydrogen fuel cell technology has already been used in short-haul buses in a number of demonstration projects and trials. Short-haul buses have many idle periods while their engines are operated far from the rated power and hence at low efficiency (e.g., less than 10%). That is why they produce more emissions than long-haul trucks. As they are mainly operated within urban areas, the potential impact on the people living in such areas is considerable.

In 2003, Folkesson et al. (2003) reported on a trial of a hydrogen fuel cell/battery bus (2001–2003) supported by Swedish National Research Programme for Green Car Research. The vehicle was a diesel-electric hybrid bus that was converted to a hydrogen/battery bus for this study. The bus had a 50 kW PEM fuel cell, lead-acid battery, and 13.2 kg high-pressure hydrogen (200 bar) on board. The result of their study showed that the bus (without using a regenerative braking system) was up to about 30% more efficient than conventional diesel-based buses of the same size and using regenerative braking can extend the range of the bus by 24–28% in the city duty cycles. The energy analysis done on the performance of the system recorded an average of 41% electrical energy efficiency for the fuel cell (based on LHV).

The reported hydrogen fuel cell bus trials in Perth, Australia, and nine European cities,* as well as Iceland and Beijing (DSEWPC 2009), was the largest scale trial of this kind to date.† In Australia, the Western Australian Department for Planning and Infrastructure (DPI), in collaboration with

---

* Amsterdam, Barcelona, Hamburg, London, Luxembourg, Madrid, Porto, Stockholm, and Stuttgart.
† Clean Urban Transport for Europe (CUTE); Ecological City Transport System (ECTOS) for Iceland; Sustainable Transport Energy (STEP) for Perth.

Daimler Chrysler and BP Australia, tested and operated three hydrogen fuel cell buses (HFCBs) between 2004 and 2007.* The Perth trial forms part of the NEFLEET project where Daimler Chrysler performed this trial program using 33 HFCBs worldwide (DSEWPC 2009). The Perth trial finished at the end of July 2007, when buses powered by 205 kW MK9 Ballard fuel cells had already travelled approximately 258,000 km, consumed over 46 tonnes of hydrogen, and carried over 320,000 passengers (Cockroft 2007).

The measurements showed 47–57% electrical energy efficiency for the fuel cells (based on LHV). However, considering motor, inverters, and other losses as well as energy required by the bus' accessories, the hydrogen to transmission efficiency (LHV-based) was measured to be ~23% (Cockroft 2007). The hydrogen consumption in the HFCBs was found to be inversely proportional to the average speed of the buses where it was measured to be higher for those with less average speed and more frequent stops, for example, those operated in city areas with more congested traffic (Cockroft 2007, CUTE 2007, Saxe, Folkesson et al. 2008).

The power drawn from each fuel cell was measured to be about 20–40 kW most of the time with some peaks of 100 kW when accelerating. Such an observation suggested some opportunities for better energy management, such as looking at the design of dump resistance or the possibility of employing a hybrid system, for example, batteries or supercapacitors (Haraldsson et al. 2005). Such hybridization provides opportunities to use a regenerative braking system as suggested by other research studies conducted by Wang et al. (2006) on three HFCBs running as a trial project in China and Gao et al. (2008).

The refueling station in the Perth trial was designed to refill each bus in less than 14 minutes. This target was achieved in 65% of refueling operations, and the average filling rate was 0.52 minutes per kg of hydrogen (Cockroft 2007). The HFCBs were found to be highly reliable: with a recorded unavailability (for maintenance) of only 5–25%, and an average rate of tow-backs to the depot of only 3.9 per 100,000 km operation, which was actually better than that for conventional buses (at ~5 tow-backs per 100,000 km [Cockroft 2007]).

In 2005, the University of Delaware demonstrated a hybrid fuel cell/battery minibus. This ~10-tonne bus employed NiCd batteries with 60 kWh capacity (capable of accepting 120 kW of peak power) together

---

* Continued into 2008 by Hamburg and Beijing.

with a 19.8 kW Ballard Mark 9 SSL fuel cell and a 12.8 kg high-pressure hydrogen storage (350 bar) on board the bus (with an equivalent electrical energy capacity of ~250 kWh at 50% fuel cell electrical efficiency). The driving range claimed was 290 km (Bubna et al. 2010). The average speed of the bus was recorded to be 17.3 km/h, corresponding to operation at an average 10–20% of the maximum power demand, while the maximum speed was 57 km/h. The minibus was equipped with regenerative braking to recover above 90% of the braking power normally, wasted to recharge batteries, and contribute to supply auxiliary demand. An average electrical efficiency of 42% (based on LHV) was reported by Bubna et al. (2010) for the fuel cell of this bus.

Ouyang et al. (2006) conducted a research study on using different energy management strategies for HFCBs using two buses trialed in Beijing. The buses were both hybridized by introducing batteries to the drive-train. Adding batteries to the system helped reduce the hydrogen consumption. The analysis done in this study showed that the buses needed 60 kW power supply to be driven at a constant speed of 60 km/h and this power requirement can be doubled (120 kW) when accelerating. Accordingly, the two buses were equipped with 65 kW (bus A) and 100 kW (bus B) fuel cells, respectively, with batteries added to the system to supplement power supply during acceleration. Bus A showed ~20% less hydrogen consumption rate than bus B. As in the earlier European trials, lower hydrogen consumption rates were recorded at higher speeds for both buses A and B. The degradation rates of both fuel cells were also measured: and the fuel cell installed in bus B showed a 10% degradation after 7000 km of operation while that in bus A degraded by only 2.5% when operated over a similar distance.

In 2008, three fuel cell/battery hybrid buses were used in a trial project in China (Li et al. 2010). One of these buses employed 80 kW PEM fuel cells and Ni-MH batteries with high-pressure hydrogen tanks, and was studied by Li et al. (2010). The rate of fuel cell degradation was a very important factor that was investigated. A 10–20% drop in maximum power of fuel cell after ~20,000 km of driving distance has been reported by Li et al. (2010), equivalent to ~0.2–0.4 W/km approximately. Gao et al. (2008) reported on another bus in this series in which both ultra-capacitors and batteries were used in conjunction with a 65 kW PEM fuel cell unit. The presence of three different energy supplies on board rendered the energy management system rather complicated, and a control system based on fuzzy logic had to be used to balance the supply to the load. Based on the driving cycle used on regular bus routes in Beijing (variable speed between 0 and 46 km/h), ~8 kg/100 km hydrogen fuel consumption was recorded under optimal operating conditions when no regenerative braking was activated. The fuel cell operated at electrical efficiencies above 50% (LHV) most of the time.

According to the National Renewable Energy Laboratory (Eudy et al. 2014) as of August 2014, there were 19 active and 8 planned HFCBs in North America. Most of these projects focus on hybrid (battery/ultra-capacitor) fuel cell systems and liquid hydrogen delivery (with compressed gas stored on board the vehicles) as the main supply method with just a few of them using on-site electrolysis or reformer.

Several research studies have investigated consumer and operator attitudes toward HFCBs as part of the CUTE HFCB project in Europe (Haraldsson et al. 2006, Saxe et al. 2007). It was found that concern about safety was generally not an issue for passengers and drivers, while both groups were quite happy with the level of comfort and low noise of the buses. Also, the operators were satisfied with the reliability of the service and were willing to include more HFCBs in their services.

The main challenges facing the commercialization of HFCBs are high capital cost, lack of the refueling infrastructure, weight, the high cost of fuel, availability, and lifetime. Currently, HFCBs are around 2.5 tons heavier than similar diesel engine buses. This affects the fuel economy and also the passenger capacity of the buses that are, in particular, important in populated areas. Hydrogen fuel cost should drop to 5–7 $/kg-$H_2$ in order to be comparable to diesel based buses (Eudy et al. 2014, Hua et al. 2014). The cost of an HFCB is around $2 million in 2014, which is planned to reduce to $600,000 by 2016; another decisive factor is the availability of buses; according to the report by NREL covering HFCB demonstration in the United States, the current availability of HFCBs is in the range of 45–72%, which ultimately should get to 90%; the bus lifetime is 2.5–5 years (80,000–240,000 km), which should be improved to 12 years or 800,000 km (Eudy et al. 2014). One of the latest reports regarding the evaluation of HFCBs is related to the American Fuel Cell Bus (AFCB) Project, which was carried out over 28 months and ended in June 2015 (Eudy and Post 2015). In this study, the performance of fuel cell, a total of four units, and conventional buses is compared. In this report, HFCBs still fall behind the CNG buses in two items: availability is just 66% for HFCBs compared to 88% achieved by CNG buses; the distance travelled between road calls— the average distance travelled between two breakdowns—for HFCBs is 6262 km whereas it is 14,013 km for CNG busses. The availability is well below the DoE's 2016 target of 85%. Also, the cost of an HFCB in this trial was $2.4 million, which is considerably higher than the DoE's 2016 cost of $1 million. Also, the fuel cell system lifetime is well below the target: 6700 hours was achieved in this trial compared to the 2016 target of 18,000 hours. Based on the outcome of these reports, cost, availability, and durability are the main challenging parameters that need to be addressed in order to successfully commercialize HFCBs.

Unlike buses, there have not been many demonstrations to date of using hydrogen fuel cell technology in heavy-duty trucks. One of the most notable trials currently in progress, however, has been of a Class 8 short-haul truck developed by Vision Motor Corporation for use in ports in California (HFCN 2011). A primary motivation for this project is to reduce smog caused by conventional diesel trucks. Vision Motor Corporation's 536-hp short-haul hydrogen fuel cell truck (called Tyrano) is claimed to be the first green Class 8 truck in the world that produces no carbon emissions while in operation. Tyrano can cover 320 km over an 8-hour shift by carrying up to 40 kg of gaseous hydrogen on board (Vision 2011), while its hydrogen tanks can be refilled in 4–7 minutes. With additional hydrogen storage capacity, the range of the Tyrano can be extended to 640 km. Although the initial cost of this demonstration vehicle is nearly 2.5 times that of a standard diesel truck of the same size, its operating cost is 30–40% less. The cost of the truck can be expected to fall considerably with higher-volume production. The torque of Tyrano is 4.5 kNm, approximately three times larger than that achieved in an equivalent diesel-powered truck.

The considerable number of demonstrations and trial projects involving HFCVs for a variety of heavy-duty applications clearly demonstrates that there is growing knowledge of and experience in the design, construction, and operation of such vehicles around the world.

7.5 OVERCOMING THE BARRIERS TO COMMERCIAL DEVELOPMENT OF ZERO-EMISSION HYDROGEN FUEL CELL FOR ROAD TRANSPORT

7.5.1 Technical Barriers

7.5.1.1 Overview

Although fuel cell technology has improved significantly in the past decade, some further technological improvements are required in order to make this technology commercially competitive with current ICEs so that they may be employed widely in the road transport sector. The main issues are as follows.

7.5.1.2 Fuel Cell Durability and Reliability

Fuel cell durability has always been one of the key technical challenges to broader adoption of hydrogen fuel cell technology for transport applications. As the technology is rapidly advancing, the fuel cell lifetime and durability have been improved considerably. A wide range of fuel cell lifetimes (between 1350 and 26,300 hours) has been reported based on constant load operation, mainly for stationary applications (Wu et al. 2008). One of the best-reported lifetimes for a fuel cell in a transport application is reported to be 2500 hours (Marrony et al. 2008). However, a recent (2011) record of >10,000 operating hours for HFCBs in the United States (UTC Power) was achieved in real trials, all with the original cell stacks and no cell replacement (DoE 2011b), equivalent to 480,000 km. This figure is comparable to lightweight diesel engine longevity. This lifetime was considerably higher than the 5000 hours of operation (~250,000 km of driving) that had been targeted by DoE (2012a). However, it is important to reproduce these long lifetimes in real-world service trials, and under conditions of rapidly changing loads, idle conditions, and numerous start-ups and shutdowns similar to typical automotive duty cycles (Ahluwalia, Wang et al. 2011).

However, in vehicles, a major factor in customer satisfaction is reliability. This is even more important than durability as unexpected vehicle breakdowns can negatively affect customer satisfaction as well as their normal life, work, business, and leisure activities. It is specifically of great importance in trucks and buses as unexpected and long downtime periods can results in significant losses for business and community. The reliability of fuel cell vehicles has not been addressed to the same extent as durability. While reliability is almost as important as (or even more important than) other factors such as durability, quality, and performance (J.D. Power 2014), surprisingly, fuel cell system reliability has not been considered in any targets. In trial experiments of buses and LDVs around the world, durability and availability have been reported while reliability has been ignored. While availability is an important factor, it does not represent the reliability of the vehicle. Hence, a successful plan for wide commercialization of HFCVs needs to address reliability. It is expected that more data can be obtained over the next years regarding the reliability of HFCVs by their commercial introduction around the world.

7.5.1.3 Systems Power-to-Weight Ratio

This performance ratio for HFCVs has been increased substantially from 10 W/kg in 1994 to 61.1 W/kg for Toyota Mirai released to the market in

TABLE 7.1   Comparison between Power-to-Weight and Torque-to-Weight Ratio
of HFCVs and Similar ICE Vehicles

Model	Power (kW)[a]	Torque (Nm)[a]	Weight (kg)[a]	Power-to-weight ratio (W/kg)	Torque-to-weight ratio (Nm/kg)
Toyota Mirai	113	335	1850	61	0.18
Toyota Corolla	103	173	1250	82	0.14
Hyundai Tucson FC	100	300	2250	44	0.13
Hyundai Tucson	121–136	203–400	1484–1622	82–84	0.14–0.25

[a] Data are obtained from manufacturers' websites.

2015 (Toyota Motor Corporation 2014b). This is becoming comparable to conventional ICE vehicles with around 70–80 W/kg (Mock and Schmid 2009).

Another important factor is the torque-to-weight ratio and towing capacity. As outdoor activities such as camping are very popular in many countries, the towing capacity is important for some buyers. Currently, there is no fuel cell vehicle with a tow hitch. Tesla's new SUV "Tesla X" is the first BEV with an optional tow hitch and a towing capacity of approximately 2300 kg due to its exceptional torque (Tesla Motors 2015). A comparison between two mass-produced HFCVs and two similar ICE vehicles is presented in Table 7.1. As it can be seen, HFCVs have considerably lower power-to-weight ratio. Torque-to-weight ratio is similar and for small vehicles, it is even higher in fuel cells thanks to the high torque provided by the electric motors in a wide range of RPM. It is worth mentioning that higher torque values are required for having better towing capabilities.

7.5.1.4 On-Board Storage of Hydrogen

Hydrogen storage directly affects the range of FCEVs, a determining factor in their successful commercialization. 5.5 wt% H_2 and 40 g-H_2/l represent the gravimetric and volumetric capacities of on-board hydrogen storage for automotive applications targeted by DoE to be achieved by 2020 (DoE 2015). As a fuel cell system is a device that provides power in the form of electricity, the associated hydrogen storage system is usually compared with batteries. Therefore, a correction factor of 50% is applied to take the fuel cell efficiency into account. Considering this efficiency factor, the 2020 DoE target can be translated to 1.08 kWh$_e$/kg and 0.79 kWh$_e$/l, respectively. A number of methods for on-board hydrogen storage are currently being investigated and developed by DoE to meet the 2020 targets.

Compressed hydrogen gas is the preferred method currently for the on-board storage of hydrogen. Toyota's mass produced Mirai is equipped with type IV pressure vessels (Figure 7.6) to contain hydrogen at 700 bar. The weight is considerably reduced by using a three-layered structure: the inside layer is a plastic liner to retain pressurized hydrogen; a carbon fiber rein-forced plastic layer is in the middle; and a glass fiber reinforced plastic layer for surface protection (Toyota Motor Corporation 2015). By this pressure vessel, they have achieved 5.7 wt%, which is over the DoE target for 2020. However, the volumetric energy density remains a challenge. While at 700 bar the hydrogen gas itself has energy density of 1.3 kWh/l (DoE target), the system energy density is around 0.95 kWh/l, which is 27% below the DoE target for 2020. Therefore, for compressed hydrogen, in order to meet the target, higher pressures are required, which poses additional challenge and cost due to the need for stronger materials and components. One method to enhance the energy density is the use of cryo-compressed hydrogen storage. In this method, sorbent materials such as synthesized composite metallic and metal organic frameworks (MOFs) are used. MOPs because of their exceptionally high surface area have very high hydrogen adsorption capacity. The adsorption increases by decrease in temperature and pressure

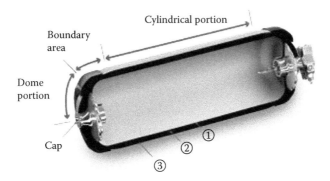

① Plastic liner
② Carbon fiber-reinforced plastic layer
③ Glass fiber-reinforced plastic layer

FIGURE 7.6 Toyota's type IV high-pressure tank for 700 bar hydrogen storage. (From Toyota Motor Corporation (2015). "Fuel Cell Vehicle." Retrieved October 8, 2015, from http://www.toyota-global.com/innovation/environmental_technology /fuelcell_vehicle/index.html.)

increase. For having a high amount of hydrogen storage, the hydrogen temperature should reach below 150 K at elevated pressure of 100 bar. Hydrogen desorption occurs when the temperature of the tank increases (Shabani and Andrews 2015).

Another method for hydrogen storage is solid state in the form of hydrides. The fine metallic powder partially fills the storage tank and hydrogen under pressure, less than 50 bar, enters the tank. In these systems, the pressure can be very low up to 5 bar. At the surface of the host material, hydrogen molecules split into atoms and diffuse into the particles and fill the interstitial sites, small voids between the basic lattice atoms, of the host crystal lattices. This process is exothermic and for optimal storage of hydrogen heat should be removed either by natural convection or by means of a dedicated cooling system. As the release of hydrogen is endothermic, during discharge of hydrogen heat should be provided to the storage tank either from the surrounding or a heating system. Metal hydride canisters are commercially available. The typical storage size of these canisters varies between 1 and 100 gr (Shabani and Andrews 2015). Based on the system requirement, a number of the canisters can be connected to each other to provide the required hydrogen. Currently, the gravimetric energy density of the commercial metal hydride canisters is around 1.6 wt%, considerably lower than the DoE target. This value can get to less than 1% for the whole storage system. However, they almost satisfy the DoE target for the volumetric energy density. As the metals used in this type of storage are relatively high, the cost of the system is usually very high. Due to these shortcomings, metal hydride storage is not being investigated for on-board storage of hydrogen for HFCVs unless a breakthrough happens to increase the energy density with a reasonable cost.

Hydrogen can be stored in liquid form to occupy much less volume. For this purpose, the temperature should be decreased to 20 K. For the storage, costly cryogenic storage tanks and insulation are required. The energy required to liquefy the hydrogen is as high as 175 of the hydrogen energy content. Considering 50% efficiency for the fuel cell the DoE target for 2020 is 1.08 kWh$_e$/kg. Cryogenic-liquid hydrogen has already passed this target (1.3 kWh$_e$/kg). However, it does not seem to be a feasible, safe, or cost-effective solution for automotive application. This is mainly because of the inherent inefficiency associated with liquefying hydrogen (equivalent to ~30% of the energy content of hydrogen stored); and the inevitable hydrogen leakage as even a small amount of heat transfer into the liquid hydrogen vessel leads to hydrogen boil-off. The evaporated hydrogen must then be released through a safety valve on the vessel to prevent a pressure build-up. According to Ahluwalia et al. (2012), the rate of hydrogen loss for cryogenic-liquid hydrogen storage can be as high as ~40% during a typical use cycle, equivalent to about 20g/h for every 1 kg of hydrogen stored. There is no such problem associated with high-pressure hydrogen gas storage. The gravimetric energy density achieved thus far with high pressure (700 bar) hydrogen storage technology is 0.95 kWh$_e$/kg, which is not far from the DoE target for 2020, considering that there are still a few years remaining to meet this target. Although the current achievement would put hydrogen in a better position compared to batteries, it needs further improvement in order to become as light as diesel-based energy storage. The approximately 40 kg hydrogen needed for a medium-haul truck (for a range of 300–350 km) (Vision 2011) may require about 1 tonne of hydrogen storage system based on current technology solutions available for high pressure hydrogen, while a fuel storage system of less than half a tonne is needed for the same driving range in diesel trucks.

7.5.1.5 Efficiency

Overall energy efficiency is another concern associated with hydrogen systems for transport. The parasitic energy associated with pressurizing hydrogen is arguably a disadvantage associated with using hydrogen. In a sustainable hydrogen economy discussed by Andrews and Shabani (2012b), decentralized production and consumption of hydrogen are proposed, in which hydrogen is either transferred to the HRSs through relatively short pipes from nearby hydrogen generation facilities or is generated on site from local renewable energy sources. However, any comparison with liquid or gaseous fossil fuels needs to take the energy involved in manufacturing these fuels in refinery facilities, truck delivery of fuels (e.g., diesel and petrol), including pumping them through within the HRS, as well as the higher energy efficiency of fuel cell systems based on hydrogen fuel compared to diesel engines. The efficiency of the hydrogen fuel cell system is also highlighted when the system is compared with battery technology. At first sight, the energy efficiency from renewable source to traction energy for BEVs appears much higher than for HFCVs. The round-trip energy efficiency of a renewable hydrogen system (electricity produced by the fuel cell over the electricity used by the electrolyzers to produce hydrogen) seems to be relatively lower than batteries in short-term energy storage applications, the reason that led some to dismiss the HFCV option outright in favor of BEVs (Mckay 2009). However, if the BEVs are charged from the grid, which to produce low-emission electricity must utilize a supply substantially from variable renewable energy sources, some form of longer-term storage on the grid would also be needed to guarantee supply throughout the year. Hence when the energy losses of this storage on the grid, which might ultimately be hydrogen based, are taken into account as well, the average round-trip energy efficiency of the overall BEV system will tend toward that of the HFCV route anyway (Andrews and Shabani 2012b).

7.5.1.6 Maximum Speed and Acceleration

A 50% increase in the top speed of fuel cell cars, from less than 100 km/h to over 180 km/h, has been achieved in the past two decades. However, it may still need some further improvement (Mock and Schmid 2009), so that the HFCVs can be designed to reach equivalent speeds to conventional ICE-based cars in the not too distant future. Toyota Mirai can reach a top speed of 178 km/h, which is acceptable for a small sedan. By further improvements and tweaks, higher speeds comparable to high performance ICE vehicles can be achieved. In terms of acceleration, while Toyota Mirai is almost 50% heavier than Corolla, due to its high torque, it can reach 100 km/h in 9.2 seconds, which is slightly better than the Toyota Corolla.

7.5.2 Economic Barriers

The per-kW cost of nearly $49 (adjusted to $55 for the increase in platinum price) has already been achieved for fuel cell systems in automotive applications, which is equivalent to more than a 30% reduction since 2008 and over 80% reduction since 2002. However, according to the 2020 DoE target, the unit cost needs a further decrease down to $40/kW (adjusted from previously estimated $30/kW) (DoE 2012b, 2013a) in order to keep the technology commercially competitive with ICEs that cost $25–35kW (Ahluwalia et al. 2011). The key contributors to the high cost of PEM fuel cells are the electrodes and associated materials. They comprise more than half the total cost (Mock and Schmid 2009). Many research studies are being undertaken globally to reduce this price, mainly by reducing the platinum catalyst loading on the cathode. The PEM fuel cell used by NASA in the 1960s had a platinum loading of 28 mg/cm^2, while today's PEM fuel cells use less than 1 mg/cm^2. DoE has set a target of <0.125 mg/cm^2 for 2017, which is expected to be achievable considering the current pace of improvement (DoE 2013b). Recent developments have shown great potential to reduce the platinum coating considerably. By applying a platinum sputter deposition method, loadings as low as 0.06 mg/cm^2 can be achieved (Çögenli et al. 2015). According to projections by a European study (zeroemissionvehicles 2009), the current high costs of hydrogen fuel cell car ownership are expected to fall considerably to make this option cheaper than BEVs and PBEVs by 2030, while the cost of the fuel cell itself is expected to drop by 90% by 2020. According to this projection, HFCVs can be competitive with internal combustion engines by 2020 with tax incentives and be cheaper than ICEs by 2050 without tax incentives.

On-board hydrogen storage is another contributor to the high overall cost of HFCVs. This is about $500/kg (Zoulias and Lymberopoulos 2007) for high-pressure hydrogen stored on board, which leads to a couple of thousand dollars for storing 4–5 kg of hydrogen for a passenger car (Honda Motor 2010). DoE target for 2020 is $333/kg and the ultimate target is $266/kg (DoE 2015). The short-haul truck Tyrano manufactured by Vision Motor Corp is a good example showing the effect of fuel cell and hydrogen storage costs on the overall price of the hydrogen fuel cell truck. In 2011, Tyrano was sold in the United States for nearly $270,000, nearly $140,000 more expensive than the same size truck with a diesel propulsion system (EV World 2011). Entering into mass production stage can minimize this gap to a great extent. Also, HFCBs currently cost around $2 million (Eudy et al. 2014), which is significantly higher than the initial cost of a typical diesel powered bus at around $300,000 (Garrett 2014).

Another factor contributing to the economic viability of HFCVs is the cost of hydrogen production and distribution through different centralized and distributed technologies and various feedstocks, which is presented in Figure 7.7 (DoE 2014b). Among different methods, the cost of water electrolysis is higher than the rest. However, water electrolysis is the only mature technology that can deliver zero-emission hydrogen if powered by renewables. Currently, hydrogen generation through reforming natural gas results in competitive prices. In the short term, it can be used to facilitate the transition to hydrogen-based economy and meanwhile the cost of water electrolysis will drop to acceptable levels.

7.5.3 Infrastructure

One of the major hurdles to the development of HFCVs or even ICEs running on hydrogen is the lack of hydrogen refueling stations, which makes people reluctant to choose this technology (Farrell et al. 2003, Paolo 2007, Kim and Moon 2008, Alazemi and Andrews 2015, Gnann and Plötz 2015). This hurdle is widely regarded as the key obstacle to fuel cell vehicle commercialization (DoE 2010). This problem is complex: on one hand, it is difficult to get investment in costly hydrogen refilling stations until there

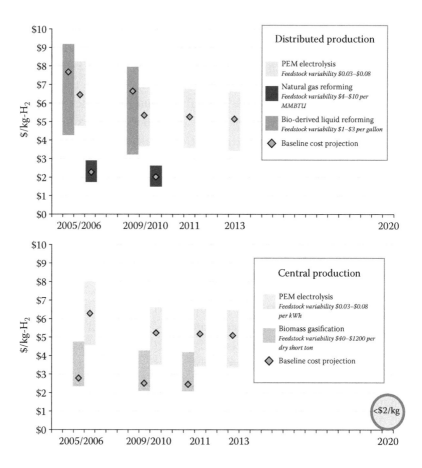

FIGURE 7.7 The estimated high-volume production and delivery costs for hydrogen produced from a range of distributed and centralized renewable energy, fossil fuel, and nuclear fission power sources. (From DoE (2014b). "Hydrogen and fuel cell program: 2014 annual progress report" http://www.hydrogen.energy .gov/annual_progress13.html.)

are many HFCVs on the roads, while on the other hand, customers will not purchase hydrogen vehicles unless adequate HRSs are available (Paolo 2007, Zapata and Nieuwenhuis 2010). Gaining insight in the required level of refueling infrastructure by policy makers can initiate the process of widespread adoption of the technology (Huétink et al. 2010). Currently, nearly 200 HRS have been established worldwide and are in operation (TÜV SÜD 2015). The United States is a leading country in establishing HRSs, mainly in California and New York, where most research and development of hydrogen fuel cell cars are in progress (DoE 2012c). In the

United States, the California government has planned for developing 100 HRSs (DoE 2014a) that is part of the measures to support their target of having 1.5 million zero-emission vehicles (ZEVs) on their roads by 2025. Countries such as Japan and South Korea have also considerable investment plans in development of their hydrogen infrastructure in order to be prepared for future transition in the automotive market. In Japan three automakers—Toyota, Honda, and Nissan—have announced a joint support for HRS infrastructure development in Japan by investing almost $48 million by 2020 (Jie and Hagiwara 2015). Figure 7.8 provides an overview of the number of HRSs operated around the world.

In many countries, the concern about lack of hydrogen refueling infrastructure is not limited to their own borders, as trucks or passenger cars that are in transit to neighboring countries would also require refueling and servicing. This matter is also important at the state level as the policies differ from state to state. For example, while California is investing around $50 million in development of 28 HRSs in addition to 10 existing stations and 16 under development (California Energy Commission 2014), many other states have no stations under development. This will potentially affect the successful implementation of HFCVs in California as it sends a negative signal to the potential customers indicating that the pricy HFCVs can only be used in their region.

FIGURE 7.8 Global hydrogen refuelling stations. (From TÜV SÜD (2015). "17 new hydrogen refuelling stations worldwide in 2014." Retrieved October 10, 2015, from http://www.tuv-sud.com/new-media/news-archive/17-new-hydrogen -refuelling-stations-worldwide-in-2014.)

HRSs are the main challenge of the production and distribution of hydrogen as production and delivery have reached the maturity stage. In the absence of sufficient and accessible number of HRSs to provide the users with a reliable fuel supply, mass commercialization of HFCVs cannot be fully realized. On the other hand, as there are a very limited number of HFCVs on the road, from an economic point of view the development of HRSs is not attractive. Therefore, supportive measures from the government and involvement of the car manufacturers are required to break through this egg and chicken cycle. Following the formation of H_2 mobility joint-venture in Germany—founding companies: Air Liquid, Daimler, Linde, OMV, Shell, and Total; partners: EnBW, Hamburger Hochbahn, Siemens, Vattenfall Europe, Intelligent Energy, BMW, Honda, Hyundai, Toyota, Volkswagen, and Nissan—with the aim of developing 400 HRSs in Germany until 2023, some other countries took similar initiatives. Countries such as Japan, the United States, the United Kingdom, France, and Norway have started the development of their hydrogen infrastructures for HFCVs (Hayter 2014).

There are two types of HRSs: HRSs with on-site hydrogen production and HRSs with hydrogen delivery (Alazemi and Andrews 2015). In HRSs with on-site H_2 production, available local energy sources and feedstock can be used to generate the hydrogen. For these kinds of stations, mostly water electrolysis and steam methane reforming are used. This type of HRS consists of the following components (Alazemi and Andrews 2015):

- Control system
- H_2 production facilities
- Distribution system
- Compressor to pressurize the hydrogen above 350 or 700 bar
- High and low pressure tanks
- Dispensers to fill the H_2 tank of HFCVs, either at 350 or 700 bar

For high-pressure storage, the hydrogen is usually pressurized to up to 875 bar (Lipman 2011). Material and components should withstand the pressure and also they should not be prone to hydrogen embrittlement.

In the stations with hydrogen delivery, instead of the hydrogen production facilities, a receiving port is incorporated into the system where the fuel is delivered in the form of liquid or compressed hydrogen. Also, for liquid hydrogen, a heat exchanger is used to heat up the liquid hydrogen and convert it to gas.

7.5.4 Skills and Product Support Availability

Another barrier is the availability of local support to maintain hydrogen fuel cell systems. Obviously, lack of wide range availability of skilled service providers (e.g., maintenance support) may discourage potential purchasers away from this technology (Chen et al. 2007). Vehicle downtime has to be kept at an acceptably low level, so investment in technical education and well-equipped HFCV service centers will be necessary (Frenette and Forthoffer 2009). This problem is more prominent in rural areas and intercity travel as the technology takes longer to penetrate in such less populated areas. Therefore, obtaining technical support and spare parts can be problematic. A research carried out by the Department of Transport, Technical University of Denmark (2015) shows that lack of service centers is one of the main challenges that needs to be addressed for mass-adoption of HFCVs from the firm managers' point of view. From a broader political-economic perspective, moving toward hydrogen fuel cell technology is partly about protecting vulnerable economics from the uncertainties and insecurity associated with importing oil; hence, investing in skill training and support services for HFCVs may be justified by these broader national plans.

7.5.5 Renewable Energy Deployment for Hydrogen Production

There are different methods and sources to produce hydrogen, the fact that is seen as a unique feature and advantage of this alternative fuel (Verhelst and Wallner 2009). Hydrogen production by using biomass, solar thermal water splitting, waste water, thermochemical cycles, fossil fuels through carbon capturing (e.g., steam reforming of natural gas), water electrolysis using electricity generated by renewables, and nuclear fission are some of the methods practiced for hydrogen production (Hoffman 2012). Nuclear fission technology is very expensive; due to previous disastrous experiences, this technology may not generally receive strong social support. Moreover, the nuclear waste, with a high level of radioactivity, can have irreversible environmental impacts and have harmful effects on human health. Hence, due to these negative scores in environmental, economic and social aspects, nuclear fission technology might not be regarded as a sustainable solution for hydrogen production.

Carbon capturing can be performed on different ranges of fossil fuels. In countries with abundant coal resources (e.g., Australia), where this fuel is widely used in coal-fired power plants, hydrogen extraction from coal might be considered as an immediately available and feasible option. However, the low hydrogen to carbon ration (0.6–0.7) of coal would make the hydrogen production through this process challenging and expensive (Hoffman 2012). Such a situation together with implications associated with finding sufficient and reliable geographical locations to store the captured carbon can make the economics of coal-fired power stations with carbon capturing and storage (CCS) quite unfavorable (Jacobson and Delucchi 2011). Hydrogen production from some fossil fuels with high hydrogen to carbon rations (i.e., natural gas), through steam reforming, has proven to be relatively viable economically. However, as also mentioned by Hoffman (2012), most of the researchers consider this method as a bridging technology only to help the market shift toward the hydrogen fuel cell technologies for transport, with the view to move to zero emission electrolysis option.

Zero-emission water electrolysis process powered by renewables can replace currently economical methods such as steam reforming of natural gas if enough renewable energy sources are available and economically deployable to be used for this purpose (Andrews and Shabani 2012b). In estimating the availability of renewable energy resources, the future energy demands by considering growth and rises in material standards of living, particularly in developing countries, have to be taken into account (Kleijn and van der Voet 2010). The global energy demand is estimated to experience a growth of 37% by 2035 (BP 2015) or 2040 (IEA 2014c) compared to its level in 2013; hence, a massive growth in the infrastructure is required to harvest from renewable energy resources in order to meet this demand (Andrews and Shabani 2012b). Jacobson and Delucchi (2011) conducted studies to investigate the potential of main renewable energy resources, including wind, water, and sunlight in meeting the global energy demand. They showed in their study that the 2008 rate of energy consumption, 12.5 TW, which will increase to 16.9 TW in 2030 (without taking any energy efficiency measures), can be kept to about 11.5 TW (in 2030) if duly-effective energy efficiency measures are carried out. They showed that this future demand can be entirely met by the electricity supplied through renewables (mainly wind, water, and sunlight) together with employing hydrogen as an energy carrier and storage medium, by occupying only 1% of the global land area. In the model developed by Jacobson and Delucchi (2011), wind turbines have the lion's share by potentially supplying 50% of the total demand, concentrating solar thermal plants, and solar PV plants would supply 20% and 14% of this total respectively, followed by rooftop PV systems (6%), hydroelectric and geothermal power (4% each), and wave and tidal (1% each). Hence, in the long run any sustainable hydrogen economy can only rely on clean primary energy sources (Ramesohl and Merten 2006). This is while other sources such as natural gas and coal (i.e., carbon capturing) can still be seen as intermediate solutions before water electrolysis through renewable energy resources at large scale becomes technically and economically feasible.

The sustainable hydrogen economy discussed by Andrews and Shabani (2012b) is set firmly in the context of zero GHG emissions in terms of both the production of hydrogen from renewables and consumption, rather than just as a response to depleting reserves of fossil fuels. This involves decentralized distributed production of hydrogen from a wide variety of renewables and feedstocks as near to the points of consumption as possible.

Such a transition will need massive investment and major energy industry restructuring that will require strong leadership by governments around the world, and indeed the United Nations, in order to make substantial progress over a 20-year period. While developed nations will need to make major changes to their energy infrastructure, and levels and profiles of consumption, developing nations will need assistance both technologically and economically to introduce additional renewable supply capacity right from the outset. It must also be acknowledged that such a pathway to a truly sustainable energy economy is radically different from the energy policies being pursued in most nations at present.

7.5.6 Political and Institutional Barriers

Effendi and Courvisanos (2011) discussed in their paper many political barriers to the growth of renewable energy supply, and suggest that some groups out of political-economic self-interest use mooted technical difficulties as camouflage in attempts to slow down the adoption of renewable energy technologies. Lack of reliability of supply through intermittent renewable energies to a centralized grid is one of the key technical barriers often put forward by those who oppose the widespread adoption of renewable energy technologies. However, we believe that this problem could be eliminated by using decentralized hydrogen/renewable energy-based power distribution systems in a sustainable hydrogen economy model (Andrews and Shabani 2012b).

Also, the policy instability, often fuelled by political competition or fossil fuel lobbies, makes the investments in alternative fuels less attractive. Political leaders change the policies when needed to stay in power or to take over, even if they have to pursue new goals, which they have not campaigned for (Rosenthal 2014).

Policies can affect the commitment of the companies regarding the implementation and investment in renewable energies. Investors will take the risk of investment in a new technology if there is clarity on market prospects. Therefore, clear and proper measures, standards, incentives, and legislations should be introduced by policy makers to reduce the risks involved for the stakeholders to an acceptable level. Well-developed incentives and legislation are able to alter the customers' preference toward zero-emission vehicles (Steenberghen and López 2008).

Commonly, governments are inclined to support private companies involved in the well-established energy industries such as oil, gas, and coal. The main reason is that the energy companies, due to their significant national level impact on the economy, usually have a strong tie with political systems and have a great influence in the policy-making decisions. For companies with a huge amount of investment—in terms of human, physical, and intellectual resources—in mature technologies bringing them a significant amount of profit, there is negligible, if none at all, interest in investing in new technologies with an unreliable feature. There is a need for more effort by hydrogen industry stakeholders to encourage the government to support the development and implementation of hydrogen technology. This can be achieved by highlighting the advantages of hydrogen technology in terms of economic, social, and environmental aspects and indeed not to forget the energy security dimension offered by this technology. The lobbying power of the hydrogen industry is increased by its expansion and commercial use. As a result, it will gain more support from the government (Andrews and Shabani 2014).

7.5.7 Other Barriers

Apart from the barriers discussed in this section thus far, there are also some other barriers that are not specific to hydrogen and have to be considered in shifting toward any other alternative fuel technology. These barriers include lack of international standards, policies and legislation, investment uncertainty connected to high switching costs and performance, and public awareness about the potential benefits of the new/alternative technology (RET 2011b). Demonstration of the alternatives would certainly raise industry and public awareness, such as the nine-day 2700-km tour of a hydrogen fuel cell car from Chula Vista in California to Vancouver in Canada supported by major car manufacturers such as GM, VW, Daimler, Honda, Nissan, Toyota, and Hyundai (DoE 2010). Public education and awareness raising have been proven to have a positive influence on people's perspective of fuel cell cars. The results from a "ride-and-drive" clinic (Martin et al. 2009) show that when potential customers are exposed to the HFCVs and HRSs in a trial, their perceptions are positively altered. For example, while before the study 30% of participants believed that HFCVs are less safe compared to ICE vehicles, this number dropped to 7% afterward. Similarly, for HRSs this number has fallen from 40% to 13%. These results imply that safety concerns can be a preventive factor in acceptance of HFCVs among the car buyers, especially for conservative customers, and it can be addressed by first-hand experience of the technology. Also, a study carried out by Lim et al. (2015) has investigated customer anxieties regarding the EVs' range and resale values. Range anxiety mainly affects the BEVs due to their inferior range compared to ICE vehicles and it is not significant for HFCVs. They have suggested that the proximity of fuelling stations can mitigate this issue. Regarding the resale anxiety, they have argued that the option of leasing is a better encouragement compared to purchase.

Additional challenges facing a potential future transition to hydrogen fuel cell technology for transport are associated with maintenance and spare parts for fuel cell systems, availability of rare-earth metals used in manufacturing of fuel cell systems (fuel cell, hydrogen storage systems, and electric motors), and setting up the required retail network (Frenette and Forthoffer 2009).

7.6 CONCLUSION

The important role of hydrogen in terms of energy security and sustainable energy strategy has been discussed. Hydrogen has a great potential to address different aspects of the energy security and can play a vital role in providing different energy sectors with sustainability. The transport sector as one of the most energy-intensive sectors, relying heavily on oil, needs to be addressed in energy policies. The challenges associated with continued use of fossil fuels in the transport sector (in particular for road transport) have been reviewed in this chapter. Biofuels, electric vehicles, and hydrogen (ICEs and fuel cells) have all been discussed as alternative solutions to conventional fossil fuel based systems for road transport. All these technologies along with the demand-side measures have a role to play in achieving a sustainable secure road transport system based on their potential and strengths and they have complementary roles in this regard. Hybrid petrol electric vehicles and biofuels may be regarded as an immediate and achievable short-term or transitional option for reducing demand for petroleum-based fossil fuels. However, biofuels seem to be a controversial solution from the sustainability point of view if there was a high-level of petroleum substitution and hence very high requirement for biofuels worldwide. This is mainly due to their negative impact on food and water supplies, and the price and availability of arable land. Therefore, in the final sustainable energy system, biofuels can have a partial contribution as long as their provision remains sustainable. While EVs might play a role in short-distance urban trips by passenger cars, and despite recent advancement of this technology (e.g., Tesla electric vehicles), the cost of this technology, the mass and volume of the batteries, and other technical challenges are yet to be addressed. We, therefore, concluded that although EVs are more likely to play a role in the overall transport sector, the future scenario of whole or even a vast majority of the road transport sector relying on this technology may not seem to be promising at this stage.

We also discussed why the hydrogen fuel cell technology, if particularly supported by renewables for hydrogen production, is a promising sustainable solution for road transport and for passenger vehicles with a driving range comparable to today's petrol and diesel vehicles. Hydrogen fuel cell vehicles employing an all-electric-drive train offer high energy efficiency option for road transportation and have encouraged many automakers to be investing on the commercial version of this technology in their products.

However, further research is still required to remove some barriers to strongly introduce this technology as a sustainable alternative to petroleum-based transport. Hydrogen storage systems still need improvement (in particular to reduce the mass). Further cost reductions of the fuel cell and storage system and availability and durability improvements are required to achieve economic competitiveness for this option. Although initiated in many countries through public and private sector investments, still far more investments are required to support the establishment of a solid hydrogen infrastructure network. Finally, the technology needs to receive further support from the governments, research institutes and industries. Such support is required in the forms of research, development, demonstration, public education, and commercialization, as well as detailed strategic policy studies that demonstrate how sustainable hydrogen and fuel cell technologies can assist in meeting national and international targets to achieve long-term GHG emission targets at the same time as reducing dependence on imported petroleum fuels and enhancing overall energy security.

Successful implementation of hydrogen technology in an energy policy can provide energy security, especially for the road transport sector, that is heavily dependent on oil. Hydrogen technology can effectively address all the four As of energy security: affordability, accessibility, acceptability, and availability. The main strengths of hydrogen energy are its potential for zero-emission energy supply (i.e., when produced through renewables), and the diversity of technologies and feedstock that can support hydrogen production. As a result, it can provide clean energy which can be sourced locally and eliminate dependency on imported fossil fuels. In addition, the price is less affected by parameters such as political and economic turmoils and natural disasters compared to other energy sources; not to mention its capacity as an effective energy storage to increase the integration of intermittent renewable energy sources such as wind and solar into the energy grid.

REFERENCES

Aftabuzzaman, M. and E. Mazloumi (2011). "Achieving sustainable urban transport mobility in post peak oil era." *Transport Policy* **18**(5): 695–702.

Ahluwalia, R. K., T. Q. Hua and J. K. Peng (2012). "On-board and off-board performance of hydrogen storage options for light-duty vehicles." *International Journal of Hydrogen Energy* **37**(3): 2891–2910.

Ahluwalia, R. K., X. Wang, J. Kwon, A. Rousseau, J. Kalinoski, B. James and J. Marcinkoski (2011). "Performance and cost of automotive fuel cell systems with ultra-low platinum loadings." *Journal of Power Sources* **196**(10): 4619–4630.

Al-Hallaj, S. and J. R. Selman (2002). "Thermal modeling of secondary lithium batteries for electric vehicle/hybrid electric vehicle applications." *Journal of Power Sources* **110**(2): 341–348.

Alazemi, J. and J. Andrews (2015). "Automotive hydrogen fuelling stations: An international review." *Renewable and Sustainable Energy Reviews* **48**: 483–499.

Amjad, S., S. Neelakrishnan and R. Rudramoorthy (2010). "Review of design considerations and technological challenges for successful development and deployment of plug-in hybrid electric vehicles." *Renewable and Sustainable Energy Reviews* **14**(3): 1104–1110.

Andrews, J. and B. Shabani (2012a). "Dimensionless analysis of the global techno-economic feasibility of solar-hydrogen systems for constant year-round power supply." *International Journal of Hydrogen Energy* **37**(1): 6–18.

Andrews, J. and B. Shabani (2012b). "Re-envisioning the role of hydrogen in a sustainable energy economy." *International Journal of Hydrogen Energy* **37**(2): 1184–1203.

Andrews, J. and B. Shabani (2012c). "Where does hydrogen fit in a sustainable energy economy?" *Procedia Engineering* **49**: 15–25.

Andrews, J. and B. Shabani (2014). "The role of hydrogen in a global sustainable energy strategy." *Wiley Interdisciplinary Reviews: Energy and Environment* **3**(5): 474–489.

Anstrom, J. R. (2014). 17—Hydrogen as a fuel in transportation. In: *Advances in Hydrogen Production, Storage and Distribution*. A. Basile and A. Iulianelli, Eds.,Woodhead Publishing, pp. 499–524.

APERC (2007). A quest for energy security in the 21st century, Asia Pacific Energy Research Centre.

Arbizzani, C., F. De Giorgio and M. Mastragostino (2015). Battery parameters for hybrid electric vehicles. In: *Advances in Battery Technologies for Electric Vehicles*. B. S. G. Tillmetz, Ed., Woodhead Publishing, pp. 55–72.

Aris, A. and B. Shabani (2015). "Sustainable power supply solutions for off-grid base stations." *Energies* **8**(10): 10904.

Audi AG (2015). "Audi A7 Sportback h-tron quattro." Retrieved October 9, 2015, from http://www.audi.com/com/brand/en/vorsprung_durch_technik /content/2014/11/audi-a7-sportback-h-tron-quattro.html.

Ballard. (2012). "Ballard fuel cell." Retrieved March 2012, from www.ballard.com.

Barfod, M. B., S. Kaplan, I. Frenzel and J. Klauenberg (2015). COPE-SMARTER—A decision support system for analysing the challenges, opportunities and policy measures: A case study of electric commercial vehicles market diffusion in Denmark, Department of Transport, Technical University of Denmark.

Behrmann, E. (2015). "BMW pushes fuel-cell car development with first street tests." Retrieved October 10, 2015, from http://www.bloomberg.com/news /articles/2015-07-01/bmw-s-first-fuel-cell-car-starts-testing-in-clean -engine-push.

Beissmann, T. (2009). "BMW abandons internal combustion hydrogen technology." Retrieved October 20, 2015, from http://www.caradvice.com.au/51099 /bmw-abandons-internal-combustion-hydrogen-technology/.

Berckmuller, M., H. Rottengruber, A. Eder, N. Brehm and G. Elsasser (2003). "Potentials of a charged SI-hydrogen engine." *SAE International* 2003-01-3210.

BP (2015). BP energy outlook 2035, BP.

Brown, S., D. Pyke and P. Steenhof (2010). "Electric vehicles: The role and importance of standards in an emerging market." *Energy Policy* **38**(7): 3797–3806.

Bubna, P., D. Brunner, J. J. Gangloff Jr., S. G. Advani and A. K. Prasad (2010). "Analysis, operation and maintenance of a fuel cell/battery series-hybrid bus for urban transit applications." *Journal of Power Sources* **195**(12): 3939–3949.

Çağatay Bayindir, K., M. A. Gözüküçük and A. Teke (2011). "A comprehensive overview of hybrid electric vehicle: Powertrain configurations, powertrain control techniques and electronic control units." *Energy Conversion and Management* **52**(2): 1305–1313.

California Energy Commission (2014). "California investing nearly $50 million in hydrogen refueling stations " Retrieved October 11, 2015, from http://www.energy.ca.gov/releases/2014_releases/2014-05-01_hydrogen_refueling _stations_funding_awards_nr.html.

California Fuel Cell Partnership (n.d.). "About fuel cell electric vehicles." http://cafcp.org/carsandbuses/aboutFCEVs.

Capros, P., A. De Vita, N. Tasios, D. Papadopoulos, P. Siskos, E. Apostolaki, M. Zampara, L. Paroussos, K. Fragiadakis and N. Kouvaritakis (2014). EU rnergy, transport and GHG emissions: Trends to 2050, reference scenario 2013.

Carter, B. (2015). "2015 Toyota CES Press Preview." Retrieved October 10, 2015, from http://toyotanews.pressroom.toyota.com/releases/2015+toyota+ces +press+preview+carter.htm.

Chen, F., T. R. C. Fernandes, M. Yetano Roche and M. da Graça Carvalho (2007). "Investigation of challenges to the utilization of fuel cell buses in the EU vs transition economies." *Renewable and Sustainable Energy Reviews* **11**(2): 357–364.

Clarke, P., T. Muneer and K. Cullinane (2010). "Cutting vehicle emissions with regenerative braking." *Transportation Research Part D: Transport and Environment* **15**(3): 160–167.

Cockroft, C. (2007). Perth's fuel cell bus trial 2004–2007, Final operational report to the department for planning and infrastructure, February 2008. Perth, Australia, Murdoch University.

Çögenli, M. S., S. Mukerjee and A. B. Yurtcan (2015). "Membrane electrode assembly with ultra low platinum loading for cathode electrode of PEM fuel cell by using sputter deposition." *Fuel Cells* **15**(2): 288–297.

Cuda, P., I. Dincer and G.F. Naterer (2012). "Hydrogen utilization in various transportation modes with emissions comparisons for Ontario, Canada." *International Journal of Hydrogen Energy* **37**(1): 634–643.

CUTE (2007). A hydrogen fuel cell bus project in Europe (CUTE), Clean Urban Transport for Europe.

Daimler AG (2007). History of fuel cell development at Mercedes-Benz, Daimler Ag.

Daimler AG (2011). "Mercedes-Benz F 125! research vehicle." Retrieved October 9, 2015, from http://media.daimler.com/dcmedia/0-921-1417474-1-1422637 -1-0-0-0-0-0-11702-0-0-1-0-0-0-0-0.html.

DoE (2007). "Angae biofuels." Retrieved April 2012, from http://www1.eere .energy.gov/biomass/pdfs/algalbiofuels.pdf.

DoE (2010). 2009 Fuel Cell Market, US Department of Energy.

DoE (2011b). Technical plans-fuel cells.

DoE (2012a). Analysis of durability of MEAs in automotive PEMFC applications, 2011 annual progress report.

DoE (2012b). Fuel cells sub-program overview.

DoE (2012c). 2011 Vehicle technologies market report, US Department of Energy, Oak Ridge National Laboratory.

DoE (2013a). "Hydrogen and Fuel Cell Program: 2013 Annual Progress Report" http://www.hydrogen.energy.gov/annual_progress13.html.

DoE (2013b). Fuel cell technical team roadmap, US Department of Energy.

DoE (2014a). 2013 Fuel cell technologies market report, US Department of Energy.

DoE (2014b). "Hydrogen and fuel cell program: 2014 annual progress report" http://www.hydrogen.energy.gov/annual_progress13.html.

DoE (2015). Target explanation document: Onboard hydrogen storage for light-duty fuel cell vehicles, US Department of Energy.

DoE (n.d.). "Compare fuel cell vehicles." Retrieved October 21, 2015, from http://www.fueleconomy.gov/feg/fcv_sbs.shtml.

DSEWPC (2009). "Hydrogen fuel cell bus trial." *Department of Sustainability, Environment, Water, Population and Communities* Retrieved June 2011, from http://www.environment.gov.au/atmosphere/fuelquality/emerging/alternative/hydrogen.html.

Dwivedi, G., S. Jain and M. P. Sharma (2011). "Impact analysis of biodiesel on engine performance—A review." *Renewable and Sustainable Energy Reviews* **15**(9): 4633–4641.

Effendi, P. and J. Courvisanos (2011). "Political aspects of innovation: Examining renewable energy in Australia." *Renewable Energy* **38**(1): 245–252.

EIA (2015). Annual Energy Outlook 2015, U.S. Energy Information Administration (EIA).

e-mobil BW (2011). Structure Study BW^e mobile 2011—Baden-Württemberg on the way to electromobility, e-mobil BW.

Eudy, L. and M. Post (2015). American Fuel Cell Bus Project evaluation: Second report, National Renewable Energy Laboratory (NREL).

Eudy, L., M. Post and C. Gikakis (2014). Fuel Cell Buses in U.S. Transit Fleets: Current Status 2014, National Renewable Energy Laboratory (NREL).

European Union (2014). EU energy in figures.

EV World (2011). "Tyrano: Moving freight beyond fossil fuels." Retrieved October 21, 2015, from http://evworld.com/article.cfm?storyid=2031.

Farrell, A. E., D. W. Keith and J. J. Corbett (2003). "A strategy for introducing hydrogen into transportation." *Energy Policy* **31**(13): 1357–1367.

Folkesson, A., C. Andersson, P. Alvfors, M. Alaküla and L. Overgaard (2003). "Real life testing of a Hybrid PEM Fuel Cell Bus." *Journal of Power Sources* **118**(1–2): 349–357.

Ford Motor Company (2014). "Hydrogen Fuel Cell Vehicles (FCVs)." Retrieved October 20, 2015, from http://corporate.ford.com/microsites/sustainability-report-2013-14/environment-products-plan-migration-fcv.html.

Frenette, G. and D. Forthoffer (2009). "Economic & commercial viability of hydrogen fuel cell vehicles from an automotive manufacturer perspective." *International Journal of Hydrogen Energy* **34**(9): 3578–3588.

Gao, D., Z. Jin and Q. Lu (2008). "Energy management strategy based on fuzzy logic for a fuel cell hybrid bus." *Journal of Power Sources* **185**(1): 311–317.

Garrett, M. (2014). *Encyclopedia of Transportation: Social Science and Policy.* Thousand Oaks, CA: SAGE Publications, Inc.

GM (2015). "Emerging technology: Driving safety, efficiency and independence." Retrieved October 20, 2015, from http://www.gm.com/vision /design_technology/emerging_technology.html.

Gnann, T. and P. Plötz (2015). "A review of combined models for market diffusion of alternative fuel vehicles and their refueling infrastructure." *Renewable and Sustainable Energy Reviews* **47**: 783–793.

Gray, E. M., C. J. Webb, J. Andrews, B. Shabani, P. J. Tsai and S. L. I. Chan (2011). "Hydrogen storage for off-grid power supply." *International Journal of Hydrogen Energy* **36**(1): 654–663.

Hal, T. (2006). "Sustainable global automobile transport in the 21st century: An integrated scenario analysis." *Technological Forecasting and Social Change* **73**(6): 607–629.

Hamut, H. S., I. Dincer and G. F. Naterer (2012). "Exergy analysis of a TMS (thermal management system) for range-extended EVs (electric vehicles)." *Energy* **46**(1): 117–125.

Haraldsson, K., A. Folkesson and P. Alvfors (2005). "Fuel cell buses in the Stockholm CUTE project—First experiences from a climate perspective." *Journal of Power Sources* **145**(2): 620–631.

Haraldsson, K., A. Folkesson, M. Saxe and P. Alvfors (2006). "A first report on the attitude towards hydrogen fuel cell buses in Stockholm." *International Journal of Hydrogen Energy* **31**(3): 317–325.

Havlík, P., U. A. Schneider, E. Schmid, H. Böttcher, S. Fritz, R. Skalský, K. Aoki, S. D. Cara, G. Kindermann, F. Kraxner, S. Leduc, I. McCallum, A. Mosnier, T. Sauer and M. Obersteiner (2011). "Global land-use implications of first and second generation biofuel targets." *Energy Policy* **39**(10): 5690–5702.

Hayter, D. (2014). Global H$_2$Mobility initiatives—What they mean for FCEV introduction, Cenex.

HFCN (2011). "Vision Tyrano truck." Retrieved June 2011, from http://www .hydrogencarsnow.com/vision-tyrano.htm.

Hoffman, P. (2012). *Tomorrow's Energy: Hydrogen, Fuel Cells, and the Prospects for a Clear Planet*, Cambridge, MA: MIT Press.

Honda Motor (2010). "2010, *FCX Clarity*" Retrieved Dec. 2010, from http:// automobiles.honda.com/fcx-clarity/.

Honda Motor (2014). "Honda unveils all-New FCV CONCEPT fuel-cell vehicle." Retrieved October 20, 2015, from http://world.honda.com/news/2014 /4141117All-New-Fuel-Cell-Vehicle-FCV-CONCEPT/.

Honda Motor. (2015). "Honda FCV concept." Retrieved October 20, 2015, from http://automobiles.honda.com/honda-fcv/.

Hua, T., R. Ahluwalia, L. Eudy, G. Singer, B. Jermer, N. Asselin-Miller, S. Wessel, T. Patterson and J. Marcinkoski (2014). "Status of hydrogen fuel cell electric buses worldwide." *Journal of Power Sources* **269**: 975–993.

Huber, C. and R. Kuhn (2015). 13—Thermal management of batteries for electric vehicles. In: *Advances in Battery Technologies for Electric Vehicles*. B. S. G. Tillmetz, Ed. Woodhead Publishing, pp. 327–358.

Huétink, F. J., A. v. der Vooren and F. Alkemade (2010). "Initial infrastructure development strategies for the transition to sustainable mobility." *Technological Forecasting and Social Change* **77**(8): 1270–1281.

Hyundai. (2015). "Tucson Fuel Cell." Retrieved October 10, 2015, from https://www.hyundaiusa.com/tucsonfuelcell/.

IEA (2011). World energy outlook. Paris, International Energy Agency.

IEA (2012). World energy outlook. Paris, International Energy Agency.

IEA (2013). Global EV outlook: Understanding the electric vehicle landscape to 2020, International Energy Agency.

IEA (2014a). Key world energy statistics. Paris, International Energy Agency.

IEA (2014b). IEA Statistics, CO_2 Emissions from Fuel Combustion Highlights, International Energy Agency.

IEA (2014c). World energy outlook 2014. Paris, International Energy Agency.

IEA (2015a). Renewables Information 2015, International Energy Agency.

IEA (2015b). Energy technology perspectives 2015—Mobilising innovation to accelerate climate action, International Energy Agency.

IEEE (2012). "Electric vehicles in the early years of the automobile." Retrieved February 2012, from http://www.ieee.org/organizations/pes/public/2004/may/peshistory.html.

IPHE (2009). "Germany: Demonstration and Deployment." Retrieved October 11, 2015, from http://www.iphe.net/partners/germany/demonstrations.html.

IRS (2015). "Plug-in electric drive vehicle credit (IRC 30D)." Retrieved October 7, 2015, from https://www.irs.gov/Businesses/Plug-In-Electric-Vehicle-Credit-IRC-30-and-IRC-30D.

Islam, M. R., B. Shabani, G. Rosengarten and J. Andrews (2015). "The potential of using nanofluids in PEM fuel cell cooling systems: A review." *Renewable and Sustainable Energy Reviews* **48**: 523–539.

J.D. Power (2014). *Reliability, durability and safety drive the purchase decision among new-vehicle owners in Germany*, McGraw Hill Financial.

Jacobson, M. Z. and M. A. Delucchi (2011). "Providing all global energy with wind, water, and solar power, Part I: Technologies, energy resources, quantities and areas of infrastructure, and materials." *Energy Policy* **39**(3): 1154–1169.

Jie, M. and Y. Hagiwara. (2015). "Japan carmakers to subsidize hydrogen station operating costs." Retrieved October 21, 2015, from http://www.bloomberg.com/news/articles/2015-07-01/japan-carmakers-to-subsidize-hydrogen-station-operating-costs.

Kia Motors Corporation (2015). "Hydrogen fuel cell cars." Retrieved October 20, 2015, from http://pr.kia.com/en/wow/eco-dynamics/eco-friendly-technologies/fuel-cell-electric-vehicle.do.

Kim, E., K. G. Shin and L. Jinkyu (2014). Real-time battery thermal management for electric vehicles. Cyber-Physical Systems (ICCPS), 2014 ACM/IEEE International Conference.

Kim, J. and I. Moon (2008). "The role of hydrogen in the road transportation sector for a sustainable energy system: A case study of Korea." *International Journal of Hydrogen Energy* **33**(24): 7326–7337.

Kleijn, R. and E. van der Voet (2010). "Resource constraints in a hydrogen economy based on renewable energy sources: An exploration." *Renewable and Sustainable Energy Reviews* **14**(9): 2784–2795.

Klein-Marcuschamer, D., P. Oleskowicz-Popiel, B. A. Simmons and H. W. Blanch (2012). "The challenge of enzyme cost in the production of lignocellulosic biofuels." *Biotechnology and Bioengineering* **109**(4): 1083–1087.

Koizumi, T. (2015). "Biofuels and food security." *Renewable and Sustainable Energy Reviews* **52**: 829–841.

Larminie, J. and A. Dicks (2003). *Fuel Cell Explained,* 2nd ed., John Wiley & Sons.

Li, X., J. Li, L. Xu, F. Yang, J. Hua and M. Ouyang (2010). "Performance analysis of proton-exchange membrane fuel cell stacks used in Beijing urban-route buses trial project." *International Journal of Hydrogen Energy* **35**(8): 3841–3847.

Liaquat, A. M., M. A. Kalam, H. H. Masjuki and M. H. Jayed (2010). "Potential emissions reduction in road transport sector using biofuel in developing countries." *Atmospheric Environment* **44**(32): 3869–3877.

Lim, M. K., H.-Y. Mak and Y. Rong (2015). "Toward mass Adoption of electric vehicles: Impact of the range and resale anxieties." *Manufacturing & Service Operations Management* **17**(1): 101–119.

Lipman, T. (2011). An Overview of Hydrogen Production and Storage Systems with Renewable Hydrogen Case Studies, The Clean Energy States Alliance (CESA).

Liu, L., F. Kong, X. Liu, Y. Peng and Q. Wang (2015). "A review on electric vehicles interacting with renewable energy in smart grid." *Renewable and Sustainable Energy Reviews* **51**: 648–661.

Maniatopoulos, P., J. Andrews and B. Shabani (2015). "Towards a sustainable strategy for road transportation in Australia: The potential contribution of hydrogen." *Renewable and Sustainable Energy Reviews* **52**: 24–34.

Marbán, G. and T. Valdés-Solís (2007). "Towards the hydrogen economy?" *International Journal of Hydrogen Energy* **32**(12): 1625–1637.

Marrony, M., R. Barrera, S. Quenet, S. Ginocchio, L. Montelatici and A. Aslanides (2008). "Durability study and lifetime prediction of baseline proton exchange membrane fuel cell under severe operating conditions." *Journal of Power Sources* **182**(2): 469–475.

Martin, E., S. A. Shaheen, T. E. Lipman and J. R. Lidicker (2009). "Behavioral response to hydrogen fuel cell vehicles and refueling: Results of California drive clinics." *International Journal of Hydrogen Energy* **34**(20): 8670–8680.

McDowall, W. and M. Eames (2007). "Towards a sustainable hydrogen economy: A multi-criteria sustainability appraisal of competing hydrogen futures." *International Journal of Hydrogen Energy* **32**(18): 4611–4626.

Mckay, D. (2009). *Sustainable Energy without the Hot Air.* Cambridge: Cambridge University Press.

Mercedes-Benz (n.d.). "Mercedes-Benz Necar 1." Retrieved October 9, 2015, from https://www.mercedes-benz.com/en/mercedes-benz/classic/museum/mercedes-benz-necar-1/.

Metz, B., O. R. Davidson, P. R. Bosch, R. Dave and L. A. Meyer (Eds.) (2007). IPCC Fourth Assessment Report (AR4), Climate Change 2007: Mitigation of Climate Change. Cambridge, United Kingdom and New York, Intergovernmental Panel on Climate Change (IPCC).

Mock, P. and S. A. Schmid (2009). "Fuel cells for automotive powertrains—A techno-economic assessment." *Journal of Power Sources* **190**(1): 133–140.

Mohammadi, M., G. D. Najafpour, H. Younesi, P. Lahijani, M. H. Uzir and A. R. Mohamed (2011). "Bioconversion of synthesis gas to second generation bio-fuels: A review." *Renewable and Sustainable Energy Reviews* **15**(9): 4255–4273.

Nissan Motor Corporation (2015). "Toyota, Nissan, and Honda agree on details of joint support for hydrogen infrastructure development." Retrieved October 10, 2015, from http://www.nissan-global.com/EN/NEWS/2015/_STORY/150701-02-e.html.

Nissan Motor Corporation (n.d.). "Fuel-cell electric vehicles (FCEVs)." Retrieved October 9, 2015, from http://www.nissan-global.com/EN/ENVIRONMENT/CAR/FUEL_BATTERY/DEVELOPMENT/FCV/.

Offer, G. J., D. Howey, M. Contestabile, R. Clague and N. P. Brandon (2010). "Comparative analysis of battery electric, hydrogen fuel cell and hybrid vehicles in a future sustainable road transport system." *Energy Policy* **38**(1): 24–29.

Okullo, S. J., F. Reynès and M. W. Hofkes (2015). "Modeling peak oil and the geological constraints on oil production." *Resource and Energy Economics* **40**: 36–56.

Ouyang, M., L. Xu, J. Li, L. Lu, D. Gao and Q. Xie (2006). "Performance comparison of two fuel cell hybrid buses with different powertrain and energy management strategies." *Journal of Power Sources* **163**(1): 467–479.

Panwar, N. L., H. Y. Shrirame, N. S. Rathore, S. Jindal and A. K. Kurchania (2010). "Performance evaluation of a diesel engine fueled with methyl ester of castor seed oil." *Applied Thermal Engineering* **30**(2–3): 245–249.

Paolo, A. (2007). "Hydrogen infrastructure for the transport sector." *International Journal of Hydrogen Energy* **32**(15): 3526–3544.

Post, W. (2008). "A promising oil alternative: algae energy." Retrieved April 2012, from http://www.washingtonpost.com/wp-dyn/content/article/2008/01/03/AR2008010303907.html.

Qin, N., A. Raissi and P. Brooker (2014). Analysis of fuel cell vehicle developments, The Florida Solar Energy Center (FSEC).

Ramesohl, S. and F. Merten (2006). "Energy system aspects of hydrogen as an alternative fuel in transport." *Energy Policy* **34**(11): 1251–1259.

Rao, Z. and S. Wang (2011). "A review of power battery thermal energy management." *Renewable and Sustainable Energy Reviews* **15**(9): 4554–4571.

RET (2011b). Strategic framework for alternative transport fuels, Department of resources, energy and Tourism, Australian Government.

Reuters (2015). "Merkel says Germany weighs further support for electric cars." Retrieved October 7, 2015, from http://www.reuters.com/article/2015/06/15/germany-autos-electric-merkel-idUSL5N0Z144720150615.

Rosenthal, M. (2014). "Policy instability in a comparative perspective: The context of heresthetic." *Political Studies* **62**(1): 172–196.

Saxe, M., A. Folkesson and P. Alvfors (2007). "A follow-up and conclusive report on the attitude towards hydrogen fuel cell buses in the CUTE project—From passengers in Stockholm to bus operators in Europe." *International Journal of Hydrogen Energy* **32**(17): 4295–4305.

Saxe, M., A. Folkesson and P. Alvfors (2008). "Energy system analysis of the fuel cell buses operated in the project: Clean Urban Transport for Europe." *Energy* **33**(5): 689–711.

Shabani, B. and J. Andrews (2011). "An experimental investigation of a PEM fuel cell to supply both heat and power in a solar-hydrogen RAPS system." *International Journal of Hydrogen Energy* **36**(9): 5442–5452.

Shabani, B. and J. Andrews (2015). Hydrogen and fuel cells. In: *Energy Sustainability Through Green Energy*. A. Sharma and S. K. Kar, Eds. Springer India, pp. 453–491.

Shabani, B., J. Andrews and S. Badwal (2010a). "Fuel-cell heat recovery, electrical load management, and the economics of solar-hydrogen systems." *International Journal of Power and Energy Systems* **30**(4): 256–263.

Shabani, B., J. Andrews and S. Watkins (2010b). "Energy and cost analysis of a solar-hydrogen combined heat and power system for remote power supply using a computer simulation." *Solar Energy* **84**(1): 144–155.

Shabani, B. and M. Biju (2015). "Theoretical modelling methods for thermal management of batteries." *Energies* **8**(9): 10153.

Sorda, G., M. Banse and C. Kemfert (2010). "An overview of biofuel policies across the world." *Energy Policy* **38**(11): 6977–6988.

Sovacool, B. K. and I. Mukherjee (2011). "Conceptualizing and measuring energy security: A synthesized approach." *Energy* **36**(8): 5343–5355.

Steenberghen, T. and E. López (2008). "Overcoming barriers to the implementation of alternative fuels for road transport in Europe." *Journal of Cleaner Production* **16**(5): 577–590.

Stoeglehner, G. and M. Narodoslawsky (2009). "How sustainable are biofuels? Answers and further questions arising from an ecological footprint perspective." *Bioresource Technology* **100**(16): 3825–3830.

Tan, K. M., V. K. Ramachandaramurthy and J. Y. Yong (2016). "Integration of electric vehicles in smart grid: A review on vehicle to grid technologies and optimization techniques." *Renewable and Sustainable Energy Reviews* **53**: 720–732.

Tesla Motors (2015). "Model X." Retrieved October 9, 2015, from http://www.teslamotors.com/modelx.

Timilsina, G. R. and A. Shrestha (2011). "How much hope should we have for biofuels?" *Energy* **36**(4): 2055–2069.

Toyota Motor Corporation (2014a). "History of Toyota's fuel cell vehicles." Retrieved October 10, 2015, from http://www.toyota-global.com/innovation/intelligent_transport_systems/world_congress/2014detroit/pdf/History_of_Toyota's_Fuel_Cell.pdf.

Toyota Motor Corporation (2014b). "Toyota ushers in the future with launch of 'Mirai' fuel cell sedan." Retrieved October 9, 2015, from http://newsroom .toyota.co.jp/en/detail/4198334.

Toyota Motor Corporation (2014c). "The future has arrived, and it's called Mirai." Retrieved October 20, 2015, from http://toyotanews.pressroom.toyota .com/releases/toyota+names+fuel+cell+vehicle+mirai.htm.

Toyota Motor Corporation (2015). "Fuel Cell Vehicle." Retrieved October 8, 2015, from http://www.toyota-global.com/innovation/environmental_technology /fuelcell_vehicle/index.html.

TÜV SÜD (2015). "17 new hydrogen refuelling stations worldwide in 2014." Retrieved October 10,2015, from http://www.tuv-sud.com/news-media /news-archive/17-new-hydrogen-refuelling-stations-worldwide-in-2014.

UN (2008). Biofuel production technologies: Statuse, prospecs, and implications for trade and development. *United Nation Conference on Trade and Development*. New York and Geneva.

van Vliet, O., A. S. Brouwer, T. Kuramochi, M. van den Broek and A. Faaij (2011). "Energy use, cost and CO2 emissions of electric cars." *Journal of Power Sources* **196**(4): 2298–2310.

Verhelst, S. and T. Wallner (2009). "Hydrogen-fueled internal combustion engines." *Progress in Energy and Combustion Science* **35**(6): 490–527.

Vision (2011). "Vision hydrogen fuel cell truck for TTSI, 100 on order." *Fuel Cells Bulletin* **2011**(8): 2.

Vision (2011). "Vision Tyrano." Retrieved July 2011, from http://www.visionmo torcorp.com/maxvision.htm.

Wang, J., Y. Chen and Q. Chen (2006). "A fuel cell city bus with three drivetrain configurations." *Journal of Power Sources* **159**(2): 1205–1213.

WEC (2013). World energy scenarios to 2050, World Energy Council.

Wild, A. (2012). "Biofuel and competition in Australia." Retrieved April 2012, from http://www.csiro.au/en/Outcomes/Food-and-Agriculture/biofuels-and -competition.aspx.

Winzer, C. (2012). "Conceptualizing energy security." *Energy Policy* **46**: 36–48.

Wu, J., X. Z. Yuan, J. J. Martin, H. Wang, J. Zhang, J. Shen, S. Wu and W. Merida (2008). "A review of PEM fuel cell durability: Degradation mechanisms and mitigation strategies." *Journal of Power Sources* **184**(1): 104–119.

Xing, M.-N., X.-Z. Zhang and H. Huang (2012). "Application of metagenomic techniques in mining enzymes from microbial communities for biofuel synthesis." *Biotechnology Advances* **30**(4): 920–929.

Yergin, D. (1988). "Energy Security in the 1990s." *Foreign Affairs* **67**(1): 110–132.

Young, K., C. Wang, L. Wang and K. Strunz (2013). Electric vehicle battery technologies. In: *Electric Vehicle Integration into Modern Power Networks*. R. Garcia-Valle and J. A. Peças Lopes, Eds., Springer New York, pp. 15–56.

Yusuf, N. N. A. N., S. K. Kamarudin and Z. Yaakub (2011). "Overview on the current trends in biodiesel production." *Energy Conversion and Management* **52**(7): 2741–2751.

Zapata, C. and P. Nieuwenhuis (2010). "Exploring innovation in the automotive industry: New technologies for cleaner cars." *Journal of Cleaner Production* **18**(1): 14–20.

zeroemissionvehicles (2009). A portfolio of power-trains for Europe: A fact-based analysis; the role of battery electric vehicles, plug-in hybrids and fuel cell electric vehicles.

Zhao, J. and M. W. Melaina (2006). "Transition to hydrogen-based transportation in China: Lessons learned from alternative fuel vehicle programs in the United States and China." *Energy Policy* **34**(11): 1299–1309.

Zoulias, E. I. and N. Lymberopoulos (2007). "Techno-economic analysis of the integration of hydrogen energy technologies in renewable energy-based stand-alone power systems." *Renewable Energy* **32**(4): 680–696.

ZWS (2015). "More than 740,000 cars worldwide powered by electricity." Retrieved October 6, 2015, from http://www.zsw-bw.de/en/support/news/news-detail /mehr-als-740000-autos-weltweit-fahren-mit-strom.html.

CHAPTER 8

Status of Biomass Gasification Technologies in Europe

Vinod Kumar Sharma and Giacobbe Braccio

CONTENTS

8.1 BIOMASS GASIFIER: AN EXTENSIVE REVIEW

There are a variety of technologies for generating modern energy carriers—electricity, gas, and liquid fuels—from biomass, which can be used at the household (~10 kW), community (~100 kW), or industrial (~MW) scale. The different technologies tend to be classed in terms of either the conversion process they use or the end product produced.

An extensive review of gasifier manufacturers in Europe, the United States, and Canada, identified 50 manufacturers offering "commercial" gasification plants from which:

1. 75% of the designs were downdraft type,

2. 20% of the designs were fluidized bed systems,

3. 2.5% of the designs were updraft type, and

4. 2.5% were of various other designs.

However, there was very little information on cost aspects, emissions, efficiencies, turn-down ratios, and actual operating hours experience. Actual operating experience is limited and there is little confidence in the technology, which is due to the general poor performance of the various prototypes.

Atmospheric circulating fluidized bed gasifiers (ACFBG) have proven very reliable with a variety of feedstock and are relative easy to scale up from a few MW_{th} up to 100 MW_{th}. Even for capacities above 100 MW_{th}, there is confidence that the industry would be able to provide reliable operating gasifiers. It appears to be the preferred system for large-scale applications and it is used by most of the industrial companies such as TPS, FOSTER WHEELER, BATTELLE, LURGI, and AUSTRIAN ENERGY. Therefore, ACFBG have high market attractiveness and are technically well proven.

Atmospheric bubbling fluidized bed gasifiers (ABFBG) have proven reliable with a variety of feedstock at the pilot scale and commercial applications in the small to medium scale; up to about 25 MW_{th}. ABFBG are more economic for small to medium range capacities. Companies promoting ABFBG are CARBONA and DINAMEC.

Pressurized fluidized bed systems either circulating (PCFBG) or bubbling (PBFBG) are complex due to both installation and the additional costs related to the construction of all pressurized vessels.

Atmospheric downdraft gasifiers (ADG) are attractive for small-scale applications (<1.5 MW$_{th}$), not only in developed but developing economies, too. However, the problem of efficient tar removal is still a major problem to be addressed and there is a need for more automated operation especially for small-scale industrial applications. Nevertheless, recent progress in catalytic conversion of tar gives credible options and ADG can therefore be considered of average technical strength.

Atmospheric updraft gasifiers (AUG) have practically no market attractiveness for power applications due to the high concentration of tar in the fuel gas and the subsequent problems in gas cleaning.

Atmospheric cyclonic gasifiers (ACG) have only recently been tested for biomass feedstock and although they have medium market attractiveness due to their simplicity, they are still unproven.

Finally, atmospheric entrained bed gasifiers (AEBG) are still at the very early stage of development.

No company is presently developing pressurized systems for downdraft, updraft, cyclonic, or entrained bed gasifiers for biomass feedstocks and it is difficult to imagine that such a technology could ever be developed into a commercial product due to the inherent problems of scale, tar removal, and cost.

In conclusion, for large-scale applications, the preferred and most reliable system is the circulating fluidized bed gasifier, while for small-scale applications downdraft gasifiers are the most extensively studied.

Bubbling fluidized bed gasifiers can be competitive in medium-scale applications. Large-scale fluidized bed systems have become commercial due to successful co-firing projects while moving bed gasifiers are still trying to achieve this.

At present, 87 gasification facilities are active. Fifty-four of them can be found in Task 33 member countries and 33 in other countries. (Austria 9, NZ 1, Denmark 7, Norway 0, Italy 0, Sweden 4, Finland 4, Switzerland 4, Germany 7, Turkey 2, Japan 2, Netherlands 6, and United States 8).

Co-firing (4 gasification facilities); CHP (37 gasification facilities), synthesis (34 gasification facilities); other innovative (12 gasification facilities).

It is worth noting that the *majority* of all 87 gasification facilities are now in operation (59%), an additional 14% are in construction, 3% are in commissioning, and 16% are planned. Only 8% of all gasification facilities are on hold. Nearly half of all gasification facilities (47%) are commercial, 27% are pilot plants and 26% are demo plants.

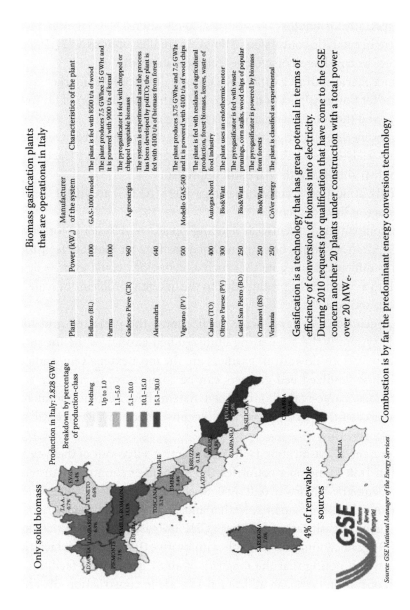

Biomass gasification plants that are operational in Italy

Plant	Power (kW$_e$)	Manufacturer of the system	Characteristics of the plant
Belluno (BL)	1000	GAS-1000 model	The plant is fed with 8500 t/a of wood
Parma	1000		The plant produces 7.5 GWhee 15 GWht and it is powered with 9000 t/a of kenaf
Gadesco Pieve (CR)	960	Agroenergia	The progasificator is fed with chopped or chopped vegetable biomass
Alessandria	640		The system is experimental and the process has been developed by poliTO; the plant is fed with 4100 t/a of biomass from forest
Vigevano (PV)	500	Modello GAS-500	The plant produces 3.75 GWhe and 7.5 GWht and it is powered with 4100 t/a of wood chips
Caluso (TO)	400	Autogas Nord	The plant is fed with residues of agricultural production, forest biomass, leaves, waste of food industry
Oltrepo Pavese (PV)	300	Bio&Watt	The plant uses an endothermic motor
Castel San Pietro (BO)	250	Bio&Watt	The pyrogasificator is fed with waste prunings, corn stalks, wood chips of popular
Orzinuovi (BS)	250	Bio&Watt	The pyrogasificator is powered by biomass from forests
Verbania	250	CoVer energy	The plant is classified as experimental

Gasification is a technology that has great potential in terms of efficiency of conversion of biomass into electricity. During 2010 requests for qualification that have come to the GSE concern another 20 plants under construction with a total power over 20 MW$_e$.

Only solid biomass

Production in Italy: 2.828 GWh

Breakdown by percentage of production-class

- Nothing
- Up to 1.0
- 1.1–5.0
- 5.1–10.0
- 10.1–15.0
- 15.1–30.0

4% of renewable sources

Combustion is by far the predominant energy conversion technology

Source: GSE National Manager of the Energy Services

FIGURE 8.1   National energy potential: current status of biomass gasification power plants.

Based on the successful operation of the Güssing plant, the FICFB gasifier has been commercialized in six plants in Europe in stages of planning, construction, or operation.

Because of the high potential awarded to this energy source, efforts are mainly focused to sharply increase the utilization of biomass in Italy.

Several projects (thermo-chemical conversion process of biomass via gasification) in cooperation with both national and international institutions have either already been completed or are in progress.

A number of experimental plants based on different technologies (fixed bed, BFB, FICFB gasifiers) and of different sizes (10 kW_{th}, 100 kW_{th}, 500 kW_{th}, 1 MW_{th}) are available at Trisaia.

The plants have been investigated experimentally to test the most promising field of application (production of fuel gas for power generation) following different possible ways such as via internal combustion engine, gas turbines, and high temperature fuel cell (MCFC).

The use of biomass gasification for syngas production to biofuels conversion has also been considered.

Development of a 1 MW_{th} reactor for the production of a fuel gas to be fed to a gas turbine is under investigation. The product gas will be produced by oxygen/steam gasification of biomass by means of a bubbling fluidized bed. The associated plant is under construction. The 1 MW_{th} reactor will be the starting point of the prototype reactor that will be developed and tested throughout the unique project (Figure 8.1, Tables 8.1 through 8.3).

8.2 CASE STUDY

Güssing is a small town with about 4000 inhabitants and located in the eastern part of Austria (Burgerland) near the Hungarian border. It is the capital of a district with 27,000 people. For a long time the Austrian-Hungarian border was called the Iron Curtain. There used to be huge deficits in infrastructure: lack of highways, roads, and railways, and therefore no industry settled there. This led to the lack of industry (Figure 8.2).

The municipality could not get much income from local business taxes. These negative circumstances led to the high rate of unemployment and migration to other cities. More than 70% of the working inhabitants became commuters. The region was very poor until biomass as a source of energy was discovered and utilized in the region. In 1989, the majority of Güssing and some experts worked out a concept for the energy supply of Güssing. The point of the concept was to satisfy the local energy demands based on local energy producers who utilize local resources. This way the

TABLE 8.1   List of Biomass Gasification Plants Investigated Experimentally by ENEA Research Centre Trisaia

	Fixed Bed Plants
Clean Energy (H₂) from Biomass: 500 kW$_{th}$ internally circulating fluidized bed (ICFB): Coordinated by University of L'Aquila with participation from ENEA and TUV Austria.	Presently, we have two fixed bed experimental plants at Tempio Pausania:
1 MW$_e$ (2 units of 500 kW$_e$) Up draft BUG with Power Generation: coordinated by CCT Legnano (VA) with participation by Guascor.	Plant No. 1
4.5 MW$_e$ downdraft gasification with exhausted olive cake using prime energy system: Coordinated by Rossano Energy, Rossano(CS), in Southern Italy (with participation from Guascor).	Gassogeno HT (horizontal type fixed bed) of capacity 1 MW$_t$ and working with triturated RSU is in operation since May 2005. It produces the synthesis gas at approximately 750°C.
3 MW$_{th}$, updraft BMG (including coal, wood, and RDF): Coordinated by Ansaldo Ricerche, Genova.	The main objective of this plant is to test different fuels, analyze the smoke from the combustion, design a treatment plant, and gas purification.
3 MW$_{th}$, updraft BMG; coordinated by Marcegaglia Group in Taranto, in Southern Italy.	Plant No. 2
15 kW$_e$ downdraft fixed bed. 80 kW$_e$ downdraft fixed bed and a multi-fuel 160 kW$_e$ fluid bed (CFB) BMG systems:	Gassogeno LT (vertical type fixed bed) of capacity 1.5 MW$_t$, and working using medium to high density briquette CDR, is in operation since October 2005. This plant comprises of tar removal and scrubber head with sub-cooling.
First two are on stand-by while the third plant is under experimentation, in China.	This plant is able to produce purified synthesis gas with low tar and dust contents, ready to be used in internal combustion engine.

TABLE 8.2   Commercial FICFB Gasifiers

Location	Electricity Production	Fuel/electr. MW, MW$_{el}$	Start Up	Status
Güssing, AT	Gas engine	8.0/2.0	2002	Operational
Oberwart, AT	Gas engine/ORG	8.5/2.8	2008	Operational
Villach, AT	Gas engine	15/3.7	2010	Commissioning
Klagenfurt, AT	Gas engine	25/5.5	2011	Planning
Ulm, DE	Gas engine/ORG	14/5	2011	Under construction
Göteborg, Sweden	BioSNG	32/20 (BioSNG)	2012	Planning

TABLE 8.3 Comparision for Different Gasification Plants in Italy: Economic Aspects

		Caerra Rivoira E++	Guascor	Bio & Watt	AG.T.	C.I.P.	Di GAS	Biosolar Flenco (ORC)
Power		1 MW	1 MW	250 kW	250 kW	400 kW	150 kW	120 kW
Plant	Mil, €	3	4	1	0.82	1.3	0.45	0.5
Installed cost/kW$_e$	£/kW$_e$	3000	4000	3200	3300	3250	3000	4000
Design	€	70,000	Incl.	Conf.	Conf.	Incl.	/	Conf.
Permit costs	€	80,000	Conf.	Conf.	/	Incl.	/	Conf.
Ancillary works	€	150,000	Conf.	Customer	/	200,000	/	Not available
Operational hours	h/day	8	24	3	/	8	/	3
Operational cost	£/year	60,000	Conf.	Customer	30,000	50,000	/	20,000
Maintenance (system/engine)	€/kWh	0.025	Conf.	Conf.	0.03	0.03	/	0.03
Biomass tq	€/t	50 (w50%)	40–30 (w40%)	30 (w45%)	20/100	50	Not available	40
Biomass ss	€/t	70 (w20%)	Not available	Not available	Not available	Not available	Not available	Not available

FIGURE 8.2   Biomass CHP plant in Güssing, Austria.

region could be independent from imported fossil energy, the changing oil prices, and the money spent on energy (oil, power, fuels, transportation, etc.) could stay in the region and the concept would have a positive effect on the local industry as well.

Those resources were essentially made up of local grown agricultural crops and residues, and wood/forest biomass.

The essence of the Güssing concept is summarized in Figure 8.3.

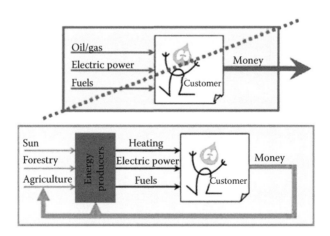

FIGURE 8.3   The essence of the Güssing concept.

First, the energetic optimization of buildings was carried out—reducing local energy demand—then demonstration energy plants were established in the region. The flagship of the most important innovation is the combined heat and power plant with fluidized bed steam gasification technology. Apart from the gasification CHP plant, there are various research projects being carried out in Güssing concerning incineration, solar energy, hydrogen generation, fuel cells, the production of methane from syngas, Fischer-Tropsch synthesis, etc. The aim of these research projects is to produce heat, electricity, and gaseous and liquid fuels to satisfy the energy demands of the region and be as independent from energy importing as possible.

The plant uses a special fluidized bed steam gasification technology which was developed at Vienna University of Technology in cooperation with AE Energietechnik and RENET. The plant started operation in 2001 and after the optimization phase it is still working perfectly.

It is the first utility-scale power plant of its kind in the world, with a rated capacity of 8 MW, producing on average about 2 MW of electricity and 4.5 MW of heat per hour.

Operating at 8000 hours per year for the last several years, the Güssing facility, together with a network of smaller district heating plants and other renewable energy units, produces more energy than the town consumes (industrial demands not included) on an annual basis.

The CHP plant utilizes 18,400 tons of wood annually. The raw materials are obtained from within a radius of 5–10 km. The biomass supply is secured by long-term contracts. The price is fixed for a duration of 10 years which is about 1.6 € cents/kWh (Figure 8.4).

The generated heat is delivered to a district heating grid which has a length of more than 20 km. The consumers are mainly private houses (300 pcs), public offices, schools, and a hospital (50 pcs). Furthermore, there is a growing demand for industrial heat which is needed the whole year around. Also, wood drying chambers have been installed in the vicinity which are additional heat consumers. Electricity is sold to the electrical grid operator with a feed-in rate of 16 cents/kWh.

In 2002 an 8 MW CHP plant based on a circulating fluidized bed steam blown gasifier producing heat and power (4.5 MW_{th}, 2 MW_{el}) with a gas engine went into operation in Güssing, Austria. In the middle of 2002 the gasifier and the gas cleaning system was coupled with a gas engine.

Rennet-Austria, a competence network on energy from biomass, consisting of experts from universities and industry started to develop this process further to a commercial stage.

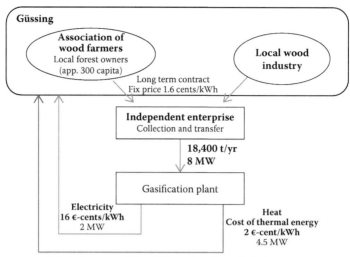

FIGURE 8.4   Useful data relevant to biomass CHP plant in Güssing, Austria.

Excellent performance has been recorded over the last few years. It is to be noted that the nearly free of nitrogen and high hydrogen content producer gas from the circulating all thermal fluidized bed gasifier is well suited for fuel cells as well as several synthesis products. Therefore, projects aiming at the development of processes for the production of synthetic natural gas and Fischer Tropsch liquids are currently carried out (Figure 8.5).

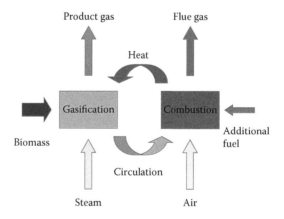

FIGURE 8.5   Basic idea of the gasification process.

The basic idea of the gasifier concept is to divide the fluidized bed into two zones, a gasification zone and a combustion zone. Between these two zones a circulation loop of bed material is created but the gases should remain separated. The circulating bed material acts as a heat carrier from the combustion to the gasification zone. The fuel is fed into the gasification zone and gasified with steam. The gas produced in this zone is therefore nearly free of nitrogen. The bed material, together with some charcoal, circulates to the combustion zone. This zone is fluidized with air and the charcoal is partly burned.

The exothermic reaction in the combustion zone provides the energy for the endothermic gasification with steam. Therefore, the bed material at the exit of the combustion zone has a higher temperature than at the entrance. The flue gas will be removed without coming in contact with the product gas. With this concept it is possible to get a high-grade product gas without use of pure oxygen. This process can be realized with two fluidized beds connected with transport lines or with an internally circulating fluidized bed.

8.2.1 Description of the Biomass CHP Güssing

In Güssing an innovative process for combined heat and power production based on steam gasification has been successfully demonstrated.

The system consists of the following main components (Figure 8.6):

- Biomass feeding system
- Gasifier (gasification and combustion zone)
- Product gas cooler
- Product gas filter
- Product gas scrubber
- Product gas blower
- Gas engine
- Water boiler
- Flue gas cooler
- Flue gas filter
- Flue gas (gas engine) cooler

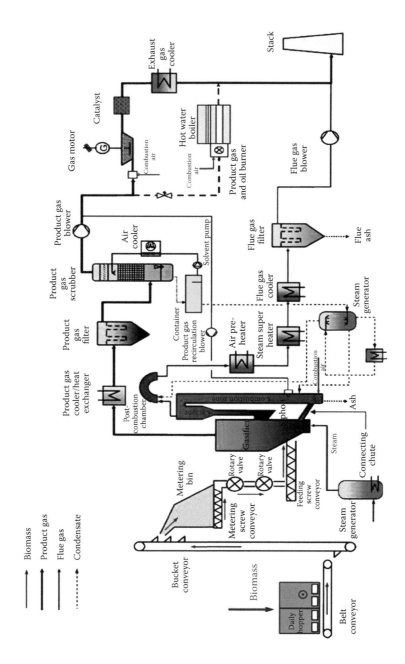

FIGURE 8.6 Schematic flow diagram of the biomass power plant in Güssing.

The fluidized bed gasifier consists of two zones, a gasification zone and a combustion zone. The gasification zone is fluidized with steam which is generated by waste heat of the process, to produce a nitrogen-free producer gas. The combustion zone is fluidized with air and delivers the heat for the gasification process via the circulating bed material.

A water cooled heat exchanger reduces the temperature from 850°C–900°C to about 150°C–180°C. The producer gas is cooled and cleaned by a two-stage cleaning system. The first stage of the cleaning system is a fabric filter to separate the particles and some of the tar from the producer gas. These particles are recycled to the combustion zone of the gasifier. In a second stage, the gas is liberated from tar by a scrubber. Spent scrubber liquid saturated with tar and condensate is vaporized and fed for thermal disposal into the combustion zone of the gasifier. The scrubber is used to reduce the temperature of the clean producer gas to about 40°C.

The clean gas is finally fed into a gas engine to produce electricity and heat. If the gas engine is not in operation the whole amount of producer gas can be burned in a backup boiler to produce heat. The flue gas of the gas engine is catalytically oxidized to reduce the CO emissions. The sensible heat of the engine's flue gas is used to produce district heat. The flue gas from the combustion zone is used for preheating air, superheating steam as well as to deliver heat to the district heating grid. A gas filter separates the particles before the flue gas of the combustion zone is released to the environment.

The plant fulfills all emission requirements. Operational experience shows that there is only one solid residue which is the fly ash from the flue gas. This fly ash fully burned out, the loss of ignition is lower than 0.5 w-%. The plant produces no condensate which has to be disposed externally.

8.2.2 Availability of the Plant

It is clear that the availability of any demonstration plant cannot be as high as for a plant that uses an already mature technology. For such an innovative technology as is used in the case of the CFB allothermal steam gasification plant and the gas cleaning system several years of operational experience are necessary to remove all the weak points within the plant. Figure 8.7 shows an increase of the availability for the gasifier and also for the gas engine for the years 2002 until 2006. It can be seen that the availability could be increased essentially over time and it reached more

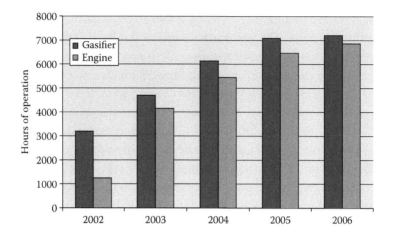

FIGURE 8.7 Increase of the availability for both gasifier and the gas engine during the period 2002–2006.

than 90% for the gasifier and more than 85% for the gas engine in the year 2006.

8.2.3 Operation Performance of the Biomass CHP Güssing

The Güssing plant has been in operation continuously since the middle of 2002. Of course, during this time there were several periods of maintenance and also periods for improvement of the construction. The production of electricity started in the middle of 2002. Heat is fed into an existing district heating system and electricity into the power grid. Data in Table 8.4 shows

TABLE 8.4   Main Characteristics of the CHP Plant

Technical Parameters

Technology: Fluidized bed steam gasification
Feedstock (type and consumption/h): Wood chips 2300 kg/h
Feedstock volume: 18,400 t/y ; Average WC : 30.0%
Plant Power: 8 MW_{th}
Output Thermal Power: 4.5 MW_{th}
Output Electrical Power: 2 MW_e
Thermal Efficiency: 56.3%
Electric Efficiency: 25.0%
Total Efficiency: 81.3%
Total operational hours until 2006: 30,000 (gasifier); 25,000 (motor)
Total operational hours in 2006: 8000 (gasifier); 7000 (motor)

the cumulative production of heat and power since January 2002. It is evident that there were only a few periods when the plant was not in operation. Furthermore, also an increase in the heat and power output can be observed.

8.3 COSTS AND ECONOMICS

The biomass CHP plant in Güssing can be operated economically under the specific Austrian frame conditions. Despite the quite high costs for the biomass feedstock, the operation of biomass CHP plants is currently quite good due to the high fixed feed-in tariffs for green electricity (up to 16.0 €-cents/kWh$_{el}$ for solid biomass) (Table 8.5).

For the next plant, 25% reduction of the investment cost can be expected due to the experience and learning gained from the demonstration plant. The operation costs can be reduced as well by unmanned operation and further operation optimization (bed material, gas cleaning).

Total heat power: Approximately 50 GWh (households, public utilities, industry)

Electricity: Approximately 20 GWh (households, public utilities)

Synthetic gas: Approximately 120 m^3/h

Synthetic fuel: 1 barrel/day

Actual added value with 47% self-sufficient use of renewable energies is € 20 million.

Potential added value with 100% self-sufficient use of renewable energies is € 38 million (Figure 8.8).

TABLE 8.5 Summary of Economic Data Sets for the Güssing Power Plant

Cost Category	Amount
Investment cost	10 Mio €
Funding (EU, national)	0.6 Mio €
Operation cost/year	1.3 Mio €/yr
Price for heat (into grid)	2.0 €-cents/kWh$_{th}$
Price for heat (consumer)	3.9 €-cents/kWh$_{th}$
Price for electricity	16.0 €-cents/kWh$_{el}$

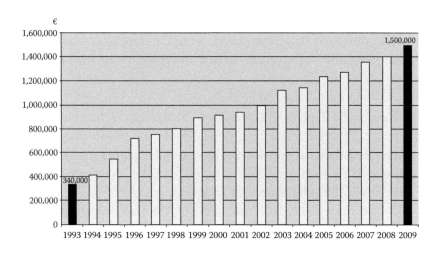

FIGURE 8.8   Growing income from business taxes (1993–2009).

8.4 OPTIMIZATION AND FURTHER DEVELOPMENT OF BIOMASS CHP PLANTS

Research in the biomass plant in Güssing also includes the further development of feedstock conveyance, the variation of bed material, and the use of additives for targeted control of gas quality.

Other goals consist of extending the range of usable feedstock, simplifying gas cleaning, and the optimization of the gas engine in order to reduce capital and operating costs.

The favorable characteristics of the product gas (low nitrogen content, high hydrogen content, H_2:CO ratio of 1.6–1.8) allow also other applications of this producer gas. Research projects concerning the production of electricity in an SOFC (solid oxide fuel cell), the synthesis of SNG (synthetic natural gas), and Fischer-Tropsch liquids have been started. Figure 8.9 gives an overview about possible applications of the producer gas from a steam blown gasifier.

In principle, all products can be obtained from the synthesis gas as this is the case for coal or crude oil. All the necessary chemical pathways have been well known for many decades. Therefore, in analogy to coal or oil chemistry, one can say now "green chemistry" if the original material is renewable (e.g., biomass) (Figure 8.10).

All these advanced applications need an ultra-clean synthesis gas. To cover with these requirements further cleaned up and conditioning steps are necessary. For this purpose a slip stream of the synthesis gas is taken, treated in a suitable way, and fed to the research installations. Figure 8.11 shows a principal scheme of this arrangement.

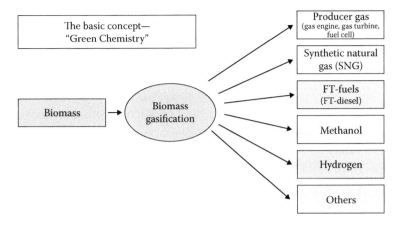

FIGURE 8.9   Possible applications of the producer gas from a steam blown gasifier.

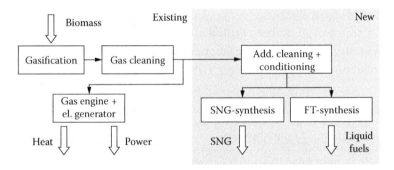

FIGURE 8.10   Extension of the Güssing plant.

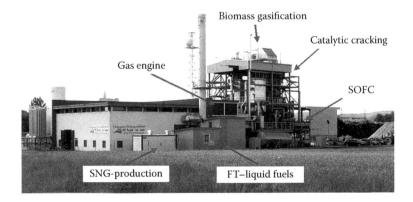

FIGURE 8.11   Principle scheme (cleaning and conditioning) to obtain ultra-clean synthesis gas.

8.5 ADVANTAGES

Advantages of this method of production are its compact construction and by using steam as the gasification medium, there is a smaller tar content in the product than when using air.

Equilibrium between combustion and gasification reactions takes place automatically, thus one can keep the operation running stably without excessive regulation and adjustment.

As already mentioned, the gasification reaction is endothermic. If the temperature in the gasification section drops, less fuel is fully decomposed and this leads to an increasing proportion of carbon or nonoxidized fuel in the combustion section.

By virtue of the increased combustion there, one transfers more energy to the bed material and this supplies in turn more energy back to the gasification section. Thus, a renewed temperature rise in the gasification section is brought about.

In this way, a stable equilibrium is maintained between the gasification and combustion chambers. Additionally, the temperature in the combustion section can be regulated by controlling the flow of product gas.

8.6 ECONOMIC ANALYSIS WITH DIFFERENT DESIGN SOLUTIONS

The economic investigation has been conducted by analyzing various cost terms associated with configurations of the plant studied. Plants of three different sizes have been considered.

- Plant with thermal power of nearly 1.3 MW_{th}, using a biomass flow rate of nearly 330 kg/h.

- Simulated plant similar to above, but with thermal power of 10 MW_{th} and biomass feed rate of nearly 2500 kg/h.

- Simulated plant similar to above, but with thermal power of 20 MW_{th} and biomass feed rate of nearly 5000 kg/h.

The economic analysis was done in a classical mode considering cost of investment, operating and maintenance costs, depreciation, and financing charges.

8.6.1 Cost of Investment (CI)

Cost of investment is the sum of both direct and indirect costs. These are broken down as follows.

8.6.2 Costs of Direct Investment (CID)

Direct cost comprises all costs relevant to construction of the plant (cost of the land, preparation of land, different components of the plants for its construction, electro-mechanical work, etc.).

The costs have been evaluated considering the data available in the literature and based on the values provided for various components by the manufacturers. These are broadly divided into two groups, namely plant components and civil works. Plant components include a system for the receipt and storage of biomass, a system to feed the gasifier, a system for the distribution of auxiliary fuels, a gasification section, a filtering section, a thermal recovery section, a metallic structure and accessories, treatment of feed water, supply and assembling of electrical, instruments, mechanical assembling and piping, separation section, and an O_2 feeding section.

On the other hand, civil works comprise building of control room and offices, floors for the machine and cemented network, preparation of area, roads, and platforms, wall enclosure, sewage of water, fire-fighting network, etc.

8.6.3 Cost of Indirect Investment

Indirect costs include expenses for the plant designing (engineering aspects), testing, etc. The cost of engineering and supervision is taken as 10–20% of the total cost of direct investment. General costs constitute 5–20% of the total cost of direct investment.

8.6.4 Total Installation Cost

Total cost investment (CI) is equivalent to 135–123% of CID. The above-mentioned costs have been stimulated by the summation of CI for gasification section, shift section, separation section, oxygen production section, energy recovery section, etc. Cost of direct investment as a function of a plant's potential variation can be obtained using an exponential relationship based on the existing cost data. If C1 is the cost of equipment or a part of plant of output M1, then the cost of a similar device, of output M2, can be calculated using the relationship:

$$C_2 = C_1 \cdot \left(\frac{M_2}{M_1} \right)^S$$

where the value of the exponential factor S depends on the type of equipment or plant. The correlation of exponential cost has been developed for specific parts and/or sections of plant. In many cases, the cost has to be correlated in terms of parameters related to the plant output.

8.6.5 Direct Cost for Gasification Plant

Cost of gasification plant on a pilot scale, including a section for heat recovery and cleaning, has been calculated based on the analysis of the cost of a pilot plant 1.3 MW_{th}. The cost calculation relevant to the plant on a large-scale has been done using values obtained from the exploitation of the pilot plant as well as literature data.

Direct cost for shift section: Prices used have been taken from the data available in the literature providing a relationship between the plant cost and actual molar flow rate of $CO + H_2$.

Direct costs for PSA separation section: Costs for the separation section have been taken from the data available in the literature, that provide a relationship between cost of the plant and actual molar flow rate of gas, in addition to data provided by companies that supply separation systems.

Compression section: Cost for the compression section appears to be nearly 70.900 k€ per kW_e, multistage cooling compressor $\beta = 15$–18.

Direct costs for the section producing oxygen: Costs for the separation section have been taken from the data available in the literature that report a relationship between plant cost and actual daily O_2 production. The data has been compared with data provided by market analysis of a small O_2 generating set based on a PSA system.

Direct cost for energy recovery section: Costs for the energy recovery section have been taken from the data provided by a market analysis of a micro- and mini-generating set based on micro-/mini-turbine system. All investment costs of a plant, in general, are summarized in Table 8.6. It is, however, to be noted that the direct cost depends on the type of plant under investigation. The same is evident from the insignificant difference between the cost of hydrogen produced, irrespective of the fact of whether the oxygen is produced on-site or elsewhere.

TABLE 8.6   Data Relevant to the Investment Cost of a Plant

Investment cost [k€]	1.3 MW$_t$	10 MW$_t$	20 MW$_t$
Direct cost			
Gasification section	921.0	4483.0	7765.8
Shift section	105.0	395.0	630.0
Separation section	500.0	1195.0	1620.0
Compression section	57.0	433.0	866.0
Oxygen section	196.0	1329.0	2300.0
Energy recovery section	150.0	900.0	1750.0
Total direct cost	1929.0	8735.0	14,931.8
Indirect cost	289.1	1310.3	2239.8
Start cost	96.4	436.8	746.6
Total investment cost	2314.9	10,482.1	17,918.2

Operational and maintenance costs: Operational and maintenance costs have been defined as the costs necessary for the functioning of the plant. The items considered include: fuels, electric energy, chemicals, different materials consumed, personnel involved, etc.

Fuel cost: The quantity of biomass needed annually to run the plants at their normal load of 330 kg/h, 2500 kg/h, and 5000 kg/h is approximately 2500, 19,500, and 39,000 T/year, respectively. The biomass is furnished using husk (nearly 20%), almond-shell (nearly 15%), and waste from the sawmill (nearly 65%). The total cost comprises the material cost (approximately 20 Euro/t) and the transport cost, which depends on the distance, type of material, and the conveyance used. Considering average distance of approximately 50 km, the overall cost of biomass inclusive of supply and transport is approximately 26 Euro/t.

Cost of labor involved: Cost of labor involved depends on so many factors such as size of the plant, automatic dependency, different existing norms relevant to the use of different machines, possibilities of realizing plants in the already existing industrial areas, etc. It is hypothesized that the plants are autonomous, that is, they do not belong to other industrial plants with number of persons engaged for the plant (1) equal to 9 while for the plants (1) and (3) are 11 and 15, respectively. The average specific cost for the specialized technical staff is of the order of 30 k€.

Electric energy: Electric energy (cost approximately 10 c€/kWh) consumed by the plant is considered jointly for the three sections with major electric power engaged:

- Gasification section around 40 kWh/t biomass

- Oxygen section is nearly 0.3 kWh/kg oxygen

- Compression section for PSA at 15–18 bar

Oxygen cost: Cost of oxygen for industrial purposes supplied by the manufacturing companies depends on various factors, in particular, annual consumption, and the distance from the main producing center. On the whole, it varies between 4 and 9 c€/kg. In the present analysis, oxygen cost of 6 c€/kg is applied.

Other relevant costs: Other relevant costs include the cost of chemicals, additives and consumables, mechanical and maintenance operations, etc. On the whole, such cost has a fixed value equivalent to nearly 4% of the cost of investment for the realization of the plant.

Fiscal and financial rate: The main fiscal and financial rates adopted in the present study are the inflation rate 2%, discount rate 5%, and taxation level 35%.

Depreciation: Depreciation of the plant under investigation is regulated for its fiscal effects under the existing norms of law. The percentage values considered appear to be constant over a period of 10 years.

Benefit derived: The benefits obtained are associated with the sale of electric energy produced and the Green Certificates. The gain derived from the sale of electric energy produced has been assumed to be 0.05€/kWh, whereas the gain relevant to the Green Certificates has been assumed to be nearly 0.08 €/kWh.

8.7 RESEARCH ACTIVITIES ON THERMO-CHEMICAL CONVERSION OF WASTE BIOMASS AT ENEA

In the framework of its research activities focused on thermo-chemical conversion of waste biomass for both thermal and electric power, ENEA has developed an industrial scale FICFB gasifier at Trisaia.

The design of the reactor and the use of steam as a gasification agent gives this process a nearly nitrogen-free product gas with a high calorific value of around 12 MJ/Nm³ dry gas. By using a natural catalyst as bed material and gasification temperature above 800°C, the tar content was reduced below 5 g/Nm³. However an adequate purification of the product gas is obtained thanks to the inclusion of a high temperature ceramic filter in the cleaning section. By adding in the reactor specific catalysts, the hydrogen content in the product gas can go over 50% and its quality can be further improved (Figures 8.12 through 8.19).

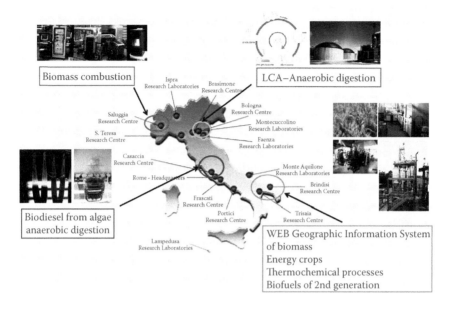

FIGURE 8.12 National distribution of the ENEA's activity regarding the biomass.

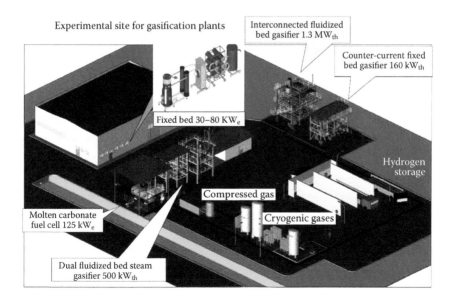

FIGURE 8.13 Experimental platform for gasification plants.

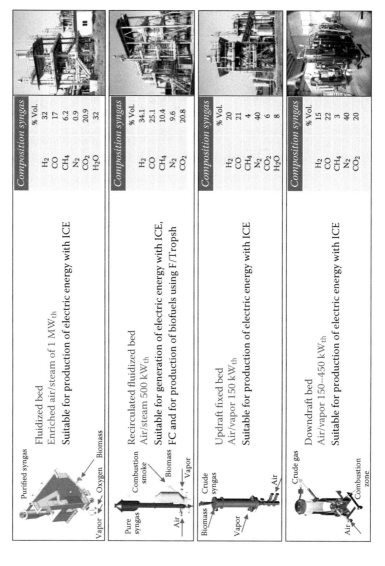

FIGURE 8.14   Development of processes to obtain syngas: ENEA Research Center Trisaia.

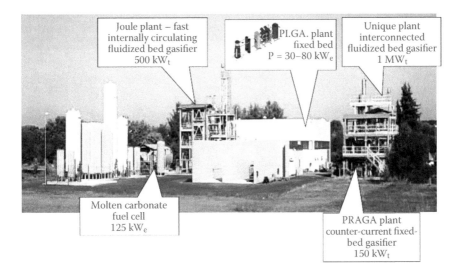

FIGURE 8.15 Current state of the technological platform for the ENEA biomass gasification.

FIGURE 8.16 The 500 KW_{th} FICFB gasifier at Trisaia.

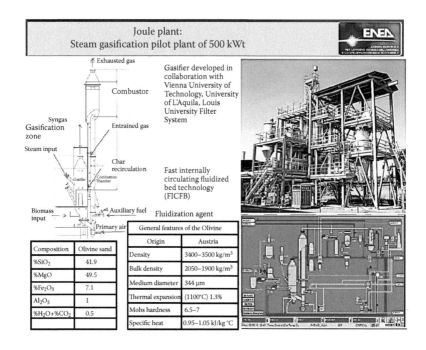

Joule plant:
Steam gasification pilot plant of 500 kWt

ENEA

Exhausted gas

Combustor

Gasifier developed in collaboration with Vienna University of Technology, University of L'Aquila, Louis University Filter System

Syngas
Gasification zone

Entrained gas

Steam input

Char recirculation

Biomass input

Fast internally circulating fluidized bed technology (FICFB)

Auxiliary fuel — Fluidization agent

Primary air

General features of the Olivine

		Origin	Austria
Composition	Olivine sand	Density	3400–3500 kg/m³
%SiO₂	41.9	Bulk density	2050–1900 kg/m³
%MgO	49.5	Medium diameter	344 μm
%Fe₂O₃	7.1	Thermal expansion	(1100°C) 1.3%
Al₂O₃	1	Mohs hardness	6.5–7
%H₂O+%CO₂	0.5	Specific heat	0.95–1.05 kJ/kg °C

FIGURE 8.17 Joule plant: steam gasification pilot plant of 500 KW$_t$.

Fixed bed gasifier plants have been developed, most appropriate for their use, especially in the developing countries as well as for their widespread diffusion at the national level. Fast Internally Circulating Fluidized Bed Gasifier of capacity 500 kWth designed and experimented by research group at ENEA research Centre Trisaia, in Italy.

8.8 CONCLUSIONS

Several economic studies have been made on biomass gasification regarding the feasibility and long-term prospects. The first demonstration projects are mostly far too expensive to become profitable. Investment figures of more than 5000 €/kW electric are not exceptional. However, it is expected that due to the learning curve, the investment costs can be reduced to approximately 2000 €/kW electric within the coming decade.

- Operational experience and value engineering is needed to achieve this goal.

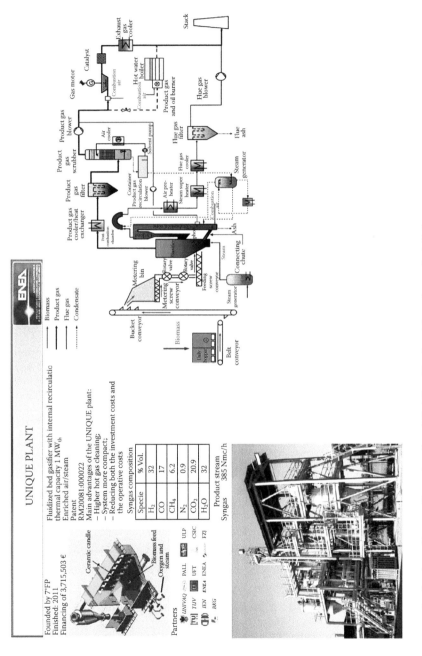

FIGURE 8.18   Joule plant: Internally recirculated fluidized bed gasifier plant of 1 MW$_{th}$.

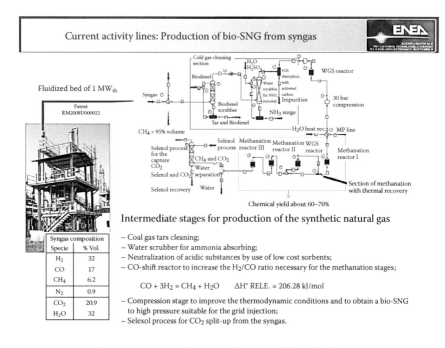

FIGURE 8.19 Current activity lines: production of bio-SNG from syngas.

- Another aspect is the operational costs, in particular the price of the feedstock. These can be expensive such as short rotation coppice (SRC) or cheap (negative) such as waste residues. Transportation, fuel handling, and processing add to the cost of the feedstock.

Furthermore, labour costs must be minimised through process control and automation.

- Practical experience is needed to determine the maintenance costs.

- Remuneration of electricity and heat can also be decisive in the overall economics.

Technical improvement and optimized production systems along with multifunctional land-use could bring biomass close to the costs of fossil fuels. Studies showed that biomass gasification can compete with other RES when capital costs can be reduced and favorable conditions are created.

ACKNOWLEDGMENTS

Valuable work of various authors worldwide reported in the present chapter is duly acknowledged.

III

Nonconventional Energy Resources

CHAPTER 9

Shale Gas in the Energy Basket

Satish Kumar Sinha and Ankit Sharma

CONTENTS

9.1 INTRODUCTION

In the beginning of the twenty-first century, a revolution in energy production came in the form of shale gas. Projections in U.S. energy imports suggest that there is potential for U.S. energy imports and exports to come into balance for the first time since the 1950s and natural gas is going to be the dominant energy export in the coming years. Taking into account different oil and gas price scenarios, Energy Information Administration (EIA) estimates that the transition from a net importer of natural gas to a net exporter is likely to be in 2017 (U.S. Energy Information Administration 2015). Contribution of shale gas production in the United States, which was just 1% of the natural gas supply in 2000, rose to 46.5% of the total natural gas production by 2013. It is expected to contribute more than

55% of the total gas supply in the United States in the next two and a half decades (U.S. Energy Information Administration 2015).

In the shale gas revolution that has changed the oil and gas industry, Barnett shale has been at the core of it and its impact has been enormous. With technological advancements, Barnett shale of Texas was the first shale play to be exploited economically. Mitchell Energy started producing shale gas from Barnett in 1981 but was initially uneconomic. Various fracturing techniques were experimented over 18 years before the slick-water fracturing method turned out to be an economically viable completion method for production of shale gas from Barnett (Miller et al. 2012). Successful development of the Barnett shale resource play is now regarded as the turning point in the shale gas revolution.

Development of shale gas play was not immediate. It has more than two decades of research behind it. The embargo imposed by OPEC countries due to the Arab-Israeli conflict in 1973 (Yom Kippur War) coupled with the rapid decline in domestic natural gas production in the 1970s (Wang and Krupnick 2013) forced the United States to invest heavily in research related to conventional and unconventional energy resources. Unconventional Gas Resource R&D Program was started by the Department of Energy (DOE) in 1976. Eastern Gas Shale Program (1976–1992) operated under the DOE with a total budget of slightly more than $92 million over its 16 years of history. During that time period, several innovative technologies were implemented which later led to commercial technologies (U.S. Department of Energy 2007). The Gas Research Institute (GRI) was established in 1976 with the purpose of management and financing of natural gas-related R&D program in partnership with DOE, USGS, industry and universities. GRI, which later became Gas Technology Institute (GTI), invested $565 million in unconventional gas R&D program until 2004 (Edelstein 2012).

The two technologies that were pivotal in the shale gas revolution are hydraulic fracturing and horizontal well drilling. Although both technologies were known and practiced in the oil and gas industry, it was the synergy between the two that made economic development of shale gas play a reality. In the year 1947, the first hydro-fracturing (or "fracking" as it is called now) was experimented in the oil and gas industry to clean up a clogged formation with drilling mud. The Klepper formation in Hugoton gas field in the United States was fractured using 1000 gallons of a napalm mixture of blended palm oil, napthenic acid, and gasoline with river sand as a proppant (Skelton 2015). During the Eastern Gas Shale Program, GRI and DOE conducted cost-shared stimulation research experiments with industry partners. Initial experiments with different fracturing fluids and proppants were unsatisfactory and cost-prohibitive. However, at the same time, George Mitchell, chairman of Mitchell Energy & Development Corp., who pioneered Barnett shale gas exploitation, made numerous attempts of fracturing shale almost for two decades before achieving economic success in 1998 with the improved slick-water hydro-fracturing technique. The hydro-fracturing technique is applied at a massive scale to propagate fracture network in shales, thus creating permeability pathways.

With the advancements in down-hole motors, down-hole telemetry systems, and other drilling equipment and technologies, horizontal drilling became commercially viable in the 1980s (King 1993). In shale gas exploitation, directionally controlled horizontal well technology is used to maximize contact shale volume per well while intersecting the natural fractures in the shale formations. Furthermore, a horizontal well drilled in a particular azimuth given subsurface stress orientation with multi-stage hydro-fracturing is state-of-the-art technology to unlocking trapped gas from impermeable shales. Propagation of a fracture network is imaged with microseismic imaging technology (Maxwell et al. 2002).

Natural gas, being the cleanest fossil fuel, is preferred among hydrocarbon-based energy sources. Current annual consumption of natural gas is about 122 Tcf for the world (U.S. Energy Information Administration 2014). EIA in its world shale resource assessments reported 7250 Tcf of technically recoverable dry shale gas from 46 countries (Figure 9.1) out of which 1144

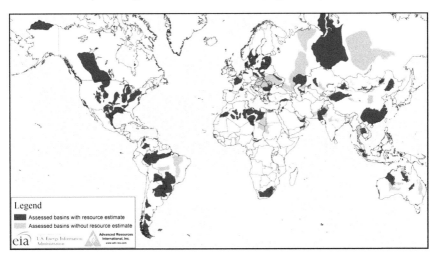

FIGURE 9.1 Map of various basins around the world assessed for shale gas resource estimate. (From https://www.eia.gov/analysis/studies/worldshalegas/.)

Tcf are from shale formations in the United States and Canada alone. Thus, shale gas is to remain an important constituent in the energy basket for decades.

9.2 SHALES AND SHALE GAS

Shales are sedimentary rocks formed from consolidation of silt and clay-sized particles or mud (i.e., grain size smaller than 62.5 μm). Shales mainly comprise clay minerals, quartz, feldspars, carbonate particles, organic material, and small amounts of sulfides and other minerals. The clay minerals, such as illite, smectite, kaolinite, and chlorite, are generally aligned giving fissile character to shales. Although the word shale refers to those mudstones that are fissile or laminated due to preferential alignment of platy clay minerals or phyllosilicates, shales are often used to mean all fine-grained sedimentary rocks (Figure 9.2). Microscopic and SEM pictures analyses provide an estimate of mineral orientation. Recently, Wenk and Houtte (2004), Wenk et al. (2007), and Lonardelli et al. (2007) used a new high-energy synchrotron X-ray method to provide a more quantitative estimate of mineral phase proportion, crystal structure, grain

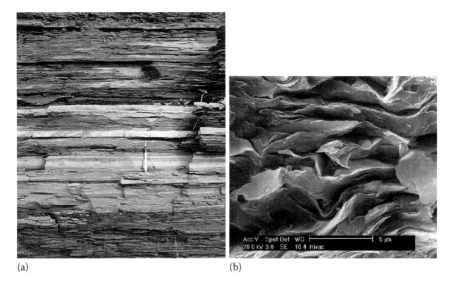

(a)   (b)

FIGURE 9.2 Shales are fissile due to alignment of clay minerals. (a) Shale outcrop with writing pen as a scale. (b) Scanning electron microscope photo of shale showing platy clay minerals. (From National Energy Board, A primer for understanding Canadian shale gas. *Energy Briefing Note*, 27 pp, ISSN 1917-506X, 2009, http://publications.gc.ca/pub?id=9.571462&sl=0.)

size, and preferred orientation of minerals present in the sample. Shales at micro- and nano-scales are being investigated using focused ion-beam (FIB) milling and SEM (Curtis et al. 2010).

Almost 75% of clastic fills of a basin are mudstones (Jones and Wang 1981). However, only organic-rich shales or mudstones are of interest for petroleum exploration and production as they are a source rock for oil and gas generation. Subject to the burial depth and geothermal gradient, shale with high organic content produces oil and gas depending on whether the source rock passed through an oil window or a gas window. Eagleford shale of Western Gulf Basin, United States produces gas from a deeper depth whereas the same at a shallower depth produces oil upon fracking (Cander 2012). Because of micropores in shales, they have very high capillary entry pressure as well as extremely low permeability (Figure 9.2b). They act as seals in conventional petroleum systems and prevent hydrocarbons from migrating across. At the same time, oil and gas have migrated from source rocks to traps through shales over the geological timescale. Thus, understanding of depositional environment and their succession through geological time in a basin is important for shale gas exploration and exploitation.

In conventional petroleum exploration for porous and permeable sandstone and carbonate reservoir rocks, wells have been drilled through volume of shales. However, not much study was done on shales as they were not considered potential reservoir rocks. Shale is often said to be a notorious rock. No two shales are similar. Even within a shale formation, there will be a lot of heterogeneities vertically as well as laterally. Shales can be investigated in different ways:

- Mineralogical and geochemical analysis
- Textural analysis using high resolution optical microscope, scanning electron microprobe (SEM) and FIB-SEM analysis
- Wireline log measurements such as natural gamma ray, resistivity, density, neutron porosity, sonic, etc.
- Laboratory measurements of porosities, permeabilities in shales
- Provenance analysis from grain size statistics and isotopic analysis
- Paleoenvironment conditions from paleontological analysis and trace element compositions

- Hydrocarbon generation potential from maturity studies of organic carbon content using vitrinite reflectance and pyrolysis

There are several books relating to physical properties of shales or mudstones, their depositional environment, clay mineralogy, and geochemistry that can be referred to for further details (Garrels and Mackenzie 1971; Potter et al. 1980, 2005; Wignall 1994; Schieber et al. 1998; Aplin et al. 1999; Harris 2005; Macquaker et al. 2007; Camp et al. 2013; Chamley 2013; Velde 2013).

9.3 GEOLOGICAL EXPLORATION OF SHALES

Faraj et al. (2004) published a brief review of shale gas plays in the United States that reveals a variety of geochemical and geological parameters unique to each play. However, total organic carbon (TOC) is a fundamental attribute of gas shale and is a measure of present-day organic richness. Typically, source rocks contain more than 2% of TOC and can go up to 20–30% of TOC (Tyson 1995). Evolution of gas from source rock could be of biogenic or thermogenic origin. Maturity of organic matter is often expressed in terms of vitrinite reflectance (% Ro), and a value of 1.0–1.1% Ro and above indicates sufficiently mature organic matter to generate gas. The TOC content and its organic maturity indicate hydrocarbon generation potential as well as gas adsorption potential. In general, more matured shale at high temperature and pressure is likely to have more gas. Thus, the thickness of organic shale and its maturity determines the volume of hydrocarbon generated, only a part of which is expelled from the source rock to be trapped in conventional reservoirs of varying porosity and permeability. Furthermore, shale gas reservoirs include not only shales, but also a wide lithological variation from mudstones to siltstones to alternations of thin-bedded shale and fine sandstone. Free gas in micropores and nanopores of shales and adsorbed gas in kerogen add up to total natural gas present in shales (Bustin 2005). Relative abundance of free gas and sorbed gas in shales is an important factor in resource estimation and gas production profile. While there may be varying degrees of existing open natural fractures in shales, permeability of the reservoir is helped by induced fractures providing additional pathways and also connecting existing fractures for gas flow. Thus, a general rule for shale gas exploration would be to target matured organic rich thick shale under high pressure (deeper depth) with high density of existing natural fractures (Rokosh et al. 2009).

The entire thick shale will not have uniform gas content as lateral and vertical lithological variations are observed in shale reservoirs. For shale characterization, it is important to establish lithofacies of shales. Slatt et al. (2008) suggested several steps to be followed for the purpose:

- Establish depositional environment based on biostratigraphic analysis
- Lithofacies characterization of shales in sequence stratigraphic framework from cores and geochemical characteristics of shales
- Calibration of well log measurements to established lithofacies
- Correlate lithofacies from one well to another and build lithofacies map of the area

Based on high resolution lithological characterization study of cores from three wells, Singh et al. (2009) identified nine lithofacies in Barnett shale. Different parasequences were mapped using well log and 3D seismic data.

9.4 GEOPHYSICAL EXPLORATION OF SHALES

Different shales have their unique petrophysical characteristics which impact their fracturing and, hence, productivity. Mineral composition, porosity, permeability, saturation, and TOC content among others affect their petrophysical properties (Sondergeld et al. 2010). Apart from these, compaction, pore pressure, and alignment of clay platelets also control mechanical properties of shales. Not only due to alignment of clays, but oriented cracks also produce anisotropy in shales (Schoenberg and Sayers 1995; Sayers 2004). Full azimuth seismic surveys with anisotropic processing have been successfully used in development of Barnett play. 3-D seismic surveys have been used to determine fracture density and their orientation (Lynn et al. 2011).

It is common to expect preferentially oriented clay minerals in shales, but is not necessarily found in all shales (O'Brien and Slatt 1990). It depends on depositional environment, state of stress, and diagenesis. Seismic attribute assisted lithofacies classification, shale characterization, and fractured zone delineation have been employed in shale gas exploration (Al-Dossary and Marfurt 2006; Zhao et al. 2014). Long-offset full-azimuth 3D seismic in Eagle Ford shale prospecting helped characterize reservoir quality variations, avoid drilling hazards, and predicting sweet spots (Treadgold et al. 2011).

9.5 PRODUCTION TECHNOLOGY

Two technologies have been the key in development of shale gas play: horizontal drilling and hydraulic fracturing (Figure 9.3). Development of polycrystalline diamond compact (PDC) bits and downhole motors led to advancement in horizontal drilling technology (U.S. Department of Energy 2007). Directional and horizontal wells are drilled to improve productivity of shale gas. Horizontal wells are drilled to maximize contact volume per well; they are oriented to intersect a large number of natural fractures and maximize lateral propagation of induced fractures. In 1986, a 2000-ft horizontal well was drilled to intersect natural fractures which resulted in increased initial flow rates that were 10 times higher than the average flow rate of vertical wells (U.S. Department of Energy 2007). In shale gas development wells, lateral section of the horizontal well may range from 1000 ft to more than 5000 ft.

Shales are extremely low permeable rocks, in the range of nanodarcy permeability, virtually making them impermeable rocks. Natural gas trapped within the micropores and nanopores of shales is produced through open natural fractures and/or hydraulically induced fractures. Given sufficient matrix permeability, shales with higher fracture density (i.e., shorter fracture spacing) should yield higher production rates (Bustin et al. 2008), a larger drainage area and, hence, a greater recovery of hydrocarbons (Walser and Pursell 2007; Cramer 2008).

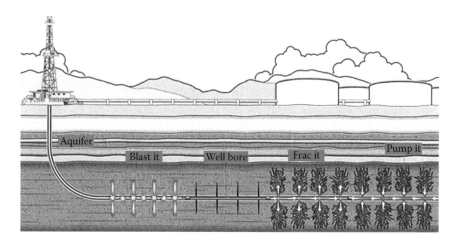

FIGURE 9.3 A schematic to show horizontal well and hydraulic fracturing. (From http://koppillustration.com/.)

In the late 1970s to early 1990s, U.S. Department of Energy (USDOE) in partnership with industry experimented with several stimulation techniques including foam fracturing, massive hydraulic fracturing, chemical explosives, propellants, or high density explosives (U.S. Department of Energy 2007). High pressure fluid is injected into the shale formation to create fractures and then proppants (usually sand) are pushed into the fractures to keep them open. The first successful use of CO_2/sand stimulation in Devonian shale wells of the Appalachian basin became one of the stimulation options in the San Juan basin on a commercial basis (U.S. Department of Energy 2007). In most basins of North America, large-scale massive hydraulic fracturing is conducted in multiple stages to fracture and create permeability throughout the drill length in the shale section. The amount of water needed for fracturing shales depends on the formation properties, well type (vertical/horizontal), the number of stages, and the operator. During the 2009 to mid-2011 period, 2.8 million gallons of water were used per well in Barnett, 4.3 million gallons per well in Eagle Ford, and 5.7 million gallons per well in Haynesville shale (Nicot and Scanlon 2012). Several chemical additives (2% or less) are used in low concentration (Figure 9.4). Functions of chemical additives are summarized in Table 9.1. Grieser et al. (2008) reported that addition of 3% HCl to induced fracturing in Barnett

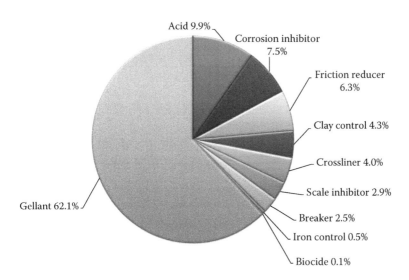

FIGURE 9.4 A typical percentage of the chemical additives used are shown in the pie chart. Chemical additives usually make up less than 2% of the fracking fluid. (Adapted from FracFocus data 2012.)

TABLE 9.1   Commonly Used Fracturing Fluid Additives and Their Purpose

Additive	Compound	Purpose
Diluted acid (15%)	HCl or muriatic acid	To dissolve minerals and initiate cracks
Biocide	Glutaraldehyde	Eliminate corrosive by product producing bacteria
Breaker	Ammonium persulfate	To delay breakdown of the gel polymers
Corrosion inhibitor	N,n-dimethyl formamide	Prevents the corrosion of the pipe
Crosslinker	Borate Salts	Maintains fluid viscosity at elevated temperature
Friction reducer	Polyacrylamide	Reduces friction between the fluid and the pipe
	Mineral oil	
Gel	Guar gum or hydroxyethyl cellulose	Provides suspension to sand by thickening water
Iron control	Citric acid	Prevents precipitation of metal oxides
KCl	Potassium chloride	Creates a brine carrier fluid
Oxygen scavenger	Ammonium bisulfate	Removes oxygen from the water to protect the pipe from corrosion
pH Adjusting agent	Sodium or potassium carbonate	To maintain the effectiveness of other components, such as crosslinker
Proppant	Quartz sand	To keep the fracture open
Scale inhibitor	Ethylene glycol	Prevents scale deposit in the pipe
Surfactant	Isopropanol	To increase viscosity of the fracture fluid

Source: GWPC, ALL Consulting (2009) Modern Shale Gas Development in the U.S.: A Primer. U.S. Department of Energy.

shale increased the daily flow rate by enhancing matrix permeability. A typical horizontal well in Barnett when stimulated with massive hydraulic fracturing would initially produce a few million cubic feet per day. Initial flow rate declines rapidly and in about 3–5 years these wells would produce 200–400 thousand cubic feet per day with no additional fracturing.

Properties of hydro-fracturing fluid, their pump rates, fluid injection points, and proppants affect fracture network, their conductivity, and connectivity. In addition to that, development of fracture geometry is also dependent on formation lithology, present-day subsurface stress condition, natural fractures, and fracture interference. Efficiency of the fracture network will depend on the growth of the fracture network, their complexity, connectivity, and permeability.

9.6 GEOMECHANICS IN SHALE GAS EXPLOITATION

Development of a fracture network in shales affects productivity of shale gas. Fractures propagate when tensile strength of the rock is overcome by the hydraulically induced pressure known as fracture pressure. Fracture gradient and brittleness of the rock is a function of its compaction history, composition (i.e., mineralogy, kerogen type, fraction of heavy hydrocarbons), microcracks, textural variation, alignment of clay minerals, etc. Fractures open in a plane perpendicular to the least principal stress orientation. In many cases, vertical propagation of fractures above or below the shale layer can be detrimental for various reasons. Competence contrast between different layers dictates if the fractures are going to be lithobound (i.e., contained within the intended shale formation).

Shale exhibits permeability lower than coal bed methane (CBM) or tight gas. Hence, not all shale is capable of sustaining an economic rate of production after fracturing. In this respect, permeability of the shale matrix is the most important parameter influencing sustainable shale gas production (Bennett et al. 1991; Davies and Vessell 2002; Gingras et al. 2004; Pemberton and Gingras 2005; Bustin et al. 2008). Therefore, induced fracturing may occur many times during the productive life of a shale gas reservoir (Walser and Pursell 2007). For refracturing of shales, it becomes imperative to build a geomechanical model of the shale reservoir with changing pore pressure and local stress modification.

Shales exhibit varying degree of strength anisotropy depending on the alignment of clay minerals. Mechanical properties of shales measured parallel to the layers are different from those measured perpendicular to the layers (Islam and Skalle 2013; Sone and Zoback 2013a,b). Also, the current state of stress needs to be considered in different tectonic settings. Usually, in extensional settings, vertical induced fractures are common, whereas in compressional settings layer parallel induced fractures may become dominant. Additionally, existing microfractures in different tectonic settings may become important for economic production (Browning et al. 2013).

9.7 IMAGING OF FRACTURES

From mapping of an induced fracture network in Barnett shale, Grieser et al. (2007) suggested that the drainage area is about 14 acres. The pertinent question is: "How do we map fracture propagation in the subsurface?" Microseismic and tiltmeter are the two technologies used for fracture mapping. With opening of hydraulic fractures, the induced deformation

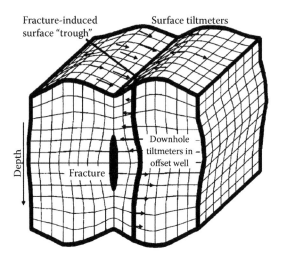

FIGURE 9.5 Displacement field around the induced fracture. The displacement can be measured using a tiltmeter on the surface or in the wellbore. (From Wright CAF, Davis EJF, Wang GF, Weijers LF (1999) Downhole tiltmeter fracture mapping: A new tool for direct measurement of hydraulic fracture growth. Paper presented at the The 37th U.S. Symposium on Rock Mechanics (USRMS), Vail, CO.)

field radiates in all directions and can be measured with a surface and/or downhole array of tiltmeters (Figure 9.5) (Wright et al. 1999). Tiltmeters cannot resolve individual fractures or complex fracture patterns. It is a tool to estimate total fracture volume, fracture azimuth, and depth of fracture. Mapping resolution of azimuth decreases with depth. Downhole monitoring of fracture development with tiltmeter was first introduced by Pinnacle in 1992 (Lewis 2009) and a six-tiltmeter array was first used in 1993 for fracture diagnostics project in the Piceance Basin of Colorado (Wright et al. 1999). Downhole tiltmeter tool is installed in an observation well (or multiple offset wellbores) and provides high resolution in fracture length and height. Resolution of fracture mapping using downhole tiltmeter tool depends on the availability of potential offset observation wells and their distance from the fracturing well. It gives poor definition of the fracture azimuth.

Generation of hydraulic fractures is akin to very small magnitude earthquakes. Thus, by sensing these microseismic events, fractures are mapped given a velocity model of the subsurface (Figure 9.6) (Abaseyev et al. 2009). Given the level of noise present, it is difficult to sense these small magnitude seismic events (−3 to −1 range on the Richter scale) on the surface geophones. Therefore, for microseismic imaging, an array of

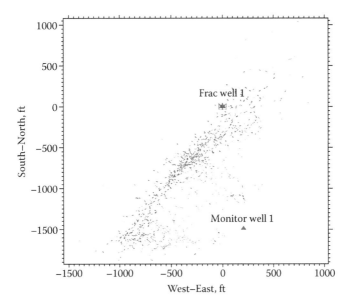

FIGURE 9.6 Mapping of microseismic events to show fracture network from hydraulic fracturing. (From Abaseyev S, Ammerman M, Chesnokov E (2009) Automated detection and location of hydrofracking-induced microseismic event from 3C observations in an offsetting monitor well. In: SEG Technical Program Expanded Abstracts 2009. SEG Technical Program Expanded Abstracts. Society of Exploration Geophysicists, pp. 1514–1518. doi:10.1190/1.3255136.)

multicomponent geophones is installed in an observation well (or multiple offset wellbores).

While the number of microseismic events picked on observed seismograms depends on signal-to-noise ratio, event location is sensitive to the velocity model built for the purpose. It is common to use an isotropic velocity model for approximate locations and hydraulic fracturing pattern recognition. However, for detailed analysis of microseismic events, anisotropic velocity model building is very important as the shales are inherently anisotropic (Thomsen 1986).

Anisotropy of shales is understood via model building for an effective medium. Alignment of clay minerals and/or pore spaces in shales causes seismic anisotropy. The depositional environment plays a huge role in the development of clay fabric in shales. Alignment of clay minerals is categorized as (a) randomly oriented microfabric, (b) poorly oriented microfabric, and (c) well-oriented microfabric (O'Brien and Slatt 1990). Furthermore, the presence of oriented cracks/fractures to enhance permeability also creates anisotropy. A crack is defined as an ellipsoidal open space having aspect ratio less than 1. Usually, anisotropy produced by the gas-filled aligned pores/cracks dominates the anisotropy caused by the alignment of clay minerals (Bayuk and Chesnokov 1998). Water-filled and gas-filled cracks/fractures for different crack porosity have a direct effect on phase velocity (Tiwary et al. 2007). Natural fractures in shale indicate paleostress condition and hydraulic fracture propagation depends on the mechanical properties and current day stress condition in the subsurface (as explained in the previous section). Therefore, fracture patterns need to be integrated in the anisotropic velocity model building process for microseismic imaging. Wave propagation in fractured shale and effect of attenuation on microseismic data caused by fluids in shale has been extensively studied by Sinha et al. (2007).

9.8 ENVIRONMENTAL IMPACT OF SHALE GAS EXPLOITATION

Natural gas, encompassing tight gas, CBM, shale gas, or conventional gas, is seen as the cleanest fossil fuel. However, tremendous development of shale gas play in the United States has come at some negative social costs. Intense drilling and fracking activity was unseen and unheard of in the past among the people of different parts of the country. Fracturing requires huge amounts of water (~2 to 8 million gallons of water per well). One horizontal well is estimated to require about 1500 to 2000 truck trips (18 wheeler trucks with 80,000 pounds of truckload each) to and from well site (Zucker 2014), which can be ruinous to roads and bridges in the towns (Figure 9.7).

When drilling activities are not conducted in accordance with the set guidelines, laws, and drilling principles, it is bound to create an adverse impact on the environment. Places where hydraulic fracturing waste fluids with hazardous chemicals are illegally discharged into surface water and ponds, dumped into open pits and surrounding jungles, environmental and health concerns arise. Contamination of groundwater aquifers is yet another environmental challenge. Groundwater resources need to be protected from hydraulic fracture treatments and subsequent migration of gas through not so well cemented zones between casing and formations. Absence of best industry practices has led to anti-fracking hysteria. The "GASLAND" documentary by Josh Fox (http://www.gaslandthemovie .com/home), which was first screened at the Sundance Film Festival in 2010 and a special jury prize winner, still remains popular and the source

FIGURE 9.7   A typical drilling site bird's eye view showing a huge number of trucks involved in hydraulic fracturing. (From: Groundwater Protection Council 2012.)

of knowledge among environmental and political activists throughout the world. The Environmental Protection Agency (EPA) has been empowered by the federal government of the United States with several regulations, such as The Clean Water Act, Safe Drinking Water Act, Resource Conservation and Recovery Act, to oversee the program. The EPA is also considering rules for mandatory disclosure of chemicals used in hydraulic fracturing (Trager 2014).

In recent years, there has been increased seismic activity in Oklahoma. In 2014, nearly 600 earthquakes of magnitude 3+ were recorded. It has now been established that these induced seismicity are not due to hydraulic fracturing of shale formations but are triggered by injecting wastewater into the deep Arbuckle formation (Walsh and Zoback 2015).

9.9 SUMMARY

Among all the fossil fuels natural gas burns cleanly and emits the lowest amount of carbon dioxide per calorie. Natural gas that can be produced from shale formations is in abundance in most of the petroliferous basins of the world. A combination of two technologies, namely, hydraulic fracturing and horizontal well drilling, made economic exploitation of shale gas possible. Revolution in shale gas production started from Barnett shale in the Fort Worth basin of Texas, and gradually spread in many parts of continental North America in a short span of time. Rapid expansion of shale gas in the natural gas energy mix has changed the energy geopolitics and governments all over the world are formulating strategy to assess and exploit shale gas resources available in their countries.

No two shale formations are similar and, therefore, systematic evaluation of their hydrocarbon generation potential should be carried out based on their geological and geomechanical properties. Shale formations with high TOC at deeper depth with high pore pressure and high fracture density (natural or induced) are likely to produce at a high initial flow rate. Decline in the flow rate over years would depend on many factors including local stress condition and type of gas (free gas versus desorbed gas) being produced. Therefore, economics of shale gas production should be carried out with prevailing gas prices in the area.

Fracturing of shale formation requires a huge volume of water, which has been a big hurdle in shale gas development around the world. Sourcing of water and wastewater disposal is a challenge. For success of shale gas exploitation, it is essential that society, in general, is taken into confidence and issues raised by environmental and political activists are addressed with scientific explanation. Following best industry practices holds the key to success of shale gas exploitation.

REFERENCES

Abaseyev S, Ammerman M, Chesnokov E (2009) Automated detection and location of hydrofracking-induced microseismic event from 3C observations in an offsetting monitor well. In: SEG Technical Program Expanded Abstracts 2009. SEG Technical Program Expanded Abstracts. Society of Exploration Geophysicists, pp. 1514–1518. doi:10.1190/1.3255136.

Al-Dossary S, Marfurt KJ (2006) 3D volumetric multispectral estimates of reflector curvature and rotation. *Geophysics* 71 (5): 41–51. doi:10.1190/1.2242449.

Aplin AC, Fleet AJ, Macquaker JH (1999) Muds and mudstones: Physical and fluid-flow properties. *Geological Society,* London, Special Publications 158 (1): 1–8.

Bayuk IO, Chesnokov EM (1998) Correlation between elastic and transport properties of porous cracked anisotropic media. *Physics and Chemistry of the Earth* 23 (3): 361–366.

Bennett RH, Bryant WR, Hulbert MH (eds) (1991) *Microstructure of Fine-Grained Sediments: From Mud to Shale. Frontiers in Sedimentary Geology.* Springer-Verlag, New York.

Browning J, Ikonnikova S, Gülen G, Tinker S (2013) Barnett shale production outlook. *SPE Economics & Management* 5 (3): 89–104. doi:10.2118/165585-PA.

Bustin AMM, Bustin RM, Cui X (2008) Importance of fabric on the production of gas shales. Paper presented at the SPE Unconventional Reservoirs Conference, Keystone, Colorado.

Bustin RM (2005) Gas Shale Tapped for Big Pay. AAPG Explorer. AAPG, Tulsa, OK.

Camp WK, Diaz E, Wawak B (Eds.) (2013) AAPG Memoir 102: Electron Microscopy of Shale Hydrocarbon Reservoirs. The Americal Association of Petroleum Geologists, Tulsa, OK.

Cander H (2012) Sweet spots in shale gas and liquids plays: Prediction of fluid composition and reservoir pressure. *Search and Discovery* Article 40936.

Chamley H (2013) *Clay Sedimentology*. Springer Science & Business Media.

Cramer DD (2008) Stimulating Unconventional reservoirs: Lessons learned, successful practices, areas for improvement. Paper presented at the SPE Unconventional Reservoirs Conference, Keystone, CO.

Curtis ME, Ambrose RJ, Sondergeld CH (2010) Structural characterization of gas shales on the micro- and nano-scales. Paper presented at the Canadian Unconventional Resources and International Petroleum Conference, Calgary, Alberta, Canada.

Davies DK, Vessell RK (2002) Gas production from shales. In: Scott ED, Bouma AH (Eds.) Depositional Processes and Characteristics of Siltstones, Mudstones and Shales: Special Symposium: 2002 GCAGS Annual Meeting. *GCAGS Transactions*, vol 52. pp. 1079–1091.

Edelstein R (2012) R&D – building the pathway to the shale gas revolution. Paper presented at the NARUC Summer Committee Meetings, Portland, OR.

Faraj B, Williams H, Addison G, McKinstry B (2004) Gas potential of selected shale formations in the western Canadian sedimentary basin. *GasTIPS* 10 (1): 21–25.

Garrels RM, Mackenzie FT (1971) *Evolution of Sedimentary Rocks*. Norton, New York.

Gingras MK, Mendoza CA, Pemberton SG (2004) Fossilized worm burrows influence the resource quality of porous media. *AAPG Bulletin* 88 (7): 875–883.

Grieser WV, Shelley RF, Johnson BJ, Fielder EO, Heinze JR, Werline JR (2008) Data analysis of Barnett shale completions. *SPE Journal* 13 (3): 366–374. doi:10.2118/100674-PA.

Grieser WV, Wheaton WE, Magness WD, Blauch ME, Loghry R (2007) Surface reactive fluid's effect on shale. Paper presented at the Production and Operations Symposium, Oklahoma City, OK.

GWPC, ALL Consulting (2009) Modern Shale Gas Development in the U.S.: A Primer. U.S. Department of Energy.

Harris NB (2005) The deposition of organic-carbon-rich sediments: Models, mechanisms, and consequences. *SEPM*, SP-82. Tulsa, OK.

Islam MA, Skalle P (2013) An experimental investigation of shale mechanical properties through drained and undrained test mechanisms. *Rock Mech Rock Eng* 46(6): 1391–1413. doi:10.1007/s00603-013-0377-8.

Jones LEA, Wang HF (1981) Ultrasonic velocities in Cretaceous shales from the Williston basin. *Geophysics* 46(3): 288–297. doi:10.1190/1.1441199.

King RF (1993) Drilling sideways—A review of horizontal well technology and its domestic application. *Natural Gas Monthly*. Energy Information Administration, U.S. DOE, Washington, DC.

Lewis J (2009) Monitoring fractures with tiltmeters and microseismics. Future Energy Publishing. http://www.findingpetroleum.com/.

Lonardelli I, Wenk H, Ren Y (2007) Preferred orientation and elastic anisotropy in shales. *Geophysics* 72(2): D33–D40. doi:10.1190/1.2435966.

Lynn HB, Veta L, Michelena RJ (2011) Introduction to this special section: Practical applications of anisotropy. *The Leading Edge* 30(7): 726–730. doi:10.1190/1.3609086.

Macquaker JHS, Taylor KG, Gawthorpe RL (2007) High-resolution facies analyses of mudstones: Implications for paleoenvironmental and sequence stratigraphic interpretations of offshore ancient mud-dominated successions. *Journal of Sedimentary Research* 77(4): 324–339. doi:10.2110/jsr.2007.029.

Maxwell SC, Urbancic TI, Steinsberger N, Zinno R (2002) Microseismic imaging of hydraulic fracture complexity in the Barnett shale. Paper presented at the SPE Annual Technical Conference and Exhibition, San Antonio, TX.

Miller R, Loder A, Polson J (2012) Americans Gaining Energy Independence with U.S. as Top Producer. Bloomberg, Feb 7, 2012.

Nicot J-P, Scanlon BR (2012) Water use for shale-gas production in Texas, U.S. *Environmental Science & Technology* 46 (6): 3580–3586. doi:10.1021/es204602t.

O'Brien NR, Slatt RM (1990) *Argillaceous Rock Atlas*. Springer, New York. doi:10.1007/978-1-4612-3422-7.

Pemberton SG, Gingras MK (2005) Classification and characterizations of biogenically enhanced permeability. *AAPG Bulletin* 89 (11): 1493–1517.

Potter PE, Maynard JB, Depetris PJ (2005) *Mud and Mudstones: Introduction and Overview*. Springer Science and Business Media.

Potter PE, Maynard JB, Pryor WA (1980) *Sedimentology of Shale*. Springer-Verlag.

Rokosh CD, Pawlowicz JG, Berhane H, Anderson SDA, Beaton AP (2009) What is shale gas? An introduction to shale-gas geology in Alberta. Energy Resources Conservation Board, ERCB/AGS Open File Report 2008-08, Edmonton, Alberta.

Sayers CM (2004) Seismic anisotropy of shales: What determines the sign of Thomsen's delta parameter? *SEG Technical Program Expanded Abstracts* 2004: 103–106. doi:10.1190/1.1845094.

Schieber J, Zimmerle W, Sethi P (Eds.) (1998) *Shales and Mudstones*. Schweizerbart'sche Verlagsbuchhandlung, Stuttgart, Germany.

Schoenberg M, Sayers C (1995) Seismic anisotropy of fractured rock. *Geophysics* 60 (1): 204–211. doi:10.1190/1.1443748.

Singh P, Slatt R, Borges G, Perez R, Portas R, Marfurt K, Ammerman M, Coffey W (2009) Reservoir characterization of unconventional gas shale reservoirs: Example from the Barnett Shale, Texas, USA. *The Shale Shaker* 60 (1): 15–31.

Sinha S, Abaseyev S, Chesnokov E (2007) Full-waveform synthetics and its spectral characteristics in multilayered anisotropic attenuating media. In: SEG Technical Program Expanded Abstracts 2007. SEG Technical Program Expanded Abstracts. Society of Exploration Geophysicists, pp. 144–148. doi:10.1190/1.2792399.

Skelton LH (2015) *Digging the roots of hydraulic fracturing.* AAPG Explorer. AAPG, Tulsa, OK.

Slatt RM, Singh P, Philp RP, Marfurt KJ, Abousleiman YN, O'Brien NR (2008) Workflow for stratigraphic characterization of unconventional gas shales. Paper presented at the SPE Shale Gas Production Conference, Fort Worth, TX.

Sondergeld CH, Newsham KE, Comisky JT, Rice MC, Rai CS (2010) Petrophysical considerations in evaluating and producing shale gas resources. *Society of Petroleum Engineers.* doi:10.2118/131768-MS.

Sone H, Zoback MD (2013a) Mechanical properties of shale-gas reservoir rocks—Part 1: Static and dynamic elastic properties and anisotropy. *Geophysics* 78 (5): D381–D392. doi:10.1190/geo2013-0050.1.

Sone H, Zoback MD (2013b) Mechanical properties of shale-gas reservoir rocks—Part 2: Ductile creep, brittle strength, and their relation to the elastic modulus. *Geophysics* 78 (5): D393–D402. doi:10.1190/geo2013-0051.1.

Thomsen L (1986) Weak elastic anisotropy. *Geophysics* 51 (10): 1954–1966. doi:10.1190/1.1442051.

Tiwary D, Bayuk I, Vikhorev A, Ammerman M, Chesnokov E (2007) Comparison of seismic upscaling methods. In: SEG Technical Program Expanded Abstracts 2007. SEG Technical Program Expanded Abstracts. Society of Exploration Geophysicists, pp. 2723–2727. doi:10.1190/1.279303210.1190/1.2793032.

Trager R (2014) Backlash as EPA considers fracking chemicals disclosure rules. *ChemistryWorld.* http://www.rsc.org/chemistryworld/2014/09/fracking-chemicals-transparency.

Treadgold G, Campbell B, McLain B, Sinclair S, Nicklin D (2011) Eagle Ford shale prospecting with 3D seismic data within a tectonic and depositional system framework. *The Leading Edge* 30 (1): 48–53. doi:10.1190/1.3535432.

Tyson RV (1995) *Sedimentary Organic Matter—Organic Facies and Palynofacies.* Springer, the Netherlands. doi:10.1007/978-94-011-0739-6.

U.S. Department of Energy (2007) DOE's Unconventional Gas Research Programs 1976–1995: An Archive of Important Results (trans: Laboratory NET). NETL, Strategic Center for Natural Gas and Oil.

U.S. Energy Information Administration (2014) International Energy Statistics. http://www.eia.gov/cfapps/ipdbproject/IEDIndex3.cfm?tid=3&pid=26&aid=2. Accessed April 15, 2015.

U.S. Energy Information Administration (2015) U.S. energy imports and exports to come into balance for first time since 1950s. http://www.eia.gov/todayinenergy/detail.cfm?id=20812. Accessed April 15, 2015.

Velde B (Ed.) (2013) *Origin and Mineralogy of Clays: Clays and the Environment.* Springer-Verlag, Berlin.

Walser DW, Pursell DA (2007) Making mature shale gas plays commercial: Process vs. natural parameters. Paper presented at the Eastern Regional Meeting, Lexington, KY.

Walsh FR, Zoback MD (2015) Oklahoma's recent earthquakes and saltwater disposal. *Science Advances* 1 (5): 1–9. doi:10.1126/sciadv.1500195.

Wang Z, Krupnick A (2013) A retrospective review of shale gas development in the United States: What led to the boom? *Resources for the Future DP* 13 (12): 1–39.

Wenk H, Lonardelli I, Franz H, Nihei K, Nakagawa S (2007) Preferred orientation and elastic anisotropy of illite-rich shale. *Geophysics* 72(2): E69–E75. doi:10.1190/1.2432263.

Wenk HR, Houtte PV (2004) Texture and anisotropy. *Reports on Progress in Physics* 67 (8): 1367.

Wignall PB (1994) *Black Shales,* vol 30. Oxford Science Publications.

Wright CAF, Davis EJF, Wang GF, Weijers LF (1999) Downhole tiltmeter fracture mapping: A new tool for direct measurement of hydraulic fracture growth. Paper presented at the The 37th U.S. Symposium on Rock Mechanics (USRMS), Vail, CO.

Zhao T, Jayaram V, Marfurt KJ, Zhou H (2014) Lithofacies classification in Barnett shale using proximal support vector machines. *SEG Technical Program Expanded Abstracts* 2014: 1491–1495. doi:10.1190/segam2014-1210.1.

Zucker HA (2014) A public health review of high volume hydraulic fracturing for shale gas development. Department of Health, New York.

CHAPTER 10

Energy Security and Sustainability through Wind Energy

Om Prakash, Saket Pratap, and Anil Kumar

CONTENTS

10.1 INTRODUCTION

In essence, wind is actually another form of solar energy. On a global scale, uneven heating of the Earth's surface combined with the rotation of the planet causes convective currents that run generally from the lower latitudes toward the higher latitudes. The sun is the source of wind energy. Solar rays come down, hit the Earth's surface, and heat it up. Wind is created by the unevenly heating of the Earth's surface. The irregularities of the Earth cause the sun's rays to heat differently from one area to the next. These areas are between the equator and the polar regions. These create areas with different pressures; nature will balance these differences by moving higher pressure air toward the lower pressure air, which is called wind. The wind is the by-product of solar energy. Approximately 2% of the sun's energy reaching the Earth is converted into wind energy (www .centurionenergy.com). The surface of the Earth heats and cools unevenly, creating atmospheric pressure zones that make air flow from high- to low-pressure areas. Solar radiation differentially absorbed by the Earth's surface is converted through convective processes due to temperature differences between the air. Conversions of kinetic energy into mechanical energy can be performed to generate electricity. Solar radiation heats the air near the equator, and this low density heated air is buoyed up (Sharma et al., 2015). Wind energy systems are energized due to the natural flow of wind; therefore, it is a clean source of energy. Wind energy does not pollute the environment. Wind turbines do not produce atmospheric emissions that can cause acid rain or greenhouse gases (Wagner and Mathew, 2009) Wind turbines working due to turning the kinetic energy of the wind into torque (a force) causes the wind turbine to turn and drives an electrical generator.

The circulation of air in the atmosphere is caused by heating of the Earth's surface at different locations, due to variation in Earth's temperature wind is generated. The nature of the terrain, the degree of cloud cover, and the angle of the sun in the sky are all factors that influence this process. In general, during the day air above the land mass tends to heat up more rapidly than the air over water. In coastal regions, this manifests itself in a strong onshore wind. At night, the process is reversed because the air cools down more rapidly over the land.

10.1.1 Wind Energy and Its Environmental Effects

Wind energy can play a critical role in saving our planet from the negative effects of energy powered by fossil fuels. Wind power alone cannot solve the world's energy crisis. For example, wind power cannot power vehicles beyond electric vehicles. But, there are definite possibilities in using wind power to both coexist with and supplant other energy sources to work as a total package in attacking the world's energy crisis. The biggest hurdle in wind energy development is how to store the excess wind for use when the wind does not blow. Typically, as the wind blows, energy is transferred to the electrical grid for immediate use. But when the wind stops blowing, grid managers must switch over to traditional electricity to maintain power. Wind power has since developed in its efficiency and its ability to produce electricity, the form of energy we most commonly associate with wind turbines today. Horizontal or vertical axis, facing into or away from the wind, the number and type of blades, and the construction materials, all aspects are variable. The basic components and processes of a wind energy conversion system are shown in Figure 10.1. Conversion of kinetic energy into mechanical energy can be performed to generate electricity.

The wind is made up of real matter with mass. When mass is moving it has kinetic energy. As the wind causes the wind turbine to turn,

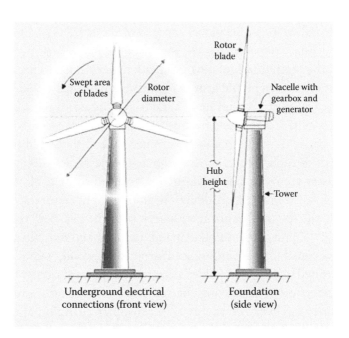

FIGURE 10.1   Wind energy conversion system. (Drawing of the rotor and blades of a wind turbine, courtesy of ESN. From http://data.naturalcapitalproject.org.)

we are reducing the energy in the wind (Wagner and Mathew, 2009). The energy removed from the wind is converted into mechanical energy that is used to drive an electrical generator and is then converted into electrical energy. The process of converting wind into mechanical energy starts with the wind turbine blades.

10.2 WORLDWIDE STATUS OF WIND ENERGY

As demand for energy increases, wind is seen as one of the key future sources of electricity generation. The installed capacity of wind power is growing rapidly. Electricity produced by wind turbines is generated with significantly lower lifetime CO_2 emissions than the global average for electricity production. There is growing awareness that increased deployment of renewable energy (and energy efficiency) is critical for addressing climate change, creating new economic opportunities, and providing energy access to the billions of people still living without modern energy services.

Solar photovoltaic (PV) is starting to play a substantial role in electricity generation in some countries as rapidly falling costs have made unsubsidized solar PV-generated electricity cost-competitive with fossil fuels in an increasing number of locations around the world. In 2014, solar PV marked another record year for growth, with an estimated 40 GW installed for a total global capacity of about 177 GW. China, Japan, and the United States accounted for the vast majority of new capacity. Even so, the distribution of new installations continued to broaden, with Latin America seeing rapid growth, significant new capacity added in several African countries, and new markets picking up in the Middle East. Although most EU markets declined for the third consecutive year, the region—particularly Germany—continued to lead the world in terms of total solar PV capacity and contribution to the electricity supply. The solar PV industry recovery that began in 2013 continued in 2014, thanks to a strong global market. Consolidation among manufacturers continued, although the flood of bankruptcies seen over the past few years slowed to a trickle. To meet the rising demand, new cell and module production facilities opened (or were announced) around the world. Although discussion is limited to date, renewables also are an important element of climate change adaptation, improving the resilience of existing energy systems and ensuring delivery of energy services under changing climatic conditions. Worldwide wind power installed capacity in year 2013 and 2014 from different countries is mentioned in Table 10.1.

TABLE 10.1   Wind Power Capacity Installation in Different Countries

Country	Installed Capacity (MW)	
	2013	2014
Morocco	487	787
Egypt	550	610
South Africa	10	570
Tunisia	245	245
Ethiopia	171	171
Cape Verde	24	24
Other	115	129
Pr China	91,413	114,609
India	20,150	22,465
Japan	2669	2789
Taiwan	614	633
South Korea	561	609
Thailand	223	223
Pakistan	106	256
Philippines	66	216
Other	167	167
Germany	34,250	39,165
Spain	22,959	22,987
United Kingdom	10,711	12,440
France	8243	9285
Italy	8558	8663
Sweden	4382	5425
Portugal	4730	4914
Denmark	4807	4883
Poland	3390	3834
Turkey	2958	3763
Brazil	3466	5939
Chile	31	836
Uruguay	59	464
Peru	2	148
Cambean	250	250
United States	61,110	65,879
Canada	7823	9694
Mexico	1917	2551
Australia	3239	3806
New Zealand	623	623
Pacific Islands	12	12

Source: www.gwec.net

10.2.1 Asia

Asia was the world's largest regional market for wind energy, with capacity additions totaling just over 26 GW (www.gwec.net).

China installed 16 GW of new capacity. China should double its wind capacity to 200 GW by the end of 2020.

India's new wind energy installations reached 2315 MW by the end of 2013, for a total of 22,465 MW (www.gwec.net).

The Japanese new installations of 130.4 MW in 2014 reached a cumulative capacity of 2788.5 MW.

The Indian wind industry has a de facto target of 5 GW per annum for the rest of the decade and into the next. We don't expect it to reach that level in 2015, but it will move in that direction and get close by the end of the five-year period. Elsewhere in Asia, we are seeing the basis for strong growth in Pakistan and the Philippines, and Taiwan and Thailand continue to surprise. Japan will start to grow again in 2015, but the slow pace of electricity market reform and the hesitation to unbundle the existing utilities means that it will be slow to realize its potential; and the slow pace of onshore development in Korea means that we will not see much from that market until the offshore market starts to get built out toward the end of the decade. Overall, however, we're expecting an additional 140 GW to be installed in the region between now and the end of 2019, a doubling of the existing installed capacity.

10.2.2 Africa

South Africa took off in 2014, installing 560 MW of new capacity, for a cumulative capacity of 570 MW. It's just a beginning of the wind market in the country.

Morocco had an exceptional year as well, as the 300 MW Tarfaya wind farm (Africa's largest) came online. They brought the total installed capacity in Morocco to over 786 MW for the first time since 2010 (www .gwec.net).

Egypt added new capacity. Egypt saw 60 MW of new installed capacity for a total of 610 MW.

Kenya added 13.6 MW at the N gong II wind farm, located 30 km west of Nairobi.

Ethiopia has two wind farms in operation: the 51 MW Adama I wind farm, which began production in 2011; another is the 120 MW Ashegoda wind farm, started in October 2013.

South Africa's "ReBid" programme. Wind energy represents 630 MW of a total of 1450 MW of renewable power in the first round of bidding and may be awarded another 1200 MW in the remaining rounds to be announced in 2012. This round was the first bidding under South Africa's long-range plan, which envisages more than 8000 MW of wind energy by 2030. Brazil benefits from unique climatic circumstances, with good complementarities between hydropower and wind, which eases the integration of wind energy to the grid. High-wind seasons are drier and low-wind seasons are humid, while average wind speeds are higher and lead to high wind capacity factors. Although the economic crisis of 2008–2009 created a lack of liquidity in the global markets, the support from BNDES allowed the wind industry to develop in Brazil. The success of the auctioning system was made possible inter alia due to the availability of cheaper and accessible domestic finance, and oversupply in the wind industry globally.

10.2.3 Australia

The climate and energy logic, as well as Australia's tremendous wind resources mean that this is going to be a strong market again. The situation has not improved in New Zealand, and although there are some projects in the pipeline in the Pacific Islands, they will take some time to mature. We expect only about 4 GW to be added in this region over the next five years. Australia's wind farms are mostly distributed along its southern coastline and to the west, which are the regions with the most favorable wind resources. Most states have multiple wind farms, with the exception of the sparsely populated Northern Territory and Queensland, which has only one small wind farm. South Australia remains the state with the highest wind power capacity, successfully capitalizing on an excellent wind resource, a relatively small population, and government policies supportive of investment. It produced more than 33% of its electricity from wind power between mid-2013 and mid-2014. Installed wind capacity in Australia by state will be increased up to 58.51% through upcoming 16 projects (www.gwec.net).

10.2.4 Europe

A total of 129 GW of wind energy capacity was installed in the European Union at the end of 2014, 9.8% more than at the end of 2013. Germany has the largest installed capacity, followed by Spain, the United Kingdom, France, and Italy. Ten EU countries have over 1 GW of installed capacity: Austria, Belgium, Denmark, Greece, Ireland, the Netherlands, Poland,

Portugal, Romania and Sweden (www.gwec.net). The offshore segment seems to be in a much healthier place than it was at this time last year, with more realistic targets and a stronger financial base, as well as a greater diversity of suppliers of the next generation of >5 MW machines which will be rolled out in earnest over the next few years. On the whole, we expect Europe to continue its march toward its 2020 targets, installing about 70 GW over the next five years.

10.2.5 North America

In Canada in 2014, 1871 MW of new wind capacity came online, making it the sixth largest market globally. Compared to 1609 MW in 2013, Canada's wind power market saw significant growth in 2014, its best year ever. Canada finished 2014 with nearly 9700 MW of total installed capacity, supplying approximately 4% of Canada's electricity demand. In 2014, wind energy projects were built and commissioned in the Canadian provinces of Ontario, Quebec, Alberta, Nova Scotia, and Prince Edward Island. The United States is the second largest market in terms of total installed capacity (www.gwec.net).

10.2.6 South America

The Latin American market installed over 1 GW of new capacity. In 2012, the region installed 1225 MW of new wind capacity of total installed capacity over 3.5 GW. In 2013, Brazil, Chile, Argentina, Dominican Republic, and Uruguay accounted for 1219 MW of new wind power capacity for a total installed capacity of 4.7 GW. Brazil has one of the cleanest energy matrices in the world with hydropower providing 67% of the total installed capacity (Aneel, 2011). In the 1990s, Brazil faced a period of rapid economic growth, which led to a rapid increase in energy demand, particularly in the northeast of the country. Brazil faced a very serious energy crisis between 2000 and 2002 (California Energy Commission, 2011). In 2014, Brazil, Chile, Uruguay, Peru, Argentina, Honduras, Costa Rica, Nicaragua, Venezuela, and Ecuador have supported many wind energy projects for electricity generation (www.gwec.net).

10.3 WIND ENERGY POLICY

10.3.1 India

The government of India to develop an offshore wind farm has decided to have a policy that would enable optimum exploitation of offshore wind energy in the best interest of the nation and to achieve the following objectives. Offshore wind energy is shown in Figure 10.2.

- Develop and promote deployment of offshore wind farms in the exclusive economic zone (EEZ) of the country.

- Spatial planning and management of maritime renewable energy resources in the EZZ of the country.

- To set aim of energy security.

- Reduction of carbon emissions.

- To promote indigenization of the offshore wind energy technology.

- Offshore wind energy is encouraged in the sector of research and development.

- Skilled manpower and employment in the offshore wind energy sector.

- Coastal infrastructure and supply chain to support heavy construction and fabrication work and the operation and maintenance activities.

FIGURE 10.2   Offshore wind energy. (From http://350nh.org.)

10.3.2 France

Ecologically responsible production and consumption. The purpose of these programs is to develop organizational and technological responses to reduce the environmental and energy impact of human activities.

- Bioenergy and bioproducts.
- Capture and storage of CO_2.
- Eco-technologies and processes for better air and soil quality and cleaner waste management.
- Generation of electricity from renewable resources.
- To promote smart grids and energy storage.

Sustainable cities and regions. These programs are designed to increase our knowledge of the effects of human activity on the environment and on human health and behavior.

- Impact of soil pollution, environmental assessment of wastes, and sustainable soil management practices.
- Socioeconomic forecasting.
- Clean and green transportation. In these major research areas, ADEME is developing forecasting exercises in cooperation with experts from public-sector research bodies and private enterprise.
- Second-generation bio-fuel.
- Positive-energy and low-carbon buildings and developments.
- CO_2 capture and underground sequestering.
- Private motor vehicles and fuels in 2050.

10.3.3 China

Environmental and social benefits will be considerable if the above targets are realized. Annual CO_2 emission mitigation will be 1.5 billion tonnes in 2050. China's energy resources are abundant, but less so on a per-capita basis; high-quality resources are limited, unevenly distributed, and difficult to develop. China has abundant coal, but oil, natural gas, and other fossil energy resources are limited. Oil shale, coal bed methane, and other unconventional fossil energy reserves may have great potential. China's coal, hydro and wind energy resources are mainly located in the west, while the principal load centers are in the east. Therefore, large-scale and long-distance transmission of coal and electricity form the basis of China's energy development and utilization. Wind power is becoming a vital part of low-carbon energy strategies aimed at dealing with energy supply and environmental challenges. According to an assessment of wind resource potential and an analysis of development costs, China has economically exploitable wind power potential of at least 1 TW in the long term, so ambitious long-term wind power development objectives are warranted. China's wind industry has seen one of the steepest learning and shortest experience curves in the wind industry. The growth of the wind industry started with the adoption of the comprehensive Renewable Energy Law passed in 2005. Thereafter, the policy frameworks were updated through five-year plans, allowing any deficiencies in the policy or incentives to be addressed on a regular basis. A series of auctions enabled to gain experience on the price of the electricity generated from wind power, and to define the level of feed-in tariffs (FIT). The government stimulated the strong existing industrial base, and enabled the creation of a strong domestic manufacturing capacity. Today, China is the market leader both in terms of cumulative installation and manufacturing capacity.

10.3.4 Germany

The government adopted the "Energy Concept," which includes long-term climate and energy targets. As a response to the nuclear disaster in Fukushima in 2011, Germany decided on the gradual phasing-out of nuclear power by 2022, greater energy efficiency, and an accelerated growth of renewable energies (Lehr et al., 2011). These decisions supplemented and accelerated the implementation of the measures set out in the "Energy Concept." The offshore wind energy capacity increased to 108 MW in 2011, and is expected to reach 3 GW by 2015. To date, the national maritime authority and the federal states have licensed 24 projects, bringing the overall capacity close to 7 GW. Germany is among the early pioneers of wind energy in Europe, with one of the most consistent renewable energy policy frameworks since the late 1980s. The desire for energy independence combined with prominent public support for addressing climate change led to a high level of commitment to developing renewable energy. The main conditions supporting the uptake of wind energy were

1. A clear and long-term price stability through the FIT mechanism.

2. Priority grid access.

3. Local and regional banks made financing available.

4. Early and strong political commitment to renewable energy.

10.4 CASE STUDY

10.4.1 Case Study 1

The vision of the UN Intergovernmental Panel on Climate Change (IPCC) is to limit the global average temperature increase to no more than 2°C (3.6°F) above the preindustrial level. This will require global CO_2 emissions to be half of 1990 levels by 2050 (Global Wind Energy Council, 2008).

This case study shows steel is contributing to the reduction of CO_2 emissions significantly, by reducing the CO_2 intensity of power generation and the dependency on fossil fuels, by being the most important material in wind energy production (Figure 10.3). The European Union Climate and Energy package includes a target that 20% of all energy production by 2020 will be by renewable means (Gipe, 2004). Wind power will play a significant role in achieving this target. Over 20 GW of wind power was installed globally in 2007, led by the United States, China, and Spain, bringing worldwide installed capacity to 94 GW, an increase of about 27%. The rate of installation is increasing, with the 2007 figure being 31% greater than the capacity installed in 2006. Wind energy now contributes to the energy mix in more than 70 countries. Germany is the largest producer of electricity.

10.4.2 Case Study 2

In Bangladesh, one 1 MW wind power generation plant is there to provide electricity to one isolated Kutubdia Island. In order to provide steady power, the plant coupled with a battery system (Azad and Alam, 2012). A flow diagram is present in Figure 10.4.

This plant replaced the diesel-based generator system. By this, this system not only decreased environmental pollution but also saved revenues. The actual site of the plant is given in Figure 10.5.

FIGURE 10.3 Climate change due to increasing of temperature (Horns Rev off-shore wind farm).

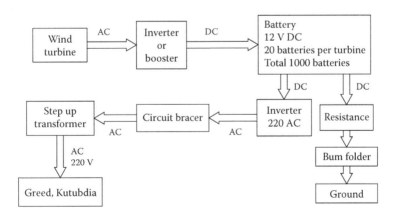

FIGURE 10.4 Flow diagram of the wind power plant with battery storage. (From Azad, A. K., and Alam, M. M. (2012). *International Journal of Advanced Renewable Energy Research*, 1(3), 172–178.)

FIGURE 10.5   Actual site of the wind plant with battery storage. (From Azad, A. K., and Alam, M. M. (2012). *International Journal of Advanced Renewable Energy Research*, 1(3), 172–178.)

10.5 CONCLUSION

At present, requirement of energy per person is increasing with a higher rate due to many reasons such as change of lifestyle, rapid industrialization, change of climate, and so on. Hence, energy security is becoming increasingly difficult due to limited nonrenewable energy sources. In this scenario, wind energy provides a continuous supply of rotary motion. This motion can be converted into generating electricity or for useful mechanical work. Government policy is being regularly updated for the smooth development of wind energy.

REFERENCES

Aneel. (2011). Banco de Informacoes de Geracao, www.aneel.gov.br/aplicacoes /capacidadebrasil/capacidadebrasil.asp.

Azad, A. K., and Alam, M. M. (2012). Wind power for electricity generation in Bangladesh. *International Journal of Advanced Renewable Energy Research*, 1(3), 172–178.

California Energy Commission. (2011). energy.ca.gov/renewables/index.html. http://data.naturalcapitalproject.org.

Gipe, P. (2004). *Wind Power: Renewable Energy for Home, Farm, and Business*. White River Junction, VT: Chelsea Green.

Global Wind Energy Council. (2008). *Global Wind 2007 Report*, 2nd ed. Global Wind Energy Council, Renewable Energy House, Brussels, Belgium.

Lehr, U., Lutz, C., Edler, D., O'Sullivan, M., Nienhaus, K., Nitsch, J., Simon, S., Breitschopf, B., Bickel, P., and Ottmüller, M. (2011). Kurz- und langfristige Auswirkungen des Ausbaus der erneuerbaren Energien auf den deutschen Arbeitsmarkt. Forschungsvorhaben DLR, DIW, GWS, FhG-ISI, ZSW im Auftrag des Bundesministeriums für Umwelt, Naturschutz und Reaktorsicherheit (BMU).

Sharma, A., Srivastava, J., and Kumar, A. (2015). A comprehensive overview of renewable energy status in India. In *Environmental Sustainability—Role of Green Technologies*. P. Thangavel, G. Sridevi, Eds. Springer India, pp. 91–105. doi 10.1007/978-81-322-2056-5_5.

Wagner, H.-J., and Mathew, J. (2009). Wind energy today, green energy and technology.

www.centurionenergy.com (accessed on May 11, 2015).

www.gwec.net (accessed on May 11, 2015).

IV

Renewable energy, Its Economics, Policy and Communication

CHAPTER 11

Renewable and Sustainable Architecture

Mahendra Joshi and Alok Kumar Maurya

CONTENTS

11.1 PRINCIPLE OF RENEWABLE ENERGY

11.1.1 Introduction

The need for a reliable energy source is required for running our daily needs, whether it is transportation, communication, heating, ventilation and air conditioning, or food-processing industries. Worldwide, all nations rely on fossil fuels, that is, coal, oil, and natural gas, for their energy; however, such types of sources of energy are finite and will be depleted eventually as per their consumption rate. Simultaneously, these resources are going to become too expensive, nevertheless producing many greenhouse gasses, which are the major reason for global warming issues. In contrast, the many types of renewable energy resources (RES) such as solar energy, wind energy, biomass, biogas, biofuels, hydro energy, geothermal energy, and so on are constantly replenished and will never run out.

The Texas Renewable Energy Industry Alliance's (TREIA) definition of renewable energy has been adopted by the Texas legislature, and is as follows:

> Renewable energy is the energy resource that is naturally regenerated over a short time scale and derived directly from the sun (such as thermal, photochemical, and photoelectric), indirectly from the sun (such as wind, hydropower, and photosynthetic energy stored in biomass), or from other natural movements and mechanisms of the environment (such as geothermal and tidal energy). Renewable energy does not include energy resources derived from fossil fuels, waste products from fossil sources, or waste products from inorganic sources [1].

REN21's 2014 report says that 19% of worldwide energy utilization is produced by renewable sources; in 2012 and 2013, energy generation was 22% by renewables. This energy utilization is isolated in the following way:

Traditional biomass	9%
Heat energy (non-biomass)	4.2%
Hydro electricity	3.8%
Electricity by wind, solar, geothermal and biomass	2%

Worldwide investment in renewable is added up to be more than US$214 billion in 2013 in which China and the United States are putting the substantial sum in wind, hydro, sun-based and biofuels [2].

11.1.2 Renewable Energy Sources and Sustainable Development

RES plays a vital role in the economic growth, progress, and sustainable development (SD), as well as poverty eradication and security of any nation. On the other hand, RES provides an opportunity for the financial advancement of the nation by the nation or other neighboring countries. SD is a process for development for getting goals although sustaining without depletion of natural sources (Figure 11.1). Nowadays, SD has become a key issue for the development in the twenty-first century. Presently, the future economic growth significantly depends on the long-term accessibility of RES that is affordable, accessible, and environmentally friendly.

RES are perfectly suitable for the SD for any country growth; in this view, each nation should move further toward RES implications. In the case of buildings, it should be planned in such a way that the workplace and living space are within walking distance. Due to this concept, a lot of time as well as fuel and other resources, which are wasted in traveling, can be saved.

Another concept for SD is the famous 3Rs, that is, Reduce, Reuse, and Recycle. In this concept, these 3Rs propose alternatives that are environmentally friendly and which can deal with overwhelming waste generation. The 3Rs are directly related to human health, economy and the natural ecosystem. This can be understood by Figure 11.2.

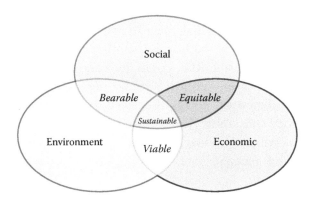

FIGURE 11.1 The traditional three pillars of sustainable development. (From Adams, W. M. (2006). The Future of Sustainability: Re-thinking Environment and Development in the Twenty-first Century. Report of the IUCN Renowned Thinkers Meeting, January 29–31, 2006. http://cmsdata.iucn.org/downloads /iucn_future_of_sustanability.pdf, retrieved February 16, 2009.)

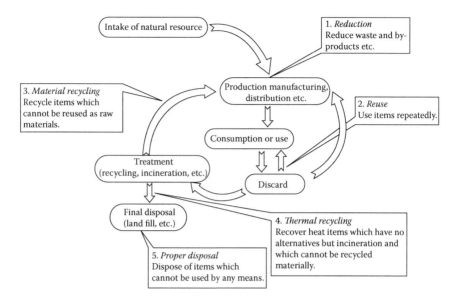

FIGURE 11.2   Steps involved in the 3Rs process. (From Japan's Experience in the Promotion of the 3Rs, for the Establishment of a Sound Material-Cycle Society. Ministry of the Environment, Tokyo, Japan, April 2005.)

11.1.3 Basic Principle

Renewable energy is characterized as green energy, that is, energy from resources that are refueled naturally with progressing time. Renewable energy replaces conventional fuels in four distinct areas: electricity generation, hot water/space heating, motor fuels, and rural (off-grid) energy services. By using RES, renewable energy flows involve natural phenomena such as sunlight, the wind, tides, plant growth, and geothermal heat. Renewable energy is derived from natural processes that are replenished constantly. However, on the other hand, non-renewable energy is known as a finite energy source because it does not reestablish itself at an adequate rate, which can meet sustainable economic extraction.

Energy is acquired from static stores of energy that stay underground unless discharged by human action. Fossil fuels (coal, oil, and natural gas), nuclear fuels are non-renewable energy sources. This energy is an isolated energy potential at the initial level, and for practical purposes, an external action is needed to start the supply of energy. This sort of energy is called brown energy. Figure 11.3 explains these two definitions.

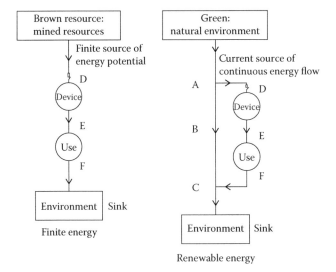

FIGURE 11.3 Contrast between renewable (green) and finite (brown) energy supplies. ABC = environmental energy flow; DEF = harnessed energy flow. (From Twidell, J. and Weir, T. *Renewable Energy Resources*. Taylor & Francis Group, New York, 2006.)

There is primarily five energy sources on Earth [1]

1. The sun

2. The motion and gravitational potential of the sun, moon, and Earth

3. Geothermal energy from cooling, chemical reactions and radioactive decay in the Earth

4. Human-induced nuclear reactions

5. Chemical reactions from mineral sources

The sun is the essential wellspring of energy from the time of evolution of the Earth. It is one of the ceaseless wellsprings of renewable energy.

11.2 SOLAR ENERGY

11.2.1 What Is Solar Energy?

The sun radiates in all regions of the spectrum, from radio waves to gamma rays. Everyday sun emanates huge amounts of energy from itself. The amount of energy created by the sun in one second is a great deal more than a human has utilized subsequent to the start of the time. Actually, the sun is similar to other stars which are chunks of gasses whose most extreme segment are atoms of hydrogen and helium. The sun produces energy in the center where hydrogen particles consolidate, helium is formed, and therefore a lot of energy is created. This procedure of generation of energy is called nuclear fusion. Sunlight reaches the Earth's surface in 8 min 19 sec; the distance is 149.6 million km. Solar energy travels at the speed of light, which is 186,000 miles per second or 3×10^8 meter per second [3]. The sun generates enormous energy, that is, 1.1×10^{20} kilowatt-hours per second [4].

11.2.2 Why Solar Energy?

The sun is a wellspring of clean, green, eco-friendly and unending energy to the universe. Solar energy originates from the thermonuclear fusion reactions, which are occurring on the sun. The solar energy is abundantly available around the globe and due to this reason, Earth's atmosphere, land, and oceans heated up; otherwise, the planet would have been frozen. This solar heat creates wind, drives the water cycle, and helps in photosynthesis. This energy can be changed over into heat and cold, electricity and in numerous different structures. Presently, solar radiation can be converted into heat, electricity at less expensive cost due to technical advancement.

11.2.3 Harnessing Solar Energy

The use of solar energy by humans is not new; its history ranges from the seventh century B.C. to today when humans utilized amplifying glass to focus the sunbeam to light the flame and to blaze the ants [5]. It was begun by concentrating the sun's warmth with glass and mirrors to light the shoot. Many applications based on solar energy are available in the worldwide market. In 2001, Power Light Corporation introduced the biggest rooftop solar power framework in the United States in 1.18 megawatt at the Santa Rita Jail in Dublin, California [6]. Solar power can be utilized in its active and passive forms, which can satisfy the energy needs like space warming and lighting, domestic hot water (DWH), power and electricity and recently space cooling.

- DHW can be generated using active solar thermal collectors.

- Space heating can be effortlessly accomplished by passive heating through windows (greenhouse effect). It can be accomplished by utilizing active solar thermal collector.

- Space cooling can be specifically rendered by the passive night ventilation (free cooling with no guide). With the innovative improvement, solar thermal systems that can change solar heat into cold have been produced. These systems are at their initial stage and are available as an experimental system for the pilot project.

- Lighting the space is done by utilizing passive sunlight, in other words daylight, photovoltaic modules can also be used where there is need of electric lighting.

- Electricity can be produced by photovoltaic modules.

Solar energy is majorly harnessed by the following technologies:

a. Active solar energy system/solar thermal technology

b. Passive solar energy system

c. Photovoltaic modules

a. Active solar energy system/solar thermal technology

Active solar heating system or solar thermal technology utilizes the solar radiation to heat the fluid, water or air, and then this energy is directly transferred to the interior spaces for thermal comfort or to a storage system for later use. On a larger scale, solar collectors in this system collects the sun energy for heating liquids; in turn, the liquid is converted to steam, which can then be used to make electricity.

b. Passive solar energy system

Passive solar heating uses free heating direct from the sun to reduce the energy consumption in the buildings for space heating and cooling. Many heating and cooling design objectives overlap but the different emphasis is required depending on the climate needs.

c. Photovoltaic modules

Photovoltaic is a combination of the photo and volt where photo stands for light and volt is a measurement of electricity. Photovoltaic modules or cells are also known as solar cells. These cells convert solar radiation into direct current (DC) using semiconductor technologies through the photovoltaic effect.

The main constituents of PV cells are silicon; it is the same substance of which sand is made. Silicon is found abundantly on the Earth. It is the second common substance on the Earth. PV cells can power anything, which is operated on batteries or electrical power. Solar cells produce the electricity when radiant energy from the sun strikes the cell, resulting in electrons moving around. Movement of the electron causes the electric current. This action takes place silently and instantly.

11.3 CONCEPT OF PASSIVE SOLAR ENERGY

In ancient times humans used to roam and hunt for food. Other than animals, humans needed security and protection from climatic conditions too. Wild animals and birds used to make their shelters by impulse and embraced themselves to climatic changes from era to era yet people made sanctuary from various natural resources, which withstand against the different climatic conditions like rain, heat, cold, etc. Gradually as time passed, the knowledge about the different building materials and construction techniques of humans increased by which finer shelters were made which were more balanced between climate and lifestyle of individuals.

Humans' first shelter was probably a cave. Caves gave shelter from the furious climatic conditions as well as from wild animals, which might have harmed them. The mass of the Earth by which the cave was built gave coolness in summer and maintained the warmth in the winter. Some of the caves found were in a direction governed by the sun's movement in a manner so that in summer, sunlight did not penetrate too much inside and in winter, sunlight could enter inside, for example, a cave dwelling in Mesa Verde (Figure 11.4).

In various parts of the world, humans discovered diverse dwellings according to various solutions for protection against the different climatic conditions. For instance, in the hot and humid conditions of Asia, Australia, and so on, the walls were not so much a concern as the roof. On the other hand, for the cold areas like the Himalayas and parts of the United States, we find well-insulated timber walls.

As per the above discussion, the primary concern of the building was better indoor quality and protection from the natural elements. In modern days, the better indoor quality is maintained by mechanical means, that is, air-conditioning for cool and warm conditions, artificial lights and so on, which consumes energy.

As the oil crisis arose in 1983, the risk of an annihilation of fossil fuel came and to conquer this issue the pursuit of the option of energy sped

FIGURE 11.4   Cave dwelling in Mesa Verde. (From kids.britanica.com.)

up and the significance of energy preservation developed. The first alternative that came to mind was solar energy and other sources like wind, geothermal, and so on. These sources were tested scientifically to fulfill the modernized need. Among all the techniques, one of the techniques based on the simple theory of heat transfer was developed which is known as "solar passive technique." A growing global concern of the SD has forced humanity to take an interest in the ecologically sustainable material, pro cesses and sources of the energy. The method of achieving the thermal comfort within a building with minimum or no use of artificial energy is known as "solar passive architecture."

The solar passive design is the method of collecting, storing, conveying, and controlling thermal energy flow by means of the natural principle of heat transfer. This method utilizes the energy directly available in the immediate environment and exchanges the heat by a natural process. This system does not have any other separate device to collect energy, storage units or any mechanical means of conveying heat. In this method, dampers, open windows, shading devices, and so on regulate the flow of natural energy.

Intellectual use of simple passive techniques in design like the orientation of the building, location and size of the window, color and vegetation considerably decreases the energy consumption and enhances the indoor quality. In extreme climatic conditions, these simple passive techniques cannot help in achieving the desired indoor quality. The passive design has other solutions for such climatic conditions such as wind towers, evaporative cooling, roof ponds, solariums, and so on that help in achieving the desired indoor comfort level within the building. Passive methods have many advantages. These methods cut down the energy consumption and lower the annual usage of the power. These techniques can be added in buildings at minimal cost. Traditional material can be used in the construction and can be maintained by people with little technical knowledge.

11.3.2 Different Techniques Adopted

Solar passive techniques can be broadly classified into two categories:

1. Simple solar passive techniques

2. Advanced solar passive techniques

11.3.2.1 Simple Solar Passive Techniques

As the name suggests, these techniques can be adopted in any design without adding too much cost. It is vital to understand these procedures for appropriate use in the design. Following design considerations must be taken care of:

Site

Building plan

Building orientation

Building envelope

11.3.2.1.1 Site   Site condition is one of the major factors of the building design. Legitimate determination of site can help in saving considerable amounts of energy and provide satisfactory indoor air quality throughout the year.

The following consideration are important:

- Macroclimate
- Microclimate

Macroclimate characterizes the atmosphere of the distinctive zones and necessities of comfort for better places. It incorporates distinctive components of the atmosphere like air temperature, humidity, wind, precipitation, and so forth.

On the other hand, the microclimate is site-specific climate. Elements of the weather like wind, sun radiation, temperature, and humidity are recorded at a particular location around the building. The building itself influences the microclimate of the region as it creates obstructions to the wind flow and casts the shadows on the ground. The designer's job is to take account of these factors while designing.

The following factors affect the microclimate of the site:

a. Landform

b. Water bodies

c. Vegetation

d. Open space and built form

e. Street width and orientation

These variables help in creating an agreeable indoor environment.

a. Landform

Landform is the topography of any site; it might be flat, undulating, contoured or sloped. Hills, mountains, and valleys are the major landforms that influence site. Each of the landforms has a diverse impact on the microclimate.

For instance, in valleys, the bottom temperature is less than the upper part as the hot air rises up and cool air settles down. Wind flow is higher along the direction of the valley than the across it due to unrestricted movement. Further, the orientation of the slope is also important as it decides the amount of solar radiation falling on the slope.

b. Water bodies

Seas, oceans, streams, lakes or wellsprings are the distinctive water bodies relying on the size. They can be vast and small. Water has a cooling impact as it has a high latent heat of vaporization; it utilizes heat as a part of evaporation. Water absorbs or releases a huge amount of heat per unit rise or fall of temperature because of its high specific heat. Water is an ideal medium for storing heat, which may be used for heating purposes.

Wind flow pattern of the site is influenced by the presence of a large water body. This is because of the heat storing capacity of the land mass, water is different, and this difference forces the wind to flow. Figure 11.5 shows the wind direction in the presence of a water body at day and night time.

In warm, humid climates, a water body adds humidity, which creates an uncomfortable indoor environment. The presence of the water body may be beneficial or disadvantageous if not taken care of while designing.

c. Vegetation

Vegetation in all structures whether a tree, plant, bush, grass and so forth have an exceptionally noteworthy part in adjusting the microclimate of a place. Trees and plants are called regular natural air conditioners of the Earth as they cut off the solar radiation and give shade. Vegetation by transpiration process discharges the water vapor in nature, which brings down the encompassing temperature. Plantation channelizes the airflow, that is, vegetation creates a different airflow pattern.

As per the climate, appropriate types of trees can be selected. For example, in a hot and dry climate west and east side deciduous trees prove to be beneficial. They provide shade from the intense and glaring morning and evening sun and they also cut off the hot breezes.

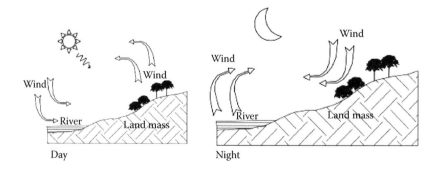

FIGURE 11.5 Direction of wind at day and night in the presence of a large water body.

d. Open spaces and built form

In any city or town, open spaces act as a lung, as these open spaces manage the airflow pattern inside the structures. Built forms are responsible for the heat gain and heat loss. Both together can modify the microclimate of the site.

In cold climates, open spaces like courtyards can be designed in a manner that the solar radiation incident on them during daytime can be reflected on the building facade for heat gain. Patios can likewise be intended to function as a heat sink if they are made green.

If buildings surround an open area, then it will be mutually shaded and air will be cold, which can be used to facilitate the proper ventilation and will promote the heat loss through the building envelope. Built forms can be arranged in such a way that the building causes mutual shading and thus will reduce heat gain.

e. Street width and orientation

How much of the solar radiation will be received by a building and street depends on the street width and orientation of an urban area. Solar radiation can be controlled by handling them. While designing large residential areas and town planning, this point should be considered.

Buildings standing on one side of the street will cast a shadow on the street. It means streets can be wider or narrower as the solar radiation is favorable or not. For example, in Egypt, most of the streets are narrow with buildings shading each other to reduce solar radiation and consequently heat gain of the building. Airflow can also be controlled by the orientation of the street. For free flow of the air, the street can be oriented in the prevailing wind direction. To avoid the flow of the air, the street can be oriented at an angle to the prevailing wind direction.

11.3.2.1.2 Building Plan   The amount of solar radiation within the building is affected by the plan form of the building and similarly by the wind flow. Hence, the plan form of the building has an important role in heat gain and heat loss.

When the building is in the wind flow, it creates an obstruction, positive pressure is created on the windward side and negative pressure at the leeward side, due to this pressure variation a new wind flow pattern is created around the building. For example, in row housing staggered pattern is adopted in place of gridiron pattern for adequate wind flow around the buildings. With proper openings connecting between pressure differences, effective ventilation can be achieved.

11.3.2.1.3 Building Orientation   Building orientation is always talked about with reference to the cardinal direction of the area, that is, North-South, East-West. This is an essential parameter in designing of any town or residence. In hot and dry climates, the building should be oriented in such a way that a minimum of solar radiation gets in the building envelope while vice versa in the cold regions. In the same way, winds can be desirable or undesirable, depending on the climate.

11.3.2.1.4 Building Envelope   The building envelope decides the amount of radiation that is going to be achieved. The following elements of a building affect the heat gain/loss:

  a. Roof

  b. Wall

  c. Openings/fenestration

  d. Shading

  e. External cladding, color, and texture

a. Roof

  In any building, the roof is an extremely pivotal part, as it receives a significant amount of the solar radiation. The design, and type of roof is a major factor in deciding the heat gain/loss, day lighting and ventilation.

  Reinforced cement concrete (RCC) slab, if it has a considerable thickness, tends to delay the heat transmission from the outer surface to the interior when it is compared to a lighter roof like asbestos cement, corrugated aluminum sheet roofing. Sometimes, to reduce heat gain from the roof, some inverted earthen pots are kept over which mud phuska (earth layer) is laid. As we know, air (trapped within the earthen pots) and earth is a good insulator of the heat, this method reduces heat gain significantly. Pitched, the curved roof has a large surface area, which allows more heat loss than a flat roof. Therefore, the material, as well as roof design, plays a significant role in the performance of the roof.

b. Walls

The second major part by which a building envelope is made up of is the walls. The walls receive a large amount of direct solar radiation. As per the climate, the wall can be designed for heat gain or heat loss, and correspondingly wall thickness can be decided. The conduction process through the wall in warmer regions achieves 25% of heat gain in India. A properly designed wall can reduce the cooling load of the building effectively. Hence, heat gain by the wall should be considered.

c. Openings/fenestration

In any building position, shape and size of opening/fenestration, which is in the form of windows and jharokhas, are important aspects of the climatic design. These are given for ventilation, daylight and heat gain which can be modified/controlled by the curtain, louvers, and so on. Intelligent use of the openings provides proper cross ventilation, daylight, and so on. Ventilation helps in lowering the indoor temperature as it allows fresh air to get in and exhaust the hot air of the room. In warm and humid climates where the outside temperature does not exceed 28–32°C, the indoor air speed of 1.5–2.0 m/s can create comfortable indoor temperature [7].

While deciding the location of the windows, simple physics about the air should be kept in mind. Hot air rises, so openings at the higher level will naturally exhaust the warm air. Orientation, shape, size of the opening will affect the pattern and flow of the air within the building envelope. For instance, opening at the windward side will have a high pressure which allows good cross-ventilation (Figure 11.6). A small inlet and large outlet will enhance the velocity and air flow of the air within the room (Figure 11.7).

Natural light in the building is taken by the glazed opening, skylights, clearstories, light shelves, and so on. The shutters, louvers, curtains, blinds, and so on can control the amount of light entering the room. On the other hand, solar transmission, absorption, and reflection can be managed by the various tints of glazing with a surface coating. For instance, 6 mm thick float glass (absorbing glass) can reduce the solar transmission by 45% (Figure 11.8) [8]. Use of reflective glass can reduce more admittance of sunlight depending

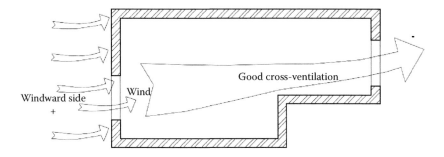

FIGURE 11.6   Good cross-ventilation if opening is at the windward side.

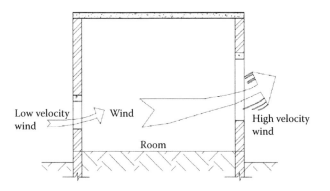

FIGURE 11.7   Increased velocity of the wind entering from a small inlet and going out by a large opening (Venturi effect).

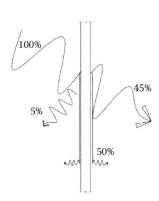

FIGURE 11.8   Transmission properties of absorbing glass.

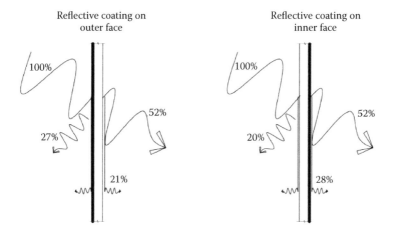

FIGURE 11.9   Transmission properties of reflecting glass.

on the coating done. Reflectivity can vary depending on the coating done on the outer or inner face of the glass (Figure 11.9).

d. Shading

Shading devices cut off the solar radiation falling on the exposed surface of buildings thus reducing the heat gain. Shading the window can significantly enhance the indoor climate of the building. In hot and dry climate, mutual shading can be beneficial for the inhabitants, that is, taller structures can be placed on the south and west to shade the other structures. Balconies, vegetation, fins, paints, and so on can shade exposed walls. Openings and windows can be shaded by the appropriate size of the sunshade, egg crate shade, and awnings. Figure 11.10 shows different shading devices.

e. External cladding, color, and texture

The character of the cladding, color, and texture of the external surface decides the amount of heat absorbed or reflected by it. Smooth textured and light-colored walls reflect more light and heat whereas rough textured surfaces create self-shading and increase the area of radiation. Dark shades of external wall absorb more radiation, which increases heat gain. Lighter shades of the wall have high emissivity, resulting in low heat gain, so these shades can be used in warmer regions.

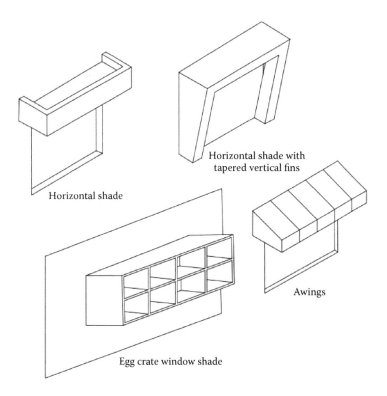

FIGURE 11.10   Different shading devices.

Tables 11.1 and 11.2 show the effect of the color of the external wall in four cities.

11.3.2.2 Advanced Solar Passive Techniques

There are a number of passive techniques that can be incorporated into the building. In this section, the authors will discuss these techniques.

11.3.2.2.1 Direct Gain   Direct gain is the simple, cheap, and effective approach for heat gain in cold climates. In this method, sunlight is allowed in the room directly through the opening or glazed window, to raise the temperature of the walls and floors, which results in rising of the indoor temperature. In direct gain, the main requirement is a glazed window or opening and thermal storage. The glazed window is placed on the southern side of the building (in the northern hemisphere) to get maximum heat gain, sometimes the glazed windows are double glazed with an insulating curtain inside which reduces the heat loss in the night time.

TABLE 11.1 Effect of Color of External Surface on Room Temperatures for Hot, Dry, Warm, and Humid Climate

Color (Absorptive, Emissivity)	Ahmadabad (Hot and Dry)					Mumbai (Warm and Humid)				
	Yearly Min (°C)	Yearly Max (°C)	Yearly Avg (°C)	H_{25}^{Y} (h)	H_{30}^{Y} (h)	Yearly Min (°C)	Yearly Max (°C)	Yearly Avg (°C)	H_{25}^{Y} (h)	H_{30}^{Y} (h)
White painted surface (0.3, 0.9)	20.6	42.2	29.7	7140	3908	24.5	34.6	29.6	8605	3350
White washed surface(0.4, 0.9)	20.8	42.5	30.0	7319	4123	24.8	34.9	29.8	8667	3654
Dark grey surface (0.9, 0.9)	21.9	44.0	31.1	7830	5599	26.0	36.1	30.9	8760	5535
Cream surface (0.4, 0.5)	21.2	43.0	30.4	7498	4739	25.3	35.30	30.2	8760	4320
Red surface (0.6, 0.9)	21.2	43.1	30.4	7498	4739	25.2	35.4	30.2	8760	4412

TABLE 11.2 Effect of Color of External Surface on Room Temperatures for Composite and Moderate Climate

	Nagpur (Composite)					Pune (Moderate)				
Color (Absorptive, Emissivity)	Yearly Min (°C)	Yearly Max (°C)	Yearly Avg (°C)	H_{25}^Y (h)	H_{30}^Y (h)	Yearly Min (°C)	Yearly Max (°C)	Yearly Avg (°C)	H_{25}^Y (h)	H_{30}^Y (h)
White painted surface (0.3, 0.9)	20.4	40.1	29.2	7067	2975	22.0	34.4	27.4	7078	1926
White washed surface (0.4, 0.9)	20.7	40.3	29.5	7220	3139	22.3	34.7	27.7	7319	1957
Dark grey surface (0.9, 0.9)	22.2	41.7	30.9	7923	4408	23.7	35.9	28.8	8171	2682
Cream surface (0.4, 0.5)	21.4	40.9	30.1	7494	3715	23.0	35.2	28.2	7894	2172
Red surface (0.6, 0.9)	21.3	40.9	30.1	7494	3687	22.9	35.2	28.1	7864	2140

Source: Nayak, J.K. and Hazra, R., Development of Design Guidelines on Solar Passive Architecture and Recommendations on Modification of Building Byelaws, Final Report, R&D Project No. 10/86/95-ST, 1999.

Note: H_{25}^Y: Number of hours for which room temperature exceed 25°C in a year. H_{30}^Y: Number of hours for which room temperature exceed 30°C in a year. min: minimum; max: maximum; avg: average.

At daytime, the wall facing the south side gets very hot, hence thermal storage mass is provided in the form of bare massive walls, concrete or water filled drums to capture the increase in room temperature. Heat arrested in these thermal walls is released at nighttime, which increases the temperature of the indoor environment.

In cold climates, direct gain techniques are used extensively for heating due to its simplicity and effectiveness. Sometimes direct heat gain technique creates undesirable heating in summer and undesirable heat loss in winter if the large glazed window and storage facility are provided. Various control measures can be adopted to prevent undesirable heating and cooling. Roof overhangs, shutters, and reflectors can be used for increasing and decreasing the solar heat gain. Vents and exhausts can be used for cooling the space through the ventilation during the summer when the temperature rises.

11.3.2.2.2 Solarium/Sunspace   Solarium/sunspace is a system that is based on passive heating and is generally used in cold regions. This system works on the concept of the direct gain and thermal storage of solar radiation. Solar radiation is allowed to enter in the sunspace, this radiation heats the air by convection, and this heat energy is transferred to the living space through the mass wall by conduction (Figure 11.11). The sunspace is also constructed on the south side of the

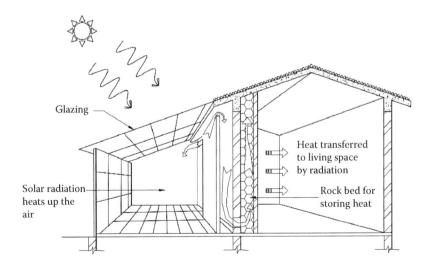

FIGURE 11.11   Solarium/sunspace.

building (in the northern hemisphere). The following elements are the basic requirements of this type of building:

a. A glazed south facing collector space

b. Thermal storage unit linking the collectors and living space for heat transfer.

11.3.2.2.3 Roof Radiation Trap   This technique traps the incident solar radiation and is utilized in heating up the air, which is trapped in the cavity. Some amount of the energy is transferred to the living space by the conduction method to raise the temperature of the room.

A south facing inclined glazing and north facing insulated sloped roof is constructed under which a trap is formed (in the northern hemisphere). Over the glazing, the projection is provided which prevents the summer sun from getting in. The solar radiation heats the cavity or gap, which is formed between the roof and the insulation. Glazing/window is provided with the shutter, which controls the amount of solar radiation getting inside. Figure 11.12 shows the phenomena of the roof radiation trap.

In the winter season, solar radiation infiltrates through the glazing and is absorbed by the blackened surface of the roof. A movable insulated shutter on the glazing can reduce the heat loss during the night. Parts of the solar radiation, which is trapped in the gap, are conducted and radiated into the living area through the roof and the remaining heat is stored in the thermal storage mass (water bags/gravel/rock bed) which can be used on nights or cloudy days (Figure 11.12a).

This technique can be used in summer for cooling purposes. The insulating slab is covered with a reflective metal sheet, which increases the emissivity. During nights of the summer, the sheet is cooled by the nocturnal radiation exchange. So, the air which is blown under is cooled. This coolness is stored in thermal storage mass, which is used in cooling the living area during hot days and nights (Figure 11.12b).

11.3.2.2.4 Isolated Gain   In this system, the designer/architect has greater flexibility in design and operation of passive concept because in this solar collector and thermal storage unit are thermally insulated from the living space. In this system, solar radiation is trapped and used to heat a fluid like water or it may be used to heat air also. This system works on the concept

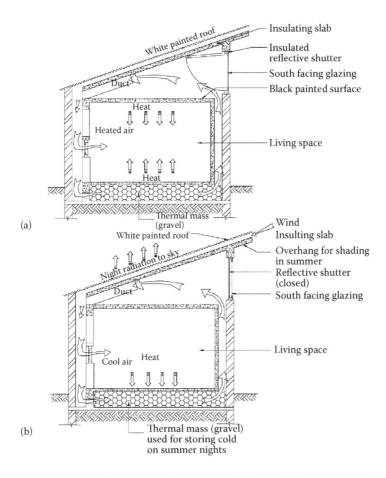

FIGURE 11.12 Roof radiation trap: (a) winter condition and (b) summer condition.

of a convective loop. In this loop, the warm air rises and passes through the storage, transferring the heat. The air/water, which has given its heat to the media, is cooled and falls to the collectors or absorber and is heated up again. This "thermo-siphoning heat flow" is explained in Figure 11.13.

This system comprises the following:

1. A collector/absorber, which traps the solar radiation to heat the fluid.

2. A storage mass/media, which absorbs the heat from the fluid and stores the heat for distribution into the living area.

3. Mechanism/techniques to distribute the heat stored in the storage mass.

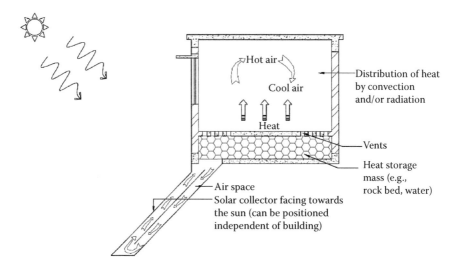

FIGURE 11.13   Thermo-siphoning heat flow.

11.3.2.2.5 Thermal Storage Wall   The thermal wall is placed between the living space and glazing. It prevents solar radiation from directly getting in the living space; solar heat is absorbed by the storage wall and then transferred to the living space. Such types of features are used in heating the space. Different types of storage wall are discussed below.

a. Trombe wall

A trombe wall is a thick solid wall with vents at both upper and lower parts of the wall. This wall is a thermal storage wall made up of concrete, masonry or composite bricks, block and sand, which is usually located on the southern side (in the northern hemisphere) of the building to receive maximum solar radiation. The face of the wall is painted black to maximize the absorptive capacity of the wall and it is placed directly behind the glazing with the air gap between. Vents are provided at the top and bottom for air circulation (Figure 11.14).

Solar radiation absorbed by the blackened massive thermal storage wall is in the form of sensible heat. Air present in the cavity between glazing and the wall gets heated up and this heated air gets in the living room from the upper vent. Cool air from the room takes its place in the cavity through the lower vent, thus establishing the natural airflow pattern. A part of absorbed solar heat is transferred to the living space by the convection and radiation. Figure 11.14a shows the

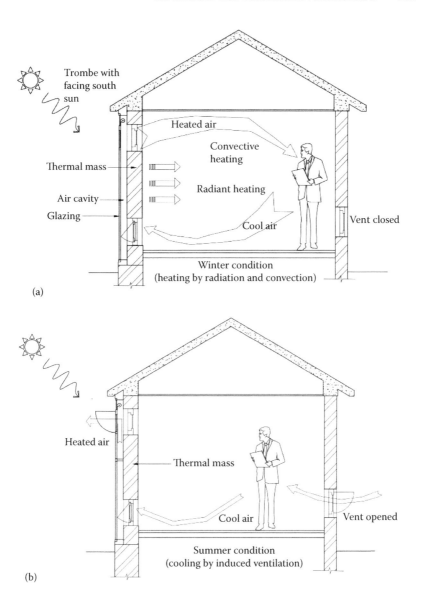

FIGURE 11.14 Principle of a trombe wall.

living room heated up. In the summer months, sun altitude is high; the overhang on the wall cuts the sun radiation falling on the surface. A trombe wall can provide the induced ventilation in summer for cooling of the space (Figure 11.14b). Here heated air in the cavity between the wall and glazing flows out through the exhaust vent at the top of the outer glazing, and air from the outer space enters

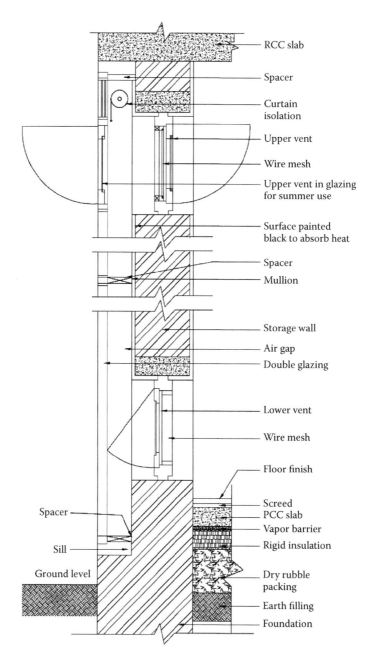

FIGURE 11.15   Detailed section of a trombe wall.

the space through the opening on the cooler side of the building to replace the hot air. This circulation of the air within the living space cools the space inside. Figure 11.15 shows the detailed section of a trombe wall.

b. Solar chimney

This system works on the same principle as the trombe wall does; therefore, it may be called a modified trombe wall. It is incorporated on the roof as a part of it. This system consists of a solar chimney and a thermal storage unit. The solar chimney is installed on the southern side of the building (in the northern hemisphere) as a collector panel with minimum thermal inertia. It absorbs the solar radiation falling on it and passes the heat to the air, which is present in absorber glazing space. A well-insulated outer layer limits the heat loss to the outer space. Heated air forces itself in the inner space and cool air takes its place and this cycle is repeated (Figure 11.16).

The storage of heat is generally in the inner structure of the building like an internal wall/partition or concrete ceiling, which is not exposed to the outside. These types of internal storage act as the buffer between the house and outer atmosphere, which eliminates the need of movable insulation which prevents the heat loss during nighttime. Figure 11.17 shows the typically detailed section of the solar chimney.

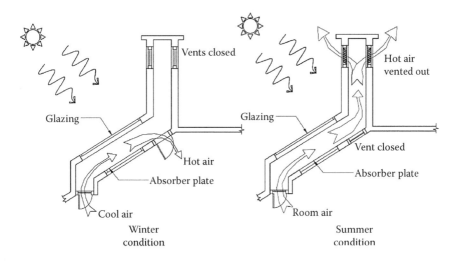

FIGURE 11.16   Solar chimney.

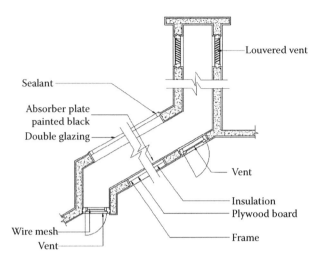

FIGURE 11.17   Details of a solar chimney.

c. Water wall

A water wall is based on the same principle as the trombe wall; the only difference is that it employs water as a thermal storage material. Figure 11.18 shows the typical arrangement of the water wall. The water wall is a thermal storage made up of drums filled up with water inside, stored behind the glazing. Drums are painted black outside to increase the absorption of the sun's radiation. The interior

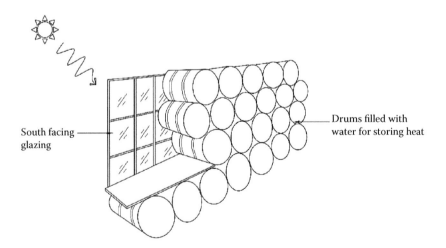

FIGURE 11.18   Water wall.

of the drum can be painted in any color. This wall can be directly in contact with the interior space or might be isolated with a thin concrete wall or any other separating layer. As storage in the water wall is a convective body of mass, heat transfer is very rapid in this case in comparison to the trombe wall/masonry wall.

11.3.2.2.6 Thermal Storage Roof   This system functions admirably in both the climates in summer as well as in winter. While this system is most appropriate for cooling it is appropriate for heating purposes in lower latitudes with high winter sun.

In this technique, a heap of water is stored on the terrace of the building. In the summer season, this mass of water is covered and insulated by the external, movable and reflective insulation. This insulation keeps the solar radiation away from the water and keeps the water cool. This mass of water takes the heat from the room below and keeps the air cool inside. At night time covers (insulation) are removed so that water can dissipate the heat to the environment by convection and radiation. This principle is shown in Figures 11.19 and 11.20 shows the construction detail of the roof pond.

11.3.2.2.7 Passive Cooling   The concept of passive cooling in the building has evoked the interest of designers and architects as it reduces the cooling load in the hot climatic regions. The main/basic concept of this system is to prevent heat gain (or at least minimize the heat gain) entering into the building or to remove the heat that has already entered in. This concept uses, besides solar energy, various other natural or eco-friendly cooling techniques. Some of these techniques are nocturnal cooling and evaporative cooling. Applicability of the above-mentioned techniques greatly depends on the climatic conditions of the area or regions of the specific place.

a. Nocturnal radiation cooling

Nocturnal radiation cooling is the procedure in which any external element of the building part is exposed to a cool night sky for cooling. In this system, heat loss occurs by emission of long wavelength radiation, so the surface must have a high emissivity. The accumulated heat during the daytime is radiated back to the atmosphere in the cool nights, hence cooling the envelope. This method works capably without using water as used in an evaporative cooling system. This procedure is illustrated in Figure 11.21.

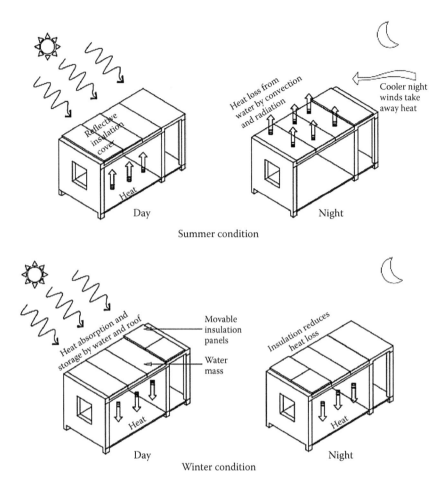

FIGURE 11.19   Principle of roof pond.

The roof, which is the element of the building envelope that is mostly exposed to the sky, is the most effective long wave radiator. The rate of exchange of heat mostly depends on the temperature difference between the building envelope which is radiating the heat and the surrounding atmosphere. This process works efficiently in regions that have high diurnal temperature variation. The condition of the atmosphere will also affect this cooling, like vapor pressure and cloud condition. The good thermal link between the emitting surface and living space is required; otherwise, cooling resulting from the exchange of radiation will only serve to cool ambient air rather than cooling the living space.

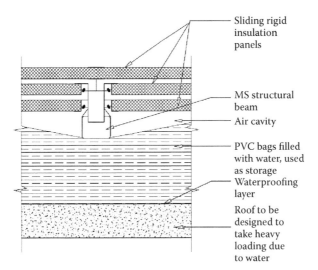

Sliding rigid
insulation
panels

MS structural
beam

Air cavity

PVC bags filled
with water, used
as storage

Waterproofing
layer

Roof to be
designed to
take heavy
loading due
to water

FIGURE 11.20   Detail of roof pond.

b. Evaporative cooling

Evaporative cooling is one of the passive cooling techniques, which
are employed in hot and dry regions or climate. In this principle,
water is evaporated by the sensible heat present in the air, which
cools the air, resulting in a cool ambient indoor temperature of the
living area. In simpler words, this principle can be understood by the
working principle of the desert cooler, which is frequently used in
North India (Figure 11.22).

This procedure can be used in many ways. In India, tropical climate is prevailing in the north zone where the solar radiation incident on the terrace is very high during the summer. This solar heat
gain from the roof can be minimized by sprinkling water on the
roof, which is evenly spread over the roof surface, resulting in lowering of temperature in the roof and heat gain of the surface is reduced.
Other than this, evaporation also cools the air present above the roof
surface. This cool air gets in the room by infiltration and ventilation,
leading to increasing the thermal comfort of the living space.

The presence of a water body like a pool, fountain, lake, river, and
so on near the building envelope or any water feature present within
the building where the smooth cross-ventilation is possible can provide a cooling effect.

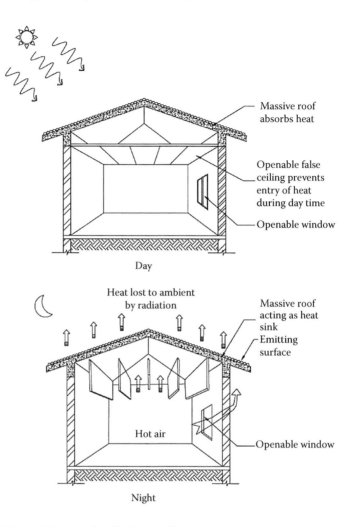

FIGURE 11.21   Nocturnal radiation cooling.

c. Wind tower

Wind towers are mostly used in hot and dry climates. Wind towers
are preferably placed where the winds are good and flow at a consistent velocity. A wind tower works in numerous ways. It works differently in the presence and absence of wind as well as in day and
night. The working principle of a wind tower lies in the change in
the temperature and thereby density of air inside and around the
tower. This difference in density generates a draft, which pulls the air
either upward or downward through the tower. Figure 11.23 shows
the workings of a wind tower.

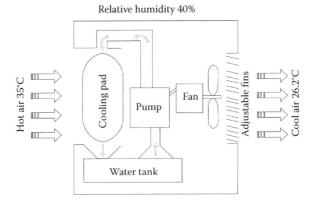

FIGURE 11.22   Principle of desert cooler.

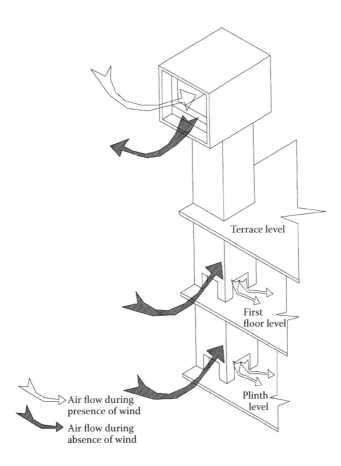

FIGURE 11.23   Workings of a wind tower.

d. Earth air tunnel

Generally, this technique is embraced for cooling in hot and dry climates whereas this technique can also be adopted for winter heating. Earth air tunnel is a special type of wind tower, which is connected to an underground tunnel. In this technique, the cooling process is based on the theory that after a few meters under the ground, the temperature is almost constant throughout the year. A wind tower is connected to an earth tunnel, which runs underground from the wind tower to the basement of the building. The wind tower catches the wind and forces the air to the underground tunnel where the air gets as cool as the temperature of the tunnel, which is lower then the ambient air temperature. This cool air is circulated into the living space. Figure 11.24 shows the schematic diagram of the earth air tunnel. During the winter season, the tunnel temperature is higher than the ambient temperature; hence, air gets warm while passing through it.

Sometimes, to reduce the underground temperature, the ground can be shaded using vegetation and can be wetted by sprinkling water. This water percolates through and dampens the tunnel wall. This results in air passing through the tunnel being cooled by the evaporative cooling.

e. Earth sheltering or berming

Earth berming/sheltering is a technique that can be used both for passive cooling as well as for heating purposes of the building. In

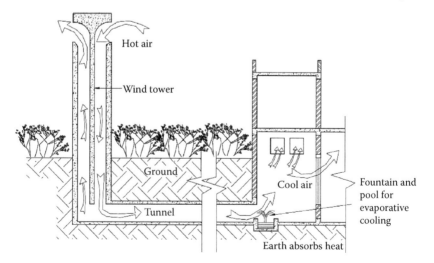

FIGURE 11.24   Schematic diagram of an earth air tunnel.

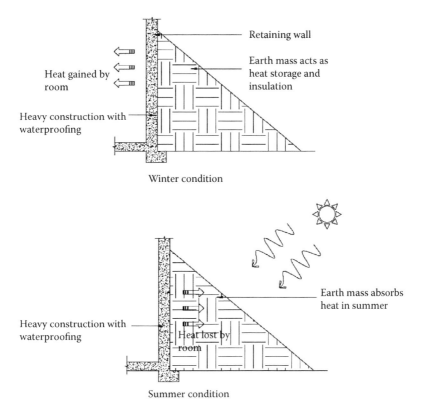

FIGURE 11.25   Principle of earth berming.

this, the building is made up of earth, which acts as a heat sink. With the increasing depth from the earth's surface, temperature variation dries out in summer as well as in winter. Building with basement or semi-basement would provide cooling (in summer) and heating (in winter) to the living areas if properly planned. Figure 11.25 shows the principle of earth berming. Earth sheltered building/structure has to be strong as it has to carry the load of earth and vegetation above. In addition, the structure should be properly treated against dampness, that is, efficient waterproofing and insulation to be provided to avoid ground moisture from rising.

f. Induced ventilation

Induced ventilation is one of the methods of passive cooling. This method acts well in hot and humid as well as hot and dry climates. In this method, temperature difference is created by heating the air

in restricted areas by solar radiation and this temperature difference forces air movement. The draft forces hot air to rise and escape
to ambient, pulling the cooler air and creating a cooling effect.
Figure 11.26 shows the air circulation by this technique.

g. Curved roof and air vents

This system works on the cooling by induced ventilation, which is caused
by a pressure difference. This phenomenon is shown in Figure 11.27. In

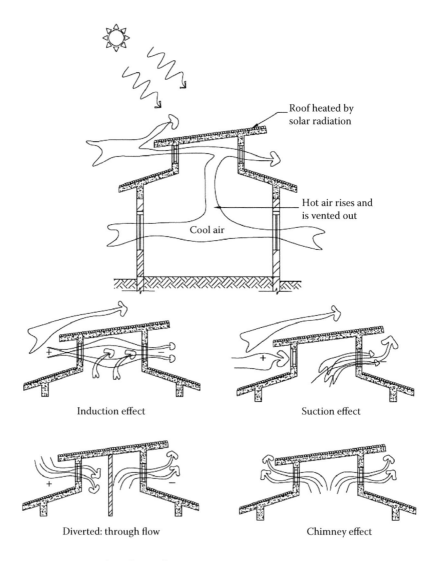

FIGURE 11.26   Induced ventilation.

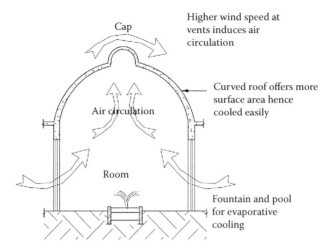

Cap

Higher wind speed at vents induces air circulation

Curved roof offers more surface area hence cooled easily

Air circulation

Room

Fountain and pool for evaporative cooling

FIGURE 11.27   Curved roof and air vent.

this technique, wind, which flows over the curved surface, creates the pressure difference around it. If the surface is provided with opening, then the air inside is sucked out from the structure.

Hence, the hot ambient air is sucked out through the vents inducing air circulation. Vents are generally designed over the living space. This cooling can be enhanced by incorporating evaporative cooling.

h. Insulation

As we know, heat gain or loss in a building occurs by building components like walls, roofs, floors, and so on, which can be regulated by insulating materials, which can be installed externally or internally. Insulating materials that can be used are polyurethane foam (PUF), thermo cool, and so on. Insulation can be done by using cavity walls in the external building envelope. Details of cavity walls and insulation are shown in Figure 11.28.

i. Passive desiccant cooling

This method works efficiently in warm and humid climates. As we all know, the human body controls or regulates its body temperature by sweating, but in warm and humid climates natural cooling of the body by sweating is not achieved. Thus, our tolerance to high temperature is reduced. To achieve the desired cooling effect, it is desirable to reduce the humidity level.

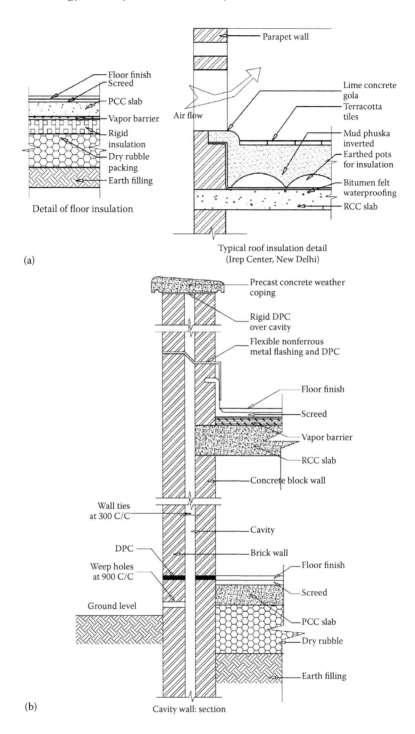

FIGURE 11.28 Details of (a) insulation and (b) cavity wall.

In the desiccant cooling system, desiccant salts or mechanical dehumidifiers are used to achieve the desired level of humidity in the surroundings. Materials that have a high affinity for water are used for dehumidification. Materials may be solid such as silica gel, activated alumina and alumina gel or liquid like tri-ethylene glycol. Humid air from outside is forced to pass through units containing desiccants and the air is dried before entering the living space. The desiccants used may be regenerated by solar energy.

11.4 DAY LIGHTING

11.4.1 Illumination Quantity

The eye responds to a range of illumination levels extending over a million orders of magnitude: from 0.1 lux (full moonlit night) to 100,000 lux (bright sunshine).

For practical situations and various activities (thus various visual tasks), detailed illumination requirements are given in various publications [9]. The values (in lux) in Table 11.3 can provide some general guidance.

11.4.2 Daylight Factor Method

The quantitative parameter that describes daylighting in a building is the daylight factor (DF) defined as

$$DF = \frac{E_i}{E_o} \times 100$$

where
  E_i = illumination indoors, at the point of observation (lux)
  E_o = illumination outdoors from an unobstructed sky hemisphere (lux)

TABLE 11.3   Illumination Requirements

Task	Illumination (lux)
Casual seeing	
Ordinary tasks, medium detail (e.g., wood machining, general office work)	100 lux 400
Severe, prolonged tasks (e.g., fine assembly, silk weaving)	900
Exceptionally severe tasks (e.g., watch making)	2000–3000

TABLE 11.4   Daylight Factors for Domestic Buildings

Building/Function	min DF
Housing	
• Kitchen, general	1.0
• Kitchen, main workshops	1.5
• Living room, general	0.5
• Living room, desk for writing	1.5
• Bedroom, general	0.25
• Bedroom, dressing table	1.0
• Circulation	0.2
Entrance halls and reception area	0.3
General offices	1.0
School assembly halls	0.2
School classrooms	1.0

Recommended values of daylight factors for domestic buildings are given in Table 11.4.

In India, it is usually taken as 8000 Lux. Once the illumination outdoors is known, the illumination indoors can be obtained by the above formula.

11.4.3 Daylight

Daylight is the visible part of the solar radiation as perceived by the eye. Daylight is composed of a spectral power distribution (SPD) of electromagnetic radiation in the visible wavelength range (380–780 nm). Daylight has two components, namely, sunlight and skylight. Sunlight is the direct component of light coming from the sun, which is variable in nature and creates glare and shadow. On the other hand, skylight is a diffuse component of light coming from the sky dome. Skylight is quite steady and does not create glare and shadow. The spectral distribution and efficacy of skylight and sunlight are found to be somewhat different [10]. The beam and diffuse solar irradiance values, obtained as a part of meteorological weather data, give the total solar radiation (from the sun and the sky) hitting the Earth at a particular place. This contains visible and invisible portions of solar radiation. The luminous efficacy (lm/W) of a light source, which is defined as the ratio of luminous flux to the radiant flux, can be estimated through luminous efficacy models that are used to convert the portion of the irradiance into the illuminance.

Daylight is found essential for all the basic needs of a human being. It has been established that the people working in a day-lit environment are less susceptible to illness and fatigue as compared to when they work under artificially lighted indoor spaces. In contrast to artificial lighting systems, which give a fixed intensity, color rendering, and texture, daylight is characterized by time-varying properties but is available only during the daytime. An intelligent mix of daylight and artificial lights is essential to meet the lighting requirements whenever it is required and to obtain best results from an energy conservation point of view.

Form and orientation of buildings play a key role in determining quality and quantity of daylight inside the building. It is usually preferred to have the larger side of the building elongated along an east-west axis to admit daylight from the north and south apertures. It may be noted that the daylight from east and west apertures is highly variable in nature from the first half of the day to the second half. The daylight from the north aperture is found to be steadier than that from the south aperture. However, the contribution of the sunlight to daylight from a south aperture is more as compared to its contribution from the north aperture. Generally, the light from the north aperture is preferred over that from the south aperture for interior illumination. However, overhangs and blinds can be used to control the contribution of direct sunlight from the south. Higher placement of windows allows deeper penetration of daylight in buildings. Once building form, orientation, and placement of windows have been decided, mathematical models may be used to quantify daylight performance of the building at the design stage itself.

Figure 11.29 shows the comparison of the efficacy of various light sources. It can be seen that luminous efficacy of daylight is the highest of that of the other light sources.

Tables 11.5 and 11.6 show the average luminous efficacies of daylight in composite climatic conditions in India.

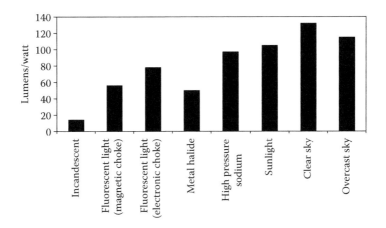

FIGURE 11.29   Comparison of the efficacy of various light sources.

TABLE 11.5 Average Global Luminous Efficacy (lm/W)

Month/Hour	6	7	8	9	10	11	12	13	14	15	16	17	18
Jan		76	92	100	101	103	104	103	101	100	92	77	
Feb		82	95	101	103	105	105	105	103	102	95	82	
Mar		93	97	104	106	105	107	105	106	105	97	93	
Apr	73	96	100	104	107	107	108	107	108	104	100	97	74
May	80	99	102	106	109	109	110	109	110	106	102	99	81
Jun	97	104	105	109	110	112	113	112	110	110	105	104	97
Jul	110	112	113	111	113	114	114	114	113	111	113	112	111
Aug	96	112	113	113	113	114	114	114	113	113	113	112	96
Sep	79	101	107	107	111	110	111	110	111	107	107	101	79
Oct		85	96	103	107	107	108	107	108	103	97	85	
Nov		78	93	101	102	104	104	104	103	102	94	79	
Dec		81	91	99	104	103	104	103	104	100	91	82	

TABLE 11.6   Average Diffuse Luminous Efficacy (lm/W)

Month/Hour	6	7	8	9	10	11	12	13	14	15	16	17	18
Jan		80	106	120	133	131	130	131	133	121	107	82	
Feb		89	108	122	130	128	126	128	131	123	111	91	
Mar		102	111	119	126	123	123	123	127	121	113	104	
Apr	74	106	114	121	127	121	120	121	128	123	117	108	75
May	89	111	119	125	131	122	122	123	133	127	121	112	90
Jun	109	115	125	127	132	134	135	135	134	128	126	116	109
Jul	110	113	115	122	122	123	123	123	122	122	115	113	110
Aug	109	113	115	116	122	122	122	122	121	116	115	113	109
Sep	64	113	117	125	126	131	131	132	128	127	117	113	63
Oct		98	115	124	132	129	128	129	133	125	117	100	
Nov		84	108	123	134	130	129	130	134	126	113	88	
Dec		73	105	119	130	132	131	132	130	120	107	74	

The annual average efficacy under the local sky conditions of the area will be useful for the architects and designers for the first estimation. From the above results, the estimated yearly average global luminous efficacy in the composite climate of India is 101.0 lm/W and the yearly average diffuse luminous efficacy is 115.0-lm/W. Diffuse luminous efficacy is higher than the global efficacy indicating that the diffuse component in day lighting design is more energy efficient [11].

Once the radiant component of daylight is known, it can be multiplied with the luminous efficacy to find the luminous energy. For example, during bright sunshine, the maximum radiant energy falling on the Earth is 1000 watts and therefore the global luminous energy and the diffuse luminous energy in the composite climate of India would be $101 \times 1000 = 101,000$ lumens and $115 \times 1000 = 115,000$ lumens, respectively.

11.5 CONCLUSION

There are different types of renewable energy sources that will end with the Earth and that can be used infinitely. The types of renewable energy that are being harnessed by countries are solar energy, wind energy, hydro energy, geothermal energy, and wave/tidal energy.

These energy sources help in the growth of countries in terms of economy, society, and the environment. Non-renewable energy sources are green and have almost no impact on the environment. They reduce the pollutants at the local and global level and provide the opportunity for socioeconomic development.

Sun radiation can be harnessed by passive ways for the comfortable indoor environment within the buildings. There are some simple and advanced passive techniques, which can be adopted. While designing the passive techniques, the considerations to be taken care of are the site, building plan, building envelope, and building orientation.

Buildings are affected by the microclimate of the area. The factors that affect the microclimate are landform, water bodies, vegetation, open space and built form, street width, and orientation.

When we talk about the simple passive techniques adopted in the building, then the following elements of the building should be taken care of which is directly linked to the indoor comfort within the building. These elements are roof, walls, opening/fenestration, shading, external cladding, color and texture.

Advanced passive techniques are sophisticated methods that are designed as per the climatic analysis of the area and under the supervision of an expert.

Daylight also falls under the category of solar passive techniques that saves artificial light. Daylight has two components: sunlight and skylight. Sunlight is a direct component of light radiating from the sun; it creates glare and shadow. On the other hand, skylight is the diffuse component of solar radiation, which is reflected from sky dome. Skylight does not create shadows and glare. The distribution of spectrum and efficacy of skylight and sunlight are different. The beam and diffuse irradiance values obtained from metrological weather data can be converted into illuminance values using the luminous efficacy models. Using the luminous efficacy model of Perez et al., the global and diffuse luminous efficacies for composite climate of India were estimated and were found to be 101.0 and 115.0 lm/W, respectively. It is evident that the diffuse luminous efficacy is higher than the global luminous efficacy indicating that the diffuse component of daylight is more energy efficient.

REFERENCES

1. http://www.treia.org/renewable-energy-defined/.
2. REN21, Renewables 2014: Global Status Report, pp. 13, 17, 21, 25, 2014. Archived from the original on September 4, 2014.
3. The NEED Project, Intermediate Energy Infobook, p. 22, Manassas, VA, 2016.
4. http://newenergyportal.worldpress.com/2009/12/01.
5. U.S. Department of Energy, Energy Efficient and Renewable Energy, The History of Solar.
6. County of Alameda, Santa Rita Jail Case Study, Smart Energy Strategies Integrating Solar Electric Generation and Energy Efficiency, A Partnership of Alameda County, PowerLight Corporation, and CMS Viron Energy Services, April 2002.
7. Givoni, B., *Passive and Low Energy Cooling of Buildings*, Van Nostrand Reinhold, New York, 1994.
8. Nayak, J.K., Hazra, R., and Prajapati, J., *Manual on Solar Passive Architecture*, Solar Energy Centre, MNES, Government of India, New Delhi, 1999.
9. Rea, M.S., Bullough, B., and Figueiro, M.G., Circadian photobiology: An emerging framework for lighting practice and research, *Lighting Research and Technology*, 34(3), 177–90, 2002.
10. Choi, U., Johnson, R., and Selkowitz, S., The impact of daylighting on peak electrical demand, *Energy and Buildings*, 387–99, 1984.
11. Muneer, T., *Solar Radiation and Daylight Models for the Energy Efficient Design of Buildings*, Architectural Press, UK, 1997.

CHAPTER 12

Renewable Energy Financing in India

Sanjay Kumar Kar and Ashok Kumar Mishra

CONTENTS

12.1 INTRODUCTION

India has sufficient renewable energy sources but currently is heavily dependent on imported sources of energy, primarily crude oil, natural gas, and coal. This is happening due to an increase in the demand for energy and the depletion of fossil fuel and coal leading to serious concerns over long-term energy security and sustainability. To satisfy the growing demand for electricity, coal is the preferred source of primary energy, but this causes serious environmental degradations. Also, energy subsidies put an enormous burden and stress on the public exchequer. On the other hand, large hydropower projects displace habitation and cause various environmental challenges. But renewable sources such as wind, solar, and bio-power pose fewer challenges and offer great opportunity.

Renewable sources such as wind and solar have source advantages over nonrenewable sources such as fossil fuel. Natural resources like solar and wind are free, available for energy generation.

12.2 STATUS OF RENEWABLE ENERGY (RE) IN INDIA

An estimated potential of 897 GW has been identified from various renewable energy sources in the country, which includes 749 GW from solar, 103 GW from wind, 25 GW from bio-energy, and 20 GW from small hydropower. As of September 30, 2015, 37.4 GW of grid connected renewable energy was installed in India. Wind contributed 65% followed by bio-power (11.8%), solar (11.6%), small hydro (11%), and waste-to-energy (0.33%).

The Ministry of New & Renewable Energy has been working on installing 175 GW of grid-connected renewable power by the year 2022, which is about 4.7 times more than the current level of 37.4 GW. The target includes 100 GW from solar, 60 GW from wind, 10 GW from bio-power, and 5 GW from small hydropower.

12.2.1 Wind

As wind is one of the cleanest forms of energy, over the last decade worldwide much emphasis has been given to this form of energy. Countries such as the United States, China, Germany, Spain, and India have made significant progress in terms of capacity addition.

Until 2007, India was the leading wind powerhouse with an installed capacity of 7845 MW. But the lead was conceded to China in 2008 when China augmented its capacity to 6.1 GW, which is almost the same cumulative capacity addition by India until 2006 (6.1 GW) (Kar and Sharma 2015b). Currently, India has a wind potential of 102 GW at 80 m height and 49 GW at 50 m height. As of June 30, 2015 about 23,762.81 (MNRE 2015) MW of wind turbines were installed in the country and another 2000 MW were to be added in the financial year 2015–2016. The government aims to achieve cumulative installed capacity of 60 GW by 2022. This means a capacity addition of 36,237 MW within 7 years with an average of 5176.7 MW addition every year.

The domestic wind turbine manufacturing industry in India is becoming globally competitive and accepted. Constant efforts have been made to increase the height of the tower, length of the blades, and power capacity (IEA 2013). With the advent of rotors designed for lower wind speed, with high mast and long blades in relation to generator size, the manufacturers are producing more efficient turbines. For instance, Suzlon is producing Hybrid Tower—a combination of lattice and tubular that can work at a hub height of 120 m and generate 10–12% higher electricity (Suzlon 2015).

Now the domestic wind turbine manufacturers are producing bigger size wind turbines (Kar and Sharma 2015a), leading to higher efficiency and lower cost. Out of the 33 domestic wind turbine producers, about 20 of them are producing turbines bigger than 1500 kW and some of them are producing turbines as big as 2650 kW.

The government is also putting equal emphasis on investment in this particular sector. In the recent reinvestment summit, 19 power producers pledged 45 GW of wind installation in the country (Kar and Gopakumar 2015).

12.2.2 Solar

Solar energy is radiant light and heat from the sun which is produced by using photovoltaic cells, solar thermal energy, and artificial photosynthesis. It is an important source of renewable energy. India is a country that enjoys maximum sun rays in a year. India is estimated to have a potential of 749 GW (MNRE 2014) to be harnessed to bridge the energy deficit in the country. Rajasthan leads in the country followed by Jammu and Kashmir. In order to reduce the carbon footprint, the present government has a clear intent and commitment. As of June 30, 2015 a grid connected solar power of 4060.65 MW has been installed (MNRE 2015), which is just about 11.1% of grid connected renewable power (Figure 12.1).

Under captive/off grid category SPV systems to the tune of 234.35 MW and solar water heating collection areas of about 8.9 million square meter are already installed.

With an estimated cost of Rs. 4050 crore the present government is trying to enhance the capacity by setting up 25 solar power plants, from 500 MW to a target of 50,000 MW in a span of 5 years, that is, from 2014–2015 to 2018–2019. In the budget of 2014–2015, the government has made a budgetary allocation of Rs. 5000 million to be provided for ultra mega solar power projects in Andhra Pradesh, Rajasthan, Tamil Nadu and Ladakh. Also, the government has budgetary support of Rs. 4000 million for solar power driven water pumping stations and solar power driven agricultural pump sets. On the banks of the canals 1 mW solar power parks will be set up with the help of additional Rs. 1000 million.

The deficit of energy requirement made India to be committed to the cause of solar energy. As a result, India attracted domestic and foreign investment in this sector. According to Thierry Lepercq, the head of Solaridirect, the cost of producing solar power in India is substantially

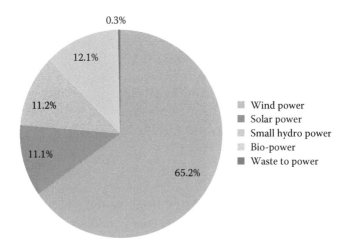

FIGURE 12.1 Renewable power mix in India (as of June 30, 2015). (From MNRE 2015.) Physical Progress (Achievements). Programme/Scheme wise Physical Progress in 2015–16 (during the month of June 2015). http://mnre.gov.in/mission -and-vision-2/achievements/ (accessed on August 08, 2015).

less in comparison to other parts of the world (Vidya 2015). That is why foreign participation could be attractive. Recently Adani group and SunEdison's solar technology entered into an agreement to make progress in the field of solar energy. The investment will be of $4 billion and will generate about 4500 direct jobs and 15,000 indirect jobs (Kar and Gopakumar 2015).

12.2.3 Small Hydro

India has a huge potential of hydropower electricity of around 20 GW. Most of the potential lies in the Himalayan states. By the end of June 2015, 4102 MW (Figure 12.2) of small hydro power with a share of 11.2% of grid connected renewable power in India, which is about 20% of the full potential.

By the end of June 2015 there were about 27 equipment manufacturers of small hydropower turbines registered with MNRE. SHP continues to be one of the most reliable, efficient, and cleanest forms of energy available among all sources and represents a flexible peak load technology to generate electricity (Sharma, Tiwari and Sood 2013). For industrial development uninterrupted power supply is necessary. Hydro power holds the key in this direction. So states that have rich hydro resources can produce affordable electricity for the furthering of industrial activity. Khan (2015) opines that these kinds of projects are viable but problems such as long gestation period and high interest rates delay the repayment period

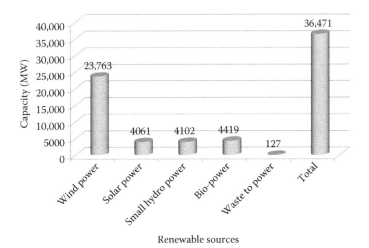

FIGURE 12.2   Grid connected renewable power in India (as of June 30, 2015).

which is also true for other renewable projects. To enhance the viability of small hydro power, the government is committed to expanding the grid connectivity and availability of finance at a cheaper interest rate. But in India, the small hydro power projects are driven by private investment. Government incentivizes the developers from private, cooperative, joint, and government sectors to install small hydro power projects.

12.2.4 Biomass

This form is a source to produce a clean form of energy and it also supports the sustainable development in developing countries (Hart and Rajora 2009). The problem that lies with this form is the availability of adequate biomass at an affordable rate. The present estimate says that in India biomass is available up to 500 million metric tons per year and the potential of producing 5 GW of power.

Biomass is used in cooking in India primarily due to lack of electricity in rural areas (Singh and Setiwan 2013). In order to popularize biomass cooking, the government has taken some initiatives such as National Biogas Manure Management Program (1981) and National Biomass Cookstoves Initiative (2009). As a result, by the end of June 2015 about 4.82 million family biogas plants were installed (MNRE 2015).

At the end of 2015, India has an installed capacity of biomass power of about 1.4 GW. Similarly initiatives have been taken for Bagasse and non-Bagasse cogeneration of 3 GW and 590 MW of power, respectively. Lower costs and higher conversion efficiency are the major reasons for biomass conversion in India (Singh and Gu 2010). Additionally, the government of India is providing a subsidy for growth of biomass energy. As an example, Biomass Gasifier for industries offered capital subsidies: Rs.0.2 million/300 KWe for electrical applications through dual fuel engines, Rs 1 million/100 KWe for 100% producer gas engines with gasifier system, and Rs.0.8 million/100 KWe for 100% gas engines alone (MNRE 2010).

The power generation from biomass will get a boost with the help of government policy to attract investment, improve tariff, and above all the price of the biomass.

12.2.5 Waste to Energy

As of June 30, 2015 waste to energy contributed (Figure 12.3) 147 MW_{EQ} (12.5%) of the off-grid/captive renewable power capacity of 1173 MW_{EQ} in India.

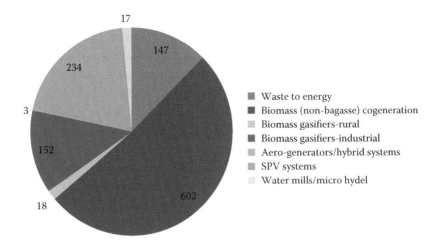

FIGURE 12.3   Off-grid/captive power capacities (MW_{EQ}) in India.

12.3 RE FINANCING: GLOBAL EXPERIENCE

12.3.1 United States

As per Wiser and Pickle (1998), the solar financing-PV industry is dominated by small private companies and wholly owned subsidiaries. Utility PV owners generally use corporate financing while electricity end users finance through internal sources. Also PV manufacturers use internal equity to finance project capital needs in a limited number of circumstances but nonutility generator development and ownership is only beginning to play a vital role in the market. Project financing arrangements have not started. The solar thermal industry developed projects through third-party financing arrangements. The source of equity is utility subsidiaries and institutional investors.

12.3.2 Germany

In Germany, closed end wind funds have become popular with the participation of local citizens. In the past, a group of local project initiators set up a company and invited local residents to join this investment project as limited partners. So partners formed a limited liability partnership that developed, owned, and operated a citizen-owned wind firm. This resulted in an increase in the demand for such projects shares and the model became quite successful. In the process project initiators eventually became project developers. Subsequently it took a different shape when the separation between project development and equity acquisition took place. Project shares became financial products. Matured market players and critical market size facilitated the evolution of a market for shares of closed end wind funds. More players made the placement of fund shares: sales subsidiaries of project developers, banks, and investment consultants. This enhanced market transparency and thereby the emergence of specialists and organizations protecting investor interests.

Private and public companies dominate the space of wind industry. In the early 1980s, all wind power development occurred through tax advantaged limited partnerships of third-party individual investors. A sale and leaseback method was also tried. But more traditional nonrecourse project financing with independent debt and equity investors became the order of the day.

In the context of Germany, Freund and Loock (2011) found that project financing is the foundation of renewable energy. The financing method has been off balance sheet financing, financing can be done looking into future cash inflows from the project which indicates the security and economic performance, and lastly a web of network of project parties and mesh of contracts are made to reduce the risk. And it has been researched that the project financing method is the best one. Most of the projects are financed by the financing institutions on the basis of premium brand technology even setting aside a better debt dervice coverage ratio (DSCR).

Trieb, Stienhagen and Kern (2011) indicate that renewable project investments are long term in nature. They require a huge sum of investments while the revenue stream is not certain, so ensuring financing for such projects becomes difficult. In many countries a power purchase agreement (PPA) is used as a mechanism to cover all types of costs ranging from investments, financing costs, insurance, personnel, and operation costs of plants.

Bobinaite and Travydus (2013) suggest that the multilateral developmental banks also provide financing to renewable projects. Most of the regional development banks provide financing and technical assistance to transition economies for investment projects and policy implementation. Together multinational development banks provide financial assistance to infrastructure projects in the form of loans and grants as well as policy-based loans to governments which in exchange for the loan take commitments to undertake particular economies and financial policies.

Basically the multilateral development banks offer two types of funds to countries; one type of fund is based on the market condition. It is basically a loan that is a nonconcessional loan and the other type is a concessional loan. The nonconcessional loan is provided at a below market interest rate and has a long repayment period. The concessional loan reduces cost of capital and ensures breathing space for repayment by the project developers.

12.4 RE FINANCING MODELS IN INDIA

12.4.1 Equity Financing

The spread between equity costs and debt costs indicates the risks and returns of respective financing. The equity cost is more as the uncertainty associated with the equity is more with the debt. So the equity finance supplier wants a premium for the risk assumed by them. For wind projects in India, the spread is 4–7%, which is very much aligned with the United States and European Union. For solar, however, the observed spread is lower (0–3%). This is surprising as solar technology is less mature in comparison to wind technology (Shrimali et al. 2013). Equity investors are assuming more risk as they want to exploit the advantage of the first mover. The availability of equity from domestic sources and international sources is better than the debt availability (Shrimali et al. 2013).

12.4.2 Debt Financing

Cost of debt financing is high in India. This is due to the high benchmark rates. The benchmark rates are significantly higher than the other developed nations. It is due to the two interplaying factors of demand and supply. Again the cost of capital is too high; enough capital is not available for deployment in the projects in a cost-effective manner. This is due to a growing economy tangled with excessive borrowing (Ambit 2010). There is a difference of 7–8 percentage points in benchmark rates of India and developed countries; the renewable projects costs vary between 5 and 7 percentage points. Again due to a lesser role of developed financial institutions, long-term loans are difficult to get (Bhandari et al. 2003). Indian banks are also funding projects that have a long gestation period. But Indian banks have average maturities of below three years (Business Standard 2012); they are not well equipped to finance longer horizon projects. In general, in India availability of debt for renewable projects is limited. In India, less than one third of the public sector banks lend to renewable projects (Shrimali et al. 2013).

12.4.3 Government Financing/Subsidy

The renewable energy services companies (RESCO) concept is most suitable for small-scale renewable energy systems such as PV solar heating systems. Dozens of RESCOs have been set up to provide sale, installation, and maintenance of solar PV systems in India. Indian IREDA provides low interest loans to wind farm developers. As the technology gains wider acceptance, the loan will be at market rates. The Indian Hilly Hydel project establishes a revolving fund, also administered by IREDA, to provide low interest rates to private entrepreneurs for small hydel projects. The Indian Hilly Hydel projects also devise national strategy and master plans with detailed investment proposals for additional small hydel projects (Liming 2009).

In India subsidies such as capital and interest subsidies are provided by the Ministry of New and Renewable Energy Sources. Import duty reduction is provided to technologies not produced in India. In India the VAT on renewable energy equipment is lower than the normal rate (Liming 2009).

12.5 IMPEDIMENTS OF FINANCING RENEWABLE ENERGY IN INDIA

12.5.1 High Risk and Moderate Return

Investing in renewable projects is perceived to be a risky proposition because returns are not as attractive as alternative options available to investors. Therefore, renewable projects do not attract sufficient investments from institutional investors (Pierpont and Nelson 2013). Furthermore, Pierpont and Nelson (2013) point out that the institutional investors find difficulty in investing in renewable energy projects for various reasons including their investment practices and regulatory issues. Due to newness of some of the renewable projects, bankers perceive the projects as risky and lending cost may be higher (UCS 1999), leading to high cost of finance and lower return compared to conventional technologies.

12.5.2 Undeveloped Bond Market

In India, companies primarily depend on financing sources such as bank financing and financing through the capital markets. Raising finance from the capital markets can be done in two ways. One way is through equity issue and through issue of bonds and debentures. Bonds are known as fixed income securities as it acknowledges debt for the borrower. Usually banks finance for short-term projects. For long-term projects having long gestation periods companies go for issuance of bonds. But the bond market is not developed as there are not adequate players in the bond market.

Reserve Bank of India (2011) observes that listed corporate debt is only 2% of the GDP. Undoubtedly this is very low in comparison to other emerging economies like Malaysia, Korea, and China (Chaudhuri et al. 2014).

In the India bond market, most of the dominant players are the government and quasi government institutions. The issues that are plaguing the bond market are limited variety in instruments, limited investor base, private placement, and limited liquidity. This usually prevents the new players coming to the market for issuing instruments for funds. Ventures such as renewable energy producers also face a tough time for getting funds from the market (Chaudhuri et al. 2014).

12.5.3 Lack of Interest/Trust of Financial Institutions

Financial institutions are not so keen on financing these projects due to lack of awareness regarding the technology, high risk perception, and uncertainties regarding the resource assessment. Investors look for a reasonable return and some sort of risk cover also looked on by the investors. Also banks and financial institutions are being extra cautious while lending to these kinds of projects. Particularly the power purchase agreements (PPA) with the state distribution companies are not viable for the banks to undertake the financing of these projects as the distribution companies are in poor financial health. Also the state governments are unable to curb the losses of these companies due to populism and political compulsions (Painuly et al. 2003).

12.5.4 Lack of Investor-Friendly Environment

Policy initiatives by the subsequent governments are not flashing a coherent message to prospective domestic and foreign investors. Any investment in this regard requires land to start with. Projects require a mechanism to have smooth flow of revenue for sustenance of the project.

12.5.5 Lack of Support from State Government

Success of renewable projects requires a high level of support from state governments and their machinery. At this point in time, the degree of support varies from very low to high. The financial condition of state power distribution companies (Discoms) is dire. India's Discoms have accumulated losses of roughly INR 3.8 trillion (US$57.8 billion) (Kenning 2015). Discom's outstanding debt nearly doubled from INR 2.4 trillion in 2011–2012 to INR 4.3 trillion (US$65.4 billion) in 2014–2015 (PIB 2015). The struggling Discoms complicate the matter further for the project developer causing concern over power purchase and payment. The grim financial health of the Discoms is known for causing long delays in payments under power purchase agreements.

Recently the central government launched a new package named Ujjwal Discom Assurance Yojana (UDAY) to help wipe out the losses of Discoms by 2019, with a view to improve distribution performance and reduce the number of blackouts. UDAY is not compulsory, but participating Discoms and states will be incentivized with various funding options.

UDAY offers four key initiatives to Discoms:

- Improving operational efficiencies
- Reduction of cost of power
- Reduction in interest cost
- Enforcing financial discipline on Discoms through alignment with state finances

Hopefully the Discoms and the states take advantage of the scheme to make the power sector self-sustainable.

12.6 INSTRUMENTS FOR CHANNELIZING FINANCING RE PROJECTS

The primary concern for financing rural renewable energy is source of finance to renewable energy project developers. Also many issues are plaguing the sector like getting low cost funds, institutional complexities that hinder the growth of the market. Though some inroads have been made in making renewable energy available at a small scale, large-scale penetration requires new financing channels and innovative financial products.

Many new methods have been tried and tested in India for the commercialization of renewable energy. These mechanisms are like a combination of government and community financing; development of a market-oriented institutional and financial model for decentralized solar systems; wind power development through combination of the clean development mechanism (CDM) and public sector financing; commercialization of solar hot water systems through a financial intermediary scheme; market development for solar lanterns in a post-subsidy regime; and developing a model for solar pumping systems (Liming 2009).

To increase penetration of renewable energy instruments can be the same kind of instruments that are used by other companies. It can be equity financing, debt financing, tax credits, grants, and prizes (Olmos et al. 2012).

12.7 RE PROGRAMS AND POLICIES IN INDIA: FINANCIAL IMPLICATIONS

Renewable energy programs and policies have direct implication on investment, project development, distribution, and consumption. Over the years, many such initiatives have been implemented with a reasonable amount of success. Some of the notable programs, incentive schemes, and policy measures (Kar and Gopakumar 2015) are listed below:

- Tax incentives for renewable energy project developers
- Feed-in tariff (FiTs)
- Accelerated depreciation benefit (ADB)
- Capital subsidies
- Renewable energy certificates (RECs)
- Generation-based incentives (GBI)

Other policy initiatives such as direct equipment subsidies and rebates, net metering, investment tax credits, preferential tariff, grid-access, banking, wheeling, third-party sales, renewable purchase obligations, and electricity duty exemptions are designed to improve renewable production, distribution, and consumption. Higher consumption of renewables means more distribution and production leading to greater need for investment. Incentive schemes like accelerated depreciation benefit and generation-based incentives reduce financial risk, increase profitability, and improve financial viability of the project.

As per the UDAY the state DISCOMs will comply with the renewable purchase obligation (RPO) outstanding since April 1, 2012, within a period to be decided in consultation with the Ministry of Power. This would certainly help better uptake of renewable power, and so would improve financial viability of renewable projects.

12.8 NEW INITIATIVES FOR RE FINANCING

12.8.1 Renewable Friendly Taxation Policy

If power generation or distribution is undertaken by any firms, a 10-year tax holiday has been offered by the government if the power generation started before March 31, 2014. However, the plant has to pay minimum alternative tax of 20–21%, based on the income, which can be offset in the future 10 years of time.

As per domestic income tax laws companies engaged in producing energy like solar and wind are provided with accelerated depreciation at 80%. However, the government limited the accelerated depreciation of 80% to windmills installed on or before March 31, 2012. Windmills installed after March 31, 2012 are eligible for depreciation of 15% instead of 80% on the written down value method (KPMG 2014).

12.8.2 Carbon Tax

The recent steep decline in international oil prices is seen by many as an opportunity to rationalize the energy prices by getting rid of the distorting subsidies while shifting taxes toward carbon use (*The Economist* 2015). The government of India (GOI) (Economic Survey, 2014–15) takes advantage of the opportune time by reinforcing fiscally prudent measures such as carbon taxes.

Carbon tax is a market-based option to cut down on the emissions level. Carbon taxes are still the most potent instruments in dealing with the threats of climate change (Economic Survey, 2014–15). GOI levies carbon tax through various forms such as excise duty (implicit carbon tax) on petrol or diesel and coal cess. The implicit carbon tax (US$140 for petrol and US$64 for diesel) is substantially above what is now considered a reasonable initial tax on CO_2 emissions of US$25–US$35 per ton. The carbon tax in the case of coal is just about US$1 per ton compared to US$0.5 in 2014. The carbon tax on coal is much lower than petrol and diesel but the intention of the government is very clear from the coal cess hike from INR 50 per ton to INR 100 per ton (2014) and INR 200/ton (2015). Still their scope is for increasing the cess close to INR 500/ton (Economic Survey, 2014–15). This has helped the government to mop up INR 17,000 crore ($2.67 billion)—which can be used for financing green energy. Carbon tax is a mechanism to encourage renewable to be cost competitive with conventional fossil fuel based energy.

12.8.3 Attracting Global Investors

Regulatory uncertainly has been identified as a major concern among renewable energy project developers and investors (Anderson 2013). Frequent policy changes can impact return on investment (ROI) of the renewable project developers and the investors. Therefore, attracting global investors demands political stability and firm long-term policy measures.

12.8.4 Green Bond

Across the globe the green bond market continues to develop; it provides public and private sector organizations with an important source of funding for activities that can bring significant benefits to the environment and society (KPMG 2015). The global green bond issuance reached $7.5 billion in the third quarter of 2015, lifting year-to-date green bond issuance to $27.2 billion and it was expected to exceed $40 billion for the full year of 2015 (Moody's Investor Services, 2015). The agency expects India to be the leader along with China in the regional green bond market. The ambitious renewable capacity addition is expected to drive the green bond market in India.

The Indian Renewable Energy Development Agency (IREDA) issued its first tax free green bond in February 2014 aggregating to Rs. 500 crore. IREDA receives equity capital and will continue to do so in the future. This means investors would have greater confidence in investing in such green bonds.

Comprising only 5.48% of GDP in 2013 and suffering from high and rising interest rates, India's bond market has room to grow and ample potential to grow green (Jaiswal et al. 2015). We are hopeful that the nascent green bond market in India is bound to flourish and fulfill the financing needs of the sector.

12.9 CONCLUSION

India's ambition to become a green energy driven economy is taking shape quite remarkably. India's strategic shift from a carbon subsidy regime to carbon tax regime is a very good sign for the growth of green energy in the country. Carbon taxation clearly disincentivizes the use of polluting fuel and encourages use of green fuel. Also, revenue generated through a carbon taxation mechanism has been used to fund green energy. The government has been very actively pursuing the objectives with serious intent and motivation. A stiffer renewable target set by the government has surprised many including the people in the government.

Achieving a stiffer target is not free from challenges and barriers. The biggest challenge seems to be making funds available for large-scale renewable projects. However, the government is in the mood to leave no stone unturned to achieve the target. All possible financial mechanisms including attracting foreign investors, developing the green bond market, and funding by domestic institutions are actively explored.

The ambitious renewable energy target of 175 GW by 2022 is very much achievable. The issue of financing renewable projects can be addressed through already initiated strategic actions.

REFERENCES

Anderson, J. (2013). Challenge and opportunity: Financing renewable energy projects. Available at http://breakingenergy.com/2013/02/21/challenge-and-opportunity-financing-renewable-energy-projects/, accessed on August 5, 2015.

Ambit. (2010). The inimical cost of debt in India. Available at http://www.Cityoflondon.gov.uk/business/support-promotion-and-advice/promoting-the-city-internationally/india/documents/BC_RS_COLAmbitCOCPosition paperFINALpdf.

Bhandari L., Dasgupta, S., and Gangopadhyay, S. (2003). Development Financial Institutions, Financial Constraints and Growth: Evidence from the Indian Corporate Sector, *Journal of Emerging Market Finance*, 2(1), 83–121.

Bobinaite, V., and Travydus, D. (2014). Financing instruments and channels for the increasing production and consumption of renewable energy: Lithuania case, *Renewable and Sustainable Energy Reviews*, 38, 256–276.

Business Standard. 2012. ECB limits for HFCs should be reasonable. http://www.business-standard.com/india/news/ecb-limits-for-hfcs-should-be-reasonable-nhb/489965/.

Chaudhari, K., Raje, M., and Singh, C. (2014). Corporate bond markets in India: A study and policy recommendation, Working Paper No 450. Indian Institute of Management, Bangalore.

Economic Survey. (2014–15). From carbon subsidy to carbon tax: India's green actions. http://indiabudget.nic.in/es2014-15/echapvol1-09.pdf, accessed on August 6, 2015.

Freund, F.L., and Loock, M. (2011). Debt for brands: Tracking down a bias in financing photovoltaic projects in Germany, *Journal for Cleaner Production*, 19, 1356–1364.

IEA. (2013). Technology roadmap: Wind energy. International Energy Agency, France.

Hart, C.A., and Rajora, M.L. (2009). Overcoming institutional barriers to biomass power in China and India, *Clean Technology and International Trade*, 9(12), 26–65.

Jaiswal, A., Heller, K., Emont, J., and Swamy, L. (2015). India's green bond: Bright example of innovative clean energy financing, available at http://switchboard .nrdc.org/blogs/ajaiswal/indias_green_bond_bright_examp.html, accessed on November 12, 2015.

Kar, S.K., and Sharma, A. (2015a). Wind power developments in India, *Renew. Sustain. Energy Rev.*, 48, 264–275.

Kar, S.K., and Sharma, A. (2015b), Insights into wind energy market developments in India, In: *Energy Sustainability through Green Energy*, Sharma, A. and Kar, S.K., Eds. Springer India.

Kar, S.K., and Gopakumar, K. (2015). Progress of renewable energy in India, *Advances in Energy Research*, 3(2), 97–115.

Kenning, T. (2015). Approved financial health package for India's Discoms will aid solar sector, available http://www.pv-tech.org/news/approved-financial-health -package-for-indias-discoms-will-aid-solar-sector, accessed on November 12, 2015.

Khan, R. (2015). Small Hydro Power in India: Is it a sustainable business? *Applied Energy*, 152, 207–216.

KPMG. (2015). Gearing for green bonds: Key considerations for bond issuers, available at https://www.kpmg.com/Global/en/IssuesAndInsights/Articles Publications/sustainable-insight/Documents/gearing-up-for-green-bonds -v2.pdf, accessed on November 12, 2015.

Liming, H. (2009). Financing rural renewable energy: A comparison between China and India, *Renewable and Sustainable Energy Reviews*. 13, 1096–1103.

MNRE. (2010). Programme on biomass gasifier for industries, available at http:// mnre.gov.in/file-manager/grid-biomass-gasification/biomass-gasifier -industries.pdf.

MNRE. (2014). State wise estimated solar power potential in the country, No. 22/02/2014-15/Solar-R&D (Misc.), http://mnre.gov.in/file-manager/UserFiles /Statewise-Solar-Potential-NISE.pdf.

MNRE. (2015). Physical progress (achievements). Programme/scheme wise phys-ical progress in 2015–16 (during the month of June, 2015). Available at http:// mnre.gov.in/mission-and-vision-2/achievements/, accessed on August 8, 2015.

Moody's Investor Services. (2015). Moody's: Global green bond issuance lags in 3Q 2015, but likely to rise in Q4, available at https://www.moodys.com /research/Moodys-Global-green-bond-issuance-lags-in-3Q-2015-but—PR _336882, accessed on November 12, 2015.

Olmos, L., Ruester, S., and Liong, J.S. (2012). On the selection of financing instru-ments to push the development of new technologies: Application to clean energy technology, *Energy Policy*, 43, 252–266.

Painuly, J.P., Lee, M., Park, H., and Noh, J. (2003). Promoting energy efficiency financing and ESCOs in developing countries: Mechanisms and barriers, *Journal of Cleaner Production*, 11, 659–665.

PIB. (2015). UDAY (Ujwal DISCOM Assurance Yojana) for financial turnaround of power distribution companies, Government of India, November 5, 2015, available at http://pib.nic.in/newsite/PrintRelease.aspx?relid=130261, accessed on November 12, 2015.

Pierpont, B., and Nelson, D. (2013). The challenge of institutional investment in renewable energy, Climate Policy Initiative Report, March.

Sharma, N.K., Tiwari, P.K., and Sood, Y.R. (2013). A comprehensive analysis of strategies, policies and development of hydropower in India: Special emphasis on small hydro power, *Renew. Sustain. Energy Rev.*, 18, 460–470.

Shrimali, G., Nelson, D., Goel, S., Konad, C., and Kumar, R. (2013). Renewable deployment in India: Financing costs and implications for policy, *Energy Policy*, 62, 28–43.

Singh, R., and Setiawan, A.D. (2013). Biomass energy policies and strategies: Harvesting potential in India and Indonesia, *Renew. Sustain. Energy Rev.*, 22, 332–345.

Singh, J., and Gu, S. (2010), Biomass conversion to energy in India—A critique, *Renew. Sustain. Energy Rev.*, 14(5), 1367–1378.

Suzlon. (2015). Suzlon Energy Limited-FY15 Earnings Presentation. May 29. Available at http://www.suzlon.com/pdf/ResultPresentationFY15.pdf, accessed on July 27, 2015.

The Economist. (2015). Seize the day. Available at http://www.economist.com/news/leaders/21639501-fall-price-oil-and-gas-provides-once-generation-opportunity-fix-bad, accessed on August 6, 2015.

Trieb, F., Stienhagen, H.M., and Kern, J. (2011). Financing concentrating solar power in the Middle East and North Africa—Subsidy or investment? *Energy Policy*, 39, 307–317.

UCS. (1999). Barriers to renewable energy technologies. Available at http://www.ucsusa.org/clean_energy/smart-energy-solutions/increase-renewables/barriers-to-renewable-energy.html#.VcIHWfcdDS4, accessed on August 5, 2015.

Vidya, R. (2015). India likely to exceed target of 100 GW of solar power by 2022: Solairedirect chief. The Hindu Business Line, January 5.

Wiser, R.H., and Pickle, J.S. (1998). Financing investments in renewable energy: The impacts of policy design, *Renewable and Sustainable Energy Reviews*, 2, 361–386.

CHAPTER 13

Energy Sustainability and Strategic Communications

Saurabh Mishra and Priyanka Singh

CONTENTS

13.1 INTRODUCTION

It is a threadbare fact that energy has been the harbinger of growth and development of the human race and civilization. Energy utilization has adapted various and many forms through this meandering course of human development. Its incremental utility to humanity has made it even more wanted today than ever. Almost everything around us is supported and functions through energy utilization. Sustainability of this prime source of progress has become an important issue; the world and the economy across its length and breadth are largely dependent on the fate of energy sustainability. For those who have not yet started to think of energy sustainability options, the walls are fast drawing closer. Our modern globalized world is sustained in the present shape because it breathes energy.

Using various kinds of fuels to obtain energy has been the oldest in the knack of things traced through the evolution and realization of energy sources around us. The human race has been since the past and even now is known to be largely dependent on the various fuel sources for the creation of energy. But the times have seen a sea change; fast depleting fuel resources have started to make a dent in the future plans of energy sustainability. As per the United Nations energy sustainability report, "One out of every five people on Earth lives without access to electricity and the opportunities it provides for working, learning, or operating a business. Twice as many—nearly 3 billion people—use wood, coal, charcoal, or animal waste to cook their meals and heat their homes, exposing themselves and their families to smoke and fumes that damage their health and kill nearly 2 million people a year." The world today has well realized that "without access to energy, it is not possible to achieve the Millennium Development Goals" (United Nations 2011).

The fulfillment of these goals tends to achieve energy sustainability which is a pertinent quotient in making the world energy sufficient and sustainable. There are various challenges in achieving this prime goal. Some of the apparent challenges being faced are in the technological sector, research and development, finance, and technical expertise. International Energy Agency (IEA) in its report of October 2011 mentioned energy for all, challenges such as: over 1.3 billion people are without access to electricity and 2.7 billion people are without clean cooking facilities. More than 95% of these people are either in sub-Saharan Africa or developing Asia and 84% are in rural areas. $48 billion per year is required for ensuring universal access of energy for all by 2030; it would increase global electricity generation by 2.5%. Demand for fossil fuels would grow by 0.8% and CO_2 emissions go up by 0.7%, both figures being trivial in relation to concerns about energy security or climate change. The prize of achieving these aims would be a major contribution to social and economic development, and helping the world to avoid the premature death of 1.5 million people per year.

But there is a bigger undiscovered challenge which baits on the future of energy sustainability for the human race. "Strategic communication" stands tall in the way of achieving energy sustainability across the world. Dependency on nonrenewable fuel resources is a big problem. Also making inroads across the existing energy habits of the world population is a herculean task. Revolutionary resurgence of renewable energy resources will not be realized until the populace is informed and persuaded to adapt the required changes in attitude and consumption patterns. Building awareness in this huge, populous, and diverse world is the real task which needs to be fulfilled before the clock ticks. Effectively communicating with the various stakeholders can help to bridge this gap and foster energy sustainability to happen on the face of earth.

The path toward energy sustainability for all by 2030, the goal established by the United Nations, that we seek is multi-forked. The challenges are diverse and multidimensional in nature. Harnessing clean and green energy will not only make the economies of the countries across the world grow but also save the lives of millions of people who are forced to use fuel that emits heavy smoke. But in most of this part of the world it is not going to be easy—regional and cultural traditions, biases, low education levels, and the economic band will pose barriers. This makes the challenge even more bitter to handle. Effectively/strategically communicating the need for change is the only step that could metamorphose the willful and eager transition among the larger world population. The Vision Statement (Nov 2011) of Ban Ki Moon, Secretary General of the United Nations also stresses the need of making all the stakeholders understand the challenge as well as the opportunity, with proper and easy access to information and knowledge.

The aim of this chapter is to plan and suggest communicative ways in which the dream of energy for all by 2030 can be realized through effectively communicating the present scenario across the diverse world by making the people: (1) become aware about the fast depleting fuel resources and methods for their efficient utilization (avoiding carbon emission) and conservation. (2) Adopting and developing technology for embarking on a shift to renewable energy sources (shifting to clean energy sources).

13.2 LOW AWARENESS

People around the world little know or are familiar with the idea of energy sustainability and security. Thus, the biggest and the foremost challenge in communicating the energy challenge to the world is the low level of awareness (Philo and Happer 2012) about the problem itself. Even in today's globalized, socialized, and information burdened world, a lot of people do not carry a fair idea about the issue. Much of what they know about science is by consuming mass media news (Wilson 1995). The citizens of the world got much of their information on energy issues during the Kyoto Protocol in the year 1997, and peaked with the Copenhagen summit in 2009. There was a large increase in the coverage of the issue, which was clearly seen in many countries across the world such as South Africa, New Zealand, the Middle East, Asia, and Eastern Europe. Roughly a mammoth presence of over 400 media organizations from all over the world was seen in Japan during the Kyoto Protocol (Leggett 2001). Studies indicate that media are the key actors in the public perception of risk (Allan et al. 2000). Hence, they are also big stakeholders in articulating public opinions in science-related matters (Nelkin 1987). Even though the media has been identified as the key player in forming the public perception, of late it has also been observed that there is a failure in communication of science to the public by the media worldwide (Boykoff and Nacu-Schmidt 2013).

Less has been said and committed by the world leaders since then; hence, it is less focused and covered by the media. This has led to people having a faint recall of the issue, but when during studies people were educated about the term and the problem they were concerned that it was not higher on the political agenda (Philo and Happer 2012). A larger and serious commitment from state stakeholders and authoritative voices from the scientific community are required on the proliferation of the issue. This would help to vaporize the dominance of nonexpert voices (Philo and Happer 2013) and inculcate the credibility and awareness among the people.

13.3 COMMUNICATING THE MESSAGE

The next big thing is how and who should communicate the message and the urgent need for the change. The decision for communicating the message is crucial; a lot would depend not on what is said, but how it is said. In sustainable energy communications, the target is aimed at first to develop understanding and empathy about the subject and second to accord a behavioral change among all the stakeholders. Constructing the social schematic representations is largely done through the various identified social elements such as political leaders, social activists, business companies, and the media (Carvalho and Burgess 2005; Favre 1992). People in general have lost trust in politicians and the political debates and media discussions on political activities have made people mundane to issues of energy security. Even the energy companies and their operations are seen hovering in doubt of corruption (Philo and Happer 2012). It has also been observed that sometimes the ideas and aspects related to energy security have been overemphasized (Zehr 2000) or are too opinionated and partisan in approach (Hmielowski et al. 2013).

People, in general, while interpreting or forming opinions and attitudes on important issues rely on cognitive heuristics (Fiske and Taylor 1991). The relative lack of awareness about the issue of energy sustainability as expressed earlier in the chapter makes people correlate on the issues largely based on their cognitive schemas. Social cognition is in a way infectious, it spreads and views and opinions based on cognitive heuristics of a small group of people tend to take shape which often is very hard to modify and preferably shape up. The process could be summarized as follows: The message recipient attends to the message arguments, attempts to understand them and then evaluates them. The person then integrates all of the information into a coherent and reasoned position (Petty and Cacioppo 1996: 256). In the current world scenario we are dealing with many such packs of opinions and ideas which are widely spread through the social, cultural, and ethnic fabric of the world population (developed, developing, and underdeveloped). With such a wide and varied set of audience, it is very possible that they may decode the communicated message through their own set of social cognition and not decode the same meanings as intended to be conveyed (Morely 1986; Burgess et al. 1991).

Much has been said and communicated via variations in degree of fear appeals (Henthorne et al. 1993; Dillard and Anderson 2004) and post their exhaustion with the takeover by guilt evocation, through self-persuasion (Burnett and Lunsford 1994; Abe 2004). Over a period of decades and the typical mundane communication lore has impacted people to adopt or even generate a negative view and response for such messages and communication strategies (Coulter and Moore 1999). The message should not be entirely based on emotional appeal, fear, shame, or guilt provoking only that has become redundant practice and much of the target audience has developed immunity toward such campaigns. It should be oriented to guide a social "norm," which is informal in nature and helps to guide and understand situations (Fazio 1990). It has been studied and observed that "perceived norms" can be guided by informational and persuasive messages to induce behavioral changes in people (Lapinski and Rimal 2005).

We should instead strategically aim at building a huge and unparched information pool with credible propagators. This would give the stakeholder's confidence by overcoming their low level of awareness and make them less reliant on their unpatched cognitive heuristics and help them make attitudinal changes in their schematic cluster of ideas and eventually guide and shape a strong and visible behavior change.

13.4 STRATEGY TO FORMULATE THE MESSAGE

Normative cognitive reaction holds the key to the formulation of a successful sustainable energy communication. It is also a deeply held notion that communication acts as a "conduit of influence" in the entire process (Lapinski and Rimal 2005). People tend to base their decisions and thereby behavior on touchstone of "norms"; creation of norms thus should be the primary target of any communication aimed at promoting energy sustainability. Much of the earlier and recent work in the field of forming messages had been based on social cognition (Bandura 1986) and cultivation (Gerbner et al. 1994) of psychological theories. Wherein focus of the work was based and targeted on providing exposure to the media messages and creating informative environment for the audiences. This mundane course led to disinterest and apathy among the audiences. The need of the time is to create subtle psychology-based messages that are aimed to seduce the subconscious mind of the audiences.

Sustainable energy communication strategy should be aimed to inculcate a worldwide and participatory oriented process at all levels of society to promote a high degree of ownership among the stakeholders, including rural and urban communities. The purpose of the strategy should be to trigger stakeholders' and beneficiaries' involvement and secure their commitments by sharing knowledge and information.

Message formulation and dissemination, in the communication process, is often taken as the end activity of the process; assuming the audiences to be passive and inert. This in fact is an unredeemable flaw that is thought to be successful in shaking and provoking the audiences, but fails to convert it to the attitude leading to the target behavioral change. The audience is the first and foremost valued component of any strategic sustainable energy communication.

Categorization of audiences on the basis of their level of awareness and behavioral patterns should be the first step in realizing what kind of message is needed to be formalized. Taylor (1999) has given divisions to this effect in his much accepted and celebrated six-segment message strategy wheel. The model has been effectively built on two communication views (Carry 1975): transmission view and ritual view. These are often synonymous with informational and transformational (Wells 1980; Laskey, Day, and Crask 1989). The model can be used for deciding on the action that is desired to be enacted by a message. Informational or transmission classification is aimed to "impart, send, transmit or give information to consumers" (Carey 1975). Transformational or ritual classification is based on the provoking self-image and importance among people (Taylor 1999).

An ideal classification of an audience should be made on the basis of their awareness, knowledge, interest, and support patterns. This could then in a further broader manner be segmented as positive, neutral, and negative stakeholders. Based on these, a stakeholder engagement plan should be chalked out wherein most effective channels of communication be identified, namely, sponsorships, exhibitions, events, newsletters, public meetings, speeches, Internet (online) postings, awards and prizes, consultative forums (symposia), clubs, VIP visits, and celebrations.

It is a general denouement of various studies that a change in people's attitude and behavior can be favorably attained by normative culturing of injunctive and descriptive norms (Lapinski and Rimal 2005). Therefore, message formulation should be strategized around influencing/changing the descriptive norm for the target audience. This would change the cognitive heuristics of the audience. Taylor's six-segment model (1999) can be converged here with the norm culturing (Figure 13.1).

Thus, if the audience classification under such a model purview would involve the level that is low on awareness, knowledge, interest, and support patterns, the transmission view is subjected to be adopted for message construction. Under a broader scaling these audiences could be scaled

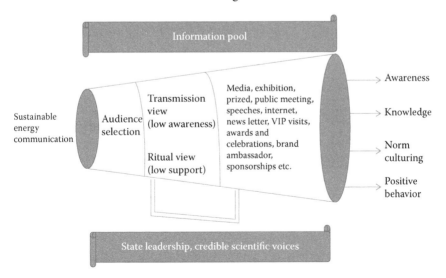

FIGURE 13.1 Depicting the suggested communication map for sustainable energy communication.

under neutral to positive, assuming all other than neutral are either negative or positive stakeholders. This section of the audience should further be targeted to be captured along their interest and routine consumption habits (Taylor 1999).

The above should be treated as the first phase of interaction with such an audience that would help to set the modified "injunctive norm." Followed by the automated triggering of themselves and their associates toward favorable "descriptive norm" and modified targeted behavior.

If the audience is high on awareness, knowledge, and interest, but low on support patterns, under broader scaling they could be scaled under neutral to negative, assuming all other than neutral are either negative or positive stakeholders. This would employ the ritual view to be adopted for message construction in accordance with Taylor's model (1999). Here the message construction should be based on targeting "ego" so as to "allow the consumer to make a statement to him/herself about who he/she is" (Taylor 1999: 13). Since this kind of message is aimed at getting social approvals, it should aim to culture the "descriptive norm."

13.5 CONCLUSION

Sense of ownership and recognition is an important part of any strategic communication. Often messages are just successful in adding to the knowledge bank/awareness about an issue or at least managing an attitude change. Journey beyond communicating vast reserves of knowledge and building attitudes is pretty doubtful. Geller (1981) has expressed, "Despite significant changes in knowledge and attitudes, behavior did not change."

It is also a fact that impact of communication and information processes on societies of every kind is going to increase rapidly in the coming decades. The volume and speed of information flows, and the number of people who have access to them, is rising fast, while costs decline (Financial Times 2007). But with this rapid bombardment and flow of information in the current scenario people are constantly scanning their surroundings, unconsciously and automatically, to determine whether there is something deserving of our focused attention. The only mental action they perform is to determine the relevance of what they perceive. They do not do much else with the data because every word and image contains more information than they are inclined to use or process further (Franzen 1999: 41).

Strategic communication works to mull interest among the stakeholders and helps to generate trust featuring the light of feasibility solutions in the requisite area. The communicative campaign should be promoted within a community framework, so that "the desired behavior should result in peer approval rather than scorn" (Harvey and McCrohan 1988: 147). There should be a possible effective dialogue initiation and wherein people's norms are formed and sustained to guide positive behavioral changes. This makes it very difficult for the stakeholders to move away in any case from the secured and sealed societal cognition which they themselves have worked to evolve.

REFERENCES

Abe, J. A. (2004). Shame, guilt and personality judgment. *Journal of Research in Personality*, 38 (2): 85–104.

Ajzen, I. and Fishbein, M. (1980). *Understanding attitudes and predicting social behavior*. Englewood Cliffs, NJ: Prentice Hall.

Ajzen, I. (1991). The theory of planned behavior. *Organizational Behavior and Human Decision Processes,* 50: 179–211.

Allan, S., Adam, B. and Carter, C. (Eds.). (2000). *Environmental Risks and the Media*. London and New York: Routledge.

Bandura, A. (1986). *Social foundations of thought and action: A social cognitive theory*. Englewood Cliffs, NJ: Prentice Hall.

Barnett et al. (1996), as cited in Borsari and Carey (2003). Descriptive and injunctive norms in college drinking: A metaanalytic integration. *Journal of Studies on Alcohol,* 64: 331–341.

Berger, C. R. and Calabrese, R. (1975). Some explorations in initial interactions and beyond: Toward a development theory of interpersonal communication. *Human Communication Research*, 1: 99–112.

Berger, C. R. (1987). Communicating under uncertainty. In M. E. Roloff and G. R. Miller (Eds.), *Interpersonal processes*. Newbury Park, CA: Sage, pp. 39–62.

Berkowitz, A. D. (2004), as cited in Lapinski, M. K. and Rimal, R. N. (2005, p. 137). An explication of social norms. *Communication Theory*, 15 (2): 127–147.

Borsari, B. and Carey, K. B. (2001). Peer influences on college drinking: A review of the research. *Journal of Substance Abuse*, 13: 391–424.

Borsari, B. and Carey, K. B. (2003). Descriptive and injunctive norms in college drinking: A metaanalytic integration. *Journal of Studies on Alcohol*, 64: 331–341.

Boykoff, M. T. and Boykoff, J. M. (2004). Balance as bias: Global warming and the US prestige press, *Global Environmental Change*, 14: 125–136.

Boykoff, M. T. (2007). Flogging a dead norm? Newspaper coverage of anthropogenic climate change in the United States and United Kingdom from 2003 to 2006, *Area,* 39 (2).

Boykoff, M. T. and Rajan, S. R. (2007). Signals and noise: Mass-media coverage of climate change in the USA and the UK, *European Molecular Biology Organisation Reports,* 8 (3).

Boykoff, M. T. and Goodman, M. K. (2009). Conspicuous redemption? Reflections on the promises and perils of the "Celebritization" of climate change, *Geoforum*, 40.

Boykoff, M. T. and Smith, J. C. (2010). Media presentations of climate change. In Lever-Tracy, C., Ed. *Routledge handbook of climate change and society*. New York: Routledge, pp. 210–218.

Boykoff, M. T. and Nacu-Schmidt, A. (2013). Cooperative Institute for Research in Environmental Sciences (CIRES), Center for Science and Technology Policy Research (CSTPR), University of Colorado.

Burgess, J., Harrison, C. M. and Maiteny, P. (1991). Contested meanings: The consumption of news about nature conservation. *Media, Culture and Society*, 13: 499–519.

Burnett, M. S. and Lunsford, D. A. (1994). Conceptualizing guilt in the consumer decision making process. *Journal of Consumer Marketing*, 11 (3): 33–43.

Carey, J. W. (1975). A cultural approach to communication. *Communication*, 2: 1–22.

Carvalho, A. and Burgess, J. (2005). Cultural circuits of climate change in U.K. Broadsheet Newspapers, 1985–2003. *Risk Analysis*, 25 (6).

Cialdini, R. B., Reno, R. R., and Kallgren, C. A. (1990). A focus theory of normative conduct: Recycling the concept of norms to reduce littering in public places. *Journal of Personality and Social Psychology*, 58: 1015–1026.

Coulter, R. H., Cotte, J., and Moore, M. L. (1999). Believe it or not: Persuasion, manipulation and credibility of guilt appeals. *Advances in Consumer Research*, 26 (1): 288–295.

Crask, M. R., Day, E., and Laskey, H. A. (1989). Typology of main message strategies. *Journal of Advertising*, 18 (1): 36–41.

Fazio, R. H. (1990). Multiple processes by which attitudes guide behaviors: The MODE model as an integrative framework. In M. P. Zanna (Ed.), *Advances in experimental social psychology* San Diego, CA: Academic Press, Vol. 23, pp. 75–109.

Financial Times. (2007). India & globalisation special report, 26: 6.

Fiske, S. T. and Taylor, S. E. (1991). *Social cognition* (2nd ed.), New York: McGraw-Hill.

Franzen, G. (1999). *Brands and advertising*. Henley-on-Thames, UK: Admap Publications.

Frazer, C. (1983). Creative strategy: A management perspective. *Journal of Advertising*, 12 (1): 36–41.

Geller, E. (1981). Evaluating energy conservation programs: Is verbal report enough? *Journal of Consumer Research*, 8 (3): 331–335.

Gerbner, G., Gross, L., Morgan, M., and Signorielli, N. (1994). Growing up with television: The cultivation perspective. In J. Bryant and D. Zillmann (Eds.), *Media effects: Advances in theory and research*. Hillsdale, NJ: Erlbaum, pp. 17–41.

Golan, G. J. and Zaidner, L. (2008). Creative strategies in viral advertising: An application of Taylor's six-segment message strategy wheel. *Journal of Computer-Mediated Communication*, 13 (4): 959–972.

Harvey, J. W. and McCrohan, K. F. (1988). Is there a better way of improving compliance with the tax laws? Insights from the philanthropic literature. *Journal of Public Policy & Marketing*, 7 (1).

Henthorne, T. L., Latour, M. S., and Nataraajan, R. (1993). Fear appeals in print advertising: An analysis of arousal and ad response. *Journal of Advertising*, 22 (2): 59–70.

Hmielowski, J. D., Feldman, L., Myers, T. A., Leiserowitz, A., and Maibach, E. (2014). An attack on science? Media use, trust in scientists, and perceptions of global warming. *Public Understanding of Science*, 23.7: 866–883.

Hwang, J., McMillan, S. J., and Lee, G. (2003). Corporate Web sites as advertising: An analysis of function, audiences, and message strategy. *Journal of Interactive Advertising*, 3.

Lapinski, M. K. and Rimal, R. N. (2005). An explication of social norms. *Communication Theory*, 15 (2): 127–147.

Laskey, H. A., Day, E. and Crask, M. R. (1989). Typology of main message strategies, *Journal of Advertising*, 18 (1): 36–41.

Leggett, J. (2001). *The carbon war: Global warming and the end of the oil era*. New York: Routledge.

Morley, D. (1986). *Family Television*. London: Comedia.

Nelkin, D. (1987). *Selling Science: How the Press Covers Science and Technology*. New York: W. H. Freeman.

Park, H. S. and Smith, S. W. (2007). Distractiveness and influence of subjective norms, personal descriptive and injunctive norms, and societal descriptive and injunctive norms on behavioral intent: A case of two behaviors critical to organ donation. *Human Communication Research*, 33: 194–218.

Petty, R. E. and Cacioppo, J. T. (1986). *Communication and persuasion: Central and peripheral routes to attitude change*, New York: Springer.

Philo, G. and Happer, C. (2012). *Climate change and energy security: Assessing the impact of information and its delivery on attitudes and behavior* (Report No. UKERC/RR/HQ/2012/002), London: UKERC.

Philo, G. and Happer, C. (2013). *Communicating climate change and energy security new methods in understanding audiences*. New York: Routledge, Taylor & Francis Group.

Plotnik, R. and Kouyoumdjian, H. (2011). *Introduction to Psychology* (9th ed.), Wadsworth: Cengage Learning.

Pluto, C. P. and Wells, W. D. (1984). Informational and transformational advertising: The differential effects of time. In Kinnear, T. C. (Ed.), *NA - Advances in Consumer Research* Volume 11, Provo, UT: Association for Consumer Research, pp. 638–643.

Price, D. J. and Anderson, J. W. (2004). The role of fear in persuasion. *Psychology & Marketing*, 21 (11): 909–926.

Rimal, R. J. and Real, K. (2005). How behaviors are influenced by perceived norms: A test of the theory of normative social behavior. *Communication Research*, 32 (3): 389–414.

Rogers, E. M. (1995). *Diffusion of innovations*. (4th ed.). New York: Free Press.

Sherif, M. (1936). *The psychology of social norms*. New York: Harper & Brothers.

Strauss, J. and Frost, R. D. (1999). *Marketing on the Internet: Principles of on-line marketing*, Paramus, NJ: Prentice-Hall.

Taylor, R. E. (1999). A six-segment message strategy wheel, *Journal of Advertising Research*, 39 (6).

United Nations. (2011). Sustainable energy for all a vision statement by Ban Ki-moon, Secretary-General of the United Nations. New York: United Nations.

Wells, W. D. (1980). *How advertising works*, Chicago, IL: Needham Harper Worldwide.

Wilson, K. M. (1995). Mass media as sources of global warming knowledge. *Mass Communications Review*, 22 (1&2): 75–89.

Zehr, S. C. (2000). Public presentations of scientific uncertainty about global climate change. *Public Understanding of Science*, 9 (2): 85–103.

END NOTES

a. Norm: In the social sciences, norms are generally defined as "the customs, traditions, standards, rules, values, fashions and all other criteria of conduct which are standardized as a consequence of contact with individuals" (Sherif 1936: 3).

b. Subjective Norm: A subjective norm refers to the pressure an individual feels to behave a certain way because of what others expect (Ajzen and Fishbein 1975). Parks and Smith (2007) conceptualize subjective norms as what important others think should be done, and/or what behavior should or should not be enacted.

c. Collective Norms: Refers to information that comes from a larger source, such as a community, the media, etc. (Lapinsky and Rimal 2005). Perceived norms refer to information that comes from an individual's social group or important others (Lapinski and Rimal 2005).

d. Descriptive Norms: Refer to belief about what is actually done by most others in an individual's social group (Lapinskyi and Rimal 2005), or the popularity of a behavior among important people.

e. Injunctive Norms: Refer to people's beliefs about what ought to be done or social approval of the act (Cialdini, Reno, and Kalgreen 1990).

f. Audience: In this chapter implies all the stakeholders of energy sustainability.

g. Message Strategy: A term that is related with message formulation in the strict sense of "what to say" rather than "how to say it" (Taylor 1999; Frazer 1983).

h. Transmission View: Transmission or informational classification is suggested as "to impart, send, transmit or give information" (Hwang, McMillan, and Lee 2003: 3), basically fulfilling the audience need for data and information.

i. Ritual View: Ritual or transformational view deals with harnessing emotional, self-gratifying, unconventional, or original means and strategies to reach audiences (Pluto and Wells 1984; Laskey, Day, and Crask 1989; Taylor 1999; Golan and Zaider 2008).

j. Schemas: Schemas are mental categories that, like computer files, contain knowledge about people, events, and concepts. Because schemas affect what we attend to and how we interpret things, schemas can influence, bias, and distort our thoughts, perceptions, and social behaviors (Plotnik and Kouyoumdjian 2011).

k. Ego: Emotionally and personally important to audiences and allow the audiences to make a statement to him/herself about who he/she is (Taylor 1999: 13).

CHAPTER 14

Policy Reforms in Indian Energy Sector to Achieve Energy Security and Sustainability

Vinayak V. Pathak, Richa Kothari,

Vineet V. Tyagi, and Balchandra Yadav

CONTENTS

14.1 INTRODUCTION

Sustainability and energy efficiency in energy systems are the main issues in the global power sector and these are the significant determinants of future energy choices and policy decisions (Jannuzzi, 2005). Developing countries are facing dual challenges to cope with the huge power demand for large population and to maintain the pace of economic development. Incorporation of clean technologies in the power sector with a market pull approach has the potential to address these challenges (Williams, 2001; Patterson et al., 2002). Reforms in the power sector have created various opportunities in the R&D sector and challenges as well; it has also motivated to innovate indigenous solutions. In the case of India, the R&D sector is out of tradition and most of the technologies are adopted from developed countries (Intarakumnerd et al., 2002). Developing countries represent an insignificant share to their GDP in R&D in comparison to developed countries. Developing countries have 0.65% share of R&D to their GDP in comparison to 3% share to GDP of industrialized countries in 1994 (Hadjimanolis and Dickson, 2001). In the last 20 years, a steady growth in expenditure in the R&D sector was observed in India, which was about 0.9% to the GDP in 2014. Despite the increment in expenditure in the R&D sector as a share to GDP, India is far behind in comparison to industrialized countries (Japan, 3.39; Korea Rep, 4.04; Israel, 3.93; Italy, 1.27; Finland, 3.55; Germany, 2.92; China, 1.98; Malaysia, 1.07) (Datta et al., 2015).

Apart from the significant role of R&D for the energy sector, the Indian power sector has also witnessed the liberalization and reform of the economy in 1991–1992. In the 1980s, the Indian power sector was rapidly growing, though issues like large distribution losses, low efficiency, reliable power supply, and a long overdue tariff policy severely affected the power sector. Economic liberalization allows private players in Indian power sectors, which has significant impact on energy generation, distribution, and pricing. Climate change issue is another driver for reform in the Indian energy sector. Rapid industrialization to achieve high economic growth has created a diverse situation for the environment. It is due to exploitation of huge fossil fuel (coal, oil, and natural gas) in the industrial sector. In 2006, India was the fifth largest importer of oil and gas in the world. Government sponsored studies have estimated that power consumption would be increased by 50% compared to the reference year of 2005, and by 2031–2032, there will be need for two- to three-fold of energy than the energy of the present scenario for sustaining economic growth. Thus, rapid economic development has contributed to greenhouse gas emission and energy security challenges. The Indian power sector has been primarily the responsibility of the Indian government through its central state driven utilities. Prior to independence, the state played a significant role in the development of power in concerned states. In this regard, the electricity act of 1948 (MoP, 1948) has issued the mandate for the state to carry the responsibility to plan and implement power development programs in their respective states. State electricity boards completely failed to achieve their objectives and raised power crisis and financial losses. This issue triggered several changes in policy and regulatory framework. Rural electrification was also a major challenge in the Indian energy sector; hence, various initiatives have been taken to achieve 100% rural electrification as given in Table 14.1. Recently, the Indian government has issued power for all initiatives in 2014, for a timeframe of 5 years. The program integrated the state-specific plan, central plans, and planned private investors (Josey and Sreekumar, 2015).

To raise the power generation capacity, the government of India formulated a policy in 1991 to encourage investment from the private sector and market development. Reforms involved private sector participation in electricity generation, with up to 100% foreign investor rights and simplified administrative procedures for clearance of projects (Singh, 2006). For further improvement, a central electricity regulation commission ordinance was issued in April 1998 to regulate the rationalization of tariff, transparent policies regarding subsidies, to promote efficient and environmental

TABLE 14.1   Initiatives and Commitments for Rural Electrification

Government Initiative	Commitment	Target Year for Completion
Electricity Supply Act (1948)	Expansion of electricity to semi urban and rural areas	No target year; 0.5% village electrification
Conference of chairman of SEBs (1976)	100% village electrification	1995
Rajadhyaksha Committee Report (1980)	100% village electrification	1995
National Development Council (1994)	100% household electrification	2010
Conference of chief ministers (2001)	Power for all	2012
National Common Minimum Program (2004)	100% household electrification	2009
National Electricity Policy (2005)	Providing 1 unit/household/ day as a merit good	2012
Rural Electrification Policy (2006)	100% village electrification, 100% village household	2009 revised to 2012
Power for all (2014)	24 × 7 power supply for all	2019

Source: Josey A. and Sreekumar N. "Power for all. Is anything being learnt from past programmes?". *Economic and Political Weekly* 41 (October 10, 2015): 13–16.

benign policies. Since then several reforms have been introduced in the Indian power sector to ensure energy security and compliance with global climate change issues. The present chapter is focused on those factors which have introduced the reforms in the energy sector and challenges in policy implementation. A critical summary of energy sector reforms is also a part of this chapter. Thus, the chapter provides actual remarks on policy reforms and suggestive measures to ensure energy sufficiency and sustainability.

14.2 MOTIVATION FOR ENERGY SUFFICIENCY AND SUSTAINABILITY

Reform in the energy sector to achieve energy efficiency shows the long-term cost-effective opportunities to cope with growing energy needs. The beginning of rapid economic development in India has led to significant power consumption and emission of carbon dioxide. In this context, the United Nation Foundation (UNF) has suggested the mutual accountability of G8 and developing countries with high consumption to achieve energy efficiency. UNF suggested that energy efficiency is the key to sustainable economical development and countries (G8 and developing) should adopt energy-efficient technology as a first priority. Climate change concern at the global level has also provided a framework to develop innovation in the energy sector. Development of renewable technologies in India has been effectively influenced by this global issue.

14.2.1 Economic Development and Energy Efficiency

Market-oriented economic reforms also affect energy efficiency (Fan et al., 2007). Energy efficiency is associated with economic status, extent of technology, living conditions, and institutional management (Wei et al., 2006). Commercial policies promote the private investment which is positively correlated with energy efficiency. This conclusion is more significant in the case of developing countries such as India (Meyers, 1998). Economic reforms in India accelerated industrial development, which was the high energy intensive development. Industrial energy demand accounts for more than 50% of the total energy demand (IEA, 1994). High energy input in the industrial sector was not sustainable; hence, an energy efficient practice was introduced to achieve sustainability. Policy reforms to promote energy efficient technology have changed conventional technology and were substituted with advance machinery. An advisory board on energy was set up in 1983, which provided the energy demand projection in different sector until 2004 by taking a variety of macroeconomic scenarios. Furthermore, the Indian Law Institute prepared a draft of an energy conservation bill in 1987 following instruction of the advisory board. The main objective of this bill was to provide a legal framework for efficient and lucid use of energy and resources. The bill also framed a Nodal Energy Conservation Organization (NECO) and the states and central government agencies are bound to follow the recommendations and assumptions of this organization (Dey, 2007). Various innovative programs were launched in 1990 by the Indian government to promote energy conservation such as National Energy Conservation Day (December 14), National Energy Conservation Award, Eco Mark to ensure environmentally friendly practices, and voluntary programs on energy efficiency (Balchandra et al., 2010).

The Bureau of Energy Efficiency (BEE) was created after the enactment of the Energy Conservation Bill, 2001. The BEE was enacted to implement the provisions of the Energy Conservation Bill; hence, as a result BEE has prepared the first energy conservation plan for implementation of standards of energy efficiency (Planning Commission, 2006). The standards cover labeling of appliances, demand side management, energy efficiency in commercial buildings, capacity building of energy managers and auditors, and energy performance code (FICCI, 2002). Energy pricing was the main barrier to promoting energy efficient technologies and programs. However, at the end of the tenth five-year plan, the government has realized that energy efficient technologies and programs are the major factors in achievement of 9.1% growth rate (Review of the Economy, 2007–2008). Thus, the government continues to promote energy efficiency programs and introduced tariffs and subsidies in energy pricing to remove the barriers. In this context, an integrated energy policy was introduced in 2006 to ensure the maximum energy efficiency and demand side management. Balachandra et al. (2010) have summarized the policy reforms to achieve energy efficiency in five phases, which is depicted by Figure 14.1.

14.2.2 Clean Development Mechanism (CDM)

Clean development mechanism is a large source for mitigation finance to developing countries (World Bank, 2009), which is the key motivation to develop clean energy technologies in the country. India has been one of the biggest implementers of CDM projects and has about 850 registered projects. India's efforts to promote clean energy have generated new governance and institutions to deal with clean energy projects. Clean energy governance deals with CDM projects and procedures with political and

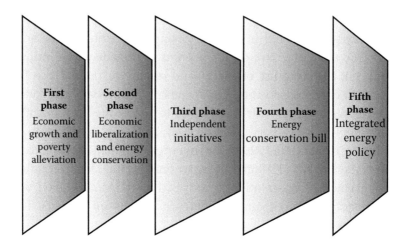

FIGURE 14.1   Policy reforms to achieve energy efficiency.

economic relations in the energy sector. Governance of clean energy in India is driven by global financial organizations as well as climate co-benefits for domestic action to meet the global commitments (Phillips and Newell, 2013). Global financial programs include Asian Developmental Bank, United National Developmental Program, and German Technical Corporation. These global programs have helped in the renewable market development, address apparent market failure, and maintain the government interest to initiate clean development mechanisms. Apart from the global pressure and financial support regulatory framework, incentives and private market development are other factors to develop renewable technologies in India. To ensure the low carbon pathway India formulated the National Action Plan on Climate Change in June 2008. This plan consists of policies and programs for climate change mitigation and adaptation. In this plan, eight missions were declared for implementation to mete out the climate change issue (PMINDIA, 2008).

State level governance has a key role in the extent of benefits from CDM. States like Maharashtra, Karnataka, Tamilnadu, and Rajasthan have more than 200 CDM projects at the validation stage while other states have no CDM projects at all (Fenhann, 2012). States enabling CDM projects have developed single window policies for clearance of CDM projects. Local governance also plays a significant role in the distribution of CDM benefits among the citizens. CDM projects require public consultation before their implementation. Opportunity of jobs, local development, and access to technology are the attractive issues to involve

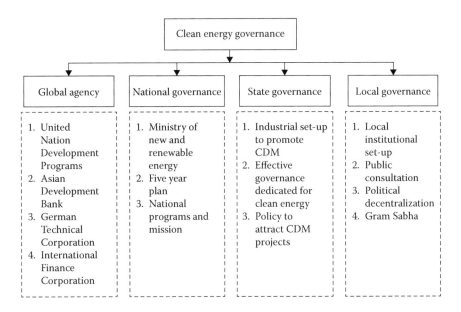

FIGURE 14.2 Framework for clean energy governance in the Indian government sector.

local citizens for public consultation. Institutional policy at the local level involves a project developer, and state and local people to mediate the CDM (Chapman, 2011). Figure 14.2 provides the framework of clean energy governance in India for effective implementation of a clean development mechanism.

14.3 CHALLENGES IN POWER SECTOR REFORMS AND SUGGESTIVE MEASURES

14.3.1 Lack of Public Investment in Renewables

India has set a voluntary commitment to follow the low carbon pathway by developing and introducing renewable energy technologies in the energy sector. In this way, India has taken a resolution to reduce the emission intensity of GDP by 20 to 25% from the level of 2005 by 2020. Public investment in the renewable energy (RE) sector is very limited, which is a major challenge in achievement of grid parity with RE technologies. According to the New Finance Report (Bloomberg, 2012), the investment in Indian energy sector is of "Asset financing," which indicates loan or equity capital. The high cost associated with RE is one of the reasons for less public investment. Public investment is essential in India to bring down the high capital cost of RE and establish effective RE markets. Attractiveness for

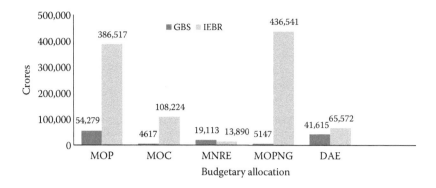

FIGURE 14.3   Budgetary allocation to various ministries in the twelfth five-year plan.

RE from the public sector can be achieved through incorporation of localized efforts in the development of off-grid connectivity for household use.

14.3.2 Inadequate Budget Allocation

A budgetary priority attached with the RE sector in the twelfth five-year plan is quite disappointing. Investment of conventional energy sources is significantly higher compared to renewable energy. In the twelfth five-year plan, the gross budgetary support (GBS) for the renewable sector is 19,113 crore, while the GBS is higher for other ministries dealing with conventional energy sources (Ministry of Power, 54,279 crore; Ministry of Coal, 4617 crore; Ministry of Petroleum and Natural Gas, 5147 crore) (Figure 14.3) (MNRE twelfth five-year plan). Apart from the GBS, the internal and extra budgetary resources to raise the resource development are also low in the case of the renewable energy sector. Thus, in the whole energy sector the renewable energy sector is a subsidiary and it needs to be mainstreamed by budgetary and policy perspectives. Besides, budgetary allocation compared to other sectors, MNRE itself has reduced symmetry in fund allocation for development of various renewable resources. The expenditure trend over the eleventh plan period shows that the solar energy sector has received about 50% of the budget, while the other sectors such as wind, small hydro, and biomass were of a lesser priority (Energy Forever, 2014).

14.3.3 Technological Challenges

Technical challenges in the Indian power sector include less efficient thermal power plants, dominated coal-based power supply, and inadequate transmission and distribution network (Garg, 2012). Efficiency in electric generation through coal-fired power plants requires integrated gasification combined cycle technology, which can enhance the energy output with reduced emission. The challenge in this way is to adopt this technology on quality of coal found in India. According to the IEA (2011), nuclear energy would increase by a factor of 30 in 2050, which requires thorium more effectively from its source. Development of fast breeder reactor and heavy water reactor will also facilitate the sufficiency of nuclear energy. Nuclear energy with a safety first slogan should be addressed by technological improvements of a less hazardous nature. Solar photovoltaics and concentrated solar power (CSP) have significant potential in bridging the country's energy supply and demand gap. However, it needs technological improvements to reduce the cost and improve the conversion efficiency. There is a significant improvement in the bioenergy sector in India, but technologies are lacking conversion efficiency and cost-effectiveness. Biomass-based energy generation is achieved through anaerobic digestion, gasification, cogeneration, or biofuel production (Garg, 2011).

14.3.4 Resource Availability and Effective Consumption

The share of domestic energy resources to fulfill the primary energy demand was about 77% in 2007, which shows a high degree of self sufficiency in comparison to other areas such as Europe (55%) and the United States (70%) (WEO, 2007). This can be easily understood by increased import of oil and coal over the recent years. Apart from resource availability, types of resource quality also affect investment in the energy sector. Despite enough coal reserve, coal import has grown over recent years to meet the technological demand for high energy efficiency and reduced emissions (Coal in India, 2015). Indigenous coal is high in ash content, and hence produces low thermal emission and high particulate emission. India has significant hydropower potential; however, only one quarter of the whole potential is harnessed (MNRE, 2010). Large hydropower plants are highly criticized in India for their adverse impact on the river ecosystem. Thus significant efforts should be taken to minimize the adverse impact that is possible with installation of mini hydropower plants. India is top in its agricultural practices compared to other countries, which generates a huge amount of biomass in the form of crop residues. On the other hand, woody biomass also has significant potential to meet the energy needs of a growing population. Thus, regionwise biomass mapping may enhance resource availability (Ramachandra TV, 2007).

14.4 CONCLUSION

In this chapter, an attempt was made to analyze reforms in the power sector to lead to energy security and sustainability with assessment of challenges to achieve policy objectives. A comprehensive discussion has been presented to track the cause and necessity of power reforms by taking the evidence from previous studies and decisions made by the government of India. India has significantly achieved energy security and efficient energy use by enabling the promoting of power generation and efforts for its conservation. Economic development in India has accelerated energy-intensive practices and caused rapid energy consumption. The realizations to overcome energy shortage and sustain use of energy resources have developed the policy for energy efficiency. The power sector reform thus follows a series of efforts to enhance the energy capacity, optimum use of resources, energy efficiency, and sustainability. Private participation in the energy market has changed the conventional energy sector of India and plays a significant role in power generation. It reduces the superiority of state electricity boards and provides more suitable power supply by centralizing the end user (consumer). Reforms such as introduction of subsidies and incentives helped in spreading electrification in rural areas. These efforts are assessed and barriers are identified. Financial budgetary allocation to promote clean energy technologies and lack of public interest toward renewable purchase have marginalized the alternative energy sector. Innovative efforts to attract the public attention toward renewable energy can be improve the situation. Public consultation is necessary while dealing with energy sector reforms especially in the case of rural electrification. These suggestions are necessary to design new energy policy to promote energy-efficient technologies.

REFERENCES

Balchandra P., Ravindranath D., and Ravidranath N.H. "Energy efficiency in India: Assessing the policy regimes and their impacts". *Energ Policy* 38 (2010): 6428–6438.

Bloomberg New Energy Finance. "Global trends in renewable energy investment 2012". FS-UNEP Collaborating Centre, Frankfurt, Germany, 2012.

Chapman S. "Assessing 'good' carbon governance in India. Good carbon governance". *Working Paper 4*. Cambridge Centre for Climate Change Mitigation Research, Cambridge, 2011.

Datta M., Neogi C., and Sinha A. "Sectoral shares in Indian GDP: How to regard it?" *Structural Change and Economic Dynamics* 35 (2015): 1–11.

Dey D. "Initiatives to improve energy efficiency of the Indian Economy: A review of the past experience sand future challenges". *Social Science Research Network*, India, 2007. www.papers.ssrn.com/sol3/papers.cfm?abstract_id=1028510.

Energy Forever. 27th Annual report of IREDA (Indian Renewable Development Agency). Ministry of New and Renewable Energy, Government of India, New Delhi, 2014.

Fan Y., Liao H., and Wei Y.M. "Can market oriented economic reforms contribute to energy efficiency improvement? Evidence from China". *Energy Policy* 35 (2007): 2287–2295.

Fenhann J. "CDM project distribution with in host countries by region and type". UNEP, Risø Centre, Roskilde, 2012.

FICCI. "International conference on strategies for energy conservation in the new millennium". New Delhi, 2002. http://www.ficci.com/media-room/speeches-presentations/2002/aug/aug23-energy-pm.htm.

Garg P. "Evaluation of water use at different scale". *Biofuels, Bioproducts and Biorefining* 5(4) (2011): 361–374.

Garg P. "Energy scenario and vision 2020 in India". *Journal of Sustainable Energy and Environment* 3 (2012): 7–17.

Hadjimanolis A. and Dickson K. "Development of national innovation policy in small developing countries: The case of Cyprus". *Research Policy* 30 (2001): 805–817.

Intarakumnerd P., Chairatana P., and Tangchitpiboon T. "National innovation system in less successful developing countries: The case of Thailand". *Research Policy* 31 (2002): 1445–1457.

International Energy Agency (IEA). "Energy in developing countries: A sectoral analysis". OECD/IEA, 1994.

Jannuzzi G.M. "Power sector reforms in Brazil and its impacts on energy efficiency and research and development activities". *Energy Policy* 33 (2005): 1753–1762.

Josey A. and Sreekumar N. "Power for all. Is anything being learnt from past programmes?". *Economic and Political Weekly* 41 (October 10, 2015): 13–16.

Meyers S. "Improving energy efficiency: Strategies for supporting sustained market evolution in developing and transitioning countries". Report LBL-41460. Lawrence Berkeley Laboratory, Berkeley, CA, 1998.

MNRE 2010. Renewable energy in India: Progress, vision and strategy. Paper Presented at the Delhi International Renewable Energy Conference (DIREC), New Delhi, October 27–29, 2010.

MoP, The Electricity (Supply) Act, 1948. http://powermin.nic.in.

Patterson W., Anton E., and Carlos E.S. "Towards sustainable electricity policy". In: Thomas B.J., Jose G. (Eds.), *Energy for Sustainable Development: A Policy Agenda*. United Nations Development Programme, Bureau for Development Policy, New York, 2002, pp. 77–114.

Phillips J. and Newell P. "The governance of clean energy in India: The clean development mechanism (CDM) and domestic energy politics". *Energy Policy* 59 (2013): 654–662.

Planning Commission. "Integrated energy policy". Planning Commission. Government of India, New Delhi, 2006.

Ramachandra T.V. "Geospatial mapping of bioenergy potential in Karnataka, India". *Energy and Environment* 6 (2007): 28–42.

Review of the Economy 2007/08. Economic Advisory Council to the Prime Minister, New Delhi, 2008.

Singh A. "Power sector reform in India: Current issues and prospects". *Energy Policy* 34 (2006): 2480–2490.

Williams R.H. "Addressing challenges to sustainable development with innovative energy technologies in a competitive electric industry". *Energy for Sustainable Development* 2 (2001), 48–73.

World Bank. "World development report 2010: Climate change and development". World Bank Group, Washington DC, 2009.

World Energy Outlook 2007. "China and India insights". *International Energy Agency* (2007). https://www.iea.org/publications/freepublications/publication/weo_2007.pdf.

CHAPTER 15

Geopolitics of Energy

Ajay Kumar Chaturvedi

CONTENTS

15.1 INTRODUCTION

Geopolitics is the study of the effects of geography (human and physical) on international politics and international relations.[1] Geopolitics is a method of studying foreign policy to understand, explain, and predict international political behavior through geographical variables. These include area studies, climate, topography, demography, natural resources, and applied science of the region being evaluated.[2] Geopolitics focuses on political power in relation to geographic space. In particular, territorial waters and land territory in correlation with diplomatic history. Academically, geopolitics analyzes history and social science with reference to geography in relation to politics. Topics of geopolitics include relations between the interests of international political actors, interests focused on an area, space, geographical element or ways, and relations that create a geopolitical system.[3] However, the term has been used to describe a broad spectrum of ideas, from "A synonym for international relations, social, political and historical phenomena"[4,5] to various pseudoscientific theories of historical and geographic determinism. However, in modern times no discussion on geopolitics would be complete without taking into account the economic aspects of the issues that are analyzed based on geopolitical impact of those issues.

15.2 NATIONAL POWER

While discussing geopolitical impact on an issue, it is essential that the concerned country's intrinsic strengths and weaknesses are taken into account. This can be done if the comprehensive national power (CNP) of a country is quantified. In simplest terms, the CNP of a nation can be defined as a putative measure of the general power of a nation-state. CNP can be calculated numerically by combining various quantitative indices to create a single number held to measure the power of a nation-state. These indices take into account both military factors (known as hard power) and economic and cultural factors (known as soft power). CNP is notable for being an original Chinese political concept with no roots in contemporary Western political theory, Marxism-Leninism, or pretwentieth century Chinese thinking. The inclusion of economic factors and soft power measures within most CNP indices is intended to prevent a nation; making the mistake of the erstwhile Soviet Union in overinvesting in the military at the expense of its economy. A fairly simplistic and effective index was developed by Chin-Lung Chang to measure the CNP.[6]

It uses critical mass, economic capacity, and military capacity as tangible measureable elements. Due to its indicators, it is often repeatable and easy to define, making it comparable to the human development index (HDI) in understanding and reliability. More abstractly, it refers to the combination of all the powers possessed by a country for the survival and development of a sovereign state, including material and ideational ethos, and international influence as well. Comparing the analysis of CNP by Chinese and other scholars as well clearly concludes that the CNP has a wider coverage, stressing comprehensiveness and all other aspects related to national security which apparently include material strength of the nation, ideational ethos, and international influence which that nation is capable of exerting. However, although CNP stresses material strength or command power, it does not ignore completely the importance of ideational ethos or soft power.[6]

15.3 NATION AND ITS EQUATION WITH THE GEOPOLITICAL ENVIRONMENT

Economic globalization has not only been accelerating the process of the integration of the world economy but it also encourages competition among/between countries, especially among big powers to optimize the value of investment. International competition manifests itself mainly in the dynamic changes in methodology to exploit the strategic resources of different countries and encourage open competition between the CNP of the contesting nations. They often come into conflict with one another and are locked in contention while being, in a complex way, interdependent and interconnected. The status (or position) of a country in the international community is in essence associated with the rise and fall of its national power, the increase and decrease of its strategic resources. Both CNP and national strategic resources focus on the study of grand strategy. In short, CNP may be simply defined as the comprehensive capabilities of a country to pursue its strategic objectives by taking actions internationally and its capacity to exploit its strategic resources, strategic capabilities, and strategic outcomes. It also entails its capacity to deny/degrade the capacity and the capability of its adversary to exploit its strategic resources. National strategic resources are defined as real and potential key resources available in realizing the strategic outcomes of a country. It also reflects on the abilities of a country in utilizing all kinds of resources worldwide. Thus, strategic resources are central in the comprehensive national power of a nation. Michael Porter lists five major resources, namely, physical resource, human resources, infrastructure, knowledge resources, and capital resources.[6] Accordingly, the national strategic resources are divided into eight categories, with 23 indictors. Those categories constitute CNP and are discussed in the succeeding subparagraphs.

a. **Economic Resources**—Economic resources are measured by the gross domestic product (GDP). It is the sum of the gross values added by all resident producers in the economy plus any product taxes and minus any subsidies not included in the value of the products. It is calculated without making deductions for depreciation of fabricated assets or for depletion and degradation of natural resources. Usually, there are two ways of measuring GDP. One is calculated by the official or nominal exchange rate. This method often underestimates the economic power of developing countries but overestimates the economic power of developed countries; the other is calculated by the purchasing power parity (PPP). The international comparison project recommended by the World Bank and the International Monetary Fund (IMF) takes 1993 as the base and calculates the gross national product (GNP) of 118 countries and uses PPP to estimate the value of the international dollar per capita GNP and per capita GDP.

b. **Human Capital**—Human capital, especially the opportunities and capabilities of education, is regarded as the decisive factor in the process of economic growth. Generally, human capital is expressed in the number CNP, which has a wider coverage, stressing comprehensiveness and all aspects, apparently including material strength, ideational ethos, and international influence. The more the number of years of education received, the more skillful the workers and the higher the labor productivity to stimulate economic growth. The rich human resources of developing countries find it easier to absorb and use new technologies imported from the developed countries.

c. **Natural Resources**—Usually, natural resources refer to the abundance, quality, ability to reach them, and costs of major natural resources. Natural resources are the necessary conditions for economic development, but they are limited, or the conditions or upper limits for restricting economic growth. It also needs to be noted that the natural resources are regressive in marginal gains, with relatively high ecological costs and external costs in their utilization. Besides, various resources play varying roles during different stages of development, generally assuming a downward trend (in contrast, the roles of knowledge resources assume an upward trend). Two of the major indicators of natural resources are, first, commercial energy use referring to apparent consumption, which is equal to indigenous production plus imports and stock changes, minus exports and fuels supplied to ships and aircraft engaged in international transport and, second, electricity production. In addition to hydropower, coal, oil, gas, nonconventional resources, and nuclear power generation, it covers generation by geothermal, ocean thermal energy conversion (OTEC), tide energy, wave energy, and waste to energy in the future. Some other aspects that also need to be taken into account are economic muscle of the nation whose indicators are growth rate of the GDP and capacity of a nation to draw foreign direct invitation and foreign institutional investment to further augment the internal financial resources.

d. **Knowledge and Technology Resources**—Knowledge and technology resources are deemed the most important strategic resources and, with the onset of the knowledge and information society, their importance is growing daily. Knowledge and technology resources are also vulnerable to impacts of international relations. For example, the United States, the technology leader of the world, has been having differential policies while dealing with different countries for sharing of critical technologies, based on their own national interests. This brings up an important issue that a country needs to invest in research and development to save itself from geopolitics restrictive regimes.

e. **Military Resources**—Military power is an important part of CNP. It reflects the abilities of a country to safeguard its territorial integrity against external and internal threats, maintaining the social fabric of the nation. By implication it means that with international tie ups efforts are made to create a situation wherein national interests are safeguarded. It also means that the international tie ups help in mustering resources to improve capability for sustained response to hostile actions and capability of a nation to exploit the international market. The latter two reflect the ability of a country to create and utilize international technologies. In this chapter, hereafter discussion will be limited to the role of natural resources; particularly energy in building the CNP of a nation and how geopolitics can leverage availability/denial of energy.

15.4 ENERGY DEMAND STATUS AND ITS FUTURE PROJECTION

Global demand for primary energy is expected to increase by between 27% and 61% by 2050.[7] Yet 1.2 billion people still do not have access to electricity and 2.8 billion lack access to clean cooking facilities.[8] It will take between US$19.3 trillion and US$26.7 trillion cumulative global investments in electricity infrastructure alone between now and 2050 to close this gap and support growing global energy needs.[9] The energy trade has seen a definite change in the pattern. Strong growth of US tight oil in recent years has had a dramatic impact, with oil increasingly flowing from West to East rather than East to West. This is likely to continue, with strong growth in China and India driving energy demand. It is expected that the gas market will become more global as gas pipelines and liquefied natural gas (LNG) integrate regional production and consumption centers (Figure 15.1).[9]

North America switched from being a net importer of energy to a net exporter last year (2015). Asia's imports of energy continue to expand, accounting for around 70% of inter-regional net imports by 2035. Among exporting regions, the Middle East remains the largest net energy exporter, but its share falls from 46% in 2013 to 36% in 2035. Russia remains the world's largest energy exporting country. Asia's import dependency rises from 23% in 2013 to 27% by 2035. Oil accounts for 60% of that rise, with

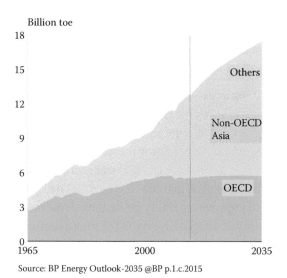

Source: BP Energy Outlook-2035 @BP p.1.c.2015

FIGURE 15.1   Consumption by region.

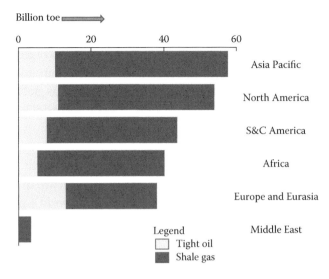

Source: Resources data © OECD/IEA 2014

FIGURE 15.2   Remaining technically recoverable resources.

imports accounting for over 80% of Asian oil consumption by 2035. Asia's oil imports in 2035 are almost as large as OPEC's[7] current entire oil production.[10] Global liquids demand (oil, bio-fuels, and other liquids) is projected to rise by around 19 million barrel/day (Mb/d), to reach 111 Mb/d by 2035. Growth slows over the period: from 1.2% p.a. in 2013–2020 to 0.7% p.a. for 2020–2035. Demand growth comes exclusively from rapidly growing non-OECD economies. Non-OECD consumption reaches around 70 Mb/d by 2035—56% higher than in 2013. OECD demand peaked in 2005 and is expected to fall further (–6 Mb/d) to around 40 Mb/d in 2035, the lowest since 1986. The increased demand is met initially by supply from non-OPEC unconventional sources and, later in the outlook, from OPEC. By 2035, on-OPEC supply is expected to have increased by 13 Mb/d, while OPEC production expands by 7 Mb/d. The largest increments of non-OPEC supply come from the United States (6 Mb/d), Brazil (3 Mb/d), and Canada (3 Mb/d), which offset declines in mature provinces such as the North Sea. OPEC supply growth comes primarily from NGLs (3 Mb/d) and crude oil in Iraq (2 Mb/d). China is the largest contributor to world demand growth: growing by 7 Mb/d to 18 Mb/d in 2035, surpassing U.S. demand (which falls by 2 Mb/d to 17 Mb/d). Even so, U.S. consumption per capita is about 3.5 times greater than China in 2035. India is the second largest contributor, growing by more than 4 Mb/d, followed by the Middle East with 4 Mb/d.

India overtakes China as the largest source of demand growth toward the end of the outlook.[9] The geopolitical importance of various geographical regions is constantly changing as technology is being leveraged to the technically recoverable resources, which are estimated to be around 340 billion barrels for tight oil and 7500 trillion cubic feet for shale gas globally. Asia has the largest resources, followed by North America (Figure 15.2).[11]

15.5 ENERGY ECONOMY RELATION

Growth of energy usage is a true indicator of the growth of a nation. Population growth and increase in income per person are the key drivers behind growing demand for energy. By 2035, the world's population is projected to reach 8.7 billion, which means an additional 1.6 billion people will need energy. Over the same period, GDP is expected to more than double, with non-OECD Asia contributing nearly 60% of that growth. Globally, GDP per person in 2035 is expected to be 75% higher than today, an increase in productivity which accounts for three-quarters of global GDP growth. Primary energy consumption will increase by 37% between 2013 and 2035, with growth averaging 1.4% per annum (p.a). Virtually all (96%) of the projected growth is in the non-OECD, with energy consumption growing at 2.2% p.a. OECD energy consumption, by contrast, grows at just 0.1% p.a. over the whole period and is actually falling from 2030. An important study on the impact of energy consumption on economic growth was conducted by Adhikari and Chen (2012).[12] The study examined the long run relationship between the two variables for 80 developing countries, divided into three income groups, from 1990 to 2009. As

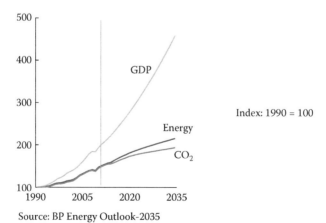

Source: BP Energy Outlook-2035

FIGURE 15.3   GDP, energy, and emissions.

per the findings of the study in upper middle income countries increasing energy consumption by 1% increases GDP by 0.82%, while for lower middle income countries a 1% increase in energy consumption increases GDP by 0.81%. For lower income countries, a 1% increase in the GDP increases energy consumption by 0.73%. Thus, major conclusions highlighted by this study are that the upper middle income countries (UMIC) and the lower middle income countries (LMIC) are more energy dependent as compared to low income countries (LIC) (Figure 15.3).[13]

15.6 SYSTEM OF COUNTRY COMPARISON BASED ON THE USE OF ENERGY

A system of energy development index (EDI)[14] was developed to track the progress in a country's/region's transition to the use of modern energy and to understand better the role that energy plays in human development. According to the EDI developed by the international Energy Agency (IEA) as published as part of the 2012 World Energy Outlook, the EDI results revealed a broad-based overall improvement in recent years except all sub-Saharan African countries with the exception of South Africa which feature in the bottom half of the EDI ranking. On the contrary, China, Thailand, El Salvador, Argentina, Uruguay, Vietnam, and Algeria and many other developing nations show substantial improvement.[15]

15.7 CORRELATION BETWEEN ENERGY USE AND CLIMATE CHANGE

There are three elements that mainly contribute to economic growth and they are agriculture (more automation leads to more production), manufacturing (it is a function of energy be it supply chain management or production or excavation/exploration), and services (which is fully energy intensive). Thus, growth in economy and growth in energy consumption are directly interlinked. Where does climate change fit in this equation? In this connection it would be important to first get a clear picture of growing emissions with the growth in energy usage. Total carbon emissions from energy consumption increase by 25% (1% p.a.) (in gross terms it would be 18 billion tons above the projected the figure by the IEA's 450 Scenarios),[9] with the growth rate declining from 2.5% to 0.7% in the period 2025–2035, although the profile of emissions would still be well above the accepted norm. Probably major change in the energy basket will be needed. More emphasis on renewable (11%) and nuclear energy (6%) as against 1% swing from coal/gas in the energy matrix will contribute substantially.[16] Such a future scenario reflects on the need to relook at the future energy scenario, related jockeying for resources, and the related geopolitics. In this connection it would be worthwhile if a case study is analyzed. Let us consider the case of India in this connection. The IMF estimates that India would figure in the world's top economies and will become its third largest carbon emitter by 2025 when the next level of enhanced climate action plans called INDGs comes into force. Most experts say that by then India will have to announce an estimated deadline for plateauing its carbon emissions which means no more use of coal, the country's primary energy source (more than 50%, which is not going to go down any time soon: refer to Figure 15.4).[9] Although India has pledged to produce two-fifths of its electricity from renewable sources by 2030, the fact is otherwise. In 2014, India was the largest consumer of coal (844 million tons).[17] The target of 1.5°C temperature rise means at best 550 gigatons of CO_2 emission which will finish by 2025 and 748 Gigatons of carbon emission by 2030 as mentioned earlier that coal continues to remain the main source of energy. In view of the agreement reached during COP-21 at Paris, India will have to peak its emission especially from coal-fired plants by 2025–2030 and therefore after 2020 India will have only five years left for coal-based emission.[18] This discussion clearly brings a few questions: How will India cope with this situation? Does India have enough funds available to make a transformation? Does India have the technology to make the transformation required? Finally, isn't it an effort on the part of developed nations

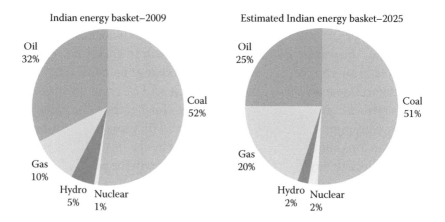

FIGURE 15.4   Indian energy basket (BP statistical review of world energy).

to put hurdles in the way of developing nations to increase energy usage based on their indigenous resources to achieve the desired economic growth? On the face of it, it appears to be an effort of developed nations to keep the developing nations under their iron grip in perpetuity.

15.8 ENVIRONMENT SCAN

The geopolitical landscape of the world is being remade by the increasing demand for energy resources from rising powers such as China and India and preserved leaders, such as the United States and Europe. That demand is resulting in a massive expansion of oil and gas delivery projects which are redrawing the battle lines of resource conflicts, both in war and in diplomacy.[7]

15.8.1 State of Demand

Energy demand will continue to rise; driven particularly by non-OECD countries. Energy infrastructure the world over will transform for optimization of available sources and evolving technologies to exploit those energy sources that are in the domain of frontier (research stage) technologies presently. Some of the areas that will have to be addressed will be development of storage of the resources like oil, development of nonpolluting technologies for the exploitation of resources like coal, and economically sustainable storage systems for renewable resources (Figures 15.5 through 15.7).

Note: China's demand reduction is on account of improved energy efficiency of systems and expansion of the service sector along with slowing down of the economy in recent times.

Note: The need for new infrastructure to meet the economic growth objectives, an expanding middle class, and 600 million new electrical connections (as part of erstwhile Rajiv Gandhi Viduytikaran's scheme and recently Deen Dayal Upadhyaya Gram Jyoti Yojna) along with campaigns like "Make in India" and "Digital India," is driving India's energy demand.

The latest World Energy Issues Monitor illustrates uncertainties on future CO_2 prices, recession, and the southward journey of all fossil fuel based energy prices.[19] It will impact the economies of Russia, Iran, Saudi Arabia, and many other OPEC countries dependent on oil and natural gas. In a recent report, it came to light that Dubai's DFM General Index ended its longest winning streak in almost three months. It closed about 1.5% lower. Similarly, Saudi Arabia lost 1.6%. It was reported that the retreats

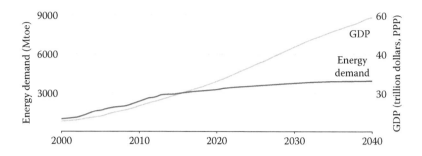

FIGURE 15.5 Energy demand in China. (From World Energy Outlook 2015, published by International Energy Agency (IEA) dated November 10, 2015, uploaded on http://www.worldenergyoutlook2015.org/151110_WEO2015_presentation.pdf.)

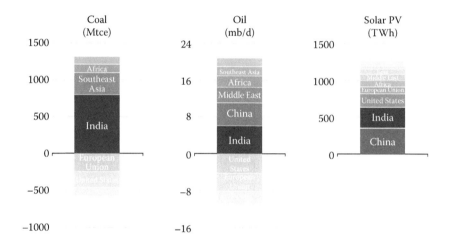

FIGURE 15.6 Change in demand for selected fuels, 2014–2040. (From World Energy Outlook 2015, published by International Energy Agency [IEA], dated November 10, 2015, uploaded on http://www.worldenergyoutlook2015.org/151110 _WEO2015_presentation.pdf.)

were on account of plunging oil prices and the Gulf countries were feeling its pinch. Kuwait and Qatar are issuing debts to cover a rising budget deficit. Saudi Arabia is trying to increase export to cover the deficit. In their appreciation one of the main contributors to this slide is the United States, which is releasing shale gas and tight oil in the energy market to signal the supply glut.[7] Saudi Arabia feels that United States' shale oil and gas flooding the supply side is dilating Washington's commitment to Persian Gulf stability.[20] The falling prices are likely to affect investment in oil and gas domain for the second year in succession. (Goldman Sachs forecasts that

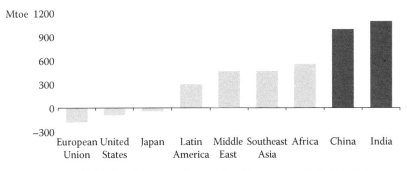

By 2040, India's energy demand closed in on that of the United States,
even though demand per capita remains 40% below the world average.

FIGURE 15.7   Change in energy demand in selected regions, 2014–2040. (From World Energy Outlook 2015, published by International Energy Agency [IEA], dated November 10, 2015, uploaded on http://www.worldenergyoutlook2015 .org/151110_WEO2015_presentation.pdf.)

the oil prices are likely to drop to US$20 per barrel[21]). It is assessed that cheap natural gas may get delink from the oil prices. In this connection, it needs to be noted that a new thrust is given to international gas pipelines. In the Asian region first is Turkmenistan-Afghanistan-Pakistan-India pipeline. It is a 1735 km long international pipeline whose groundbreaking ceremony was held at Mary in South Eastern Turkmenistan on December 13, 2015 and will cost about US$10 billion. When completed, it will deliver 33 billion cubic meters of natural gas to Afghanistan, Pakistan, and India.[22] Although it passes through some of the most volatile regions, Afghanistan and Pakistan have given guarantees for its safety and security (Figure 15.8).[23]

While the Iran-Pakistan-India gas pipeline (a lifeline for Pakistan because of its present critically deficient energy state[21]) is still not out of the woods because India is still not fully committed to this project due to security concerns,[24] India is trying to explore the possibility of a new alignment of the pipeline which is under water, based on rapid advances in undersea technology, along with recent big geopolitical shift post P5+1 and the Iran nuclear agreement[25] and consequent lifting of a ban on trading with Iran, which are opening up new fuel sources for energy-starved India. Construction of this proposed ultra-deepwater natural gas pipeline across the Arabian Sea, from Iran to India's west coast, is known as the SAGE pipeline (for South Asia Gas Enterprises Ltd., the Indian company leading the project) or the Middle East to India Deepwater Pipeline (MEIDP). It

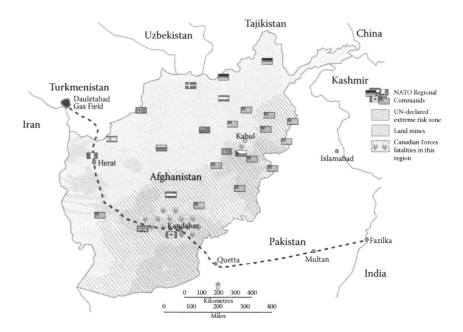

FIGURE 15.8 Alignment of TAPI. (From www.businessinsider.com/the-15-oil
-and-gas-pipelines-changing-the-worlds-strategic-map-2010-3?IR=T#us-influ
ence-tapi-pipeline-1.)

will be one of the longest and deepest oil or gas pipelines ever built, running
for 1400 km (870 miles) at depths of more than 2 miles underwater. This
pipeline, which is projected to cost $4.5 billion, is likely to be completed by
2018–2019. When completed it would transport 1.1 billion standard cubic
feet of gas every day to India. Thus, roughly doubling the country's gas
imports and bringing much-needed energy to the country.[26]

Coal prices will also be affected due to slowing down of the Chinese
economy. The cost of solar energy will also get reduced substantially but
the cost of nuclear energy is likely to see an upward trend due to emerging
needs for more stringent safety precautions post-Fukushima accident.[17]
On the contrary, there is a greater optimism with respect to shale gas with
the implication that the center of gravity on the supply side may shift to
new sources and as such jockeying for resources control may intensify.
While considering the impact of decisions during the recently concluded
COP-21, it will have to be factored in that with the settlement reached the
developing economies would become more dependent on the developed
world, as the onus to mitigate global warming will be more on developing
nations without having finances or technology to do that (Figure 15.9).

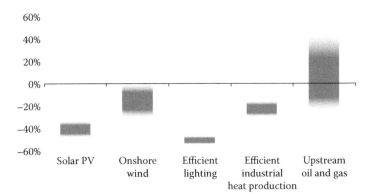

FIGURE 15.9 Costs in 2040 for different energy sources/technologies, relative to 2014. (From World Energy Outlook 2015, published by International Energy Agency [IEA], dated November 10, 2015, uploaded on http://www.worldenergy outlook2015.org/151110_WEO2015_presentation.pdf.)

15.8.2 Impact of Geopolitical Situation on Pricing

The advent of ISIS (which controls substantial areas rich in oil and natural gas with adequate refining capacity) with the emerging geopolitical equations of thawing of hostilities between Iran and the United States and isolation of Russia post-Crimea and East Ukraine developments (economic sanctions by the European Union and the United States is taking its toll on the Russian economy) (increasing dependence of Iran and Russia on oil and gas resources thus affecting the price structure in the world), economic growth of energy-starved India and the slowing down of the economy of China is bringing out the need for a more inclusive and fact-based dialogue between the nations of the world. It may be appreciated that although innovations will reduce the costs of low carbon emitting technologies and may enhance the energy efficiencies of the systems adopted for the production, storage, and transportation of the energy, the nuclear, oil, and gas sectors will need much more nuanced analysis. The cost of infrastructure, which will continue to remain stable in these sectors, will have bearing as far as pricing mechanism is concerned (it is pertinent to note that these are technical requirements and are unlikely to be affected due to geopolitical considerations). As far as the nuclear domain is concerned, the policy of selective denial of supply of raw material as well as technology through restrictive regimes by the Nuclear Suppliers Group (NSG) and "Nuclear Haves" will remain in vogue. As far as the oil and gas sectors are concerned, the role of OPEC is increasingly becoming irrelevant because economic considerations and the supply side are inundated with shale gas and tight oil, it will have to continue pumping more and more even if that amounts to a lower price for their product.

15.8.3 Future Scenario

International Energy Agency (IEA) in their annual report, World Energy Outlook (WEO)-2015 has stated that the developing Asia, a region in which India takes over from China as the largest source of consumption growth, is the leading demand center for every major element of the world's energy mix in 2040—oil, gas, coal, renewables, and nuclear. By 2040, China's net oil imports will be nearly five times those of the United States, while India's will easily exceed those of the European Union. The report also underlines that the single largest energy demand growth story of recent decades is near its end: China's coal use reaches a plateau at close to today's levels, as its economy rebalances and overall energy demand growth slows, before declining. India—the subject of an in-depth focus in WEO-2015—moves to center stage in global energy, with high levels of economic growth, a large (and growing) population and low (but increasing) levels of energy use per capita all pushing energy demand to two-and-a-half-times current levels. Overall, world energy demand will grow by nearly one-third between 2013 and 2040 in the central scenario of WEO-2015, with the net growth driven entirely by developing countries.[27]

15.8.4 Conclusion

The future scenarios suggest that either efforts of mitigation would be needed to meet the energy demands or need to go for adaptation; to the new emerging scenario which will be full of scarcity/denial of the current energy bearing resources (by going for renewable sources or nuclear energy) and the need for identifying new resources (like waste to energy, algae, thorium route for exploitation of nuclear energy, OTEC, and many others). Both of these scenarios call for more investment and research to develop new technologies that are commercially viable and safe to use.[15]

15.9 GEOPOLITICS OF ENERGY

15.9.1 Energy Dependency

The energy availability imbalance in the world is resulting in trade/acquisition of energy bearing assets. Sometimes it is country to country and sometimes it is through energy MNCs that have their assets all across the globe. While most of the energy-deficient countries are either developed or fast developing countries, many of those countries that are energy rich are not so developed as such are affected by the geopolitics of energy and that at times results in tensions and coercion by big powers. Table 15.1 illustrates the energy dependency of selected countries/group of countries.

Many of these countries that not only depend on resources but also on technology like India have a long way to go as far as technologies related to nuclear energy exploitation across all the possible sources. Similarly as far as coal and renewable sources are concerned, India has to depend on imported technology to a large extent for optimal utilization of indigenous resources.

This dependency makes these countries vulnerable to pulls and pressures exerted by supplier countries. The entire demand supply matrix becomes a captive of the geopolitics. With the advent of shale gas, the United States is now the next exporter of energy.[28] A number of important threads in the whole supply chain mechanism appear, which are as follows:

a. Shipping lines of communication (SLOC) in Indian Ocean play an important role.

b. Russia, Middle East, Africa, and Iran are important sources for energy-starved countries.

c. The United States now has an energy surplus and has rendered the world energy market quite vulnerable to price wars.

d. Need for greater research in areas like thorium exploitation and other sea-based sources.

e. Vulnerability of energy-starved countries and economically not so strong countries may call for new tie ups like gas; Turkmenistan-Afghanistan-Pakistan-India (TAPI) pipeline.

To appreciate the geopolitics of energy, the energy rich areas need to be identified. Some of these areas and the related issues are as follows:

a. **Caspian Sea Region**, particularly Azerbaijan, Central Asia, Iran, and Russia. The relationship of Central Asian republics with the United States and India and its bearing over the interests of Russia and China needs to be factored in the "demand supply matrix."

b. **People's Republic of China (PRC)**, which is employing its economic diplomacy to strengthen its relations with Bangladesh, Pakistan, and

TABLE 15.1 Energy Dependency

Ser No	Country/Group of Country	Energy Deficiency (in %)	Type of Energy	Source	Authority
1.	Europe	54	–	–	http://www.euractiv.com/sections/energy/europes-energy-dependence-day-getting-earlier-each-year-302171 updated 08/06/2015
			Oil	Middle East, Russia, Africa	Edited by Dennis Rumley and Sanjay Chaturvedi, "Indian Ocean in Geopolitics of Energy," Chapter 3, uploaded on http://books.google.co.in/books?id=V:Y-CgAAQBAJ&pg=PT35+jpg=PT35&dq=Indian+Ocean+in+geopolitics+of+energy+source=b1&ots=4mW9404mB4&sig=EG-6ZM
			Gas	-Do-	-Do-
2.	China	31	Oil	Kazakhstan, Russia, Venezuela, Angola, Middle East, Iran, Columbia, Congo, Brazil, South Sudan, Myanmar	Energy Import, net (%of energy use)data:worldbank.org/indicator/EG.IMP.CONS.ZS FACTS Global Energy, Global Trade Information Services Inc
			Gas	Middle East, Malaysia, Nigeria, Equatorial Guinea, Algeria, Indonesia and Australia	IHS Energy
			Coal	Vietnam, Australia	FT.com/Asia-Pacific/China- "Australia loses market share in China's Coal" uploaded on http://en.wikipedia.org/wiki/coal-in-china

(Continued)

TABLE 15.1 (CONTINUED) Energy Dependency

Ser No	Country/Group of Country	Energy Deficiency (in %)	Type of Energy	Source	Authority
3.	Japan	91	Nuclear (Uranium)	Kazakhstan, Niger	Vladimir Basov, "Uranium: China's Chase," published in MINING.com dated 29 Jan 2013 BP Statistical Review of World Energy-2015
			Oil	Middle East, Iran, Russia	Japan's Ministry of Finance, global Trade Info Services
			Gas	Indonesia, Malaysia, Nigeria, Russia, Middle East, Australia, Brunei	EIA: BP Statistical Review of World Energy-2014
			Coal	Australia	World Coal association: Coal statistics, page accessed on Dec 2014
			Nuclear (Uranium)	Canada, Australia, Kazakhstan	World Nuclear association, "Japan's Nuclear Fuel Cycle," www.world-nuclear.org/info/country-profiles /countries-G-N/japan-nuclear-fuel-cycle/ BP Statistical Review of World Energy-2015
4.	South Korea	93	Oil	Middle East, Russia,	EIA: Global Trade Atlas, Korea Customs Trade Development Institutions
			Gas	Indonesia, Middle East, Russia, Malaysia, Nigeria, Australia	BP Statistical Review of World Energy-2015
			Coal	Canada, Australia, Indonesia, Russia, Vietnam, China, United States	EIA, UN/World Trade Org, International Trade Centre
			Nuclear (Uranium)	Kazakhstan, Canada, Australia, Niger	www.world-nuclear.org/info/country-profiles/countries -O-S/south-korea

(Continued)

TABLE 15.1 (CONTINUED) Energy Dependency

Ser No	Country/Group of Country	Energy Deficiency (in %)	Type of Energy	Source	Authority
5.	India	38	Oil	Middle East, Iran, Venezuela, Nigeria, other African countries, other Western Hemisphere countries	India is increasingly dependent on imported fossil fuels as demand continues to rise, published in Today in Energy, uploaded in http://www.eia.gov/todayin energy/detail.cfm?id=17551
					US Energy Information Administration, Global Trade Atlas
			Gas	Middle East, Nigeria, Australia, United States, Oil MNCs	http://www.eia.gov/beta/international/analysis.cfm?iso =IND
			Coal	Indonesia, Australia, South Arica, others	EIA: Global Trade Atlas
			Nuclear	Canada, Australia, Niger, Mongolia, Kazakhstan, Namibia	Maj Gen AK Chaturvedi, "Nuclear Energy in India's Energy Security Matrix: An Appraisal", page 124, Vij Books India Pvt Ltd, Feb 2014

Sri Lanka. Simultaneously it has been employing a coercive diplomacy with countries like Vietnam and cooperative diplomacy with Indonesia and the Philippines in the South China Sea.

c. **Northeast Asia**. China and Japan are engaged in a regional power struggle. Japan, with the support of the United States, is determined not to allow China to dictate terms. This power struggle has a profound bearing on the smooth flow of energy and at the end of the day it counts whether energy flow is uninterrupted or is affected by the prevailing geopolitical tensions.

d. **Iran** with a large reserve of natural gas and oil is uniquely placed to positively support energy needs of Eurasia with the recent P5+1 and Iran Nuclear Accord.[29]

e. **In the case of China**, oceans of the world are increasingly becoming important for uninterrupted flow of energy particularly South China Sea, Straits of Malacca, Hormuz, Nine Degree Channel, Ten Degree Channel, Six Degree Channel, Luzon, and Taiwan.[20]

15.9.2 Importance of Central Asia in the Emerging Energy Supply System

Central Asia includes the five post-Soviet states of Kazakhstan, Kyrgyzstan, Tajikistan, Turkmenistan, and Uzbekistan, as well as Afghanistan and the Caspian basin. These republics are still politically vulnerable to Russian interference as most of their connectivity as well as supply system is integrated with Russia. Despite these political vulnerabilities, investors and governments in the United States, the United Kingdom, France, Italy, Russia, China, and the Middle East still seem eager to lay claim to the hydrocarbon resources of Central Asia. One of the most attractive features of Central Asian oil and gas is that there are deposits that have yet to be explored or developed, and the national governments are reliant on foreign investors to provide the capital to undertake such costly projects. Geopolitical considerations are another key concern as Central Asia continues to evolve as a highly important strategic area, especially for the United States, Russia, China, Iran, and India. Political instability in other major oil- and gas-producing locations—the Middle East, Venezuela, and Nigeria—and increasing economic nationalism in Russia are also fueling the drive to claim a share of Central Asian resources. The hydrocarbon reserves of Central Asia are concentrated in the Caspian

FIGURE 15.10 Energy resources of the Caspian Region. (From US Energy Information Administration.)

region. Azerbaijan is therefore a principal actor, despite its location in the Caucasus. It has considerable oil and gas resources in its own right and is central to non-Russian energy transit from Central Asia to points west. The bulk of Central Asian-Caspian hydrocarbons is located in Kazakhstan, Azerbaijan, Uzbekistan, and Turkmenistan. Both Tajikistan and the Kyrgyz Republic have limited reserves of oil and gas in amounts that thus far have not warranted much attention from foreign investors. Future gas transit projects include the Trans-Afghan Pipeline (TAPI) and the South Caucasus (Baku-Tbilisi-Erzerum, or BTE) Pipeline. The BTE is currently under construction. It will run parallel to the BTC oil pipeline from the Shah Deniz gas fields in Azerbaijan to Greece and presumably will then be linked to Nabucco, a planned gas pipeline to bring Central Asian and Caspian gas through Greece, Italy, and Austria. The BTE's planned initial capacity is 1.5 bcf/y, to be increased to 3 bcf/y.[30] Although Russia controls the majority of oil export routes from reserves in Central Asia and the Caspian, recent developments particularly the Baku-Tbilisi-Ceyhan (BTC) pipeline, as well as current and planned investments in the Central Asian oil sector by India and China, have yielded more options for non-Russian export routes and diversification of the customer base. These developments may help to break the Russian energy-transit monopoly, but they also open the region to intensified competition over energy resources on the part of other energy-hungry economies (Figures 15.10 through 15.12).

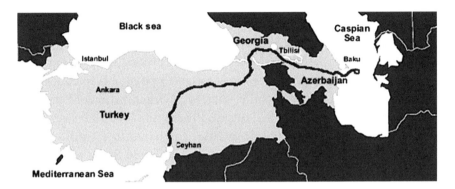

FIGURE 15.11   Alignment Baku-Tbilisi-Ceyhan (BTC) pipeline. (From Wikipedia, http://en.wikipedia.org/wiki/South_Caucasus_pipeline.)

FIGURE 15.12   Baku-Tbilisi-Erzurum (BTE) pipeline. (From Wikipedia, http://en.wikipedia.org/wiki/Baku-Tbilisi-Ceyhan_pipeline.)

15.9.3 The Interests of the United States

Central Asia plays an important part in U.S. global strategy in view of its proximity to Russia, China, India, Pakistan, Iran, and other key regional actors. No less important are its ethno-religious composition and vast deposits of oil, gas, coal, and uranium. The United States has varied and at times competing interests in Central Asia. U.S. interests in Central Asia can be summarized in three simple words: security, energy, and democracy. The United States is waging an enduring struggle to safeguard its interests, not only from terrorist threats emanating from Afghanistan, but also from overreliance on unstable sources of hydrocarbons in the Middle East. The Caspian region is a significant alternative source of fossil fuels. To put things in perspective, however, it must be noted that while the Caspian Sea's production levels are considerable, with peak production comparable to that of Iraq and Kuwait combined, they are much smaller than total Organization of Petroleum Exporting Countries (OPEC) output. Production levels have reached 4 million barrels per day (bbl/d) in 2015, compared to 45 million bbl/d for the OPEC countries.[27] Other issues the United States will have to contend with will be political and geographic conditions, including continued Russian influence, limited access to waterways beyond the Caspian Sea, and limited export infrastructure. Despite these likely challenges, the United States cannot afford to ignore the geopolitical importance of Central Asia and the Caspian Sea. The United States is not likely to become a single dominant power in Central Asia, nor is there any reason why it should attempt to achieve such a status. Realistic goals—energy security; proximity to the main theaters of operation in the war on terrorism, Afghanistan, and Pakistan; combating the traffic in drugs, weapons, and weapons of mass destruction technology; and encouraging participatory and transparent social and economic development—require a sustainable engagement. This is especially the case as the United States focuses its resources and attention elsewhere, primarily in the Middle East.[27]

15.9.4 China's Interest

China is steadily increasing its involvement in the energy sector, as demonstrated by the purchase of the Petro Kazakhstan oil company last year, acquisition of Canada-based Nations Energy by China International Trust and Investment Corporation (CITIC) in the fall of 2006, and the signing of several significant pipeline agreements.[27]

Russia and China have been cooperating to reduce U.S. influence in the region and, as they accrue more Central Asian energy assets, will have more leverage with which to prevent U.S. encroachment into their alleged spheres of influence. China is a major consumer of energy sources of Central Asia and the Caspian region and has shown interest in a pipeline to the Arabian Sea.[20] China's Northwest province Xinjiang is extremely important in the energy matrix of China. The Tarim Basin of this province has a proven reserve of 1 billion tons of crude oil and 59 billion cubic meters (BCM) of natural gas.[20] Keeping view of the importance of the area, China has settled border disputes with Kazakhstan, Kyrgyzstan, and Tajikistan to ensure sustainability, safety, and security of energy flow. China is using the Forum of SCO[31] to meet its strategic objectives in the Caspian region and Central Asia. However, they have a major conflict of interest with Russia. Russia wants it to transform into an energy club with the ultimate aim of forming a gas cartel, which would control gas prices in the world market, whereas China wants it (SCO) to become like NATO[32] or ASEAN.[33] Russia considers Central Asia and the Caspian region as its backyard and does not want China to become strong in this region. The overbearing attitude of Russia has created tensions between Russia and the United States, Russia and India, beside Sino-Russian tensions. The recent improved relations between China and Central Asian countries are being perceived by Russia as a threat to its strategic objectives. China has its own problems. China's Energy Research Institute anticipates a 7% annual growth in natural gas demand between 2000 and 2020.[20] China has two pipelines transporting natural gas from Central Asia and Russia. These are a 1833-km long Turkmenistan-Uzbekistan-Kazakhstan-China (ending in Xinjiang Region) pipeline transporting 55 billion cubic meters (bcm) of natural gas[34] and the second is 2800-km long Russia (from Purpeyskaya) to China (ending in Xinjiang) pipeline[35] which transports 30 bcm of natural gas (Figures 15.13 and 15.14).

15.9.5 Role of Iran

Iran with almost 10% of the proven world's oil reserve and the world's second largest gas reserve is an important player not only in the geopolitics of the world but more importantly in Central Asia and the Middle East. With lifting of sanctions by the western world and a highly volatile Middle East due to the advent of ISIS,[36] it has further assumed greater importance. Both China and Russia are trying to woo Iran. In this Sino-Russian power

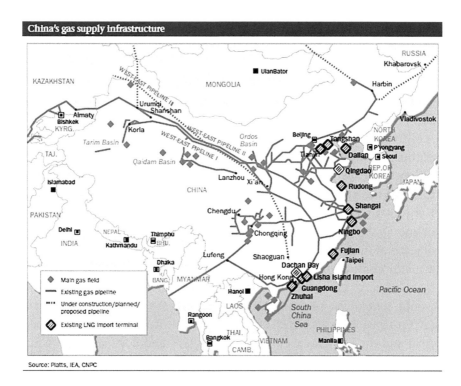

China's gas supply infrastructure

Source: Platts, IEA, CNPC

FIGURE 15.13 Gas pipeline from Central Asia to China. (From Platts, IEA, CNPC, available at http://www.platts.com/news-feature/2014/naturalgas/china-coal -to-gas-projects/china-gas-supply-infrastructure.)

equation, Iran has synergy with Russian objectives. A Russian-Iranian hydrocarbon cartel will cause a major shift and reduce the importance of Organization of Petroleum Exporting Countries (OPEC[37]), which is already getting weakened due to U.S. energy independence. However, it also needs to be taken into account that China and Iran have a consumer and supplier relationship.

15.10 A CRYSTAL GAZING FOR THE FUTURE OF THE ENERGY SCENE AS IT PERTAINS TO CHINA

a. Over the next 15 years, the United States and People's Republic of China (PRC) will be the prime movers in the international energy market. U.S. energy production and exports will increase, while China will have a difficult time matching production with growing demand in the absence of economic and energy reform.[38] However, China's energy consumption growth rate will be tempered by a

FIGURE 15.14   Altai gas pipeline—Russia to China. (From https://www.google
.co.in/search?q=altai+gas+pipeline&tbm=isch&imgil=1dXNuCBhOCoBJ
M%253A%253Bq53GA_IZ2lZE0M%253Bhttp%25253A%25252F%25252F;
www.altaiproject.org%25252F2011%25252F08%25252Faltai-gas-pipeline
-and-ukok-plateau%25252F&source=iu&pf=m&fir=1dXNuCBhOCoBJM%
253A%252Cq53GA_IZ2lZE0M%252C_&biw=1366&bih=657&ved=0ahUK
EwisqPTdxp_KAhXRGo4KHSrXC-UQyjcIMg&ei=v3eSVuzMO9G1uASqrq
-oDg&usg=__qrQFbef7EUkTJPetY3EovZTWjzk%3D#imgrc=1dXNuCBhOCo
BJM%3A&usg=__qrQFbef7EUkTJPetY3EovZTWjzk%3D.)

slowing economic growth rate. Since the energy order is a subset of the larger American-dominated world order, there are two essential questions for the future of energy: Will the PRC continue to accept, however grudgingly, the world order in most of its dimensions, or more aggressively try to reshape it in accordance with its own perceived interests? For the United States, the main strategic question is whether it will devote the economic and diplomatic resources necessary to preserving the liberal order it helped create.

b. The new energy story is twofold.[36] First, the United States is becoming a major energy producer and exporter. While this will not lessen American interest in a low and stable oil price derived on the global market, it will change the nature of America's relationship with existing suppliers and new purchasers. Second, China's economy is stagnating and its relative external demand is slowing. China could develop relatively greater interest in a preferential or even strategic relationship with Iran, Iraq, or Russia. The U.S. may be less interested in bilateral energy and strategic relationships that it has had with countries such as Saudi Arabia, while retaining an interest in stability in the Middle East. The PRC is developing capabilities to protect its energy interests in three ways.[30] First, it is growing its submarine force by beginning to foray into the Indian Ocean and the Gulf. Second, China is engaging in SLOC protection missions. Third, China is acquiring a large number of oil tankers as part of its contingency planning.

c. China has a number of transnational oil or gas pipelines with Kazakhstan, Uzbekistan, Turkmenistan, and Russia. China also revived its plans to construct an oil-import pipeline from Myanmar through an agreement signed in March 2009 and began importing gas in September 2013.[30]

d. The U.S. energy revolution is pushing the energy system back in a free-market direction by breaking the artificial production quotas favored by OPEC and undermining Russia's ability to use energy as a weapon. China would have to accrue more power to pose this type of systemic challenge. It could do so by translating more of its resources into military power or by achieving diplomatic breakthroughs—for example, by allying with a major country such as Russia or Iran. If China manages to create such a new alignment, it is doubtful that the energy system status quo will endure. But it is a pipe dream which is unlikely as in Central Asia as it is having a kind of open conflict with Russia over the Caspian and Central Asian resources. One of the possible outcomes of the present energy price war could be the balkanization of the international energy market, which will further affect negatively the price and availability of energy. With the apprehension of such a possibility China may opt for coming to terms with Moscow on energy. That could lead to the setting aside of both historic and current mistrust in favor of a strategic alignment between the two nations. In theory, this makes great sense; however, it is unlikely keeping view of its long term interests in Central Asia more importantly in Shanghai Cooperation Organisation (SCO) and also in East and South China Sea. Where it appreciates it has a better chance to succeed. Its current geopolitical stance is mainly because of the consequences for Chinese power, but also because it is unlikely to reform its energy sector, meaning it will still be dependent on energy imports (though at a slower rate of growth) but with less relative national power.[38]

15.11 INDIAN OCEAN IN THE ENERGY MATRIX

The Indian Ocean region contains 40% of oil and gas reserve of the world.[39] Energy security and geopolitics is converging in the Indian Ocean because roughly two-thirds of the petroleum traffic and 30% of total trade of the world traverses through this body of water. In addition to petroleum, the Indian Ocean per se and littoral countries are quite rich in energy sources other than petroleum and as such invite attention of those powers that are energy deficient and thus in coming years the Indian Ocean will continue to remain a place for geopolitical power struggle.[40] Besides the United States, India and China are also part of this great game rivalry. Since 2013, China is the world's largest oil importer.[41] Japan and South Korea, who get their substantial quantity of energy from Middle East,[42,43] are also important stakeholders in the smooth flow of energy through the Indian Ocean. All this makes the Indian Ocean increasingly vital for China, India, Japan, and South Korea. In recent times though U.S. interest with the advent of commercially viable shale gas has reduced, however suddenly Indonesia and Australia have started assuming greater importance (Figure 15.15).

Control of resources and energy security are going to be of increasing concern, which will affect the global flows of energy. In both cases, states around the Indian Ocean take on an even greater geopolitical significance; both as supplier as well as in many cases as a destination because of uneven spread of energy bearing resources and high demand of energy in some cases.

Such an uneven spread of resources and increasing demand by the Indian Ocean littoral countries as well as countries located in the Far East who depend on the safe transit through the Indian Ocean sets a perfect stage for interstate conflict as well as competition for the control of energy bearing resources. Some of the relevant issues in this connection are as follows:

a. The world's voracious appetite for energy is likely to fuel competition for diminishing supplies of fossil fuels and heighten national anxieties in energy deficient states about long-term energy security. Competition for energy among developing states will become more intense, particularly among the nations of the northern rim of the Indian Ocean and in Northeast Asia.[44]

b. Such accounts of energy security are common; they countenance the projection of forceful engagement with nations who by dint of their misfortune have energy resources but little sovereignty.[45]

c. As prices rise, contending countries/companies holding resources will have greater incentive to seize and retain control of valuable mines, oil fields, and timber producing forests.[46]

d. Access to new sources of energy which are available aplenty in Indian Ocean rim countries or in the bed of the Indian Ocean, like thorium, shale gas, ocean thermal energy conversion (OTEC), gas hydrates (still in the realm of research), hydro energy of fast flowing streams, will stir national ambitions, motivate corporate interests, rekindle historical claims, and fuel international rivalries.

All the above aspects very clearly flag the need to maximize economic and political stability because it is a strange coincidence that resource-rich countries in this region suffer from one or the other kind of vulnerabilities/instabilities. The rising aspirations of the resource holding countries with a view not to get controlled by bigger powers or large international corporate and exponentially rising energy demands of countries like China and India call for a new world order or a strong and effective regional grouping that can help the orderly control of energy bearing resources and its

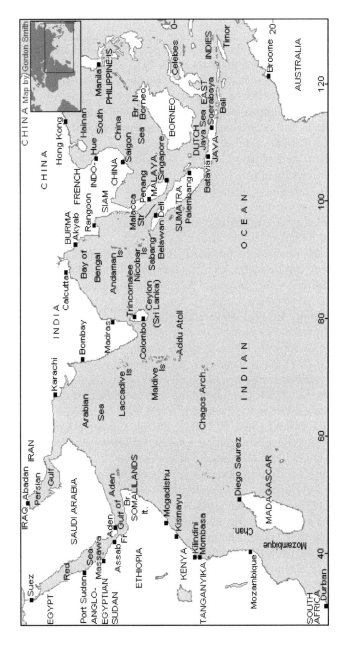

FIGURE 15.15   Indian Ocean. (From www.naval-history.net/WW2campaignsindianocean.html.)

equitable distribution through a mechanism that is fair, just, efficient, and above all has universal support.[28]

REFERENCES

1. Devetak, R., Burke, A., and George, J. (Eds.), *An Introduction to International Relations*, Cambridge University Press, 2012, p. 492.
2. Evans, G. and Newnham, J., *The Penguin Dictionary of International Relations*, Penguin Books, London, 1998.
3. Toncea, V. Geopolitical evolution of borders in Danube Basin, 2006.
4. GoGwilt, C. L. The Fiction of Geopolitics. Stanford University Press, 2000. ISBN No. 978-080-4737319.
5. Dittmer, J. and Sharp, J. (2014). Geopolitics. An Introductory Reader. *Journal Geopolitics*, vol. (II/I), p. 64 Routledge in 2006.
6. Bajwa, J. S. Defining elements of comprehensive national power, *CLAWS Journal Summer*, 156, 2008.
7. World Energy Council, World Energy Scenario: Composing Energy Futures in 2050, 2013.
8. Sustainable Energy for All (SE4All), Global Tracking Framework, 2013.
9. BP Energy Outlook 2035, Energy_Outlook_2035_booklet.pdf, p. 4.
10. Organisation of the Petroleum Exporting Countries (OPEC) is a permanent intergovernmental organization, created at the Baghdad Conference on September 10–14, 1960 by Iran, Kuwait, Saudi Arabia, and Venezuela. Presently it has 13 members, namely, Algeria, Angola, Ecuador, Indonesia, Iran, Iraq, Kuwait, Libya, Nigeria, Qatar, Saudi Arabia, United Arab Emirates (UAE), and Venezuela. As of 2014 three-quarters of the world's proven reserves are located in the member countries of the OPEC and two-thirds of the OPEC oil is located in the six Middle East Countries. Source: Wikipedia, http://en.wikipedia.org/wiki/OPEC.
11. Adhikari, D. and Chen, Y. (2012). Energy Consumption and Economic Growth: A Panel Cointegration Analysis for Developing Countries. School of Economics, Dalian University of Technology.
12. Economic Consulting Associates, Correlation and Causation between Energy Development and Economic Growth, January 2014, http://dx.doi.org/10.12774/eod_hd.january2014.eca.
13. EDI: The enhanced energy development index (EDI) is a multidimensional indicator that tracks energy development country-by-country, distinguishing between developments at the household level and at the community level. In the former, it focuses on two key dimensions: Access to electricity and access to clean cooking facilities. When looking at the community level access, it considers modern energy use for public services (e.g., schools, hospitals and clinics, water and sanitation, and street lighting) and energy for productive use, which deals with modern energy use as part of economic activity (e.g., agriculture and manufacturing). The EDI can be split by indicator and shown over time, helping a range of decision

makers to track progress in important elements of individual countries' energy development. (From World Energy Outlook, IEA, http://www .worldenergyoutlook.org/resources/energydevelopment/measuringenergy anddevelopment/.

14. Measuring Energy and Development, International Energy Agency as part of World Energy Outlook, http://www.worldenergyoutlook.org/resources /energydevelopment/measuringenergyanddevelopment/.

15. IEA's "450 Scenarios." World Energy Outlook 2014, www.worldenergyout look.org/media/.../methodology-for-450-scenario.pdf.

16. Chauhan, C., India's responsibility to rise as it progresses, *Hindustan Times*, New Delhi, Dec. 21, 2015.

17. Malik, A., Few options but to go with coal, *Hindustan Times*, New Delhi, Dec. 21, 2015.

18. Canadian Centre for Policy Alternatives, www.businessinsider.com/the -15-oil-and-gas-pipelines-changing-the-worlds-strategic-map-2010-3?IR=T# us-influence-tapi-pipeline-1.

19. Bloomberg Report, Sliding oil sinks West Asian stocks, Dec. 20, 2015.

20. Chaudhury, P. P., Crude stocks in 2015: Riyadh vs. Texas to be oil story in 2016, *Hindustan Times*, New Delhi, Dec. 24, 2015.

21. Chaturvedi, A. K., *Role of Pakistan in India's Energy Security*, Vij Books India Private Limited, May 2013, p. 51.

22. TAPI pipeline project inaugurated, *Natural Gas Asia*, Dec. 13, 2015, www .naturalgasasia.com/tapi-pipeline-project-inaugurated-17234.

23. Project focus: Iran-Pakistan-India gas pipeline, www.gulfoilandgas.com /webpro1/projects/3dreport.asp?id=100730.

24. The Joint Comprehensive Plan of Action (JCPOA) is an international agree-ment on the nuclear program of Iran reached in Vienna on July 14, 2015 between Iran, the P5+1 (the five permanent members of the United Nations Security Council—China, France, Russia, United Kingdom, United States— plus Germany), and the European Union. Under the agreement, Iran agreed to eliminate its stockpile of medium-enriched uranium, cut its stockpile of low-enriched uranium by 98%, and reduce by about two-thirds the number of its centrifuges for 13 years. For the next 15 years, Iran will only enrich uranium up to 3.67%. Iran also agreed not to build any new heavy-water facilities for the same period of time. Uranium-enrichment activities will be limited to a single facility using first-generation centrifuges for 10 years. Other facilities will be converted to avoid proliferation risks. To monitor and verify Iran's compliance with the agreement, the International Atomic Energy Agency (IAEA) will have regular access to all Iranian nuclear facili-ties. The agreement provides that in return for verifiably abiding by its com-mitments, Iran will receive relief from the United States, European Union, and United Nations Security Council nuclear-related sanctions.

25. Martin, R., With nuclear deal, India looks to Iran for natural gas, *MIT Technology Review*, July 27, 2015, www.technologyreview.com/news/539701 /with-nuclear-deal-india-looks-to-iran-for-naturalgas/.

26. Low prices should give no cause for complacency on energy security, IEA says, published as part of IEA Press Release, Nov. 10, 2015, http://www.iea .org/newsroomandevents/pressreleases/2015/november/low-prices-should -give-no-cause-for-complacency-on-energy-security-iea-says.html.

27. Rumley, D. and Chaturvedi, S., (Eds.), *Indian Ocean in Geopolitics of Energy*, 2015, http://books.google.co.in/books?id=ViY-CgAAQBAJ&pg=PT35&Ipg =PT35&dq=Indian+ocean+in+geopolitics+of+energy&source=bI&o+s=4 mW9404mB4&sig=EG6ZM, Chapter 3.

28. A deal known as P5+1 and Iran Nuclear Deal was signed between a group consisting of five permanent members of the Security Council and Germany and Iran on July 14, 2015. The scope of the deal entails to limit Iran's sensitive nuclear activities and block all pathways by which Iran could acquire material for development/fabrication of nuclear weapons. In return Iran will get relief from the sanctions imposed by UNO since 2008 and thus will be able to resume its energy trade with the rest of the world. (From A press relief dated July 14, 2015 by the Arms Control Association, P5+1 nations and Iran reach historic nuclear deal, http://www.armscontrol.org/press-release/2015-07-14 /P5-Plus-1-Nations-and-Iran-Reach-Historic-Nuclear-Deal).

29. Marketos, T. N. *China's Energy Geopolitics: The Shanghai Cooperation Organization and Central Asia*, Routledge Taylor & Francis Group, 2009.

30. Cohen, A. U.S. interests and Central Asia energy security, file:///C:/Users /aa/Desktop/U.S.%20Interests%20and%20Central%20Asia%20Energy%20 Security.html.

31. The Shanghai Cooperation Organisation (SCO) is a Eurasian political, economic, and military organization that was founded in 2001 in Shanghai by the leaders of China, Kazakhstan, Kyrgyzstan, Russia, Tajikistan, and Uzbekistan. These countries, except for Uzbekistan, had been members of the Shanghai Five, founded in 1996; after the inclusion of Uzbekistan in 2001, the members renamed the organization. On July 10, 2015, the SCO decided to admit India and Pakistan as full members, and they are expected to join by 2016.

32. The North Atlantic Treaty Organization (NATO), also called the North Atlantic Alliance, is an intergovernmental military alliance based on the North Atlantic Treaty which was signed on April 4, 1949. The organization constitutes a system of collective defense whereby its member states agree to mutual defense in response to an attack by any external party. NATO's headquarters are located in Haren, Brussels, Belgium, where the Supreme Allied Commander also resides. Belgium is one of the 28 member states across North America and Europe, the newest of which, Albania and Croatia, joined in April 2009. An additional 22 countries participate in NATO's Partnership for Peace program, with 15 other countries involved in institutionalized dialogue programs.

33. The Association of Southeast Asian Nations (ASEAN) is a political and economic organization of 10 Southeast Asian countries. It was formed on August 8, 1967 by Indonesia, Malaysia, the Philippines, Singapore, and Thailand. Since then, membership has expanded to include Brunei,

Cambodia, Laos, Myanmar (Burma), and Vietnam. Its aims include accelerating economic growth, social progress, and sociocultural evolution among its members, protection of regional peace and stability, and opportunities for member countries to resolve differences peacefully.

34. Wikipedia, http://en.wikipedia.org/wiki/Central_Asia-China_gas_pipeline.
35. Wikipedia, http://en.wikipedia.org/wiki/Altai_gas_pipeline.
36. The Islamic State of Iraq and the Levant (ISIL), alternatively translated the Islamic State of Iraq and Syria or Islamic State of Iraq and al-Sham (ISIS) is a Salafi jihadist militant group that adheres to an Islamic fundamentalist, Wahhabi doctrine of Sunni Islam. The group has referred to itself as the Islamic State. It proclaimed a worldwide caliphate in June 2014 and as a caliphate, it claims religious, political and military authority over all Muslims worldwide. As of December 2015, the group has control over vast landlocked territories in Iraq and Syria with population estimates ranging between 2.8 million and 8 million people, where it enforces Sharia law.
37. Organisation of the Petroleum Exporting Countries (OPEC) is an intergovernmental organization headquartered in Vienna, Austria. OPEC was founded by five petroleum-exporting nations at a conference held September 10–14, 1960 in Baghdad, Iraq. The formation of OPEC represented a collective act of sovereignty, and marked a turning point toward state control over natural resources, at a time when the international oil market was largely dominated by a group of multinational companies. According to the United States Energy Information Administration (EIA), OPEC crude oil production is an important factor affecting global oil prices. After major disruptions in the 1970s, OPEC started setting production targets for its member nations; and, generally, when OPEC production targets are reduced, oil prices increase. Within their sovereign territories, the national governments of OPEC members are able to impose production limits on both government-owned and private oil companies.
38. Blumenthal, D., China, the US, and the geopolitics of energy, American Enterprise Institute/InFocus Quarterly, July 7, 2015.
39. Jaiswal, P., Energy Geopolitics in Indian Ocean Region, June 17, 2014, https://www.linkedin.com/pulse/20140617101625-21195043-energy-geopolitics-in-the-indian-ocean-region.
40. Chaturvedi, A. K. and Ghosh, A. K., Indian Ocean: Need for a Fresh Policy Initiative, Strategic View Point, 2(1 & 2), Jan–July 2014, DDU University Gorakhpur.
41. Samaranayake, N. The Indian Ocean: A Great Power Danger Zone, The National Interest May 30, 2014, ///C:/Users/aa/Desktop/The%20Indian%20Ocean_%20A%20Great-Power%20Danger%20Zone_%20_%20The%20National%20Interest.html.
42. Japan's Energy Supply Situation and Basic Policy, FEPC, http://www.fepc.or.jp/english/energy_electricity/supply_situation/ and Overview by EIA, https://www.eia.gov/beta/international/analysis.cfm?iso=JPN.

43. An EIA report updated on October 5, 2015, https://www.eia.gov/beta/inter national/analysis.cfm?iso=KOR.
44. Dupont Annual Report, 2001, p. 70, http://media.corporate-ir.net/media _files/nys/dd/reports/ar2001.pdf.
45. Barnett, J. Security and Climate Change, Tyndall Centre for Climate Change Research, Oct. 2001, http://tyndall.ac.uk/sites/default/files/wp7.pdf.
46. Klare, M. T., *Resource Wars- The New Landscape of Global Conflict*, Henry Holt and Company, 2002.

Index

Page numbers followed by f and t indicate figures and tables, respectively.

T - #0146 - 230425 - C448 - 234/156/21 - PB - 9780367574451 - Gloss Lamination